The Child in ICC Proceedings

SCHOOL OF HUMAN RIGHTS RESEARCH SERIES, Volume 70

The titles published in this series are listed at the end of this volume.

The Child in ICC Proceedings

Helen Beckmann-Hamzei

intersentia
Cambridge – Antwerp - Portland

Intersentia Ltd
Sheraton House | Castle Park
Cambridge | CB3 0AX | United Kingdom
Tel.: +44 1223 370 170 | Email: mail@intersentia.co.uk

Helen Beckmann-Hamzei
The Child in ICC Proceedings

ISBN 978-1-78068-339-3
D/2015/7849/103
NUR 828

Cover image: Clara Constanze Otto (2015)

British Library Cataloguing in Publication Data. A catalogue record for this book is available from the British Library.

ACKNOWLEDGMENTS

Generous funding from the Gieskes foundation paved the way for this seven-year study on child participation in the proceedings before the International Criminal Court which was carried out at the Grotius Centre for International Legal Studies, Leiden University.

Being part of the department of Public International Law provided me with the opportunity to discuss the many questions I was confronted with during my research but also enabled me, as a lecturer, to have plenty of fruitful exchanges in the Bachelor and Master programmes. I would therefore like to thank all my colleagues and students for providing me with numerous insights and such valuable feedback. I have always experienced the combination of research and teaching as extremely helpful in developing my own thoughts and views. The wonderful opportunity to spend time at with the Office of Public Council for Victims at the ICC constituted a significant period which enabled me to see the constraints children face when participating in proceedings. Furthermore, the possibility to participate in numerous national and international conferences alongside my teaching obligations enabled me to discuss the topic with many experts in the field far beyond Leiden and the Netherlands.

I am particularly thankful to three persons who accompanied me on my path during the past years. The inspiration and enthusiasm of Karel Wellens triggered and encouraged me to apply for the PhD position at Leiden University. Liesbeth Zegveld's faith in me and her mentoring as my '*Doktormutter*', and Larissa van den Herik's support as my daily supervisor constitute the core pillars of this research project. The numerous meetings in Amsterdam and Leiden always provided me with what I needed and beyond, in order to successfully bring this project to a conclusion.

Words cannot describe how lucky I am to be part of my family and that of Johannes. Thank you for being my fellows in life and being with me on my journey throughout this research project. Most of all, I am thankful to Johannes for being there, taking me as I am and sharing joy and challenges every single day with me. Our children are our future. Since we are so blessed to live in a place where children can grow up without being threatened by any form of armed conflict or large-scale violence, I dedicate this book to all children who find themselves in less child-friendly environments. May this book contribute to the strengthening of their procedural status and encourage adults to implement child-friendly justice.

June 2015

CONTENTS

LIST OF ABBREVIATIONS

ACHR	American Convention on Human Rights
ACHPR	African Convention on Human and Peoples' Rights
ACRWC	African Charter on the Rights and Welfare of the Child
AFRC	Armed Forces Revolutionary Council
AIDS Behav	Aids and Behavior
AJIL	American Journal of International Law
Am. J. Dis. Child	American Journal of Diseases of Children
Annals, AAPSS	Annals of the American Academy of Political and Social Science
ASP	Assembly of States Parties
Beijing Rules	UN Standard Minimum Rules for the Administration of Juvenile Justice
Br J Psychiatry	British Journal of Psychiatry
Br Med J	British Medical Journal
Can J Nurs Res	Canadian Journal of Nursing Research
CAT	Convention against Torture and Other Cruel, Inhuman or Degrading Treatment or Punishment
CEDAW	Convention on the Elimination of all Forms of Racial Discrimination against Women
Child Dev.	Child Development
CMLR	Common Market Law Review
COE	Council of Europe
Colum. L. Rev.	Columbia Law Review
CRC	UN Convention on the Rights of the Child
CRC Committee	UN Committee on the Rights of the Child
DDR	Disarmament, Demobilization and Reintegration
DRC	Democratic Republic of the Congo
ECCC	Extraordinary Chambers in the Courts of Cambodia
ECHR	European Convention of Human Rights and Fundamental Freedoms
ECOSOC	United Nations Economic and Social Council
ECtHR	European Court of Human Rights
EJIL	European Journal of International Law
ETS	European Treaty Series
FIDH	Fédération Internationale des ligues des Droits de l'Homme
FORDHAM INT'L L.J.	Fordham International Law Journal

GA	United Nations General Assembly
GC	General Comment of the CRC Committee
GYIL	German Yearbook of International Law
HRC	Human Rights Committee
HRLR	Human Rights Law Review
HRQ	Human Rights Quarterly
IACHR	Inter-American Court of Human Rights
ICC	International Criminal Court
ICC Statute	Rome Statute of the International Criminal Court (see also, Rome Statute)
ICCPR	International Covenant on Civil, and Political Rights
ICESCR	International Covenant on Economic, Social and Cultural Rights
ICJ	International Court of Justice
ICRC	International Committee of the Red Cross
ICTR Statute	Statute of the International Criminal Tribunal for Rwanda
ICTY	International Criminal Tribunal for the Former Yugoslavia
ICTY Statute	Statute of the International Criminal Tribunal for the Former Yugoslavia
IDP	Internally displaced persons
ILM	International Legal Materials
INT J. Child Right	International Journal of Children's Rights
Int J Ment Health	International Journal of Mental Health
Int J Refugee Law	International Journal of Refugee Law
IJTJ	International Journal of Transitional Justice
Int. Rev. Psychiatry	International Review of Psychiatry
ISIL	Indian Society of International Law
ISQ	International Studies Quarterly
IRRC	International Review of the Red Cross
J CLIN PSYCHIAT	Journal of Clinical Psychiatry
J Int Criminal Justice	Journal of International Criminal Justice
JILPAC	Journal of International Law of Peace and Armed Conflict
J. Traum. Stress	Journal of Traumatic Stress
JPCH	Journal of Paediatrics and Child Health
JPR	Journal of Peace Research
JRS	Journal of Refugee Studies
LJIL	Leiden Journal of International Law
Med Confl Surviv	Journal of Medicine, Conflict and Survival
MONUC	United Nations Organization Mission in the Democratic Republic of the Congo
N Engl J Med	New England Journal of Medicine
Neth.Y.B.I.L.	Netherlands Yearbook of International Law
OAU	Organization of African Unity

OPCV	Office of Public Counsel for Victims
OTP	Office of the Prosecutor
PCIJ	Permanent Court of International Justice
PTSD	Post-traumatic stress disorder
RES	United Nations Resolution
RICR	Revue international de la Croix-Rouge
Rome Statute	Rome Statute of the International Criminal Court (see also, ICC Statute)
RPE	Rules of Procedure and Evidence
SC	United Nations Security Council
SCSL	Special Court for Sierra Leone
TFV	Trust Fund for Victims
TIL	The International Lawyer
TRC(s)	Truth and Reconciliation Commission(s)
UDHR	Universal Declaration of Human Rights
UN	United Nations
UNESCO	United Nations Educational, Scientific and Cultural Organization
UNICEF	United Nations Children's Fund
UNTS	United Nations Treaty Series
US	United States
VPRS	Victims Participation and Reparation Section
VWU	Victims and Witnesses Unit
Yb	Yearbook
YIHL	Yearbook of International Humanitarian Law

Introduction

CHAPTER 1

INTRODUCTION

1.1 INTRODUCTORY OBSERVATIONS ON THE CHILD IN INTERNATIONAL LAW

The particular vulnerability of children and their need for specific protection has been translated in legal protection under international law. The main source of legal protection of the child is provided under human rights law.[1] Independent of the situational background, numerous human rights documents address children's need for protection and their particular vulnerability in substantive terms. Children are provided with rights that are intended to protect the material needs of the child, such as nutrition, shelter, education and health care. The Convention on the Rights of the Child (CRC) provides for the most child specific protection in substantive terms.[2] In addition to the general protection guaranteed to the child under human rights law, specific protection is also provided to children during armed conflict and large scale violence. In this regard, human rights law also includes the specific call to protect children from being recruited as child soldiers.[3] The Optional Protocol to the CRC on the Involvement of Children in Armed Conflict focuses in particular on this aspect.[4] International human rights law and international humanitarian law also include specific calls to protect children from suffering during conflict situations.[5]

International criminal law incorporates child specific protection under distinct crime headings. The Statutes of the different international criminal courts and tribunals vary in this regard. The Statutes of the *ad hoc* tribunals are the most limited. They only contain one crime, which explicitly include the victimisation of children as an

1 UN General Assembly, Report of the Special Representative of the Secretary General for Children and Armed Conflict, UN Doc. A/F95/219 2010, para. 3. Flinterman 2006, 303-313; Ayissi 2002, 5-16; Hamilton & El-Haj 1997, 1-46; Dixit 2001, at 12-35; Heintze 1995, at 200.

2 See, e.g., arts. 9, 22, 24, 27-29 1989 Convention on the Rights of the Child, 1577 UNTS 3. For further child specific protection under Human Rights Law, see, e.g., art. 3 of the 2000 Convention Concerning the Prohibition and Immediate Action for the Elimination of the Worst Forms of Child Labor (ILO Convention no. 182), 2133 UNTS 161; art. 22 of the 1990 African Charter on the Rights and Welfare of the Child, OAU Doc. CAB/LEG/24.9/49.

3 See in this regard, art. 38 CRC.

4 See, e.g., arts. 1-6 of the 2000 Optional Protocol to the Convention on the Rights of the Child on the Involvement of Children in Armed Conflict, 2173 UNTS 222.

5 See, e.g., arts. 14, 17, 23-27, 49-51, 68, 81-82, 85, 89, 94 of the 1949 Geneva Convention relative to the Protection of Civilian Persons in the Time of War, 75 UNTS 287; arts. 70, 74-75, 76-78 of the 1977 Protocol Additional to the Geneva Conventions of 12 August 1949, and Relating to the Protection of Victims of International Armed Conflicts, 1125 UNTS 3; arts. 4-6 of the 1977 Protocol Additional to the Geneva Conventions of 12 August 1949, and Relating to the Protection of Victims of Non-International Armed Conflicts, 1125 UNTS 609.

element of crime. This is the crime of transferring children from one group to the other as an act of genocide which was copied literally from Article III of the Genocide Convention.[6] A more explicit mention of children as victims of international crimes can be found in the Statute of the SCSL. For the first time in the history of international criminal law, the Statute of the SCSL criminalises the use of child soldiers as a war crime.[7] Another step further in terms of child protection has been achieved with the coming into force of the Rome Statute. The Statute enshrines child specific crimes within the elements of the crime of genocide, crimes against humanity and war crimes.[8] The child specific crimes as *actus reus* of genocide and crimes against humanity do not specify age limits nor do they provide other indicia that may concretise the concept of childhood. In contrast, the war crime of recruitment does specify age limits. This crime protects children below the age of fifteen years.[9]

The forcible transfer of children when constituting an element of the crime of genocide (Article 6(e) Rome Statute) and the enslavement of children as a crime against humanity (Article 7(2)(c) Rome Statute) do not have child specific age limitations. Given the express age limit for recruitment as a war crime, it may be inferred that for these crimes, the age limit is the generally accepted age of eighteen years of age. This conclusion is in line with the Elements of Crimes (EoC). As regards child victims of the forcible transfer as an element of the crime of genocide the EoC define that,

> 'The person or persons were under the age of 18 years.'[10]

In addition to these child specific crimes, there are other international crimes to which children often fall victims. Sexual violence and trafficking as crimes against humanity constitute two such additional crimes.[11] Amongst civilians who became victims of sexual violence during armed conflict, children, in particular, girls, are specifically targeted by perpetrators.[12] This can to some extent be explained by the

6 Art. 4(2)(e) ICTY Statute, art. 2(2)(e) ICTR Statute. See for more, Schabas 2000, at 281.
7 Art. 4 SCSL Statute states that '[c]conscripting or enlisting children under the age of fifteen years into armed forces or groups or using them to participate actively in hostilities' is a serious violation of international humanitarian law. Justice Robertson was not convinced that this crime was considered a crime under customary international law when allegedly committed by Sam Hinga Norman, dissenting opinion Justice Geoffrey Robertson, SCSL-2004-14-AR72(E), paras. 3-5.
8 Arts. 6(e), 7(2)(c), 8)2)(b)(xxvi), 8(2)(e)(vii) Rome Statute.
9 Arts. 8(2)(b)(xxvi) and (e)(vii) Rome Statute. For further information, see, Cottier & Zimmermann 2008, at 470-475, 496-497.
10 Art. 6(e)(5) EoC.
11 Ibid., paras. 45-46, 91. See, for instance, arts. 7(1)(g), 7(2)(c), 8(2)(b)(xxii), and 8(2)(e)(vi) Rome Statute; art. 2(g) of the Statute of the SCSL.
12 The documentation of young boys being the victim of sexual violence is poorly documented, which does not alter the fact that young boys become victims of sexual violence. See, e.g., UN General Assembly, Report of the expert of the Secretary-General, Ms. Grac'a Machel submitted pursuant to General Assembly resolution 48/157, UN Doc. A/51/306 (1996), para. 93. Honwana 2006, at 58-63; Wessels 2006, at 94-101.

fact that young girls because of their virginity are expected to carry no, or fewer, sexually transmitted diseases.[13]

Next to the legal protection of the child under international law, the United Nations Security Council permanently monitors the situation of children during armed conflict. The Council has adopted resolutions and it has taken note of reports provided for by the Special-Representative of the Secretary General on Children and Armed Conflict.[14] These resolutions and reports examine the risks and threats children face during conflict situations and call in particular for state action.[15] On a regular basis, a specifically established working group of the Security Council for children and armed conflict monitors and reports on the recruitment of child soldiers.[16] International attempts on various levels to prevent that children are victimised also underline that children are seen as special not only given their vulnerability but also because they embody the future.[17]

Considering that international law and state practice mirrors the recognition of children's particular need for protection during peacetime but also in situations in which international crimes are being committed, the prosecution of international crimes committed against children before international courts and tribunals is well embedded. While international prosecutions are thus in line with the overall development of protecting children from the consequences of armed conflict and large scale violence, the involvement of the child in international criminal proceedings also gives rise to new questions which relate to the procedural involvement of the child. Questions which relate to the child sensitivity of ICC proceedings constitute the central subject of this research.

---

13 UNICEF, UNICEF, The State of the World's Children 2005, Childhood under Threat, www.unicef.org/sowc05/english/sowc05_chapters.pdf, at 45. UN General Assembly, Report of the Special Representative of the Secretary-General for Children and Armed Conflict, UN Doc. A/65/219 (2010), paras. 19-20. The Special Representative of the Secretary-General for Children and Armed Conflict underlined in her 2010 report that, '[s]exual violence against children, particularly in the context of armed conflict, continues to be of utmost concern. Such violations are exacerbated in conflict situations by the general security vacuum and the lack of administrative, law enforcement and judicial infrastructures, among other factors. Sexual violence is often used to achieve military, political and social objectives through, for instance, the targeting of specific ethnicities or terrorizing populations for force displacement. Data indicate that children are particularly vulnerable to sexual violence in and around refugee and internally displaced population settings, and when they are directly associated with armed forces and groups. Child survivors of sexual violence suffer both physical and psychological consequences, which are often debilitating. This is particularly true for girls who have been raped or forced to "marry" combatants, as well as for their children born of rape.'

14 See, e.g., UN Doc. A/68/267 (2013); UN Doc. A/65/256 (2012); UN Doc. A/65/219 (2010); UN Doc. S/RES/1882 (2009); UN Doc. S/RES/1612 (2005) ; UN Doc. A/60/335 (2005); UN Doc. A/55/163-S/2000/712 (2000); UN Doc. S/1999/957 (1999).

15 Ibid..

16 See for instance, UN Doc. A/65/256 (2012), S/2011/793 (2011), UN Doc. A/65/219 (2010), UN Doc. A/60/335 (2005). For more specific information, see www.un.org/sc/committees/WGCAAC/.

17 Parmar *et al* 2010; UNICEF 2005b.

1.2 THE CHILD AND THE ICC

Among the international criminal courts and tribunals, the Special Court for Sierra Leone (SCSL) and the International Criminal Court (ICC) are the first courts which specifically focus on crimes committed against children. The SCSL included, amongst other charges, the charge of the recruitment of child soldiers in all cases.[18] The first case before the ICC, the proceedings against *Thomas Lubanga Dyilo*, solely charged the war crime of child recruitment.[19] Trial Chamber I (whose decision was upheld by the Appeals Chamber on 1 December 2014) convicted *Thomas Lubanga Dyilo* for having recruited child soldiers in the conflict in the Democratic Republic of the Congo.[20] Other cases before the ICC have also included the war crime of child soldiering in their indictments.[21] As a consequence of this charging policy, children have been involved in the proceedings before the SCSL and the ICC in different capacities.[22] In addition to their involvement as witnesses in the proceedings, children can participate as victims of international crimes in the criminal and reparation proceedings before the International Criminal Court.

The International Criminal Court is the first permanent international criminal court. Prior to the establishment of the ICC, the *ad hoc* tribunals in the 1990s and hybrid courts, including the Special Court for Sierra Leone, played a major role in the renaissance of international criminal law.[23] The primary objective of these institutions is of a punitive nature.[24] Through the prosecution of international crimes, the courts and tribunals aim in particular to avoid impunity of such crimes.[25] This purpose is also restated in the Preamble of the Rome Statute of the ICC.[26] In addition to the punitive objective of the earlier criminal courts and tribunals, the ICC and international criminal law more generally also serve other purposes, such as deterrence, prevention, education and acknowledgement.[27] These

---

18 See, for instance, SCSL-03-01-T, SCSL-04-15-A; SCSL-04-16-A; SCSL-01-14-A.

19 ICC-01/04-01/06-2.

20 ICC-01/04-01/06-2842; ICC-01/04-01/06-3121.

21 ICC-01/04-01/07-717; ICC-01/04-02/06-2.

22 Prior to the establishment of the ICC, children also participated in truth and reconciliation proceedings in , for instance, Sierra Leone and Liberia. Truth and Reconciliation Commissions are established on a temporal basis in order to establish a historical record of human rights violations and to examine the roots of the conflicts and the consequences of such violations. In order to establish the truth, such commissions organise public and closed hearing sessions in which statements are taken from all parties involved: victims, witnesses and perpetrators. Individual criminal responsibility is thus not an objective of such commissions. See, for example, Hayner 1994, 597-655; Chapman & Ball 2001, 1-43; Evenson 2004, 730-767; UNICEF 2010a, ix-x.

23 Cryer, Friman & Robinson 2010, at 122; Triffterer 2008, at 16-21. Sloane 2007, at 39, Fletcher& Ohlin 2005, at 540, Robinson 2003, at 482.

24 Sloane 2007, at 39, Fletcher & Ohlin 2005, at 540, Robinson 2003, at 482.

25 Van den Wyngaert 2011, 495.

26 Fletcher & Ohlin 2005, at 540.

27 Gradoni *et al.* 2013, at 55-67; Drumbl 2012, 162; Akhavan 2001, at 8; Meron 1994, at 78; Bassiouni 1983, at 30.

remedial goals, and in particular the purpose of acknowledgement introduced a greater role for victims before the ICC.

As this greater role for victims in the course of the proceedings also entails the potential of greater child involvement in ICC proceedings, it is necessary to briefly address the underlying debate of victim participation in ICC proceedings in order to situate child victim participation within the broader context and debate.

The procedural status of victims of international crimes was limited before the earlier institutions. Victims were only involved as witnesses who gave testimony during examination and cross-examination.[28] The Rome Statute provides for additional procedural capacities. It enables victims, including children, for instance, to become procedural participants pursuing their own interest.[29] Victim participation is not limited to the criminal proceedings. Victims may also participate in reparation proceedings which are to be held when alleged perpetrators have been found individually responsible before the commission of international crimes.[30] Remedial goals and a particular focus on reconstruction of post-conflict societies have in this way entered the court room of international criminal proceedings.[31] These other purposes and expectations of international criminal justice have put the punitive nature of international criminal law and the ICC under pressure. In contrast to this strict criminal law approach which is, for instance, also argued in favour for by ICC Judge van den Wijngaert, another ICC judge, Judge Odio-Benito upheld a victims-orientated approach.[32] In her separate and dissenting opinion to Trial Chamber I's judgment in the *Lubanga* case, the judge argued that,

> 'that the Majority of the Chamber addresses only one purpose of the ICC trial proceedings: to decide on the guilt or innocence of an accused person. However, ICC trial proceedings should also attend to the harm suffered by the victims as a result of the crimes within the jurisdiction of the Court. It becomes irrelevant, therefore, if the prosecution submitted the charges as separate crimes or rightfully including them as embedded in the crimes of which Mr. Lubanga is accused. The harm suffered by victims is not only reserved for reparations proceedings, but should be a fundamental aspect of the Chamber's evaluation of the crimes committed.'[33]

The human rights approach is of the view that the involvement and participatory status of victims is as important as the criminal prosecution of alleged perpetrators in the course of ICC proceedings.[34] In contrast to the human rights perspective,

---

28 Olasolo 2009, at 513-514; Sloane 2007, at 48.

29 Art. 68(3) Rome Statute. Donat-Cattin 2008, at 1288; Jorda & Hemptinne 2002; Bitti & Friman 2001, at 459.

30 Art. 75(3) Rome Statute in conjunction with Rules 86, 89 and 90 RPE and Regulation 86 of the Regulations of the Court. Henzelin, Heiskanen & Mettraux 2006, at 321-327.

31 Keller 2007, at 189-190; also see Fletcher & Ohlin 2005 criticising this development, at 552.

32 Van den Wijngaert 2012.

33 ICC-01/04-01/06-2842, Separate and Dissenting Opinion of Judge Odio Benito, para. 8.

34 Ibid., paras. 22-35.

scholars have argued that international criminal proceedings are not the right forum for victims to elaborate on their experiences. It has been suggested that truth commissions constitute a better forum for victims' views. Robinson provides a critical analysis of a victim-focused approach in international criminal proceedings. This scholar addresses in particular the potential negative implications for the accused when a victim-focused approach determines the course of the criminal proceedings.[35] Worth mentioning in this regard is the dissenting opinion of ICC Judge Van den Wyngaert in the proceedings against *Germain Katanga*.[36] The judge, by vehemently disagreeing with the majority decision, upheld that a fair trial for the accused constitutes the core objective of ICC proceedings.[37] This ongoing debate has repercussions for the interpretation of the substantive and particularly procedural rules of the ICC. It is within this dialectic that the current thesis looks at the position of the child in ICC proceedings.

1.3 Research Aim, Statement of the Problem and Research Questions

We can thus witness a growing attention for the child as a victim of international crimes. Whereas the child hardly featured in the crimes catalogue of the *ad hoc* tribunals, the SCSL and the ICC Statutes contain more specific child crimes and at both courts the prosecutors made use of these provisions. In line with this, and possibly as a result of the silence of the law, the *ad hoc* tribunals did not have a child focus in their charging policies. The indictments did not include any child specific crimes. A similar increase in attention can be discerned at the procedural level.

The procedural rules of the *ad hoc* tribunals hardly refer to the child. Neither were children extensively involved in their practice as witness or otherwise. The practice changed with the establishment of the SCSL. As the Sierra Leonean conflict is known for the wide recruitment of child soldiers and given the inclusion of this crime in the Statute, the indictments charged, amongst others, crimes committed against children.[38] Consequently, children also participated quite considerably in the procedures of the SCSL as witness. The increased focus on and participation of the child at the SCSL may thus well be explained by the character of the conflict and by the type of crimes committed.

As indicated, the ICC continued this focus on the child in terms of substantive law and charging policy. In fact, the charges in the very first case, the case against *Thomas Lubanga Dyilo*, are limited to the charge of child soldiering. While all indictments before the SCSL included the recruitment crime in addition to other

---

35 Robinson 2008, at 938, 961.

36 ICC-01/04-01/07-3388-Anx.

37 Robinson 2003, at 484. ICC-01-04-01/07-3319, paras. 25-36. See also, Wyngaert 2011, at 488; Vasiliev 2015.

38 See, for instance, SCSL-03-01-T, SCSL-04-15-A; SCSL-04-16-A; SCSL-01-14-A.

crimes, the first case before the ICC is unique. The prosecutorial decision to focus on the recruitment crime gives room for greater involvement of children in the procedure compared to cases in which other crimes have also been charged.[39] Both the SCSL and ICC procedural framework do not include express bars or limitations to involve children in the procedures.

The above anticipates, that in addition to children's role as beneficiaries of substantive protection under international law, their status seemed to have gained another component: the child as procedural player. Whether the child is also in need of particular procedural protection as a result of being a child, has not been comprehensively addressed under international law and is therefore the subject of this research. The Special Representative of the Secretary General for Children and Armed Conflict underlined in the 2010 report to the United Nations General Assembly the imperative of child participation in transitional justice and in particular that

> 'procedures to protect the rights of children involved in transitional justice processes should include a specific focus on adolescents and should be constituent with the evolving capacities of the child.'[40]

Providing for child participation which is constituent with the evolving capacities of the child presupposes in the context of this research that the child is able to increase his or her own participation in the decision-making process.[41]

In contrast, under domestic law, the special status of children in both practical and legal terms has been translated into special child-sensitive procedures. This is particularly the case because children are often not accepted in legal systems as subjects with full legal capacity and competence to act.[42] These procedures recognise the inherent difficulties for children to have access to justice and their need for particular protection when involved as a procedural actor. Children who participate in ICC proceedings may equally be confronted with specific childhood related procedural particularities. These may arise at various stages in the proceedings before the ICC.

In light of the aforementioned, the research aim of this is twofold: Firstly, it analyses whether and to what extent the proceedings are child-sensitive. Secondly, a

---

39 Drumbl 2012, at 19. Women's Initiatives for Gender Justice 2012.

40 UN General Assembly, Report of the Special Representative of the Secretary-General for Children and Armed Conflict, UN Doc. A/65/219 (2010), para. 45 and Annex Principles for child protection and participation in transitional justice, principle 6. In addition, the European Union also only recently started to focus more intensively on the procedural legal status of the child, see, Stalford & Drywood 2009, 143-172.

41 Ibid., at 50. See also, Breen 2007, 71, at 81. O'Kane, Feinstein & Giertsen 2009, at 261.

42 Strode, Slack & Essack 2010, at 247-249; Cunningham 2006, 275, at 277; Hafen & Hafen 1996, 449, at 453.

lack of child-sensitivity might lead to child participation which cannot be considered to be in the best interests of the child, meaning in particular that the legal or factual consequences of child participation threaten the well-being of the child. Consequently, where necessary, this research aims to establish whether additional child-specific regulation and awareness is necessary in order to accommodate the particular needs of the child.[43] It thereby also aims to establish whether it is at all possible that ICC proceedings are sufficiently child-sensitive. If not, it might be necessary to reconsider the possibility that children participate. Summarising the foregoing, the concrete objective of this research reads as follows:

The research aims to provide informed insights into whether and to what extent participation in ICC proceedings is in the best interests of the child.

When addressing these aims, it is to be kept in mind that, even if victims, including children, may participate in the proceedings before the Court and claim reparations, the author agrees with the perspective that the ICC has as its primary objective to ensure a fair trial for alleged perpetrators. Accordingly, the punitive nature is of foremost importance when balancing the best interests of the child to participate against the core objective of international criminal justice. One may therefore as such still question the principal relevance of child participation in ICC proceedings.

In light of this research aim and considering the fact that child development is not a static process, the problem statement reads as follows:

To what extent is the ICC procedural framework child-sensitive taking account of the evolving capacities of the child?

With a view to shedding light on this problem statement, some concrete research questions have been formulated that guide the evaluation in respect of the different capacities in which children participate. As child participation in the proceedings before the ICC constitutes a matter of fact, one may raise the question whether such participation is a welcome development. Is it in the best interests of the individual child? Should it be appraised positively if viewed from broader angles such as the role of children in processes of post-conflict reconstruction? These questions are not purely legal in nature. Instead, they are part of a broader debate that cannot be limited to a legal analysis but is also involving other fields such as psychology and sociology. With this caveat in mind, the current research intends to contribute to the debate by offering legal views and perspectives. It is therefore not aimed at providing final and conclusive answers to these questions but wishes to contribute to the debate on whether child participation in different procedural capacities is in the best interest of the child.

A detailed analysis of other aspects, such as the psycho-social constitution of the child during and after armed conflict and how cultural and geographical

[43] See also in this regard, Doek 1992, at 632.

circumstances of a particular case at issue influence the child's capacity to recover, is not the focus of this research. Instead, this research departs from the factual observation that children currently participate in judicial proceedings before international criminal courts and tribunals.

1.4 TERMINOLOGY AND CONCEPTS

1.4.1 The child in ICC proceedings

Children can participate in the following five procedural capacities in international criminal and reparation proceedings at the ICC:

In criminal proceedings:

- child witness
- child victim
- child perpetrator
- child of an (alleged) perpetrator

In reparation proceedings:

- child claimant

Child witness

Children frequently become witnesses of international crimes during conflict situations.[44] Seeing acts of torture, killing, shelling and shooting constitute typical experiences of children who find themselves in situations of armed conflict.[45] Witnessing international crimes occurs in three constellations: children are either eyewitnesses, become victims themselves or witness because they commit crimes themselves.[46] Children might thus be called into the witness stand in order to give testimony on international crimes.[47]

Child victim

Armed conflicts and situations of large-scale violence lead to numerous child victims of international crimes. Children might therefore have an interest to be

---

44 Children and armed conflict, Report of the Secretary-General, G.A. 58/546 – S.C. 2003-1053 UN Doc. A/58/546-S/2003/1053 (Nov. 10, 2003); Promotion and Protection of the Rights of Children – Impact of armed conflict on children, note by the Secretary-General, addendum, G.A. 51st Sess., 4, UN Doc. A/51/306/Add.1 (Sept. 9, 1996).

45 See, e.g., Macksoud & Aber 1996, at 75-76.

46 Sanin & Stirnemann 2008, at 7.

47 Beresford 2005, at 722.

involved in the course of international criminal proceedings. As has been indicated, certain international crimes are specifically child-oriented and other crimes, such as sexual violence, tend to victimise children in particular. With the establishment of the ICC, victims may indeed participate in international criminal proceedings. When victims convince the Court that they have suffered harm as a result of a crime within the jurisdiction of the Court, they might present their views and concerns during the course of the criminal proceedings.[48] The Rome Statute does not exclude children from this form of participation.

Child perpetrator

Children may also be perpetrators of international crimes.[49] In particular, children are identified as perpetrators of international crimes if they have been recruited as child soldiers.[50] The theoretical international criminal prosecution of child perpetrators has been introduced through the establishment of the SCSL. Minors that have committed crimes at the age of 15-18 could have been confronted with international criminal proceedings[51] The Prosecutor of the SCSL, however, never charged children.[52] This prosecutorial decision does not alter the fact that the question of prosecuting children at international level raises may nevertheless be raised. If not before the ICC as a result of Article 26 of the Rome Statute of the ICC which excludes persons under 18 from the jurisdiction of the Court, a specifically established international criminal court for child perpetrators could constitute a form for the prosecution of minors. For this research, this procedural capacity is thus not as such relevant. It may, however, have to be taken into account when child victims claim reparations while having themselves committed international crimes as former child soldiers.

Child of an (alleged) perpetrator

The final capacity in the course of international criminal proceedings relates to the child of an (alleged) perpetrator. Children, whose parents are prosecuted before the ICC might be confronted with numerous consequences of their parents' involvement. While this procedural capacity is of an indirect nature as it is the result of their parents' (alleged) perpetration of international crimes, decisions taken in the course of the proceedings against their parent might bear consequences for the child and are therefore also addressed.

---

48 Rule 85 RPE and art. 68(3) Rome Statute.
49 Redress 2006, at 5-22.
50 Child Soldiers Global Report 2008, at 36.
51 Art. 7 Statute of the SCSL.
52 See Press release SCSL, Kendall & Staggs 2005, at 7.

Child claimant

In addition to the possibility of child participation in the course of the criminal proceedings before the ICC, children may also participate in reparation proceedings. Prior to the establishment of the ICC, international claims for breaches of international humanitarian law could not be brought by victims before an adequately mandated international court or tribunal. Human rights bodies have been found to be less equipped to adjudicate these claims.[53] As a result, victims of international crimes were for a long time not able to claim reparations for their suffering before an international judicial body.[54] The first conviction before the ICC, the conviction of *Thomas Lubanga Dyilo*, paves the way for reparation proceedings. As with regard to child participation in the criminal proceedings, the Rome Statute does not entail a bar of child claimant participation in the reparation proceedings.

1.4.2 Childhood

Why are child participants to be distinguished from adult participants? The central concept of this thesis is the concept of childhood. The definition of this concept is under discussion.[55] The factor age, start of a working life or the completion of educational training have been referred to as criteria which determine the end of childhood.[56] While the end of this period of life and the entrance into adulthood might vary, depending on socio-economic aspects, such as living in a developed or underdeveloped country it is agreed upon that childhood refers to a particular time in life which should provide sufficient room for play, school and a safe and caring environment.[57] Article 1 of the CRC is helpful in defining the benchmark of this concept as it provides for an upper age limit. It states that 'every human being below the age of eighteen years' is considered to be a child.[58] Accordingly, irrespective of the factors of a rather substantive nature, the age of a young human being can be considered as a criterion which can be referred to in order to distinguish children from adults.

The clear cut definition of article 1 of the CRC seems to be attractive at first sight and useful to be transposed to the ICC framework when distinguishing between child and adult participation in the proceedings. The Rome Statute and the Rules of Procedure and Evidence refer to the child in various provisions.[59] However, explicit

53 Krieger 2006.
54 Zegveld 2003.
55 See, for a general discussion, Prucnal 2012, at 70-72; Mousavi, Rastegari, & Nordin 2012.
56 Boyden & Levison 2000.
57 Brocklehurst 2006, at 8.
58 See also, art. 2 of the 1990 African Charter on the Rights and Welfare of the Child, OAU Doc. CAB/LEG/24.9/49.
59 See, for instance, arts. 6(e), 7(2)(c), 8(2)(b)(xxvi), 8(2)(e)(vii), 36(8)(b), 42(9), 54(1)(b), 68(1), 68(2) and 84(1) Rome Statute; 17(3), 19(f), 75(1), 86, 88(1), 89(3) and 112(4) RPE.

reference to a particular age can only be found twice in the Rome Statute. Firstly, Article 26 of the Rome Statute refers to children below the age of eighteen years. This provision determines that the ICC does not have jurisdiction over persons younger than eighteen years of age. Secondly, the war crime of child recruitment criminalises the recruitment of children below the age of fifteen years. The remaining provisions refer to the child without further age specification. The exclusion of the Court's jurisdiction from persons below the age of eighteen years might reflect an understanding of childhood as being terminated when the age of eighteen years is reached. Alternatively, the absence of general criteria that apply to the concept of childhood across all provisions also offers leeway to take a more encompassing approach, and to differentiate between different stages of childhood, such as early, middle childhood and adolescence.[60]

Bearing in mind the aforementioned different stages of childhood and considering the major focus of international criminal proceedings on the war crime of child soldiering, one may argue that children are particularly involved in the proceedings during a particular stage of childhood, namely their teenage years or young adulthood. Very young children, at least in these cases, are not likely to participate as the recruitment of babies or toddlers simply seems to lack any purpose as they cannot be expected to be capable of being used for the spectrum of tasks child soldiers perform.

Yet, in light of the potential of youth and next generations in processes of post-conflict reconstruction and the explicit limitation of the Court's jurisdiction to persons above the age of eighteen years (Article 26 Rome Statute), child participants within the ambit of this research are understood to be those persons who have been below the age of eighteen years when the triggering moment of, for instance, witnessing international crimes or victimisation, took place. This leads to the logical consequence that their procedural status of being a child participant does not differ despite the fact of having reached majority before the commencement or during the course of the proceedings. It should therefore be mentioned in this regard that keeping the term *child* participant instead of *adolescent* participant does not mean to imply that the current research is limited to minors.[61] Instead, having reached majority while still being involved in ICC proceedings does not alter the legal status of being a child participant within the ambit of this research.

Thus it is possible, that despite having reached majority, young persons may still come into consideration for child specific procedural treatment because they were a child at the triggering moment. It is therefore to be examined whether not only those who are *during* the proceedings minors are in need of child-sensitive procedural treatment but also whether those who have reached majority are still in need of a child-sensitive approach when the triggering moment took place during childhood.

---

60 See in this regard, Brocklehurst 2006, at 1.
61 See for similar criticism Drumbl 2012, at 3-25.

1.4.3 The particular vulnerability of the child

Children are particularly vulnerable human beings. The Preamble of the Convention on the Rights of the Child points out that,

> 'the child, by reason of his physical and mental immaturity, needs special safeguards and care, including appropriate legal protection, before as well as after birth.'[62]

According to the Convention, the need for special protection is, vested in two childhood-related characteristics, namely children's physical and mental immaturity. These are two child specific features which exist irrespective of the situational background of the child.

The determination of the degree of the child's vulnerability is based on various factors. The capacity of the child to express and communicate, the dependence on adults, reading skills, but also the educational levels of parents are decisive in this regard.[63] At the same time, not all children are equally vulnerable and children cannot always be considered as being the *most* vulnerable.[64] It is generally accepted that *being vulnerable* means, that a person is not able to protect him/herself. However, this does not imply that vulnerability should be understood as a static concept. [65] Even if children are understood to be particularly vulnerable as a consequence of their physical and mental immaturity, there are children who are capable of protecting themselves.[66] The varying degrees of child vulnerability do not diminish the overall need to distinguish children and adolescents from adults as potentially more vulnerable and in need of special procedural protection. The Committee on the Rights of the Child held in this regard that children should not be seen as *mini adults*.[67]

---

62 Preamble CRC.

63 For further information, see, Werner 2000, 115-132. The author provides an extensive overview of the available studies on factors determining children's vulnerability. Jensen & Shaw 1993, 697-708. Similarly, Skinner and Tsheko determined the vulnerability of the child in light of the basic needs of the child. A variety of factors have been pointed out as being crucial, including the physical or mental condition of the child, the educational background and family situation. See, Skinner *et al* 2004, 11. See similarly in relation to Palestinian children affected by political violence, Punamäki 1989, 63-79. For a comprehensive overview of all relevant aspects, see Committee on the Rights of the Child, General Comment No. 7, at 16.

64 Drumbl 2012, at 93-101.

65 Skinner *et al* 2006, 619, at 624.

66 UN Committee on the Rights of the Child, General Comment No. 7, at 8.

67 The Committee on the Rights of the Child underlined that, '[c]hildren differ from adults in their physical and psychological development, and their emotional and educational needs.' UN Committee on the Rights of the Child, General Comment No. 10, at 5. In the same tenor, see UNICEF 2009b, at 23.

1.4.4 The best interests of the child and child-sensitive procedures

The main objective of this research is to examine whether the law and practice of the ICC is child-sensitive. But what does child sensitivity mean in relation to ICC proceedings? Guidance on what is to be understood under child-sensitivity can be found in the principle of the best interests of the child. This principle has been codified in article 3 of the CRC. Article 3 CRC provides that,

> '[i]n all actions concerning children, whether undertaken by public or private social welfare institutions, courts of law, administrative authorities or legislative bodies, the *best interests of the child shall be a primary consideration*' (emphasis added).

The call that in all actions concerning children the best interests of the child shall be a primary consideration presupposes that the actors involved, such as judges, prosecutors, defence lawyers and legal representatives, are aware of what is to be considered in the child's best interests, i.e. that the proceedings are child-sensitive.

Various aspects are acknowledged as being important when measuring the best interests of the child.[68] The values of societies, for instance, play a decisive role in the determination of the best interests.[69] The culture and religion in a concrete situation are also of particular relevance, which may lead to different applications of the principle depending on the particular context of a case.[70] It should also be remembered that the assessment of the best interests of the child may be difficult to determine when examining today's and tomorrow's best interests. The child-specific difficulty relates to the fact that what today might be considered to be in the best interests of the child, may not be considered to be so in the future.[71] Furthermore, other issues might override the best interests of the child in the decision-making process as the best interests are only *a* primary consideration.[72]

The *Guidelines of the Committee of Ministers of the Council of Europe on child-friendly justice* provide the, to date, most explicit yardstick for assessing the best interests of the child. The *Guidelines* suggest that the assessment should include the following elements:

---

68 For an overview of the views raised regarding the difficulty of finding a coherent definition, see Detrick 1999, at 88-90; Freeman 2007, at 27; Van Rossum 2010, 33, at 36. Charlow 1987, 267, at 268. See also, UNICEF 1996, at 15; Artis 2004, 769, at 769.

69 Sund 2006, 327, at 330.

70 Van Bueren 1998, at 45. Freeman 2007, at 2. Van Rossum 2010, at 44-47.

71 Freeman 2007, at 3. See for an assessment of the concept within the African context, Himonga 2001, 89-122.

72 Van Bueren 1998, at 48. See also, Comment by the United Nations Children's Fund, UN Doc. E/CN.4/1989/WG.1/CRP.1 (1989), at 13-14 (UN Office of the High Commissioner for Human Rights, Legislative History of the Convention on the Rights of the Child, Volume I, UN Doc. HR/PUB/07/1 (2007), at 343-344); and the report of the 1989 open-ended Working Group to the Commission on Human Rights on the question of a convention on the rights of the child, UN Doc. E/CN.4/1989/48 (1989), paras. 117-126; Committee on the Rights of the Child, 51st session. UN Committee on the Rights of the Child, General Comment No. 12, para. 71.

> 'all other rights of the child, such as the right to dignity, liberty and equal treatment shall be respected at all times; a comprehensive approach shall be adopted by all relevant authorities so as to take due account of all interests at stake, including psychological and physical well-being and legal, social and economic interests of the child.'[73]

The Committee on the Rights of the Child recently published a General Comment on the interpretation of this principle.[74] The Committee held that,

> '[t]he concept of the child's best interests is complex and its content must be determined on a case-by-case basis. It is through the interpretation and implementation of article 3, paragraph 1, in line with the other provisions of the Convention, that the legislator, judge, administrative, social or educational authority will be able to clarify the concept and make concrete use thereof. Accordingly, the concept of the child's best interests is flexible and adaptable. It should be adjusted and defined on an individual basis, according to the specific situation of the child or children concerned, taking into consideration their personal context, situation and needs. For individual decisions, the child's best interests must be assessed and determined in light of the specific circumstances of the particular child.'[75]

The Committee continued stating that,

> '[t]he full application of the concept of the child's best interests requires the development of a rights-based approach, engaging all actors, to secure the holistic physical, psychological, moral and spiritual integrity of the child and promote his or her human dignity.'[76]

The Committee also stated that,

> '[w]henever a decision is to be made that will affect a specific child, an identified group of children or children in general, the decision-making process must include an evaluation of the possible impact (positive or negative) of the decision on the child or children concerned. Assessing and determining the best interests of the child require procedural guarantees. Furthermore, the justification of a decision must show that the right has been explicitly taken into account.'[77]

Bearing the above in mind, child-sensitivity in light of the research aim is in particular understood to refer to the degree of the Court's awareness in law and in practice of the procedural particularities of child participants. In order to ensure that, if desirable and possible at all, child participation can be considered to be in the best interests of the child, a child-sensitive approach is indispensable. This implies that

73 Council of Europe Guidelines 2010, principle B(2)a.-c..
74 UN Committee on the Rights of the Child, General Comment No. 14.
75 Ibid., para. 32.
76 Ibid., para. 5.
77 Ibid., para. 6.

the potential implications of child participation for the individual child but also for the proceedings as such are to be taken into account. Child-specific regulation and procedural treatment might constitute a tool to determine whether child participation is in the best interests. The preceding elaboration of the CRC Committee also points out, that the awareness of the child-specific particularities should not be limited to the organs of the ICC. Instead, the Court, but equally parties and participants should adopt a child-sensitive approach when engaging with children in the course of the proceedings.

The research therefore aims to examine in particular, whether the actors involved adopt a case-by-case approach when children are involved in ICC proceedings. Again, this research is in need of a yardstick to evaluate international practice. Bearing in mind that the principle of the best interests could constitute such a yardstick, the suggested assessment of the CRC Committee is helpful to be referred to. The Committee suggested in particular to assess the best interests as follows:

> 'Assessing the child's best interests is a unique activity that should be undertaken in each individual case, in the light of the specific circumstances of each child or group of children or children in general. These circumstances relate to the individual characteristics of the child or children concerned, such as, inter alia, age, sex, level of maturity, experience, belonging to a minority group, having a physical, sensory or intellectual disability, as well as the social and cultural context in which the child or children find themselves, such as the presence or absence of parents, whether the child lives with them, quality of the relationships between the child and his or her family or caregivers, the environment in relation to safety, the existence of quality alternative means available to the family, extended family or caregivers, etc. [...].'[78]

The above alludes that the assessment of the best interests is not limited to a legal assessment and should generally be made on a case-by-case basis. However, this research is premised on the idea that the proceedings can also be tested against this yardstick in a more generic and abstract manner. The best interests are thereby to be assessed in light of the other rights of the child. An interdisciplinary examination scrutinises the non-legal fields of interests, such as the psycho-social constitution of the individual child. This assessment, in particular the non-legal aspects, clarifies why this research does not aim to provide a definite answer to the overreaching question whether child participation in the proceedings is in the best interests of the child. It is limited to providing an assessment as far as the legal aspects are concerned for all actors involved, in particular judges, when deciding on whether and how children should participate. The limitation to an examination of the child-sensitivity from a legal perspective also explains why this research does not try to give a final and definite conclusion on whether child participation should generally be encouraged or not.

---

[78] Ibid., para. 48.

In sum, child-sensitivity is intended to entail that all actors involved in ICC proceedings approach child participants on a case-by-case basis and are aware of the special needs of children. In light of the foregoing it is necessary to bear in mind that participation in the best interests of the child can only be at stake, if desirable at all, when the multiple facets that are inherent to being a child are taken into account.

1.4.5 The evolving capacities of the child

Closely related to the question whether ICC proceedings are to be considered in the best interests of the child, is the principle of the evolving capacities of the child.[79] It has been explained before that childhood is not a static concept. Instead, depending on the individual capability and circumstances of the child, the capacities of the child might vary. As a matter of fact, a child-sensitive approach generally needs to take into account that the capacities of the child are evolving. It is therefore necessary to determine the factual capacity of the child at the time of the procedural involvement. The principle of the evolving capacities is, again, a principle which can be found in the Convention on the Rights of the Child. Article 5 CRC states that,

> 'States Parties shall respect the responsibilities, rights and duties of parents or, where applicable, the members of the extended family or community as provided for by local custom, legal guardians or other persons legally responsible for the child, to provide, in a *manner consistent with the evolving capacities of the child*, appropriate direction and guidance in the exercise by the child of the rights recognized in the present Convention' (emphasis added).[80]

The concept of evolving capacities aims to ensure that the limited autonomy of the child is gradually to be increased to full autonomy, and thereby enables the child to increase his or her own participation in the decision-making process. It ensures in this manner the progression of the child from a legal subject, which possesses a limited autonomy to a subject whose autonomy is unlimited.[81] Such an approach implies that childhood is seen as a dynamic process of human development.[82] The Committee on the Rights of the Child held in this regard, that

> 'according to their evolving capacities, [children] can progressively exercise their rights.'[83]

The assessment of the best interests of the child in the light of the evolving capacities concept guarantees that the best interests are determined in relation to the individual capacity or developmental stadium of the child at the time of decision-

79 Van Bueren 1998, at 49.
80 See also, Van Bueren 1998, at 49.
81 Ibid., at 50. See also, Breen 2007, 71, at 81. O'Kane, Feinstein & Giertsen 2009, at 261.
82 Van Bueren 2007, at 37.
83 UN Committee on the Rights of the Child, General Comment No. 4, para. 1.

taking.[84] Having said this, an increasing capability of the child lessens his or her need to be supervised or guided by others.[85] As a result of the developmental progression of the child, the respective actors involved should provide the child gradually with greater responsibilities for decisions that affect him or her.[86]

Factors that have an impact on the capacity of the child are, for instance, the gender of the child, the financial situation, the ethnical or cultural background, the geographic position of the child and also socio-political factors, such as living in times of armed conflict or large scale violence.[87] It needs to be noted that the age of the child, again, is excluded from these factors.[88] The underlying reason for excluding the age as a relevant factor is reflected in the words of van Bueren, who stated that

> '[a] young child can be mature beyond his or her years.'[89]

Bearing the research aim in mind, the assessment of the law and practice of the ICC is therefore also made in light of the question whether the actors involved take, as part of a child-sensitive approach, the evolving capacities of the child participant into consideration.

1.5 Methodology

1.5.1 Sources and approach

Legal research is usually conducted through an analysis of the *lex lata* with reference to Article 38 of the Statute of the International Court of Justice which lists the sources of international law.[90] This thesis focusses on procedure. This focus on procedure has direct ramifications for the approach and identification of relevant sources. Given that procedure is jurisdiction-specific, customary international law is generally not the most suitable source.[91] Hence, the analysis in this research will mostly rely upon and be informed by treaty law, whereby the ICC legal framework obviously functions as the most immediate point of departure.

The primary source for this research is therefore the ICC legal framework. Firstly, the Rome Statute is examined. As supplementary source, the Elements of Crimes (EoC) and Rules of Procedure and Evidence (RPE) are analysed and used in this

84 Van Bueren 1998, 50.
85 Detrick 1999, at 120.
86 UNICEF 2005b, at 3.
87 O'Kane *et al* 2009, 267; UNICEF 2005b, 9.
88 Ibid., 4.
89 Van Bueren 1998, at 136-137.
90 1945 Statute of the International Court of Justice, 33 UNTS 993.
91 Van den Herik (forthcoming).

regard as interpretative guidance for the Rome Statute.[92] Following the same methodology, the Statutes and procedural regulations of the *ad hoc* tribunals and the Special Court for Sierra Leone are scrutinised in order to clarify to whether and to what extend child participation has been explicitly addressed in the procedural regulation.

An additional primary source of this research is human rights law. The relevant human rights conventions are scrutinised in light of the question whether these documents can provide guidance for child participation in ICC proceedings.[93] Important to note is that this source is not understood to be directly applicable but may constitutes a primary source which could be referred to as yardstick for child participation in ICC proceedings.

The Convention on the Rights of the Child is the most relevant human rights treaty. Concepts from this Convention are used as a source of inspiration and in particular as a yardstick for the determination of the procedural status of the child participant in ICC proceedings. Bearing the aim of this research in mind, it refers in particular to two core principles of the CRC: the principles of the best interests (Article 3) and the evolving capacities of the child (Article 5). As a matter of fact these principles are used for guidance in a different judicial and situational setting. Firstly, as regards the judicial setting it is held that while the proceedings before the ICC are determined by international criminal law, the CRC principles, as set out in the Convention on the Rights of the Child mainly address a domestic setting, in particular proceedings, such as cases being based on domestic family or adoption law. As a result of the different judicial settings, also the legal questions addressed differ. In contrast to the proceedings before the ICC, which cover questions relating to situations of gross human rights violations, mass victimisation and individual criminal responsibility, domestic proceedings with a CRC-component involve individual cases brought, for instance, in relation to family law issues.

Secondly, the transposition of the two core principles of the CRC can also not be considered to be a direct application of the Convention on the Rights of the Child as the situational background is of major difference. The CRC relates to the largest extent to peacetime situations in which children might find themselves. ICC proceedings, however, are per definition held in light of a (sometimes even still ongoing) armed conflict or situation of large scale violence.

Bearing thus the different judicial and situational setting in mind, seeking guidance in the CRC core principles of the best interests and evolving capacities of the child may not necessarily lead to the same implications for the child participant in the course of ICC proceedings.

While the Convention itself does not extensively refer to the child as a procedural actor, the General Comments of the CRC Committee elaborate upon

---

92 Dörmann 2003, at 350. Art. 9(1) of the Rome Statute states that, the 'Elements of Crimes shall assist the Court in the interpretation and application of articles 6, 7 and 6.'

93 See the subsequent section for more on the applicability of human rights law to ICC proceedings.

procedural aspects and implications of child participation in judicial proceedings. These comments are therefore looked at in order to determine whether guidance for child participation in ICC proceedings can be found despite their non-binding force. The almost universal acceptance of the Convention on the Rights of the Child stands for a broad recognition of the rights of the child as entailed by the Convention.[94] It is recognised though that principles and concepts being introduced by the CRC may not always be directly applicable since they are tailored to be used in the domestic setting. There may thus be a need to transpose the concepts and adjust them to the specific features of an international setting.[95]

The fact that these documents, including the Convention on the Rights of the Child, are mainly drafted for individual cases in a domestic and in particular peacetime context does not necessarily constitute a problem or constraint. Procedural particularities of the child participant might, after all, mainly exist as they might be inherent to being a child – a developmental status which is distinguished from adulthood. The elaboration on the concept of childhood also stipulates in this regard, that children are to be distinguished from adults. This distinction has not been found to exist as a result of a particular situational setting, such as a peacetime environment or a domestic setting. It is recognised that children might be considered to be in need of particular protection because of factors which are inherent to being a child, regardless of whether they participate in domestic or international proceedings.

Next to the legal and other authoritative documents referred to, the case law of the International Criminal Court constitutes the second source of this research. While Article 38(1)(d) classifies judicial decisions as a subsidiary source, it is, due to the major silence of the relevant treaty law, of particular importance for this research. The case analysis is thereby not limited to the decisions of the ICC, but encompasses as a supplementary or comparative guiding source, the case law of the other international criminal courts and tribunals. Equally, questions which arose in domestic proceedings in relation to the child participant in criminal and reparation proceedings are examined if relevant and useful. For the same purpose, the case law of human rights courts is referred to as yardstick and inspiration for a comparative analysis of the procedural particularities of the child participant.

As a third and also supplementary source for this research, scholarly writing is examined. A constraint with regard to this source is reflected in the limited availability of scholarly writing on child participation in international criminal and reparation proceedings. Scholarly writing in related fields of research is therefore

---

94 193 States are currently parties to the CRC, see http://treaties.un.org/Pages/ViewDetails.aspx?src=TREATY&mtdsg_no=IV-11&chapter=4&lang=en. The importance of the CRC beyond a domestic legal context is also reflected in the practice of the European Court of Human Rights which frequently refers to the CRC in its case law. Daly 2012, at 443.

95 Raimondo 2008, at 58-69.

used for a comparison. Academic literature on the procedural status of the individual under international law, in particular on victim participation in ICC proceedings is available. Similar problems which have generally occurred in relation to victim participation, for instance, might bear particular consequences for the child participant and are therefore interesting to be used for a comparison and further inspiration.

1.5.2 Relevance of human rights law in ICC proceedings

The relevance of human rights law in ICC proceedings finds its justification in the interrelationship between human rights law and international criminal law. While human rights law primarily aims to protect the rights of individual human beings against states, international criminal law first and foremost intends to prevent impunity of individual perpetrators for violations of such rights in situations of gross human rights violations and mass victimisation.[96] This means *in concreto* that violations which constitute war crimes, crimes against humanity or genocide fall within the ambit of international criminal law.[97] Safferling states in this regard that:

> '[h]uman rights are thus protected through criminal prosecution. [...] Yet the concept of how human rights influence proceedings is complex and multi-dimensional.'[98]

In relation to ICC proceedings, the choice to be inspired by human rights and in particular children's rights and to use concepts developed in this area of law as a yardstick is informed and endorsed by Article 21 of the Rome Statute. Article 21(1)(b) of the Rome Statute provides that the Court shall apply international treaties. Paragraph 3 calls upon the Court to ensure that,

> 'the application and interpretation of law pursuant to this article must be consistent with internationally recognized human rights.'

The exact implications of this provision have been discussed extensively in scholarly writing. It has been argued, that Article 21 of the Rome Statute is not to be understood to imply that the ICC is bound to *apply* those treaties as such.[99] Instead, it is suggested that reference to international treaties by the ICC is a possibility for the Court to be assisted by such treaties when formulating a decision.[100] It has been pointed out in this regard that,

---

96 See generally in relation to human rights law Alston & Goodman 2013, 58-155; Bassiouni 2012, at 59; Safferling 2004, at 1471.. In relation to international criminal law, see, Morrissey 2012, at 65; Alvarez 2009, at 33; Sloane 2007, at 39, Fletcher & Ohlin 2005, at 540, Robinson 2003, at 482.

97 Cassese 2009, at 489; Safferling 2004, at 1476.

98 Safferling 2012, at 62-63.

99 Nolte 2013, at 288; Grover 2012, at 90; Schabas 2010, at 385; Bitti 2009, at 287-288; Politi & Gioia 2008, at 105.

100 McAuliffe deGuzman 2008, 'Article 21 Applicable Law', at 706; see also, Pellet 2002, at 1067-1070.

> '[w]hile the distinction between interpretation and application is not always easy to make, it is clear that the Court is duty bound ('must') to interpret the Statute consistently with internationally recognized human rights.'[101]

Accordingly, based upon Article 21(1)(b) and (3) of the Rome Statute, the ICC is invited to interpret the Rome Statute and its Rules of Procedure and Evidence in light of other international treaties. The Court may therefore rule upon child participation in light of the internationally recognised interpretation of the Convention on the Rights of the Child. Using for this research the core principles of the CRC as a yardstick for child participation in ICC proceedings does not therefore constitute an approach which is either farfetched or in conflict with the sources the Court may rely upon when formulating a decision.

The possibility that Article 21(3) invites the use of human rights as a yardstick for an assessment of ICC law and practice has also been addressed by Arsanjani. She pointed out that,

> '[w]hile the original intention behind this paragraph may have been to limit the court's powers in the application and interpretation of the relevant law, it could have the opposite effect and broaden the competence of the court on these matters. It provides a standard against which all the law applied by the court should be tested. This is sweeping language, which, as drafted, could apply to all three categories in Article 21. For instance, if the court decides that certain provisions of the Elements of Crimes or the Rules of Procedure and Evidence are not compatible with the standards set out in paragraph 3 of Article 21, it would not have to apply them.'[102]

Sluiter also seems to prefer such approach, as he stated that Article 21(3) of the Rome Statute,

> 'offers a starting point in filling the blanks within the Statute on the basis of human rights law.'[103]

Fletcher and Ohlin argued in relation to Article 21(3) that,

> '[t]hough this phrase obviously refers to the rights of the accused, it can also be read to include the rights of the victims, which opens the door to a more aggressive mode of prosecution.'[104]

A more modest and criminal law approach has been suggested by Grover. She pointed out by reference to the drafting history that this provision was primarily drafted with the intention of ensuring the principle of legality and the fairness of the

---

101 Vagias 2011, at 83.
102 Arsanjani 1999, at 29.
103 Sluiter 2009, at 466.
104 Fletcher & Ohlin 2005, at 552.

proceedings for the alleged perpetrator. Broadening the protection of others, such as victims, has, according to the author, not been the intention of the drafters.[105]

Delmas-Marty, by contrast, suggested that reference and inspiration from human rights law is not limited to the principle of legality and fair trial for the accused. She held that,

> '[t]his provision adds interactions between international criminal law and international human rights law [...] and grants official status to cross-references between these bodies of law. But it may also introduce a hierarchy in favour of human rights, while international judges have until how rejected any such hierarchy. [...] The mechanism of Article 21(3) [...] could encourage them to give greater weight to international human rights instruments.'[106]

As the yardstick of human rights law in this research is predominantly suggested for an interpretation of the procedural provisions concerning child participation in ICC proceedings and not for an interpretation of the substantive provisions that aim to protect victims, including children, from international crimes, one may assume that fair trial concerns are not as likely as regards the interpretation of the substantive law. This assumption, however, cannot be relied upon without further research as one can imagine that also a victim-oriented interpretation of the procedural provisions might indeed give rise to fair trial concerns. While this question is not part of the current research due to its general nature, it is a question to be kept in mind within the overall discussion of victim participation in ICC proceedings.

The case law of the International Criminal Court has also addressed the possibility to use human rights law as yardstick – be it without explicitly distinguishing between the substantive and procedural provisions under the ICC system. Direct reference to human rights law has indeed also been made with regard to victims. In the decision of 18 January 2008, Trial Chamber I ruled that,

> '[i]n light of Article 21(3) of the [Rome] Statute, and taking into consideration the decision of the Appeals Chamber that it "makes the interpretation as well as the application of the law applicable under the Statute subject to internationally recognised human rights", the Trial Chamber has considered the Basic Principles and Guidelines on the Right to a Remedy and Reparation for Victims of Gross Violations of International Human Rights Law and Serious Violations of International Humanitarian Law ("Basic Principles") [...].'[107]

The Chamber explicitly referred to Articles 3 and 12 of the CRC as relevant provisions which need to be considered for victims' participation.[108] The reference

---

105 Grover 2010, at 559, 561-562. The Appeals Chamber also referred to art. 21(3) in relation to the right to a fair trial , ICC-01/04-01/06-772, para. 37-38.

106 Delmas-Marty 2006, at 3.

107 ICC-01/04-01/06-1119, para. 35.

108 Ibid., para. 36.

of the Court itself to the Convention on the Rights of the Child and related human rights documents indicates that, where necessary, the Court does refer to human rights law in relation to others than the accused.[109] In this tenor, Schabas pointed out that,

> '[h]uman rights sources have proven to be particularly useful in developing issues relating to victim participation and protection. In this context, reference has been made to the Convention on the Rights of the Child, as well as to so-called soft law instruments such as the Declaration of Basic Principles of Justice for Victims of Crime and Abuse of Power and the Basic Principles and Guidelines on the Right to a Remedy and Reparation for Victims of Gross Violations of International Human Rights Law and Serious Violations of International Humanitarian Law.'[110]

Accordingly, the Rome Statute, ICC practice and scholarly writing permit the approach chosen in this research, namely to use the CRC and related documents as a yardstick for an evaluation of ICC practice in relation to the child participant.

1.6 Structure of the Thesis

This book is divided into three parts. Pursuant to the primary aim of this research (the examination of the child-sensitivity of the ICC procedure), Part I (criminal proceedings) and Part II (reparation proceedings) address the procedural particularities of the child participant. Both parts focus on the question whether and to what extent ICC proceedings are child-sensitive. The analysis of the law and practice focusses in particular on the question to what extent procedural insensitivities exist when children access and are involved in ICC proceedings. Pursuant to the second research aim (to determine whether there is a need for child-specific regulation), the examination of the procedural status of the child within each capacity seeks to provide not only an overview of the procedural rights and protection of the child, but also to scrutinise those fields in which additional procedural regulation, child-focused awareness and practice is needed.

As the procedural particularities might vary depending on the specific procedural capacity in which children are involved, each capacity is addressed in a separate chapter. *Chapter Two* analyses the procedural capacity of the child witness. Questions relating to the legal status and credibility of the child witness are addressed. *Chapter Three* focuses on the child as participating victim. It examines child-specific procedural particularities which are in particular the result of the child's limited legal capacity. Questions relating to the application criteria and the procedure as regards the ability to file an application on his/her own behalf or the

[109] See, for instance, ICC-01/04-01/06-1119, paras. 34-37. See also, ICC-01/04-01/06-1556, paras. 49-50; ICC-01/04-01/06-2035, para. 26. Pre-Trial Chamber III refers to arts. 2(3)(a) and 14(1) of the ICCPR, arts. 6(1) and 13 ECHR, art. 7(1)(a) ACHPR and arts. 8(1) and 25(1) ACHR. See ICC-01/05-01/08-320, paras. 16-17.

[110] Schabas 2010, at 399-400.

possibility to be represented by a legal representative in the course of the proceedings are also addressed. *Chapter Four* looks at the possibility of the procedural capacity of the child perpetrator and the derived procedural capacity of the child of a(n) (alleged) perpetrator. Subsequently, *Chapter Five* scrutinises the child in international reparatory justice mechanisms. Particular attention is paid to the law and practice of the International Criminal Court in relation to child claimants. Finally, *Part III* provides a concluding and comparative evaluation of the procedural capacities of the child in the proceedings before the ICC. It connects and evaluates the core conclusions reached within each chapter and offers some overreaching reflections on the position of the child as procedural actor in international criminal law (*Chapter Six*). As a final point, the research concludes with a view to the future and in particular calls for further research and procedural regulation of the procedural particularities in relation to child participation in ICC proceedings.

PART I

THE CHILD IN INTERNATIONAL CRIMINAL PROCEEDINGS

CHAPTER 2

THE CHILD WITNESS

2.1 INTRODUCTION

Witness testimony in international criminal proceedings is a crucial but not unproblematic means by which evidence is provided. While the criminal prosecutions before the Nuremberg Tribunal largely relied on documentary evidence, a shift to using eye-witness testimony occurred before the later established international courts and tribunals.[111]

Child witness testimony can be expected in international criminal proceedings when children are the direct victims of the crimes that are prosecuted. A child may also be able to provide insider information on other alleged crimes as a result of his or her specific and unique knowledge. It will be analysed in this chapter whether child witness testimony might encounter additional procedural difficulties compared to adult testimony which might deem it necessary that child-sensitive procedural treatment is provided for. This chapter presupposes that adult testimony prevails in proceedings which do not entail indictments of child focused crimes or in proceedings where crimes have been charged about which children cannot provide insider information. This means that child witness testimony is expected especially in cases in which, for instance, the recruitment of child soldiers below the age of fifteen years is charged. And indeed, as it will be seen, children, more specifically (alleged) former child soldiers have testified at the different international courts and tribunals.

The conflict in the Democratic Republic of the Congo is known for the tremendous numbers of child soldiers.[112] The first case before the ICC is unique as the ICC Prosecutor chose to charge *Thomas Lubanga Dyilo* solely with the crime of recruitment. This prosecutorial decision underlines that the Prosecutor deemed it necessary to focus on crimes committed towards children in armed conflict. Calling children to the witness stand in such cases seems to be considered a *conditio sine qua non* and inherent to a prosecutorial strategy in order to prove the charged crime. Such practice alludes that first-hand evidence from former child soldiers is likely to constitute one of the most direct methods of proof.

---

111 Combs (2013), 11-12.

112 For an overview of the alleged numbers of child soldiers worldwide, see, Child Soldiers – Global Report 2008, at 389-407.

A child who has witnessed atrocities may thus be able to provide information which parties or participants in international criminal proceedings wish to introduce as evidence into the court record.[113] Bearing this in mind and since there is no bar to child testimony in the Rome Statute or the Rules of Procedure and Evidence, children may be called to testify. Age is not referred to as a potentially excluding factor for testimony. Rule 65 RPE only states in this regard that '[a] witness who appears before the Court is compellable by the Court to provide testimony […].'

The aim of this chapter is to analyse the relevant provisions and practice governing witness testimony in ICC proceedings. Two research questions guide this chapter. Firstly, do child-specific provisions exist or should they be developed? Secondly, are child-sensitive interpretations given or needed to apply the general rules to child witnesses?

The chapter commences with an overview of the international practice followed by an analysis of the general and child-specific rules governing witness testimony. As the most extensive practice of calling children into the witness stand occurred during the proceedings against *Thomas Lubanga Dyilo*, this case is of particular relevance for the legal analysis in the current chapter. In this regard, questions relating to the capability of the child to provide informed consent, a potential need for child-specific protective measures and the danger of self-incrimination are addressed. Specific attention is paid to the risk of self-incrimination when children testify as the exclusion of the prosecution of minors under the Rome Statute does not prevent domestic criminal proceedings against alleged minor perpetrators. After this examination, the research assesses the trustworthiness of children and the impact of conflict situations as two potential factors which might influence the credibility of the child witness. It investigates in particular whether the ICC, the Court which is focussed upon in this research, refers to these two factors as grounds for the unreliability of child witness testimony. The chapter continues with an overview of those measures which could enhance the credibility of child witness testimony, in particular witness familiarisation and age determination. This analysis thereby pursues to provide insights to the underlying question whether the rules should be applied differently compared to adults when the child witness testifies. Finally, some concluding observations are offered.

2.2 Child Witnesses in International Criminal Proceedings

Until the first indictments before the ICC, child witnesses were either not at all or to a very limited extent called to testify in international criminal proceedings. In addition to the practice of international criminal courts, child witnesses testified

[113] Beresford 2005, at 722. For further explanation on the examination procedure before the International Criminal Court, see Schabas 2011, at 313-314.

before the Sierra Leonean, Liberian and South African Truth and Reconciliation Commissions.[114]

Publicly available information on the overall numbers of child witnesses is not easy to access. On the one hand, exact numbers are difficult to track as a result of protective measures applied in the course of the proceedings.[115] On the other hand, the respective Registries did not publish statistics on child witnesses. Neither were they willing to share this information upon request. An estimation of the number can, nevertheless, be traced from decisions taken within the course of the proceedings and also judgments.

Before the ICTY, only two young witnesses gave testimony while in total more than 6,000 witnesses testified.[116] In the *Galic* case, for instance, a witness gave testimony on how she was injured by a bullet.[117] Children were not called to the witness stand before the International Criminal Tribunal for Rwanda.[118] The limited amount of practice indicates that child witness testimony was not a widespread practice before the *ad hoc* tribunals.

---

114 The TRCs addressed the situation of children in their final reports. The aforementioned TRCs specifically included children in their mandates and invited them to statement sessions. See, for instance the final reports of the following TRCs: South Africa, Guatemala (Commission for Historical Clarification, CEH), Guatemala (Recovery of Historical memory Project, REMH), Peru, Timor-Leste, Sierra Leone and Liberia. See generally in this regard, UNICEF 2010a, at 86. See also, for instance, the children's hearings before the South African TRC, http://www.justice.gov.za/trc/special/index.htm#ch.

115 See, for instance, in regard to the proceedings against *Thomas Lubanga Dyilo*, in which pursuant to Rule 81(4) of the 2002 Rules of Procedure and Evidence, the Chambers may order redactions in order to protect the identities of child witnesses if their safety could be at risk. Rule 81(4) provides that, '[t]he Chamber dealing with the matter shall, on its own motion or at the request of the Prosecutor, the accused or any State, take the necessary steps to ensure the confidentiality of information, in accordance with articles 54, 72 and 93, and, in accordance with article 68, to protect the safety of witnesses and victims and members of their families, including by authorization the non-disclosure of their identity prior to the commencement of the trial.' See also in this regards, ICC-01/04-01/06-773, paras. 21, 33 and 34; ICC-01/04-01/06-774, paras. 31-33.

116 More than 6,000 witnesses gave testimony before the ICTY. Young witnesses therefore only amount to 0.0005% of the testimonies. More than 6% of the witnesses were under the age of 30 at the moment of testimony. 12% were older than 60 years. More than 70% were between 30-60 years of age. See, Witness Statistics as of 31 July 2010, http://www.icty.org/sid/10175.

117 The Witness Unit of the ICTY produced statistics between 1996 and 2007 which list how many witnesses testified at the ICTY who were 21 years or younger. In 2002 the Prosecution called a 16-year-old witness in the case of *The Prosecutor of the Tribunal against Stanislav Galic* (IT-98-29-I) and in 2007 a 15-year-old minor in the case of *The Prosecutor of the Tribunal against Ramush Haradinaj, Idriz Balaj & Lahi Brahimaj* (IT-04-84). Witness E testified in the *Galic case* that she was hit by a sniper bullet, *Galic case* transcript of 19 February 2002, http://www.icty.org/x/cases/galic/trans/en/020219ed.htm, at 4028-4080, see also, transcript of 20 February 2002, http://www.icty.org/x/cases/galic/trans/en/020220ED.htm, at 4134. Witness 54 testified about the last time he saw his father - *Haradinaj case* transcript of 11 September 2011, http://www.icty.org/x/cases/haradinaj/trans/en/070911ED.htm, at 8274. Surprisingly, D. Tolbert states in his contribution that child witnesses did not appear before the ICTY until 2006. Tolbert 2006, at 149.

118 UNICEF 2010a, at 17.

A larger, though still limited and, compared to the overall number of witnesses, rather small number of child witnesses gave testimony before the SCSL. Until June 2009, among the more than 500 hundred witnesses, twenty former child soldiers had given testimony.[119] Accordingly, child testimony before the SCSL was limited to the direct victims of international crimes.

Different conclusions can be drawn from the pending cases before the ICC – in particular from the practice of the competent Chambers and the Office of the Prosecutor in the case against *Thomas Lubanga Dyilo* and the combined cases against *Germain Katanga and Mathieu Ngudjolo Chui*. In these cases the recruitment of children below the age of fifteen years was a prominent charge.[120]

The first case before the ICC, the proceedings against *Thomas Lubanga Dyilo*, is of particular importance in this context. In this case, children were the direct victims of the single crime charged, the recruitment of child soldiers. In order to achieve a conviction for the recruitment of children below the age of fifteen, an essential part of the prosecutorial strategy was to call victim witnesses who could testify on their personal experiences as former child soldiers.[121] Consequently, a high number of child witnesses gave in-court testimony.[122]

---

119 Information received from the SCSL Press and Outreach Officer. 5 in the AFRC case (in total 146 witnesses: 59 prosecution witnesses, 87 defence witnesses); 5 in the CDF case (in total 119 witnesses: 75 prosecution witnesses, 44 defence witnesses); 4 in the RUF case (in total 160: 75 prosecution witnesses, 85 defence witnesses); 6 in the Taylor case (in total 111 witnesses: 91 prosecution witnesses, 20 defence witnesses). Information about the overall number of witnesses called by the Prosecution and Defence is available on the website of the SCSL http://www.sc-sl.org/CASES/tabid/71/Default.aspx. See, for example, the following transcripts: *The Prosecutor of the Special Court v. Issa Hassan Sesay, Morris Kallon, Augustine Gbao*, Case No. SCSL-04-15-PT, Trial Chamber I, transcript of 19 July 2004, witness TFI-199: first witness of the prosecution of Category B; witnesses of this category are child witnesses, at 38, lines 15-17. Same case, transcript of 20 July 2004, at 9, lines 16-21; the boy witness is 17 at the time of testimony, at 13, line 25. He gave testimony about his recruitment at the age of 12 into the Small Boys Unit, at 21, line 5; see also, transcript of 27 July 2004, at 2, lines 34-35. *The Prosecutor of the Special Court v. Alex Tamba Brima, Brima Bazzy Kamara, Santigie Borbor Kanu*, Case No. SCSL-2004-16-T, Trial Chamber II, transcript of 8 July 2005, witness TF-180: at 2, lines 21-22. The exact number varies slightly depending on the sources referred to. For a statistical overview of the number of child witnesses called until 2006, see Sanin & Stirnemann 2008, at 13-14. According to this study, approximately 13 child witnesses testified up to March 2006. Another source states that there have only been five prosecution child witnesses while the defence did not call children into the witness stand, see, Horn, Charters & Vahidy 2009, 135, at 143. Witness TFI-199 was a child witness in the AFRC Trial before Trial Chamber II who claimed to be 18 years old at the moment of testimony and 11 at the moment of recruitment, see K. Sanin, *Special Court Monitoring Program Update #57 Trial Chamber II AFRC Trial*, 5 October 2005 http://www.ocf.berkeley.edu/~changmin/SL-Reports/057.pdf.

120 ICC-01/04-01/06-803; ICC-01/04-01/07-717.

121 See, for example, testimony of victim witness DRC-OTP-WWWW-0007, ICC-01/04-01/06-T-148-ENG.

122 It needs to be noted that the following calculation, as far as the *Katanga* case is concerned, is only preliminary due to the ongoing proceedings: nine young witnesses below the age of 21 gave

The importance of the statements of child witnesses in ICC proceedings is also reflected in the decisions confirming the charges: Pre-Trial Chamber I in the *Lubanga* case, for instance, repeatedly referred to statements provided by former child soldiers.[123] At the trial stage of the same case, one third (9 out of 28) of the Prosecution witnesses were young former child soldiers.[124]

---

testimony in the proceeding against *Thomas Lubanga Dyilo*, and four child witnesses testified in the proceedings against *Germain Katanga* and *Mathieu Ngudjolo Chui*. The testimony of the young witnesses is elaborated in more detail below. For general information on the number of witnesses called, see ICC-01/04-01/06-2842; Case Information Sheet of 15 October 2010, *The Prosecutor v. Thomas Lubanga Dyilo*, ICC-PIDS-CIS-DRC-01/004/10; see also, http://www.lubangatrial.org/background/. For general information on the number of witnesses called, see Case Information Sheet of 15 October 2010, *The Prosecutor v. Germain Katanga & Mathieu Ngudjolo Chui*, ICC-PIDS-CIS-DRC2-03-004/10; ICC-01/04-01/07-1665, para. 7; see also, http://www.katangatrial.org/2011/03/parties-prepare-for-start-of-defence-case/. In the ongoing proceedings against *Germain Katanga and Mathieu Ngudjolo Chui* at least four children (out of 26 witnesses) have been called by the prosecution to give testimony with regard to the charge of using child soldiers below the age of fifteen, ICC-01/04-01/07-1665, para. 7. The following witnesses are child witnesses: witness 157 and 280, ICC-01/04-01/07-692, paras. 16, 18; witness 28 and 279, ICC-01/04-01/07-699-tENG, paras. 51, 53. Witness 28 (was also called to testify in the *Lubanga* case), 157, 279 and 280 are all former child soldiers, ICC-01/04-01/07-T-42-ENG, paras. 142-143. ICC-01/04-01/06-T-107-ENG, at 33-34. For the identification numbers of the nine former child soldiers, see ICC-01/04-01/06-1650-Anx, para. 9. See, for instance, statement of witness 007, ICC-01/04-01/06-T-148-ENG, 13 March 2009, at 24, line 3; statement of witness 008, ICC-01/05-01/06-T-135-Red-ENG, 25 February 2009 see also, commentary on the witness's testimony http://www.aegistrust.org/images/reports_briefings_2009/lc02.pdf; statement of witness 011, ICC-01/04-01/06-T-138-ENG, at 47-76. Witness 007 and 0294 were also called in the *Germain Katanga* case, *Situation in the Democratic Republic of the Congo in the case of the Prosecutor v. Germain Katanga and Mathieu Ngudjolo Chui*, Public Redacted Version of the Decision of the Prosecutor's Application to Redact Information Falling under Rule 77 of the Rules of Procedure and Evidence (Witness 007 and 294) of 17 June 2009 (ICC-01/04-01/07-1214-Conf-Exp), ICC-01/04-01/07-1240, 23 June 2009, para. 28.

123 ICC-01/04-01/06-803, paras. 250-251; ICC-01/04-01/07-717, paras. 255-256. *Situation in the Democratic Republic of the Congo in the case of The Prosecutor v. Thomas Lubanga Dyilo*, Decision on the confirmation of charges, ICC-01/04-01/06-803-tEN, 29 January 2007, paras. 250-251. See in particular paras. 385-390: interview of MONUC protection officer with a 14 year old child. From reading the decision on the confirmation of charges in the *Germain Katanga & Mathieu Ngudjolo Chui* case it becomes clear that child witnesses were involved. The Chamber underlines, for instance that 'the VWU shall give due regard to the particular needs of children [...] In order to facilitate the participation and protection of children as witnesses, VWU may assign, as appropriate, and with the agreement of the parents or the legal guardian, a child support person to assist a child through all stages of the proceedings; [...]', ICC-01/04-01/07-717, para. 144. Furthermore, the Chamber relied on evidence provided by young witnesses. The Chamber stated in para. 260 of the same decision that, '[i]n reaching this finding, the Chamber takes into account, *inter alia*, the following evidence: i. the statements of Witness 28, who was a child soldier and actively participated in the hostilities against the village of Bogoro on 24 February 2003. Witness 28 [REDACTED] was approximately thirteen years old during the attack on Bororo on 24 February 2003. [...] iii. The statement of Witness 280, who was a child soldier and actively participated in the hostilities. [...] Witness 280 [REDACTED] was twelve years old during the Bogoro attack on 24 February 2003; and iv. the statement of Witness 279, who was a child soldier and actively participated in the hostilities on the village of Bogoro on 24 February 2003. Witness 279 [REDACTED] was approximately eleven years old during the Bogoro attack on 24 February 2003.'

The practice of the SCSL and the ICC establishes that, thus far, children gave testimony in cases against alleged perpetrators who were responsible for the war crime of recruiting child soldiers. Furthermore, all institutions have in common that they only called young adolescents into the witness stand. Infants were not called to testify.[125]

Currently, it is too early to draw definite conclusions as regards the percentage of child witness testimony compared to adult testimony. Tendencies are visible. International practice alludes that the prosecution teams tend to call witnesses other than children for crimes that do not particularly address child victims. The overview of the international practice also shows that the overall number of child witnesses called in international proceedings is increasing while not constituting a majority compared to other witness testimony.

2.3 Rules Governing Witness Testimony During Trial Proceedings

Rules governing witness testimony during trial proceedings serve as the point of departure for an analysis of the legal status of the child witness. In turn, both, the general rules applying to witness testimony and the few regulations which are child-specific are for this reason briefly described.

Under the Rome Statute, the Prosecution may call witnesses.[126] Equally, one of the core rights of the accused is the right to call for the presence and examination of witnesses.[127] Article 64(6)(b) of the Rome Statute empowers the Court to call witnesses. The provision states that the Trial Chamber may,

> '[r]equire the attendance and testimony of witnesses [...].

It is debated whether this provision, in conjunction with the earlier mentioned Rule 65 RPE can be understood to compel witnesses to provide testimony.[128] In contrast to the silence of the Rome Statute and the Respective Rules in this regard, the Rules of the SCSL explicitly provide in relation to children that they cannot be forced to give testimony.[129]

---

124 ICC-01/04-01/06-2842.

125 In contrast, children have been called to give testimony in national proceedings in cases of child sexual abuse where young children are the only witness, See, Coolbear 1992, 151-167; Yung 1983, 1745-1766.

126 Art. 54(3)(b) Rome Statute.

127 Art. 67(1)(e) Rome Statute.

128 For an overview of the debate, see Alamuddin 2010, at 250.

129 Rule 90(c) RPE of the SCSL.

The first practice of the ICC mirrors that witnesses, other than the suspect or the accused, have not been compelled to provide testimony.[130] It thus seems that the Court follows the principle of the voluntary appearance of witnesses in its practice.[131] In this regard, Schabas also underlined that children, like any other witnesses, have to appear on a voluntary basis before the Court and cannot be compelled to provide testimony in ICC proceedings.[132]

Prior to their testimony, witnesses have to make the solemn undertaking that they will speak the truth.[133] Paragraph 2 of Rule 66 RPE provides an exception for child witness testimony. It states that,

> 'A person under the age of 18 or a person whose judgment has been impaired and who, in the opinion of the Chamber, does not understand the nature of a solemn undertaking may be allowed to testify without this solemn undertaking if the Chamber considers that the person is able to describe matters of which he or she has knowledge and that the person understands the meaning of the duty to speak the truth.'

A particular situation exits when victims are called to give testimony. As a result of the novelty of victim participation in the criminal proceedings before the ICC which is addressed later (*Chapter Three*), a selected number of witnesses may, as established in the proceedings against *Thomas Lubanga Dyilo*, also take part as participants.[134]

The ICC recognised that some witnesses may hold a so-called *dual status* – individuals who qualify as victims within the meaning of Rule 85 RPE and who are at the same time called as witnesses are classified as *victim-witness*.[135] The participation of victims, including children, enjoying a dual status gives rise to procedural issues which are particularly related to their protection and communication between the parties, participants and organs of the Court. Since this particular aspect of dual status witnesses is of a more general nature and therefore less child specific, a deeper analysis falls outside the ambit of the present research.[136]

---

130 In the Lubanga case, for instance, 62 witnesses were called, among these witnesses were *inter alia* two alleged former child soldiers, a head of school, victim witnesses and expert witnesses, ICC-01/04-01/06-2842, at 101-230; see also, http://www.lubangatrial.org/background/.

131 Sluiter 2005, at 218.

132 Schabas 2011, at 316.

133 Rule 66(1) RPE.

134 Art. 68(3) Rome Statute; ICC-01/04-01/06-1379, para. 72.

135 Eikel 2012, at 100; Borda 2010, at 10.

136 For further information, see International Criminal Court, Representing Victims Before the International Criminal Court 2010, at 152-158.

2.4 Ability to Provide Informed Consent and the Protection of the Child Witness

The practice of international criminal courts and tribunals established that children participate in the capacity of child witnesses. It will be established in turn that the ability to provide informed consent and the protection of the child constitute the two pillars of their participation. The questions addressed in relation to the ability to provide informed consent of the child are formulated as follows: what are the rules on consent to testify and consent to disclose medical records? How are these rules interpreted by the Court, and do we need new rules or a more child-sensitive interpretation? As regards the protection of the child witness, it is examined what protective measures exist to protect the child against re-traumatisation, the accused and self-incrimination. How are these rules interpreted and applied in practice, and do we need a more child-sensitive approach?

2.4.1 Informed consent of the child witness

The ability of the child witness to give consent is governed if not even limited by a number of legal matters. Firstly, testifying in ICC proceedings presupposes that the child witness is able to provide informed consent to testify. Secondly, as child testimony thus far only occurred in relation to children as direct victims of the crime of recruitment, the determination of the child's age calls for particular attention in relation to the child's consent to disclose medical records. Consent to disclose medical records is important as the crime definition of the recruitment crime requests that it is proven that the victim has been below the age of fifteen years at the moment of victimisation. Without the disclosure of age determination results it might be impossible to prove beyond reasonable doubt that this particular element of crime is fulfilled.

The need to obtain an informed decision has only occasionally been explicitly addressed in the procedural rules of the International Criminal Court. Remarkably, not the child's but the parent's or legal guardian's consent is referred to. In order to question children, the Prosecution is explicitly obliged to obtain the consent of the caretaker of the child. [137] Regulation 38 of the Regulations of the office of the Prosecutor states that,

---

137 With regard to the legal representation of participants/claimants, Article 15 of the *Code of Professional Conduct for Counsel* states that, '[c]ounsel shall provide the client with all explanations reasonably needed to make informed decisions regarding his or her representation.' The wording of this provision does not answer the question whether legal counsel may obtain an informed decision from children. Bearing the above-mentioned elements of an informed decision in mind, the following aspects must be covered: children need to be informed, for instance, about the procedure itself, the role of the legal representative and the possible implications of participation in ICC proceedings through a legal representative. This information is to be provided in order to enable the child to voluntarily decide whether to be represented. The code of conduct is

'[w]hen a person is under the age of eighteen, the Office shall obtain consent [to testify] from his or her parents, guardians or other relevant adult before questioning. In considering whether to question such a person, the Office shall take into account his or her best interests in accordance with article 68.'[138]

The legal incompetence of children to give an informed decision with regard to their participation as child witnesses is also reflected in the Regulations of the Registry. The admission of child witnesses into the Court's protection programme, for instance, which is decided upon by the Registrar, requests the prior consent of the representative of the child. Regulation 96(5) of the Regulations of the Registry states that,

'[b]efore being included in the protection programme, the person or – where the person is under the age of eighteen or otherwise lacks the legal capacity to do so – his or her representative, shall sign an agreement with the Registry.'

The wording does not clarify whether the representative of the child is solely understood to be the next of kin or legal guardian of the child or whether the legal representative is also recognised as being competent to provide such consent. Unquestioned seems to be that children themselves are not legally competent in this regard. As a result, the procedural regulations under the Rome Statute require that either the parent, the legal guardian or other relevant adult provides informed consent to the child's testimony. A need to gain the informed consent of the child concerned is not mentioned in the respective regulations.

The requirement to obtain prior consent from a parent or legal guardian as established in Regulation 38 has not always been recognised to be indispensable by the Prosecution. Prior to the entry into force of the Regulations of the Office of the Prosecutor, it has been argued by the Office in the *Germain Katanga and Mathieu Ngudjolo Chui* case that,

'there was no legal requirement in the Court's judicial framework requiring the consent of a parent or guardian prior to interviewing a witness under eighteen years of age. The Prosecution further explained that despite the absence of such requirement, it had obtained consent of a parental authority or legal guardian whenever possible.'[139]

The Defence counsel, on the other side, challenged in the same case that,

'the statements of witnesses who were minors on the ground that the interviews of these witnesses were conducted without certain procedural safeguards in place. In

applicable to the defence counsel and the legal representative of a victim, see art. 1 of the 2006 Code of Professional Conduct for Counsel, ICC-ASP/4/Res.1.

138 2009 Regulations of the Office of the Prosecutor.

139 ICC-01/04-01/07-717, para. 143; ICC-01/04-01/07-692, paras. 15-20.

> particular, the Defence for Mathieu Ngudjolo Chui argues that: (i) Witness 28, who is a minor, was interviewed without the prior consent of a guardian; (ii) as to Witness 157, it is unclear if the person who consented to the witness's interview had the authority to give his consent; (iii) although Witness 279's statement indicated that it was taken after consent had been given, no information was provided as to the capacity of that person to give his consent. The Defence [...] asserted that because minors are especially vulnerable, the consent and presence of a legal guardian is a minimum requirement to ensure the credibility of their testimony.'[140]

In contrast to the later adopted procedural rules and practice, Pre-Trial Chamber I concluded that,

> 'no statutory provision makes the prior consent of a parent or a guardian a condition for a child's testimony. In addition, in regions which have been or are being ravaged by conflict, parental consent can often be unavailable due to, *inter alia*, the disappearance of the child's parents, the separation of the child from his parents in the course of the conflict and/or the death of the child's parents. In the present case, notwithstanding the fact that the Prosecution had no legal obligation under the Statute or the Rules to do so, it took additional measures to secure the consent of a parent or legal guardian when such persons were available.'[141]

Does the above allude that neither the consent of the child witness nor the consent of the caretaker is necessary to be obtained when children are involved in ICC proceedings? Furthermore, can the child's or caretaker's consent never be considered to be sufficient in individual cases?

Extensive legal research addresses the elements of informed consent. Difficulties in defining this doctrine nevertheless remain.[142] The Nuremberg Code of 1947, as the first internationally recognised document, codifies this doctrine as one of its principles.[143] The Code underlines that,

> '[t]he voluntary consent of the human subject is absolutely essential. This means that the person involved should have the legal capacity to give consent; should be so situated as to be able to exercise free power of choice, without the intervention of any element of force, fraud, deceit, duress, over-reaching or other ulterior form of constraint or coercion; and should have sufficient knowledge and comprehension of the elements of the subject matter involved as to enable him to make an understanding and enlightened decision.'[144]

---

140 ICC-01/04-01/07-717, para. 142.

141 Ibid., paras. 146-147.

142 See, e.g., Fadden, Beauchamp & King 1986; Berg *et al.* 1987; Levine 1991, 207-213. Levine 1991, at 207-213.

143 Vollmann & Winau 1996, 1445-1449.

144 Nuremberg Code, Directives for Human Experimentation, http://ohsr.od.nih.gov/guidelines/nuremberg.html.

The elements of this definition are addressed in more detail by Meisel and Roth, who argue that the doctrine of informed consent is comprised of five components, namely: information, competency, understanding, voluntariness and decision.[145]

As regards the first component it is required that children, in order to formulate a decision based on informed consent, be provided with the information needed to understand the implications of their decision.

Closely related to the above are the second and third component: the child's competency to provide informed consent and its capacity to understand the implications of this act.

With regard to the competency of the child, it is noted that an increasing capability of the child calls for more child involvement and lessens his or her need to be supervised or guided by others and thereby not being involved in the decision-making process.[146] As a result of the developmental progression, the child should gradually be provided with greater responsibilities for decisions that affect him or her.[147] One should recall in this regard that the analysis of the evolving capacities of the child (*Chapter One*) underlines that a general presumption of children being able to understand the given information is difficult to make – an assumption which, by contrast, is usually made with regard to adults. Factors that have an impact on the capacity of the child to comprehend the implications of providing consent are, for instance, the gender of the child, the financial situation, the ethnical or cultural background, the geographic position of the child and also socio-political factors.[148] The age of the child is not among these factors.[149] Closely related to the individual capability of the child is his or her ability to foresee the consequences of the decision (in particular in relation to potential self-incrimination, section 2.4.4). The remaining two components request that the decision to provide informed consent is not only taken, but is taken voluntarily.

Under numerous national jurisdictions, children, particularly those who are very young, such as babies and toddlers, are frequently seen as not being legally competent to provide an informed consent. Instead, the consent is to be obtained from parents or legal guardians.

The circumstances of the proceedings before the ICC, such as war crimes and crimes against humanity, lead to situations in which these care takers may not be at the disposal of the child. Difficulty contacting these caretakers could give rise to procedural difficulties when a party intends to call a child witness. Indeed, it may not be possible at all for a legal representative, the Prosecution or Defence counsel to approach the parents and caretakers.[150] The question therefore arises whether and

---

145 Meisel & Roth 1983, 265, at 271-272.

146 Detrick 1999, at 120.

147 UNICEF 2005b, at 3.

148 O'Kane *et al.* 2009, 267; UNICEF 2005b, 9.

149 Ibid., 4.

150 See for instance under Swiss law: UN Committee on the Rights of the Child, CRC/C/78/Add.3, Switzerland, Consideration of Reports Submitted by States Parties under Article 44 of the

if so, under which circumstances children themselves can give informed consent to testify or disclose medical records in ICC proceedings?

Bearing the above in mind, it should also be remembered that, at the same time, *Chapter One* pointed out that the children involved in ICC proceedings, thus far, have been mainly adolescents and not very young children. It can therefore be held that the need to obtain informed consent of child witnesses in ICC proceedings mainly arises from two particular circumstances.

Firstly, as anticipated before, when the parents or legal guardians are not at the disposal of the child – a scenario that is not unlikely during or in the aftermath of armed conflicts.

Secondly, the informed consent is to be obtained from the child when a conflict of interest is likely to exist between the child and the caretakers. This possibility is not unlikely as a similar need exists in national proceedings which can, to a certain extent be compared with the proceedings before the ICC. This is the case with domestic adoption cases. A conflict of interest between the parent and the child has been an issue in such cases.[151] Similar situations might arise before the ICC. This is because a conflict of interest between, e.g., a former child soldier and his or her caretaker is not unlikely to occur when parents or legal guardians refuse to support the wish of the child to be a witness in the proceedings before the ICC.[152]

That there might indeed be a need to obtain the consent of a child has already been recognised in the course of proceedings before the SCSL. It has been acknowledged in particular that the child's consent is to be obtained in addition to parental consent.[153] UNICEF prepared the *Principles for child protection and participation in transitional justice*. The *Principles* request that,

> '[c]hildren have the right to participate in decisions affecting their lives. The Participation of children should be voluntary, with the informed consent of the child and a parent or guardian.[154]

Convention, Initial reports of States parties due in 1999, Switzerland, 19 October 2001, para. 47; UN Human Rights Council, Working Group on an optional protocol to the Convention on the Rights of the Child, First Session, Geneva 14-18 December 2009, UN. Doc. A/HRC/WG7/1/CRP.5 of 11 December 2009. The possibility that the defence counsel in ICC proceedings is unable to obtain informed consent from caretakers, such as parents or legal guardians is rather unlikely due to the procedural stage in which the defence usually calls child witnesses – that is at an advanced stage of the proceedings. As a consequence, the reunification of children with their families or the availability of legal guardians is more likely to have been arranged in the meanwhile. In other jurisdictions (e.g. England, Australia, Canada), this presumption may be rebutted through proof that the minor is 'mature' (the 'Gillick standard'). See, e.g., D'Cruz & Holmes 2006, 807.

151 For example, Wertheimer 2006.

152 Schabas 2011, 316.

153 Sanin & Stirnemann, 2008, at 35.

154 UNICEF 2010b, 407-411. The Principles have also been referred to by the Special Representative of the Secretary-General for Children and Armed Conflict, UN General Assembly, Report of the

An indication that the Victims and Witnesses Unit is also of the view that a child's consent might be necessary to be obtained is visible in relation to the disclosure of medical records. A report of the Victims and Witnesses Unit of the ICC established that the disclosure of medical records is clearly to be consented to by the child *and* the next of kin or legal guardian of the minor child. It is not sufficient to only obtain the consent of the legal caretaker.

> 'When seeking informed consent to disclose medical records, the patient should be informed of the nature of the information to be revealed, to whom it will be revealed, the purpose for which the information will be used and the consequences. In order to be able to provide informed consent the individual, *or in the case of a minor also the legal guardian*, should be able to comprehend, retain, believe and balance the information provided before arriving at a decision' (emphasis added).[155]

While the foregoing example refers to the need to obtain in addition to the caretaker's consent the informed consent from the child in order to disclose medical records, one can raise the question whether the combined consent of the adult and the child should not generally be preferred when the minor cannot be expected to be capable of providing an informed decision on his or her own.

More recently, UNICEF similarly underlines the need to obtain the consent of the child witness.[156] Does this mean that both the child and the adult consent is to be given, or, alternatively, could, as has just been anticipated, there also be situations in which the consent of the child is sufficient? The latter implies that there could be situations in which adult consent is not necessary at all.

Bearing in mind that the evolving capacities of the child are understood to be dynamic, it is indeed imaginable that adult consent could be dispensable. Secondly, though related to the above, is the question whether in situations in which adult consent is necessary, this consent is limited to the next of kin or legal guardian. Such limitation could be problematic as persons from these two categories might not necessarily be at the disposal. It might also be the case, as has been elaborated upon before, that a conflict of interest exists between the child and the next of kin or legal guardian. It is then necessary to examine whether, and if so, which persons would be suitable to provide the necessary consent. Community members or child rights NGO's could, for instance, come into consideration.

One may conclude that the need to obtain the consent of the next-of-kin or legal guardian when adolescents wish to participate as witnesses can, bearing in mind the evolving capacities of the individual minor, not generally be upheld. It rather seems to be adequate to examine on a case-by-case basis whether such adult consent is

---

Special Representative of the Secretary-General for Children and Armed Conflict, UN Doc. A/65/219 (2010). See also, more recently UNICEF 2009b.

155 ICC-01/04-01/06-2166.

156 UNICEF 2010c, at 16.

dispensable when a child could indeed be presumed to be able to provide informed consent.

2.4.2 Protection of the child witness

The need to protect witnesses prior and during testimony in international criminal proceedings is obvious. Taking into account that witness testimony before the International Criminal Court will generally be conducted during conflict or post-conflict, witnesses are in need of procedural protection in order to prevent that their testimony threatens their well-being.[157] This threat may not only arise from the presence of the accused, but may also, considering the potential risk-of retraumatisation, exist when actors who engage with the witness, such as the Judges, Prosecutors, the Registry, in particular staff from the Victims and Witnesses Unit (VWU) and lawyers do not adequately address and accommodate the witness. The Rome Statute and the respective rules regulate to a certain extent the protection of witnesses. Uncertainty exists, however, as regards the question when exactly is which actor responsible for the protection of the witness.[158]

Particular in relation to child witnesses and in addition to the general aspects and concerns relating to witness protection, there might be a special need that the involvement of the child witness in the course of the investigation phase but also when the child appears in the court room is accommodated by child-sensitive protective measures. Disregarding the child's need to benefit from particular measures of protection might not only entail the risk of re-traumatisation during testimony, but also prevent the child from giving a credible testimony. In order to minimise the negative implications of being questioned on the traumatic experiences and being close to the accused, protective measures may constitute an adequate and necessary tool which aims to comfort the child witness in the court room.

An early example of the awareness regarding the need to apply child-specific procedures and in particular protective measures can be found in the mandate of the Liberian and Sierra Leonean TRC. Sections 24 and 26 of the Liberian mandate state that,

> '[t]he TRC shall consider and be sensitive to issues of human rights violations, gender and gender-based violence [...] and that special mechanisms are employed to handle women and children victims and perpetrators, not only to protect their dignity and safety but also to avoid retraumatization. [...] The TRC shall take into account the security and other interests of victims and witnesses when appearing for hearing, design witness protection mechanisms on a case-by-case basis as well as special programs for children and women both as perpetrators and victims under burdens of

157 Eikel 2012, at 97-98.
158 Ibid., at 97.

> trauma, stigmatization, neglect, shame, ostracization, threats, etc. and others in difficult circumstances who may wish to recount their stories either in privacy or public, subject to the discretion of the TRC.'[159]

Turning next to the legal regime of protective measures under the ICC system, Article 68(1) points out in this regard that the Court is called upon

> 'to take appropriate measures to protect the safety, physical and psychological well-being, dignity and privacy of victims and witnesses.'

In accordance with the principal rule which is provided for in Rule 86 RPE, the Court should take into account the needs of all witnesses, in particular children. In this regard, the Victims and Witnesses Unit has an important task. The VWU is mandated to assist the Court in the protection of witnesses and victims who appear in the courtroom.[160] The Unit should, in particular,

> 'give due regard to the particular needs of children, [...]. In order to facilitate the participation and protection of children as witnesses, the Unit may assign, as appropriate, and with the agreement of the parents or the legal guardian, a child-support person to assist a child through all stages of the proceedings.'[161]

The Rules of Procedure and Evidence of the ICC provide for a variety of general protective measures. Upon request of the parties or participants, the relevant Chamber may, for instance, order the redaction of identifying information and the use of voice distorting technology – measures which could be ordered in order to prevent risks for the witness as the identification of the witness by the accused could threat the well-being of the witness.[162] Article 68(2) of the Rome Statute explicitly calls for *in camera* proceedings when children give testimony – a potential method which could be applied in order to prevent the child witness from being re-traumatised. Other measures which could be applied when children give testimony can be found in Article 69(2) of the Rome Statute. This provision allows

---

159 Truth and Reconciliation Commission of Liberia Mandate, enacted on May 12, 2005, by the National Transitional Legislative Assembly, the TRC Mandate is the Act That Established the Truth and Reconciliation Commission (TRC) of Liberia, http://trcofliberia.org/about/trc-mandate. Less extensive but nevertheless child specific regulation can also be found in the mandate of the Sierra Leonean TRC. Section 7(4) provides that, '[t]he Commission shall take into account the interests of victims and witnesses when inviting them to give statements, including the security and other concerns of those who may wish to recount their stories in public and the Commission m ay also implement special procedures to address the needs of such particular victims as children or those who have suffered sexual abuses as well as in working with child perpetrators of abuses or violations.' See, The Truth and Reconciliation Commission Act 2000, Being an Act to establish the Truth and Reconciliation Commission in line with Article XXVI of the Lome Peace Agreement and to provide for related matters; http://www.sierra-leone.org/Laws/2000-4.pdf.

160 Art. 43(6) Rome Statute, Rules 16 and 17 RPE.

161 Rule 17(3) RPE.

162 Rule 87 RPE.

> 'the giving of viva voce (oral) testimony or recorded testimony of a witness by means of video or audio technology, as well as the introduction of documents or written transcript.'

In addition, the RPE explicitly refer to children as witnesses who might be in need of special measures such as *in camera*, redaction of identifying information or *ex parte* hearings.[163] Rule 88 also refers to special protective measures which may in particular be applied to traumatised children. In this regard, a legal representative, psychologist or family member may be allowed to also attend the hearing. It can be concluded from the aforementioned that the responsibility to accommodate the child in the course of the court-proceedings through the application of protective measures lies with the respective Bench and the Registry, in particular the Victims and Witnesses Unit.

The ICTY was the first international criminal tribunal which recognised the child as a vulnerable witness who is in need of particular procedural protection.[164] The application of protective measures was, due to the lack of procedural regulation, left to the discretion of the particular Bench in each case. In the practice of the ICTY, protective measures have been applied to witnesses of the age of 21 or under.[165] The Trial Chamber in the *Tadic* case elaborated on the particular vulnerability of children and their need of specific protection alongside the example of domestic practice in relation to child victims of sexual assault. The Chamber held that,

> '[f]our of the witnesses who are sought to be protected by the confidentiality measures ordered by the Trial Chamber are allegedly victims of, or witnesses to, cases of sexual assault. The Prosecutor has requested, in Prayer 7, pursuant to Rule 75 (B)(i)(c), that all of the pseudonymed witnesses be permitted to give testimony through closed circuit television and thereby be protected from seeing the accused. This is intended to protect them from possible retraumatization. The Trial Chamber regards such measures as particularly important for victims and witnesses of sexual assault. 46. [...]. The need to show special consideration to individuals testifying about rape and sexual assault has been increasingly recognized in the domestic law of some States. *(See id.* at 22-28, *and see* Brief of Professor Chinkin at 5-6.). [...] South Africa allows the use of closed circuit television in cases of sexual offences where a child witness is involved. *(See* Joint U.S. Brief at 23.) In the United States, several of the constituent states allow closed circuit television in the courtroom, and the Supreme Court held in *Maryland v. Craig* that one-way closed circuit television can be used without violating the Sixth Amendment right to confrontation when the court finds it necessary to protect a child witness from psychological harm. (497 U.S.

---

163 Arts. 68(2), (5) Rome Statute, Rules 87(3), 88 RPE.

164 The ICTY underlined in this regard the need for particular protection of children, see, e.g., *The Prosecutor v. Dusko Tadic A/K/A "Dule"* (IT-94-1-T), Decision on the Prosecutor's Motion Requesting Protective Measures for Victims and Witnesses, 10 August 1995, paras. 45-48. See also, Tolbert, 'Children and International Criminal Law: The Practice of the International Tribunal for the Former Yugoslavia (ICTY)', Arts & Popovski 2006, at 151-152.

165 Statistics provided for by the ICTY. Available upon request.

> 836 (1990).) 48. Another such method is the use of depositions and video conferences. For example, in the United States thirty-seven constituent states permit the use of videotaped testimony of sexually abused children.[166]

Such an approach can also be found in the procedural rules of the SCSL which applied numerous protective measures to child witnesses.[167]

A question which is not answered in the procedural rules under the Rome Statute relates to the eligibility of child specific measures of protection: which witnesses are entitled to benefit from child specific measures of protection? International practice might therefore serve as a useful yardstick. As far as the eligibility of the child witness for specific measures of protection is concerned, the SCSL established that child witness related measures of protection, such as voice-distortion, were not limited to children below the age of eighteen years at the moment of testimony. Instead, it applied a broader age concept of this category.[168] If the Prosecution was uncertain about the age of young witnesses, their classification was determined upon the belief that the potential witnesses were former child soldiers.[169]

In practice, Trial Chamber II followed the categorisation of the Prosecution and applied protective measures for the listed witnesses in the child category, even if they were above the age of eighteen.[170] Such practice indicates that the Court handles a separate category for young witnesses. A deeper inquiry into the age of the young witness was not deemed necessary.[171]

On the other hand, Trial Chamber I of the SCSL applied a stricter approach by requiring a vulnerability assessment of persons above the age of eighteen before applying child-specific protectionist measures.[172] The practice of this Chamber

---

166 *The Prosecutor v. Dusko Tadic A/K/A "Dule"* (IT-94-1-T), Decision on the Prosecutor's Motion Requesting Protective Measures for Victims and Witnesses, 10 August 1995, paras. 45-48.

167 See, for instance, Rule 90(C) of the RPE of the SCSL. For an overview of the rules and practice of the SCSL with regard to child witnesses, see, Sanin & Stirnemann 2008.

168 See, for example, *The Prosecutor of the Special Court v. Alex Tamba Brima, Brima Bazzy Kamara, Santigie Borbor Kanu*, Case No. SCSL-2004-16-T, transcript of 26 September 2005, witness TF-157, at 25-26. Sanin & Stirnemann, 2008, at 4.

169 *The Prosecutor of the Special Court v. Sam Hinga Norman Moinina Fofana Allieu Kondewa*, Case No. SCSL-2004-14-T, transcript of 9 March 2005, at 3-6. The Prosecution distinguished between different categories of witnesses. Child witnesses fell within category B, see for further information with regard to the SCSL, Sanin & Stirnemann, 2008, at 8, 12. All indictments released contain the charge of using child soldiers, http://www.sc-sl.org/CASES/tabid/71/Default.aspx. For explanation of the categories of prosecution witnesses, see, *The Prosecutor of the Special Court v. Issa Hassan Sesay, Morris Kallon & Augustine Gbao*, Decision on Prosecution Motion for Modification of Protective Measures for Witnesses, Case No. SCSL-04-15-PT-180, 5 July 2004, para. 1: I. Witnesses of Fact, Categories within this group: A. Witnesses who are victims of sexual assault and gender crimes, B. Child witnesses, C. Insider witnesses; II. Expert Witnesses and witnesses who have waived their right to protection.

170 Ibid., at 12.

171 Ibid., at 4.

172 *The Prosecutor of the Special Court v. Sam Hinga Norman Moinina Fofana Allieu Kondewa*, Case No. SCSL-2004-14-T, transcript of 9 March 2005, at 10-14.

underlines once more that children and young persons can be placed within a separated category of witnesses to which child-specific measures may be applied.

Having been a child at the moment of crime commission but having reached majority in the meanwhile did not therefore exclude a young witness's eligibility for child-specific protective measures. Granting young persons above the age of eighteen child-specific protective measures indicates that the Special Court felt (at least in some instances) a need to treat these young witnesses as children as far as their procedural protection was concerned.

In light of the limited available practice of the ICC, it seems that the Prosecution recognises former child soldiers (irrespective of their age at the moment of testimony) in terms of protection, as witnesses of particular vulnerability. The Prosecutor underlined, for instance, the need to recognise that former child soldiers are vulnerable witnesses in his opening statement in the *Lubanga* case.[173] The nine young witnesses called by the Prosecution in this case were all classified as vulnerable witnesses – irrespective of whether they were children or young adults at the moment of testimony.[174]

The practice in the Lubanga case therefore indicates that the Office of the Prosecutor and Trial Chamber I recognise former child soldiers (irrespective of their age at the moment of testimony) as particularly vulnerable witnesses in terms of procedural protection.

The protective measures the Court ordered in relation to the first child witness in the *Lubanga* case were threefold: voice and face distortion were applied and the witness was referred to by means of a pseudonym. As a special measure, a support person accompanied the child witness.[175] In the course of the examination by the prosecution, the child witness changed his account by stating that what he said before was not true and in particular, that he had lied about being recruited as a child soldier.[176] Due to the behaviour of the child witness, Trial Chamber I saw an urgent need to order additional measures.[177] The Chamber recognised that,

> '[o]ne of the difficulties that's been brought to our attention is the possibility, and I (the Presiding judge) put it no higher than that, that the witness has been simply overwhelmed by the number of different people who have been speaking to him and the amount of information that's been provided to him.'[178]

173 ICC-01/04-01/06-T-107-ENG, 34-35.
174 ICC-01/04-01/06-T-107-ENG, 33.
175 Ibid., at 11-12.
176 Ibid., at 41.
177 ICC-01/04-01/06-T-111-ENG, 29 January 2009, at 1-2; ICC-01/04-01/06-T-122-ENG, 9 February 2009, at 56-57.
178 ICC-01/04-01/06-T-111-ENG, 29 January 2009, at 5, lines 3-9.

The findings of Trial Chamber I are to some extent surprising, since the same Chamber held in an earlier decision that,

> '[t]here must be awareness of the particular characteristic of a witness which may cause the court environment to be particularly foreign and uncomfortable. In the context of the present case, for example, particular attention should be paid to any children who are called as witnesses to ensure that their psychological well-being is considered as a matter of paramount importance, pursuant to Article 68 of the Statute and Rule 88 of the Rules.'[179]

In this case, the confrontation of the child witness with the accused in the court room had a negative impact on the child's ability to testify. A prior awareness that care is necessary when children provide testimony and therefore ordering those protective measures which could have prevented direct eye-contact could have prevented the strong reaction of the witness. Bearing in mind that the relationship between children and adults is of a hierarchical nature, despite differences depending on the regional environment, the confrontation in the courtroom is also dominated by this vertical relationship.

It might be necessary, bearing in mind the aforementioned example of the *Lubanga* case, to ensure that the courtroom setting is adjusted to the particular needs of the child. Such adjustment, though the application of protective measures could, for instance, ensure that the child witness does not have direct eye contact with the accused. The expert witness on child soldiers and trauma specifically underlined in this regard, that – irrespective of the traumatic experiences – children should not testify when the alleged perpetrator is present. According to the expert witness,

> 'African children in general, but child soldiers in particular have been socialized in highly hierarchical, for the latter even life-threatening environments during their childhood and time in captivity. Even in a normal context, an African child will rarely have been asked to talk about personal experiences or reveal autobiographical memories in detail to an adult listener; especially not to a stranger. A commander will always be an anxiety-including figure; a chief commander is often even perceived as a person with supernatural powers. [...] It needs to be understood that children are conditioned by the military hierarchy and are reticent to betray their commanders, who often remain important figures in their lives even after initial demobilization.'[180]

Barabara Bennet Woodhouse illustratively refers to the practice of the US Supreme Court by stating that,

> 'Although the Sixth Amendment of the Constitution typically requires that a criminal defendant has the opportunity to confront witnesses testifying against him

179 ICC-01/04-01/06-1049.

180 See also, ICC-01/04-01/06-1729-Anx1, 25 February 2009, at 37.

> at trial, the Court has approved the use of television monitors to present the testimony of young children who may be frightened by the prospect of confronting a defendant in person. The Court has continued to interpret rules of evidence broadly wherever possible to keep child witnesses from being subject to traumatic court proceedings.[181]

The presence of *Thomas Lubanga Dyilo* was indeed partially relevant for the initial recantation of the statement of the first Prosecution witnesses.[182]

Furthermore, UNICEF already warned in 2002 that the giving of testimony is likely to harm the child if the particular needs of the child are not taken into account.[183] UNICEF underlined that,

> '[p]articular attention should be paid to *the likely effect on children of testifying in front of the person accused of causing them harm*. Thus *measures designed to shield the child from seeing the accused could be employed*, such as sight-screens to separate child witnesses and the accused, or using closed-circuit television or video links that allow children to testify from outside the courtroom. In addition, while the right to a fair trial dictates that testimony must be tested to ensure it is as accurate as possible, children should never be exposed to the aggressive forms of questioning that may otherwise be employed during cross-examination' (emphasis added).[184]

Bearing in mind that UNICEF explicitly suggested (based in particular on the experience of child witness examination under national jurisdictions) that the child witness should not have direct eye contact with the accused, it seems that the ICC did not properly assess the implications for the first child witness in the *Lubanga* case.[185] Whether similar challenges have been dealt with before the Special Court for Sierra Leone could not be examined as the relevant court records are not as publicly available as the ICC court records.

While the respective Bench and the Victims and Witnesses Unit thus carry a statutory responsibility as regards the protection of child witnesses in the course of the court-room proceedings, a responsibility to protect is also recognised, while not as such being explicitly regulated under the RPE, prior to the involvement of the young witnesses in the courtroom setting. Noteworthy in this regard is the Court's strategy in relation to victims. The 2009 Report of the Court on the strategy in relation to victims stresses that,

> '[i]nterviews with investigators and any other interactions between victims and staff members of the Court must be carefully managed in order to avoid retraumatisation or other problems. The OTP will conduct assessments before interviewing

181 Bennett Woodhouse 2006, at 59-60.
182 A detailed description of the incident is given below. ICC-01/04-01/06-2434-Red2, para. 7-10.
183 UNICEF 2002, at 51-52.
184 Ibid., at 52.
185 Ibid., UNICEF 2009b, at 81-82.

vulnerable witnesses in order to determine if they are physically and psychologically fit to go through the interview, and will ensure that a psycho-social expert is available in case an intervention is needed. The OTP, as well as other relevant organs and bodies of the Court, will also ensure that their staff receive training on techniques when interviewing children […].'[186]

Clearly, this approach constitutes an attempt by the Court to ensure better protection of child witnesses by requesting that particular treatment is expected from the Registry and the OTP when conducting interviews with vulnerable witnesses. An equivalent as regards the responsibility of lawyers and legal representatives has not yet been formulated, while, considering the aforementioned, there might also be a corresponding need as regards these actors.

Related to the protection of the child witness is the risk of self-incrimination. Appearing as a child witness in relation to the crime of recruitment might lead to self-incrimination or threat of national criminal proceedings against the child if domestic law allows for the criminal prosecution of minors in this crime context. It is analysed in this regard whether the risk of self-incrimination and threat of domestic criminal proceedings against the child witness constitutes a factor which should lead to the exclusion of child witness testimony. It is to be remembered that self-incrimination or the potential of domestic proceedings equally exists for adult witnesses. A corresponding principle as the principle of the best interests does, however, not exist for adults. While adult witness participation thus is not assessed on the basis of a best interests principle, it may, taking into account the risk of self-incrimination and the threat of domestic criminal proceedings, lead to an exclusion of child witness testimony from the outset.

The discussion held during the previously addressed testimony of the former child soldier indicated that the fear of the child witness to face criminal proceedings before national courts in the DRC made the child change his account.[187]

In this specific case the fear of the child witness was unfounded as the criminal prosecution of minors for war crimes, crimes against humanity or genocide is excluded under Congolese law. The Chamber discussions established, however, that child witnesses in other situations before the ICC may nevertheless be exposed to such a risk as the possibility of domestic proceedings might exist when being provided for in national criminal codes – a possibility which might be provided for in societies which share the view that the criminal prosecution of former child soldiers is to be provided for.[188] Accordingly, while the fear of the young witness in the *Lubanga* case was unfounded, it cannot be said that child witnesses in general cannot be expected to face domestic prosecutions as a result of their statement

---

186 Assembly of States Parties, Eighth session, The Hague, 18-26 November 2009, Report of the Court on the Strategy in relation to victims, ICC-ASP/8/45, 10 November 2009, para. 38.

187 ICC-01/04-01/06-T-110-ENG, 28 January 2009, at 44.

188 ICC-01/04-01/06-T-113-Red-ENG, 30 January 2009, at 8-9.

within the course of ICC proceedings. As a consequence, the risk of self-incrimination and the possibility of domestic criminal proceedings against the witness should generally be assessed by the Court before children are called to give testimony.[189]

The possibility of self-incrimination is in particular not unlikely when former child soldiers testify on international crimes. A prior assessment before in-court testimony of the best interests of the child witness in the light of the other rights of this particular child, such as the right to 'object to making any statement that might tend to incriminate' (Rule 74(3)(a) RPE) might have been helpful. It could have prevented, in particular, the confusion during testimony.[190] Accordingly, if the child is likely to incriminate him or herself, involvement in proceedings before the ICC cannot straightforwardly be considered to be in the best interests of the child. This is because national criminal prosecutions could be opened on the basis of the statement given before the ICC.

2.5 CREDIBILITY

Can a child be considered to be a credible witness? Child witness testimony is accompanied by a number of factors which could be assumed to be decisive for the child's credibility to provide truthful testimony in international criminal proceedings. The trustworthiness of the young witness and the likelihood that the child has been traumatised in the course of the conflict are important in this regard. A child-sensitive approach might be adequate in order to enable the child to provide truthful testimony. Furthermore, various measures are at the Court's disposal to enhance the credibility of young witnesses. Those measures which played a role in the currently most advanced case, the proceedings against *Thomas Lubanga Dyilo*, are addressed in this section.

---

189 Next to the obligation of the Chambers and VWU to ensure the protection of the child, an assessment of the individual constitution of the child is also made by the Office of the Prosecutor. Art. 54(b) of the Rome Statute obliges the Prosecutor to '[t]ake appropriate measures to ensure the effective investigation and prosecution of crimes [...], and in doing so, *respect the interests and personal circumstances of victims and witnesses*, including age [...], in particular where it involves sexual violence, gender violence or violence against children [...]' (emphasis added). It is therefore that the Office of the Prosecutor established the Gender and Children Unit that is mandated to advice the Prosecutor 'in all areas related to sexual and gender violence and violence against children and shall contribute to preliminary examinations and evaluations, investigations and prosecutions in those areas.' See, Regulation 12 Regulations of the Office of the Prosecutor. A publicly available prosecutorial strategy on the assessment of children during the investigation phase is, unfortunately, not available. UNICEF 2010c, at 11-13.

190 Rule 74(3)(a) RPE provides that, '[a] witness may object to making any statement that might tend to incriminate him or her.'

2.5.1 Factors influencing the credibility of the child witness

The *Lubanga* case raises the pertinent question whether children should be deemed incapable to act as credible witnesses at the ICC because of a possible lack of trustworthiness which could be related to their immaturity or potential previous traumatisation in light of the nature of the cases that come before the ICC. This question will be addressed in light of existing literature, scholarly views on this matter as well as views offered by the Bench. In addition, it will be analysed whether other case-specific procedural matters led to the finding of incredibility in the *Lubanga* case, which do not necessarily have broader ramifications beyond this case.

The following analysis thereby aims to discuss the question whether children, bearing in mind their evolving capacities, can be considered to be a credible witness. In addition, the section has as an objective to also further the debate on whether child witness participation is in the best interests of the child and if so, how to welcome the child in a child-sensitive manner in the court room. Child witnesses could, for instance, benefit from witness familiarisation measures. Child-specific procedural accommodation might also be necessary when the accused is in the court room and the child at risk is to have, for instance, direct eye contact with the accused. The trustworthiness of the child and the impact of conflict situations are addressed in turn.

2.5.1.1 Trustworthiness of the child witness

If doubts exist in relation to the trustworthiness of the child due to the fact that children are, compared to adults, more at risk of being influenced if not even manipulated by others before and during testimony, the calling of children into the witness is to be thought through. Furthermore, as children might not understand the importance of telling the truth and tend to lie child testimony might not at all be considered trustworthy.[191] It could also be argued on the other hand, that a general assumption that children are not credible witnesses due to their young age is not accurate. Instead, as the maturity of the minor witness is understood to grow in a dynamic process, child witnesses cannot generally be considered not trustworthy.

The judgment of Trial Chamber I in the *Lubanga* case, which has been upeld by the Appeals Chamber on 1 December 2014, raises the specific question whether child witnesses should indeed be called into the witness stand.[192] In this case, the Chamber refused to rely on evidence provided by former child soldiers. The Chamber explained in relation to each former child soldier why it was unable to

---

191 For further information regarding the suggestibility of children during testimony, see, Candel *et al.* 2004, 9-18; Memon & Vartoukian 1996, 403-415; Ceci & Bruck 1993, 403-439.

192 ICC-01/04-01/06-3121.

rely on the testimony. The reason for exclusion was always found to be the result of the unreliability of the witnesses' statements. In relation to witness P-0298, for instance, the Chamber held

> 'Notwithstanding the prosecution's suggestion that P-0298's initial testimony was merely the result of his anger, the evidence overall before the Chamber creates a real doubt as to his honesty and reliability. Additionally, the real possibility exists that he was encouraged and assisted by P-0321 to give false evidence. P-0298 is not a witness on whom the Chamber is able to rely.'[193]

The ruling invites a reconsideration of the actual importance of child witnesses in international criminal proceedings. Trial Chamber I and the Appeals Chamber have been convinced beyond reasonable doubt that *Thomas Lubanga Dyilo* has recruited children below the age of fifteen years without relying on evidence provided by child witnesses. The statement that child witness testimony is to be the *condition sine qua non* in selected cases might therefore not be valid. Child witness testimony could even be said to be not as relevant as argued by the Office of the Prosecutor in the *Lubanga* case despite the fact that child specific crimes have been charged.[194]

The credibility of the child witness has, prior to the existence of international criminal proceedings, been addressed within the course of domestic proceedings.[195] The approach of the United States, for instance, has been explained by Barbara Bennett Woodhouse who clarified that,

> '[t]he changing status of children is also reflected in their role as witnesses in court proceedings. Traditionally, children were deemed incompetent to testify because they could not appreciate the oath, required of all witnesses to tell the truth. The modern rules allow admission of very young children's testimony and allow judges and juries to determine how well the child can process information.'[196]

The general recognition of the child as a potential credible statement provider is also reflected in the procedural rules of the SCSL and ICC by not questioning his or her reliability.[197] Neither has age been introduced as a factor which determines whether children are capable of providing truthful testimony.[198] Paragraph 18 of the

---

193 ICC-01/04-01/06-2842, para. 441. See in the same tenor the Chamber's conclusion in relation to the other former child soldiers who gave testimony: witness P-0213, paras. 394-406; witness P-0294, paras. 407-415; witness P-0297, paras. 416-429.

194 See for strong criticism Appeals Chamber Judge Anita Ušacka's dissenting opinion relating to the implications of the exclusion of child witnesses' evidence for the conviction of *Thomas Lubanga Dyilo* by Trial Chamber I, ICC-01-04-01/06-3121, paras. 17-18.

195 See, for instance, the calling of children into the witness stand under Dutch law, Rassin & van Koppen 2002, at 507-530. Whitcomb 2003, 149, at 153; Whitcomb 1986, 90, at 93; Bruck, Ceci & Hembrooke 1998, 136-151.

196 Bennett Woodhouse 2006, 51, at 59.

197 As regards national law, see, for instance, Rassin & van Koppen 2002, at 509.

198 See, for instance, Rule 90(C) of the RPE of the SCSL.

UN *Guidelines on Justice in Matters involving Child Victims and Witnesses of Crime* underlines in this regard that,

> '[a]ge should not be a barrier to a child's right to participate fully in the justice process. Every child should be treated as a capable witness, subject to examination, and his or her testimony should not be presumed invalid or untrustworthy by reason of the child's age alone as long as his or her age and maturity allow the giving of intelligible and credible testimony, with or without communication aids and other assistance.'[199]

Scholars have noted in relation to domestic practice that, leaving the capacity of very young children to give a statement aside, the age of the child is not decisive for the child to provide testimony. Children are not less capable than adults of providing truthful testimony.[200] This does not diminish the need that all actors who engage with the child witness are trained in particular skills in order to ensure that the child is adequately addressed.[201] Domestic practice established that an individual assessment is indispensable when examining the child's credibility.[202] Instead of age, other factors have been acknowledged as relevant when determining a child's maturity. The developmental stage, a constrained ability to concentrate due to a psychological disease, the shamefulness of the traumatic experience, the magnitude of traumatic events or the educational background of the child have been mentioned as important aspects when assessing the ability of the child to give truthful testimony.[203] Next to the traumatic experience of the child (which is addressed in more detail below), failing to take into account the child's specific background, may hinder the child to give reliable testimony in the courtroom.[204]

Turning next to the case law of the ICC, it is noted that the analysis focuses on the practice in the *Lubanga* case. Only in this specific case did child witness testimony play a major role in the course of the proceedings. In line with the foregoing, the presiding judge of Trial Chamber I, for example, reminded the Defence of *Thomas Lubanga Dyilo* to formulate questions in a more child-suitable manner.[205] When the witness repeatedly stated that he did not understand the question posted by the Defence, Judge Fulford held that,

---

199 ECOSOC Guidelines 2005, para, 18. See for further explanation, UNICEF 2009b, at 25-26.

200 Fote 1985, 157, at 158-159. Very young children are not likely to be called to the witness stand for the simple reason that numerous elder witnesses can be expected to be available to testify about international crimes. *Chapter One* established that child participation is thus far limited to the participation of juveniles. Therefore the current research does not elaborate further on the capability and credibility of very young child witnesses.

201 See, for instance, Saywitz, Snyder & Nathanson 1999, 58-68; Walker & Nguyen 1995, 1587-1618; Poole & White 1991, 975-986.

202 See, for instance, Walker & Nguyen 1995, 1587-1618; Fote 1985, 157-184.

203 Ibid..

204 Tufnell 2003, 431, at 439.

205 Committee on the Rights of the Child, General Comment No. 12, para. 64. See also, Alink & van Zeden 2006, at 147.

> 'I think the rather formal procedure that certainly works when questioning bankers and financiers and others of formally putting your case may work with witnesses of that kind. I think for others, who are completely unused to trial proceedings of this nature, it is actually quite a difficult concept to understand and to know what the appropriate response is. [...] I think a more direct form of questioning is better than going through the slightly more baroque style of putting your case.'[206]

This position underlines that the Chamber is aware of the fact that questions must also be phrased in a manner that children can be expected to understand.[207]

The appearance of the first Prosecution witness in the ICC proceedings against *Thomas Lubanga Dyilo*, on the other hand, gives rise to questioning the generally presumed credibility of child witnesses. This case shows in particular that children can easily be influenced by others in relation to their testimony. Witness 298 started his testimony on 28 January 2009. He initially explained that he had been recruited on his way home from school. At a later stage in his testimony, he recanted his earlier statement concerning his recruitment and held that it was not true and that he had been trained by someone regarding the statement he had provided. After an adjournment of his testimony for two weeks, the same witness continued on 10 February 2009 when he announced – contrary to his previous statement – that his primary statement on his alleged recruitment was the truth and that he had not been trained to lie.[208]

The Defence of *Thomas Lubanga Dyilo* underlined in the opening statement of 27 January 2010 that,

> 'the Defence intend to provide the Chamber with the results of our inquiries, in particular, we intend to demonstrate that all the individuals who were presented as child soldiers, as well as their parents in some cases, deliberately lied before this Court. The Defence intend to show that six of them were never child soldiers. The seventh lied about his age and the conditions in which he enrolled and the eighth never belonged to the UPC.'[209]

During the proceedings, the Defence challenged the testimony of the nine witnesses called by the Prosecution who held that they had been child soldiers.[210] Numerous contradictions between the statements of child witnesses and the witnesses called by the Defence have been established.[211] The Defence team argued in particular that four intermediaries of the Prosecution were

---

206 ICC-01/04-01/06-T-229-Red-ENG, 19 January 2010, at 5-6.
207 Rassin & van Koppen 2002, at 526.
208 ICC-01/04-01/06-2434-Red2, paras. 7-10.
209 ICC-01/04-01/06-T-236-Red-ENG, 27 January 2010, at 21.
210 ICC-01/04-01/06-2842, para. 37.
211 ICC-01/04-01/06-2434-Red2, paras. 7-54. See also, SCSL proceedings in which Defence has challenged the credibility of the witness: *The Prosecutor of the Special Court v. Alex Tamba*

> 'involved in soliciting false testimony from all prosecution witnesses who were called to give evidence as former child soldiers [...]'.[212]

In response to the allegations raised by the Defence of *Thomas Lubanga Dyilo*, Trial Chamber I, recognised the potential relationship between the reliance of the Prosecution on intermediaries and the alleged false statements of the child witnesses. The Chamber ordered the Prosecution to disclose the identity of intermediary 143 and the appearance of intermediaries 316 and 321.[213]

In the course of the proceedings it became clear that these intermediaries (human rights activists) had established contact between the child witnesses and the Prosecution.[214] For protectionist reasons, the Office of the Prosecutor decided to communicate with the witnesses through intermediaries. The Prosecutor argued that direct contact between the Prosecution and the child witnesses could, according to the Prosecution, constitute a threat to the well-being of the witnesses.[215] The practice of the Prosecution in relation to intermediaries has been summarised as follows by Trial Chamber I:

> 'from the outset of the investigation, human rights activists gave the investigators the names of potential witnesses, since they had "seen these people and they knew what they were going to say". Because of their long-term presence, it was considered that the activists were better placed than the investigators, and particularly it did not cause any surprise when the activists spoke with representatives of MONUC or had discussions with villagers. The investigators could not move about freely without being threatened and witnesses were endangered if the investigators spoke directly with them. As a result, the investigating team or some of the activists suggested the latter should act as intermediaries. Therefore, from early on, even with the assistance of the intermediaries, the investigators were restricted as to the timing and the location of any meetings, and they had to act discreetly.'[216]

Brima, Brima Bazzy Kamara, Santigie Borbor Kanu, Case No. SCSL-2004-16-T, testimony of witness TF1-157, transcript of 26 September 2005, at 25:

Q. At the time you were taken from Bo-Ngieha were you at school?
A. Yes.
Q. What class were you in?
A. Class two.
Q. And at class two you would be able to tell the days of the week; not so? At that time you could tell the days of the week; you could read them or name them?
A. At that time I was not going to school.
Q. When they took you from Bo-Ngieha you weren't going to school at all?
A. No.

212 ICC-01/04-01/06-2842, para. 38.

213 ICC-01/04-01/06-2434-Red2, paras. 138-150.

214 Intermediary 143 established contacts between the OTP and witnesses P-0007, P-0008, P-0010 and P-001, see judgment, para. 291. Intermediary 321 introduced witnesses P-0157, P-0213, P-0294, P-0297 and P-0298, see ICC-01/04-01/06-2842, para. 383.

215 Ibid., paras. 183-184.

216 Ibid., para. 167.

In its judgment, Trial Chamber I decided that,

> 'given the pattern of unreliability as regards the witnesses introduced by Intermediary 143 and called to give evidence during the trial (P-0007, P-0008, P-0010 and P-0011), the Chamber accepts that there is a real risk that he played a role in the markedly flawed evidence that these witnesses provided to the OTP and to the Court. Bearing in mind this consistent lack of credibility as regards the trial witnesses he introduced to the investigators, and particularly focussing on the cumulative effect of their individual accounts, it is likely that as the common point of contact he persuaded, encouraged or assisted some or all of them to give false statement. The Chamber accepts that the accounts of P-0007, P-0008, P-0010 and P-0010 were or may have been truthful and accurate in part, but it has real doubts as to critical aspects of their evidence, in particular their age at the relevant time. Although other potential explanations exist, the real possibility that Intermediary 143 corrupted the evidence of these four witnesses cannot be safely discounted.'[217]

The Chamber did not only assess the potential influence of intermediaries. Trial Chamber I examined in detail the credibility of each former child witness who gave testimony on his or her alleged recruitment. The Chamber's conclusion in relation to witnesses P-0007 and P-0008 illustrates that the testimony of former child soldiers have not been relied upon mainly because of contradictions in relation to the name and age of the witnesses, but also as regards facts concerning their recruitment and stay in the Union des Patriotes Congolais (UPC). The Chamber recalled that,

> '[i]n August 2005, the witness (P-0007) apparently told the IEC that his year of birth was 1986, and he gave them a name that differed from the one provided by him to the prosecution. His birth certificated (dated November 2005) records the year of his birth as 1990. Although the witness gave his names in evidence, he explained that his parents, brothers and sisters call him by different names, and later in his testimony he indicated that he had used two further names. He also stated that he was born in 1987 [...]. In these circumstances his reliability is profoundly called into question, given the considerable, and essentially unexplained differences as to the date of birth of this witness, in his oral testimony and in the documentary evidence. The witness gave contradictory testimony concerning the names of his father. [...] It is suggested by the defence that P-0007 gave an implausible account regarding certain aspects of his time in the UPC.'[218]

In relation to witness P-0008 Trial Chamber I pointed out that,

> 'he gave a name that differs slightly from the one on his voting card. He said he was born in 1989 and he provided the names of his parents. P-0008's testimony before the Court on this issue partially contradicts the information on his birth certificate (obtained by P-0143 [intermediary] on 11 August 2005), which states that he was

217 Ibid., para. 291.
218 Ibid., paras. 223-227.

> born in 1991 and lists names for his parents that, to an extent differ from those given in Court. The witness's electoral card indicates that he was born in 1987. P-0008 suggested that soldiers from the UPC forcibly enlisted him at the beginning of 2003, whilst he was attending school. He underwent military training for two weeks at the UPC camp in Irumu, at the conclusion of which he was deployed as a bodyguard. He fought at the battles of Libri and Barrière. However, this account, viewed overall, is contradictory and implausible. The description of his abduction changed significantly […].'[219]

The Chamber furthermore ruled that,

> 'documentary evidence tends to demonstrate that P-0007 and P-0008 lied about having attended school in a particular town in the year 2001-2002 and at the beginning of the 2002-2003 academic year, because the records establish they were both at school in a different location. [...] Witnesses P-0007 and P-0008 were re-interviewed by the prosecution on 7 and 8 January 2010, following their evidence before the Chamber. They accepted that the family relationships were significantly different from the description provided by each of them earlier. […] During their re-interviews with the prosecution, P-007 and P-008 accepted that they had lied about the relationships within their family.'[220]

In conclusion Trial Chamber I held that,

> '[t]he Chamber's assessment of these two witnesses is that the weaknesses and contradictions in their evidence (particularly as to their ages and true identities) along with the evidence of D-0012 undermine the reliability of their testimony. The difficulties with their accounts are not satisfactorily or sufficiently explained by fears for their safety or that of their family. The Chamber is unable to rely on the evidence of either witness in these circumstances.'[221]

The Chamber concluded that it could not rely on any statement provided by alleged former child soldiers in the *Lubanga* case.[222] The general standard which Trial Chamber I applied when assessing the relevance of the oral evidence provided by witnesses reflects that the Chamber applied a comprehensive assessment which also addressed the particularities of child witnesses:

> 'When evaluating the oral testimony of a witness, the Chamber has considered the entirety of the witness's account; the manner in which he or she gave evidence; the

219 Ibid., paras. 213-232.

220 Ibid., paras. 237-238, 244.

221 Ibid., para. 247.

222 Ibid., see the following rejections by Trial Chamber I in the judgment: testimony of P-0007 and P-0008 declared unreliable, para. 247; testimony (with the exception of video material) of P-0010 declared unreliable, paras. 257, 268; testimony of P-0011declared unreliable, para. 288; AAA; testimony of P-0157 declared unreliable, para. 473; testimony of P-0213 declared unreliable, para. 406; testimony of P-0294 declared unreliable, para. 415; testimony of P-0297 declared unreliable, para. 429; testimony of P-0298 declared unreliable, para. 441.

> plausibility of the testimony; and the extent to which it was consistent, including as regards other evidence in the case. The Chamber has assessed whether the witness's evidence conflicted with prior statements he or she had made, insofar as the relevant portion of the prior statement is in evidence. In each instance the Chamber has evaluated the extent and seriousness of the inconsistency and its impact on the overall reliability of the witness. The Chamber has made appropriate allowance for any instances of imprecision, implausibility or inconsistency, bearing in mind the overall context of the case and the circumstances of the individual witnesses. For example, the charges relate to events that occurred in 2002 and 2003. Memories fade, and witnesses who were children at the time of the events, or who suffered trauma, may have had particular difficulty in providing a coherent, compete and logical account. [...] The Chamber called a psychologist who gave expert testimony on the psychological impact of a child having been a soldier and the effect of trauma on memory.'[223]

Each testimony of child witnesses has thus carefully been assessed. Trial Chamber I did not exclude their testimony from the outset. Additional legal consequences, besides the refusal of the Chamber to rely on the statements provided by these witnesses were only formulated in relation to those child witnesses who were also participating as victims in the course of the criminal proceedings. The Chamber was no longer convinced that the these participants were victims of the charged crime. Thus those children who gave evidence as witnesses in the criminal proceedings while participating as victims at the same time, were also to be excluded from further participation.[224] The Chamber did not rule further on possible legal consequences for the child witnesses for providing false information. Instead, the Judges only pointed out in this regard that the possibility to instigate proceedings against the intermediaries under Article 70 of the Rome Statute for alleged offences against the administration of justice remains with the Prosecution.[225]

Keeping in mind that next to the *Lubanga* case, the experience of the ICC in relation to child witnesses is thus far rather limited it is stated with the necessary caution that nevertheless more accuracy during the investigation phase, in particular better monitoring of intermediaries by the Prosecution by, for instance, introducing a transparent procedure and qualification requirements for the appointment of intermediaries, could perhaps have made a difference and enabled the Chamber to rule other than not relying on these testimonies. In the end, the entire exclusion of children's testimony in the *Lubanga* case might give rise to at least two questions. Firstly, are, according to the Chamber, children in general or child soldiers, as particular group of child witnesses, prone to be unreliable witnesses or was the unreliability only the result of inadequacy of the Prosecution's investigations and strategy and should no general conclusion be drawn from this? Secondly, is child

223 Ibid., paras. 102-105.
224 Ibid., paras. 478-484.
225 Ibid., para. 483.

testimony in fact actually indispensable when crimes committed against children are prosecuted?

With regard to the first question, the Chamber clearly states that it disapproves of the inaccuracy in the selection of child witnesses by heavily criticising the Prosecution for its delegation of investigative tasks to intermediaries. It did not generally exclude the use of child witnesses. The Chamber unmistakably formulated its dissatisfaction. It stated that,

> '[t]he Chamber is of the view that the prosecution should not have delegated its investigative responsibilities to the intermediaries in the way set out above, notwithstanding the extensive security difficulties it faced. A series of witnesses have been called during this trial whose evidence, as a result of the essentially unsupervised actions of three of the principal intermediaries, cannot safely be relied on. The Chamber spent a considerable period of time investigating the circumstances of a substantial number of individuals whose evidence was, at least in part, inaccurate or dishonest.'[226]

With regard to the second question, it is important to note that the conviction of *Thomas Lubanga Dyilo* was instead based on statements provided by adult witnesses (NGO workers or witnesses closely related to *Lubanga*) and documentary evidence, in particular video footage.[227] The evidence of child witnesses was thus not necessary in order to achieve a conviction – child witness testimony was not relied upon at all, despite the fact that it considered a case in which children were the only direct victims.

Since the exclusion of child witness testimony was mainly the result of inaccurate research done by the Prosecution prior to the children's testimony, it seems to be too drastic to conclude that child witness testimony is also beyond the *Lubanga* case not important at all. Instead, there might, after careful assessment, be cases in which the testimony of children could be considered to be highly relevant when, for instance, children are the only witnesses. Cases in which sexual violence has allegedly been committed against children might constitute such cases.

In contrast to the judgment in the *Lubanga* case, the SCSL did rely on former child soldiers' testimony in its judgments after assessing the credibility of the witnesses. Trial Chamber I, for instance, in the case of *The Prosecutor v. Issa Hassan Seay, Morris Kallon and Augustine Gbao* held that,

> '[s]everal of the witnesses who testified were former child combatants who had been captured by the RUF at ages as young as ten. Many of these child witnesses experienced serious physical and mental trauma both during and after the war. Many were forced to consume or use drugs throughout their time in the RUF. Due to the fact that the events they attempt to recount took place largely during their childhood,

226 Ibid., para. 482.

227 Ibid., paras. 632-916. The strong criticism of Judge Anita Ušacka in her dissenting opinion to the Appeals Chamber judgment of 1 December 2014 is addressed in more detail in section 2.5.3.2.

> their ability to recall such events is compounded by the passage of time. This means that such witnesses generally experienced difficulty in remembering specific details about such events, and various minor discrepancies are identifiable in their evidence. However, the Chamber has generally accepted the evidence of former child soldiers, especially as it relates to their own experiences. [...] [228]

Without ignoring the fact that some testimony of former child soldiers contained discrepancies, Trial Chamber I clarified in its judgment that evidence which related to acts and conduct of the accused (thus not describing the personal experiences of the child witness) could only be relied upon when supported by corroborating evidence as it concerned the testimony of a child.[229]

Accordingly, while maturity factors (and not age as such) of the individual witness are to be examined in order to assess the relevance of the testimony, the ICC did not refuse to rely on child testimony due to a presumed lack of maturity. Instead, the Chamber held in the *Lubanga* case, that while maturity as such might put children at risk of manipulation, it does not constitute a cause to exclude their testimony. Instead, the misuse of children by others as a result of their developing maturity can be seen as a factor which made the Chamber exclude child testimony. In other words, such practice seems to recognise that children, despite being minors, can indeed, if their evolving capacities permit for this, provide credible testimony.

2.5.1.2 Impact of conflict situations and trauma

It is generally agreed that PTSD, can have an impact on the ability of the child to recall and describe traumatic events in judicial proceedings.[230] Next to the trustworthiness factor of the child witness, conflict situations as such might therefore bear particular consequences for child witnesses' credibility. Conflicts may traumatise children. Experiencing violence in the course of large scale violence is, in most of the cases, traumatising – irrespective of whether the violence amounts to international crimes.[231]

Research underlines that the effects of armed conflict on the well-being of the child are far-reaching.[232] Numerous scholars have pointed out that children are

---

228 Case No. SCSL-04-15-T, para. 579.

229 Case No. SCSL-04-15-T, paras. 580-594.

230 Rassin & van Koppen 2002, 507, at 510. Cashmore & Bussey 1996, 313-334; Fivush 1998, 699-716. See also, ICC-01/04-01/06-1729-Anx1, 25 February 2009, at 35.

231 Drumbl critically points out that not necessary all child soldiers see themselves as victims. Drumbl 2012, at 37.

232 UN General Assembly, Report of the expert of the Secretary-General, Ms. Grac'a Machel submitted pursuant to General Assembly resolution 48/157, UN Doc. A/51/306 (1996), para. 2; UN Security Council, Report of the Secretary-General to the Security Council on the protection of civilians in armed conflict, UN Doc. S/1999/957 (1999), para. 16; General Assembly/Security Council, Report of the Secretary-General, Children and armed conflict, UN Doc. A/58/546-S/2003/1053 (2003), para. 64; UNICEF 2005c, at 39 and 55. Beresford 2005, 721, at 722; Machel 2000, at 23. See, for example with regard to Sri Lanka, Elbert *et al.* 2009, 238, at 241; in regard to

especially at risk of suffering from post-traumatic stress disorder (PTSD) caused by the traumatic events experienced during conflict situations. This is particularly because armed conflicts may destabilise the protective environment of children. Armed conflict may lead to major changes in their social environment, such as family and school life – components, which are crucial for the healthy development of a child.[233]

The particular vulnerability of children is reflected in the disproportionate consequences of the full or partial denial of their fundamental needs.[234] Violations of basic needs during childhood frequently lead to permanent damage.[235] Research on Palestinian children suffering from PTSD caused by the Al-Aqsa Intifada in the Gaza Strip established that,

> '[t]he most prevalent types of trauma exposure for children in "hot" areas (those in which there is a great deal of shooting) are: for those who had witnessed funerals 94.6%, witnessed shooting 66.9%, saw a friend or a neighbor being injured or killed 61.6% or were tear gassed 36.1%. [...] Traumatic experiences among children led to a high level of neurotic symptoms and behavioral problems: 80% were moody; 63.3% became disobedient; 58.6% were unhappy; 58.8% were squirmy; and 52% were irritable.'[236]

Children that have witnessed the most violent acts and have had their rights, such as their rights to family life, education and health care, violated, often experience the

Gaza, see, Murthy & Lakshminarayana 2006, 25, at 27. Qouta *et al.* 2007, 699, at 700; for Sudan, see, Paardekooper, de Jong & Hermanns 1999, 529-536.

233 See for an overview, Stichick Betancourt, Tanveer Khan 2008, 318-319. For further information on post-traumatic stress disorder, see, Yehuda 2002, 108-114; Brewin *et al.* 1999, 360-366; Honwana 2006, at 152. ICC-01/04-01/06-1729-Anx1, 25 February 2009, at 3. Somasundaram & van de Put 2006, 64-73; Dawes 1990, 13-31; Jensen & Shaw 1993, 697-708; Honwana 2006, at 152.

234 The Unite Nations repeatedly expressed their concern, see, for instance, UN Security Council, Resolution 1261 (1999), UN Doc. UN Doc. S/RES/1261 (1999) and Report of the Secretary-General on women, peace and security, UN Doc. S/2002/1154 (2002), para. 6. Kar 2009, 5-11; Macksoud & Aber, 1996, at 70-88; G.H. Aldrich, van Baarda & Kalshoven 1995, 851; Nylund 1998, 23-54; Honwana 2006, at 2; Goldson 1996, 809-819. See also, ICRC 2009, at 1. Stichick Betancourt & Khan 2008, 317, at 317-319. The *EU Guidelines on Children and Armed Conflict* point out that, '[i]n the past decade alone, armed conflicts estimated to have claimed the lives of over two million children and physically maimed six million more. Conflict deprives children of parents, care-givers, basic social services, health care and education. There are some twenty million displaced and refugee children, while others are held hostage, abducted or trafficked. Systems of birth registration and juvenile justice systems collapse. At any given time, there are estimated to be at least 300,000 child soldiers participating in conflicts.' European Union 2003, para. 1.

235 Smith *et al.* 2001, 395-404; Dyregrov *et al.* 2000, 3-21; Gararina & Kostelny 1993, 23-39.

236 Qouta & El Sarraj 2006, at 118.

psychological consequences of such actions throughout their entire lives.[237] In this regard, medical science holds that,

> '[d]epending upon the developmental stage, level of cognitive and emotional maturity, and limited coping strategies, the psychological reactions in children are expected to be different from those in adults [...] and one can not generalize adult findings to children.'[238]

The need to distinguish between adults and children is furthermore justified by the factor of the young age of children. It is established that the younger the child, the more likely are scatter and long-lasting effects of the traumatic experience.[239]

It has, however, also been argued that, depending on child specific-characteristics, such as intelligence, coping skills and temperament, children might be resilient to the negative implications of armed conflict. In particular the dynamic developmental stadium of the child might constitute a protective feature which can lead to an enhanced resilience of the child.[240] Drumbl points out that child soldiers should not be seen as one group. Instead, he calls for an intra-group assessment as not necessarily all children might have suffered to the same extent. This approach mirrors a critical re-assessment of the image of the child soldier as victim.[241]

Furthermore, post-traumatic stress disorder constitutes a major threat to the healthy development of the child and leads in particular to a delay in development.[242] Studies on post-war refugees established that PTSD was/is observable in 30% to 70% of adolescent refugee populations.[243] The final report of the South African Truth and Reconciliation Commission similarly describes the long-lasting effects of gross human rights violations. It held that,

> 'Political and community violence characteristically expose children and adolescents to suffering long after the event. Whilst many are able to recover with the support of friends, family and community; others may suffer lasting psychological damage. [...] including post-traumatic stress disorder, depression, substance abuse and anti-social behaviour.'[244]

---

237 Delfos 2007, 39, at 40; Pynoos *et al.* 1993, 239-247; Baker 1990, 237-247; Zivcic 1993, 709-713; Berman 1999, 89-109. On the potential positive development after traumatic experiences see, for instance, Woodward & Joseph 2003, 267-283; Tedeschi & Calhoun 1996, 445-471.

238 Kar 2009, at 5; Kar, Jagadhisha & Murali 2001, 7-14; see also, Abu Hein *et al.* 1993, 1130.

239 Research on the potential positive effects of post-traumatic stress disorder has only recently been carried out, see, Woodward & Joseph 2003, 267-283; Tedeschi & Calhoun 1996, 445-471. Delfos 2007, at 39; Punamäki 2002, 181-204; Elbedour, ten-Bensel & Maruyama 1993, 33-52; UNICEF 2010a, ix.

240 Betancourt, Tanveer Khan 2008, 318-319.

241 Drumbl 2012, at 43.

242 Eth & Pynoos 1985, at 36-52; Pfefferbaum 1997, 1503-1511; Thabet & Vostanis 2000, 291-298; Allwood, Bell-Dolan & Husain 2002, 450-457; Joseph, Cairns & McCollam 1993, 471-473. See generally, Apfel & Aimon 1996.

243 Kar 2009, at 6. Similarly, up to 77% children suffered from PTSD, see, Thabet & Vostanis 1999, 385-391.

244 South African TRC Volume 4, at 271.

It is also to be kept in mind that child witness testimony as such may also pose another risk for the well-being of the child (secondary victimisation) as the witness has to recapitulate the negative experiences during testimony.[245] On the other side, child testimony may also bear positive implications such as the possibility to talk about the suffering which may have a constructive effect on the rehabilitation of the individual child.[246]

Due to the impact PTSD can have an impact on the ability of the child to recall and describe traumatic events in judicial proceedings, it needs to be examined whether a traumatised child is also capable of providing truthful testimony.[247] The difficulty of a young witness to recall, for instance, a particular period is exemplified by the following testimony before the SCSL:

> Q. And how long did you stay there?
> A. How long?
> Q. Yes, how long did you stay there?
> A. I am confused.
> Q. Have you forgotten?
> A. If you say a week, maybe I can remember. But when you talk about time, I cannot understand; I am confused.
> Q. Did you stay there for one week, two weeks, three weeks? How many weeks did you stay there for?
> A. Three weeks..
> Q. So when did you join the CDF?
> A. I joined the CDF between '97 and '98. I do not know the right month that I joined the CDF. At that time I was a small boy.[248]

As children are particularly likely to be called into the witness stand in relation to the recruitment crime (Article 8 Rome Statute), the child should, first of all, be able to recall his/her experiences and to testify about the particular moment of the alleged recruitment.

---

245 Dezwirek Sas, Wolfe & Gowdey 1996, 338-357; Avery 1983, 1-48.

246 The positive effects of child participation on the well-being of the child are particularly addressed in Chapter Six, as Part III.

247 The capability of the child to recall and describe traumatic events is, however, not only important with regard to the trustworthiness of the testimony of child witnesses before the SCSL and ICC, but also relevant when considering the credibility of child participants (*Chapter Three*) and child claimants (*Chapter Five*) in relation to their explanations as contained in the application form or even provided in person in the courtroom. Due to the fact that more extensive ICC practice exists with regard to the credibility of the child witness and the impact of trauma on the ability of the child to provide testimony, this particular issue is addressed in the current Chapter.

248 *The Prosecutor of the Special Court v. Alex Tamba Brima, Brima Bazzy Kamara, Santigie Borbor Kanu*, Case No. SCSL-2004-16-T, transcript of 26 September 2005, testimony of Witness TF1-157, at 27. See also, CDF Trial Transcript, Trial Chamber I, 6 June 2005, p. 24: Testimony of Witness TF2-080.

The expert witness (psychologist) on child soldiers and trauma who has been invited by Trial Chamber I of the ICC in the *Lubanga* case to report and testify on various issues concerning child soldiers and trauma pointed out that former child soldiers have difficulties recalling their experiences and the time or period when these took place.[249] The expert witness underlined in her report that,

> 'a child or also an adult […] with a developed PTSD […], will find it difficult to narrate in detail a particular traumatic experience. The information is certainly not lost to the survivor and can be recovered in clear order, completeness and chronology. This might however in some cases call for a therapeutic testimonial process before giving evidence in court […].'[250]

This conclusion is backed up in academic literature and the practice of Trial Chamber I.[251] It prompts questioning in particular whether, as will be elaborated upon below (section 2.5.3.1), witness familiarisation is indeed sufficient or whether witness proofing should be recognised and accepted as an exceptional measure needed to prepare children for their testimony.

This Chamber, even prior to the report of the expert witness, addressed the difficulties of young witnesses to recall their exact age or to elaborate upon the precise moment of recruitment.[252] In order to comfort a young witness in the courtroom, the presiding judge explicitly emphasised that the witness should not feel ashamed and thereby showed that he takes the difficulty of the child to recall memories during testimony into account. Judge Fulford stated that,

> '[w]e understand that obviously with questions about dates and ages, particularly if they're some years ago, you're going to need to take time to think about them. Don't be embarrassed about needing to think about when things happened and, obviously, do your best and answer the question if you can, but if you can't remember any dates, of course you'll say. […] These issues are important, and we're grateful to you for your assistance. But don't feel any embarrassment.'[253]

Accordingly, as with regard to the maturity factor, neither is the traumatisation as such, to date, recognised to generally prevent the child from giving truthful and

249 ICC-01/04-01/06-1671; ICC-01/04-01/06-1729-Anx1.
250 ICC-01/04-01/06-1729-Anx1, 25 February 2009, at, 35.
251 Rassin & van Koppen 2002, 507, at 510. Cashmore & Bussey 1996, 313-334; Fivush 1998, 699-716.
252 Rosenberg 2001, 33, at 47-48; Moradi *et al.* 1999, 357-361; Rassin & van Koppen 2002, at 510. Witness 0225 had difficulties recalling his age, ICC-01/04-01/06-T-228-Red-ENG WT, 15 January 2010, at 34. See also, statement of witness 0229, ICC-01/04-01/06-T-229-Red-ENG, 19 January 2010, at 5-6.
253 ICC-01/04-01/06-T-228-Red-ENG WT, 15 January 2010, p. 34.

credible testimony. In its judgment in the *Lubanga* case, Trial Chamber I did state that,

> '[i]rrespective of the Chamber's conclusions regarding the credibility and reliability of these alleged former child soldiers, given their youth and likely exposure to conflict, they were vulnerable to manipulation.'[254]

Accordingly, the combination of a child's maturity and his or her potential exposure to traumatising situations do, in the Chamber's view, constitute two factors which may constitute an incentive for manipulating children.

2.5.2 Measures enhancing credibility

The above permits the conclusion that the Court is of the view that children, despite their developing maturity and the potential impact of conflict situations, can be considered to be credible witnesses. In turn, it is examined whether, and if so which, measures have been introduced by the Court in order to welcome the child in the court room and thereby enhance the child's credibility.

2.5.2.1 Witness familiarisation

As the court environment can be considered to be alien to witnesses and child witnesses in particular, the preparation of witnesses by witness proofing or witness familiarisation could constitute effective measures prior to their testimony.

Witness proofing is understood to constitute a means of preparing a witness for testimony. The party who calls the witness meets the witness and discusses substantive matters of the testimony prior to the witness's appearance in the court room. The purpose of this meeting is to ensure a more accurate statement from the witness.[255]

Witness familiarisation, in contrast to the former, is understood to prepare the witness for testimony as regards the formalities of the court room proceedings. This preparation is intended to make the witness familiar with the court room setting in order to enable the witness to provide testimony.[256] Accordingly, the latter does not entail any discussion of evidence which is to be provided by the witness. Trial Chamber V defined the terms in a rather recent decision as follows:

> 'The terms "witness preparation", "witness proofing" and "witness familiarisation" are all used, sometimes interchangeably, throughout the submissions of the parties and the Victims and Witnesses Unit ("VWU"). In this Decision, the Chamber will use the term "witness preparation" to refer to a meeting between a witness and the party calling that witness, taking place shortly before the witness's testimony, for

---

254 ICC-01/04-01/06-2842, para. 482.
255 Ambos 2009, at 600.
256 Ambos 2009, at 599.

> the purpose of discussing matters relating to the witness's testimony. The term "witness familiarization" will be used to describe the support provided by the VWU to witnesses as set out in the Registry's "Unified Protocol on the practices used to prepare and familiarize witnesses for giving testimony" ("Familiarisation Protocol").'[257]

It will be established in the following paragraphs that the legal basis for witness familiarisation can be found in the Rome Statute and the respective rules. A legal basis for witness proofing is less straightforward.

Looking for a legal basis for the practice of witness proofing, the Rome Statute constitutes the first source which is to be examined. Guidance on this aspect can be found in part VI of the Statute. This part regulates the trial proceedings. Concerning the general organisation of the proceedings, Article 68 of the Statute addresses *inter alia* the protection and participation of witnesses in the proceedings. Paragraph 1 states in particular that

> '[t]he Court shall take appropriate measures to protect the safety, physical and psychological well-being, dignity and privacy of victims and witnesses.'

Article 68(1) of the Rome Statute in conjunction with human rights law could be referred to as a legal basis for witness proofing. Firstly, this provision unmistakably states that the Court's task is to protect witnesses. Secondly, the relevance of human rights law and the possibility to be referred to in the context of ICC proceedings has been explained in the first chapter. Human rights law can therefore be relevant in the context of ICC proceedings. Thirdly, as witness proofing can be said to aim 'to protect the safety, physical and psychological well-being, dignity and privacy of victims and witnesses', the referral to human rights law does not seem far-fetched.[258] After all, human rights law seeks to pursue similar protective goals as have been formulated in paragraph 1 of Article 68 Rome Statute.

Despite the possibility that witness proofing could indeed be provided with a legal basis which can be found in the Rome Statute and human rights law, Pre-Trial Chamber I and Trial Chamber I rejected the possibility to prepare witnesses for testimony by witness proofing – a practice which departs from the permissive approach taken by the *ad hoc* Tribunals and the SCSL.[259] Before the aforementioned Court and Tribunals, the practice of witness proofing was used as

257 ICC-01/09-01/11-524, para. 4.
258 Art. 68(1) Rome Statute.
259 Vasiliev 2009, at 194-195; Ambos 2008, at 912. The practice of witness-proofing has elsewhere been argued to be a legitimate practice in international criminal trials, see, e.g., Karemaker, Taylor & Pittman 2008. ICC-01/04-01/06-679; ICC-01/04-01/06-1049. *The Prosecutor v Karemera et al*, ICTR-98-44-T, Decision on Defence Motions to Prohibit Witness Proofing, 15 December 2006, para 10; *The Prosecutor v Milan Mihanovic et al*, IT-05-87-T, Decision on Ojdanic Motion to Prohibit Witness Proofing, 12 December 2006, para 10. *The Prosecutor v Limaj et al*, IT-03-66-T, Decision on Defence Motion on Prosecution Practice of 'Proofing' Witnesses, 10 Dcember 2004, 3.

pointed out in the *Limaj* case in order to 're-examine the witness's evidence to enable more accurate, complete and efficient testimony'.[260] The Prosecution underlined in its submission to Trial Chamber I in the *Lubanga* case that witness proofing serves in particular the purpose to establish the truth and should therefore indeed be used by prosecution and defence teams. A refreshment of the memory of the witness by the means of witness proofing is understood to also remind the witness of the importance to tell the truth.[261] Bearing in mind the earlier addressed difficulties of former child soldiers to recall their memory and the concerns about young persons' ability to understand the importance of telling the truth, one could argue that as regards minor witnesses, the Court should depart from the prohibitive position of Pre-Trial Chamber I and Trial Chamber I as regards witness proofing. Preparing young witnesses for testimony by means of witness proofing could constitute a means to further the credibility of the witness. The risk of re-traumatisation during witness proofing could, as suggested by the Prosecution, be minimised by seeking the assistance of child professionals.[262] This assistance should, however, not as suggested by the Prosecutor be provided by experts from within the Office of the Prosecutor, but should be given by qualified staff members of the Registry as this organ is impartial and not at risk of overseeing the best interests of the young witness due to the professional commitment of prosecution or defence teams. Furthermore, the earlier addressed risk of manipulation of the child could further be prevented if not the party who intends to call the witness prepares the witness for testimony but an independent organ of the Court carries out this task.

The practice in the *Lubanga* case, however, did not permit such approach. The Prosecution was therefore prohibited from discussing the content of the witnesses' testimony prior to the court session. The Chambers ruled that witness proofing with respect to substantive parts of the testimony is not provided for in the Rome Statute and the respective Rules.[263] The provisions request instead that in the case of testimony, appropriate protective measures are applied to (traumatised) children (see section 2.4.2).[264] By explaining the reasons of its restrictive approach as regards witness proofing, Trial Chamber I pointed out that the aforementioned objectives, namely to establish the truth and to refresh the memory of young witnesses can be achieved by witness familiarisation as the latter also includes this objective and possibility to review the earlier made statement without, however, taking away the equally important spontaneity of the testimony.[265] The suggested

260 ICC-01/04-01/06-1049, para. 7.

261 ICC-01/04-01/06-1049, para. 12.

262 ICC-01/04-01/06-1049, para. 16.

263 ICC-01/04-01/06-679, paras. 28, 53, 35-41.

264 Art. 68(1) Rome Statute in conjunction with Rules 87-88 of the Rules of Procedure and Evidence and Regulation 96(5) of the Regulations of the Registry. The unified protocol on the practices used to prepare and familiarise witnesses for giving testimony at trial as suggested by the Victims and Witnesses Unit recognises that children are to be specifically protected due to their particular vulnerability, ICC-01/05-01/08-1081-Anx, paras. 20, 90. See also, ICC-01/04-01/06-1049, paras. 16-32.

265 ICC-01/04-01/06-1049, paras. 49-51.

restrictive approach of Pre-Trial and Trial Chamber I cannot be said to reflect the overall approach of the ICC. Trial Chamber V, in line with the Prosecution's argumentation in the *Lubanga* case, issued a decision at the beginning of 2013 stating that the Rome Statute does not prohibit witness preparation.[266]

Irrespective of the answer to the question whether witness proofing will be introduced as a general practice before the Court, it is argued that, witness familiarisation is crucial to make the witness, in particular young witnesses familiar with the proceedings and court room settings.[267] All Chambers, thus far, ruled that witness familiarisation has to be conducted by the Victims and Witnesses Unit of the Registry. Pre-Trial Chamber 1 held that the responsibility to familiarise witnesses with the Court proceedings is laid down in Article 43(6) of the Rome Statute in conjunction with Rule 17 RPE.[268] Rule 17(2)(b) provides that the Victims and Witnesses Unit's task with respect to witnesses is:

> '(i) Advising them where to obtain legal advice for the purpose of protecting their rights, in particular in relation to their testimony;
>
> (ii) Assisting them when they are called to testify before the Court;
>
> (iii) Taking gender-sensitive measures to facilitate the testimony of victims of sexual violence at all stages of the proceedings.'

With respect to children, paragraph 3 underlines that,

> '3. In performing its functions, the Unit shall give due regard to the particular needs of children, elderly persons and persons with disabilities. In order to facilitate the participation and protection of children as witnesses, the Unit may assign, as appropriate, and with the agreement of the parents or the legal guardian, a child-support person to assist a child through all stages of the proceedings.'

In order to familiarise witnesses with the proceedings before the Court, Trial Chamber I also underlined that specific attention must be paid to the particular vulnerability of the child as such. The Chamber held that,

> '[t]here must be awareness of the particular characteristics of a witness which may cause the court environment to be particularly foreign and uncomfortable. In the context of the present case, for example, particular attention should be paid to any children who are called as witnesses to ensure that their psychological well-being is considered as a matter of paramount importance, pursuant to Article 68 of the Statute and Rule 88 of the Rules'.[269]

---

266 ICC-01/09-01/11-524, paras. 31-50.
267 Vasiliev 2009.
268 ICC-01/04-01/06-679, para. 22.
269 ICC-01/04-01/06-1049, para. 32.

It has become clear that two factors are particularly important when it comes to child witness testimony. Firstly, the impact of armed conflicts in combination with the particular vulnerability of the child places the child in a particular position. This position is not limited to children's need for specific protection in substantive terms. Instead, children, including child witnesses, also find themselves in a particular procedural position. Child witness testimony is therefore to be held in a manner which reflects that child-specific aspects are taken into account. Secondly, the evolving capacities of the child, which mirror the dynamic progression of the child from an immature to a mature legal person calls for another child-specific treatment of child witnesses.

Bearing these thoughts in mind one may raise the question whether, at least with regard to children, the strict limitations concerning witness familiarisation in ICC proceedings as suggested by Pre-Trial Chamber I and Trial Chamber I sufficiently accommodates child testimony. In other words, it might be necessary to reconsider the possibility to at least permit witness proofing in relation to child witnesses as the formalistic means and methods of familiarisation might not be sufficient in order to ensure that children are capable of providing credible testimony. This is because a lack of child-specific preparation for the testimony entails the risk of not taking the two abovementioned factors into account. On the other side, it is also to be kept in mind, as has been pointed out before, that children are, due to their developmental status, at risk of being manipulated or influenced by others if being prepared for testimony in particular when the preparation techniques go beyond the rather formalistic preparation in the context of witness familiarisation. A general applicable clear cut position as regards witness proofing of child witnesses should therefore not be taken. Instead, a case-by-case assessment, again, is advisable.

2.5.3.2 Age determination

The determination of the age of a child witness or participant is particularly relevant when being called to testify on his/her recruitment as a child soldier (victim witness).[270] Making use of age determination techniques could constitute a method

[270] Appeals Chamber Judge Anita Ušacka criticised Trial Chamber I for the approach taken in relation to evidence establishing age of those children who did *not* appear in the courtroom in person, thus *not* being physically present and thereby not falling into consideration for medical age determination techniques. As this aspect is not part of this research since it does not have implications for the best interests or evolving capacities of the child in relation to child participation, it is not addressed in further detail.
It is nevertheless interesting to briefly refer to the dissenting opinion of Judge Anita Ušacka to the Appeals Chamber Judgment, see ICC-01/04-01/06-3121. The Judge strongly criticised the methods used by Trial Chamber I in relation to the age determination of children who did not appear in person in the courtroom. In contrast to the majority opinion, the Judge was not convinced that video material and non-expert witness statements which have been accepted by Trial Chamber I, proved beyond reasonable doubt that the recruited children were below the age of fifteen years (paras. 23-78). The Judge dissented in particular that the Trial Chamber could not have concluded, based upon the physical appearance of the young human beings being shown in

which could enhance the credibility of the witness by proofing a witnesses' alleged age.

Obviously, only those witnesses who were below the age of fifteen years at the time of recruitment might provide evidence on the alleged crime as a direct victim. The Prosecution in the *Lubanga* case held in the closing statements that,

> 'the Prosecution presented nine former child soldiers as witnesses. They had to remember and relive yet again the details of the horrors that they were trying to forget, to leave behind. They had to tell this Court and, indeed, the whole world the miseries they had suffered. They are not on record, and we hope we can help them to understand that they are not alone, that the failure to protect them will not be repeated by this Court. [...] [a]ll of the former child soldiers participating in this trial have no doubt undergone psychological damage because they lived through an atrocious experience and traumatizing because they were soldiers. Many of them – many of these former child soldiers underwent physical damage and wide range of injuries, violent acts against them including sexual violence.'[271]

For the Defence counsel, an attempt to question and disprove the evidence of the established age submitted by the Prosecution (or child participant) constitutes a self-evident defence strategy when arguing that this specific element of crime is not ed. The *Lubanga* Defence underlined in this regard concerning a Prosecution witness that

> '[l]es témoins D01-0005 et D01-0006, [EXPURGÉ], confirment que W-0010 n'était pas âgée de moins de 15 ans en 2002 [...].'[272]

The reason why age determination receives particular attention in international criminal proceedings is that armed conflicts often make it impossible to refer to official documents in order to establish age and identity.[273]

---

the video excerpts, that the recruits were below the age of fifteen years (paras. 37-45). The Judge also pointed out that evidence provided by non-expert witnesses did neither establish the exact age as most of these witnesses relied on age estimates and hearsay (paras. 29, 68-76). The Judge therefore came to the conclusion that *Thomas Lubanga Dyilo* should have been acquitted (paras. 22, 79). As regards the age determination method applied by Trial Chamber I in relation to children not being physically present in the courtroom, namely, age determination based on the physical appearance of young human beings, non-expert witness and hearsay it could be held that such a low-threshold assessment could also be an approach being in the best interests of the child by enabling children in a more child-sensitive manner to apply for participation. While this indeed would be the case, it is held that such low threshold for child participation constitutes a threat to the right of the accused to a fair trial – as it is also validly pointed out by the dissenting Judge already in relation to the above addressed 'child-evidence' accepted by Trial Chamber I. For this reason, a balanced application of the best interests principle and fair trial considerations should lead to the conclusion that this approach is not to be followed in relation to child participation in the course of the criminal and reparation proceedings. It should, in light of the convincing dissenting opinion, perhaps even not be followed in future proceedings in relation to evidence which is submitted in order to prove the age of those children who do not appear in the courtroom.

271 International Criminal Court, Office of the Prosecutor, Prosecutors Closing Statements of 25 August 2011, http://www.icc-cpi.int/iccdocs/doc/doc1210316.pdf, at 5, 61.

272 ICC-01/04-01/06-2773-Red, para. 151.

The age determination of former child soldiers has already confronted the SCSL with major difficulties.[274] In order to broaden its knowledge on age determination assessments, the Special Court invited an expert witness on child soldiers to various cases. The witness testified *inter alia* on age determination and gave an opinion on the official age determination process that was undertaken during the disarmament process in Sierra Leone.[275] This testimony could have provided interesting insights into the assessment standards of the SCSL. These insights were not accessible, since the entire testimony was given in closed session.

The overall approach of the SCSL towards age determination is also not visible from publicly available documents. From reading selected testimonies of former child soldiers which are publicly available, it seems that the SCSL relied in particular on situational circumstances (such as reference to a particular (rainy) season, school year or information provided by the parents to the witness) as described by the witnesses in order to determine their birth date.[276] Defence criticisms on the circumstantial assessment of the age of alleged child soldiers are reflected in the closing arguments. Defence counsel in the case of *The Prosecutor of the Special Court v. Sam Hinga Norman, Moinina Fofana, Allieu Kondewa*, for instance, underlined that,

> '[o]ne point I would like to make straight away is that the evidence and the exhibits invariably refer merely to child soldiers without particularizing the age group of children which are subject matter of the indictment. Most of the evidence that has been given in this respect does not specify that it refers to children below the age of fifteen but rather just to child soldiers [...].'[277]

---

273 For further discussion, see *Chapter Three*. See also, Kamara 2008.

274 Sanin & Stirnemann 2008, at 12.

275 *The Prosecutor of the Special Court v. Issa Hassan Sesay & ORS*, Written Reasoned Ruling on the Preliminary Characterization of Expert Witness TF1-296, Case No. SCSL-04-15-T (2006), 14 July 2006.

276 See, e.g., *The Prosecutor of the Special Court v. Alex Tamba Brima, Brima Bazzy Kamara, Santigie Borbor Kanu*, Case No. SCSL-2004-16-T, transcript of 8 July 2005, witness TF1-180, at 35; The Prosecutor of the Special Court v. Charles Chankay Taylor, Case No. SCSL-2003-01-T, transcript of 21 October 2008, witness TF1-158, at 31-34; *The Prosecutor of the Special Court v. Issay Sesay, Morris Kallon, Augustine Gbao*, Case No. SCSL-2004-15-T, transcript of 11 April 2005, witness TF-141, at 51, 59. See also, *The Prosecutor of the Special Court v. Issay Sesay, Morris Kallon, Augustine Gbao*, Case No. SCSL-2004-15-T, judgment Trial Chamber I (2 March 2009), paras. 509-510.

277 *The Prosecutor of the Special Court v. Sam Hinga Norman Moinina Fofana Allieu Kondewa*, Case No. SCSL-2004-14-T, transcript of 29 November 2006, at 7-8, 29-31. Trial Chamber I in its judgment was convinced that the accused Kondewa is guilty of having recruited children below the age of fifteen. The Chamber agreed that the crime has been proven beyond reasonable doubt on the basis of the testimony of witness TF2-021, who testified on his own recruitment and declared furthermore that he witnessed the recruitment of at least 20 other children. See *The Prosecutor of the Special Court v. Sam Hinga Norman Moinina Fofana Allieu Kondewa*, Case no. SCSL-01-14-T, Judgment, 2 August 2007, paras. 968-972.

Similarly, the conviction of alleged perpetrators by the ICC requires that the Prosecution establishes *beyond reasonable doubt* that the crime has been committed.[278] This requires not only that children are below fifteen years of age but also that perpetrators knew or should have known that the children were below the age of fifteen years at the moment of recruitment.[279]

In this context, the Defence counsel of *Thomas Lubanga Dyilo* contested the age of Prosecution witnesses who were called to testify on their recruitment as child soldiers as to counter argue that the elements of the recruitment crime have been established. Such Defence strategy is, for instance, reflected in the questioning of witness 10:

> Q: If I were to suggest that you were enlisted by the APC and not the UPC in 1999 until the year 2003, what would you say? Do you agree? Is that untrue?
> A: I know nothing about what you're saying. I was enlisted by the UPC. What you're talking about, I know nothing about that.
> Q: If I were to suggest that – well, let me rephrase that. If you re-think about the period when you joined the ranks of the UPC, rather than being 13 years of age, isn't it true that in fact you were much older than that and most likely already an adult?
> [...]
> A: I told you that when I was enlisted in the UPC I was 13 years old. I don't understand what counsel is saying to me.[280]

At a later stage in the Prosecution case, Trial Chamber I – upon request of the Prosecution – invited two medical expert witnesses on age determination.[281] The experts prepared an opinion, which establishes the age of the nine victim witnesses called by the Prosecution.[282] Both underlined in their testimony that the determination of the age of a person is not a straightforward exercise. The expert witness pointed out that,

> 'At the present time we consider that there may be one year of variation between the actual age and the estimated bone age. That is why we generally specify an age bracket. [...] This is why the intra-and inter-individual variability is so significant, but in our clinical use the method what really happens is that somebody comes saying he's 12. A colleague wants us to look at the bone age and see whether this is

278 Art. 66(3) Rome Statute.

279 Kurth 2010, at 493-496.

280 Witness DRC-OTP-WWW-0010, ICC-01/04-01/06-T-145-Red-ENG, 6 March 2009 at 72-73.

281 ICC-01/04/01/06-1311-Anx2; ICC-01/04/01/06-1625; ICC-01/04-01/06-T-172-Red-ENG, 12 May 2009.

282 ICC-01/04-01/06-T-172-Red-ENG, 12 May 2009, at 38. Ibid., indirect reference that OTP submitted individual reports on witness 7, at 38-40, 45 – at least 19 years of age; witness 8, at 47 – at least 19 years of age. ICC-01/04-01/06-T-173-ENG, 13 May 2009, at 24. Age determination has been requested for nine prosecution witnesses, ICC-01/04-01/06-1274, para. 3. The expert report on age determination of prosecution witnesses has been submitted to defence counsel and is not publicly available, ICC-01/04-01/06-1145, ICC-01/04-01/06-109Anx.

compatible with alleged age. If we find that he's 10 or 14, to within a year, we're going to say that his pathology is slightly above or slightly under his actual age, and that's the way we usually use the method.'[283]

When being asked by a legal representative to answer whether the current age determination technique establishes a reliable age, the expert witness replied that,

'[i]t gives us an age bracket with a notion of probability, but it would be a mistake to want to use this method to have an absolutely sharp assessment of the age. We currently do not have the medical means to give you such precision. It gives a fairly reliable bracket for a normal subject as regards his age.'[284]

The expert underlined that, to date, the age of a child can only be assessed based on x-ray images of their bones, in particular images of the wrist and hand, supplemented by a dental assessment.[285] The age of a very young child (3 months) and an 'adult' (17-year-old girl, 19-year-old boy) based on x-ray images can be determined with great certainty due to the early or finished stadium of growth cartilage.[286]

Assessing the exact age of girls and boys between the ages of fifteen and seventeen/eighteen years of age is less easy to determine for three major reasons: Firstly, expert witness Catherine Adamsbaum pointed out that a precise age cannot always be assessed due to *intra* variability between different medical disciplines which may lead to different age determinations of up to one year. Secondly, inter-individual variability is also not unlikely – notwithstanding the fact that the individual variability of the examining doctor is deemed to be less than one year. Thirdly, the age determination atlas referred to when assessing the age is based on images which are older than 50 years and limited to the white population of Northern America; an African equivalent does not exist.[287] It was also held that social and economic factors, such as diseases and insufficient nutrition also have an impact on age determination.[288] As a result of these factors, the variability is greater between the ages of fifteen and seventeen/eighteen.[289]

The expert witnesses concluded in regard to the victim witnesses who had undergone age examinations that two of them were between the ages of fifteen and sixteen years at the moment of examination (December 2007 and January 2008)

283 With regard to the expert witness on age determination based on x-ray images of bones, ICC-01/04-01/06-T-172-Red-ENG, 12 May 2009, at 80.

284 Ibid., at 82-83.

285 Ibid., at 12.-14. ICC-01/04-01/06-T-173-ENG, 13 May 2009, at, 20, 37.

286 ICC-01/04-01/06-T-172-Red-ENG, 12 May 2009, at 25-26, for girls, at 49. For girls: females mature faster than males. Consequently, there is no cartilage growth from the age of 17 years onwards.

287 Ibid., at 34-35, 86.

288 Ibid., at 78.

289 Ibid., at 90-92. A precise age determination based on dental assessment is particularly difficult between the ages of 15 and 20, see ICC-01/04-01/06-T-173-ENG, 13 May 2009, at 36.

while the others were at least nineteen years.[290] The period in which *Thomas Lubanga Dyilo* has been charged with the recruitment of children lasts from early September 2002 to 2 June 2003,[291] and 13 August 2003 respectively.[292] Relying on the reports of the experts and counting back from the determined ages, the witnesses would therefore have been approximately between nine and fourteen years, with a majority of the witnesses close to the latter age at the moment of recruitment.

Considering the lack of precision with regard to those witnesses who were at least nineteen years at the moment of x-ray examination, the probability remains that these young witnesses were above the age of fifteen at the moment of recruitment. The Defence of *Lubanga* submitted in this regard that Trial Chamber I has to assess evidence relating to the age determination of child witnesses with caution.[293]

Since the Rome Statute does not criminalise the recruitment of children above the age of fifteen years, the Bench in the *Lubanga* case was confronted with the difficulty of determining whether the alleged recruitment of those witnesses indeed, constitutes a crime within the jurisdiction of the International Criminal Court and whether the perpetrator should have had knowledge about the age.[294]

It can be concluded that medical science does not enable the Court to draw definite conclusions regarding the age of young witnesses. Bearing this lack of preciseness in mind one, may question whether children should expose themselves to the necessary examinations if in the end, the Court may not be able to use the medical results for convicting alleged perpetrators.

2.6 Conclusion

Children have appeared as witness before the ICTY, the SCSL, the ICC and TRCs. As has been pointed out throughout this chapter, the particular focus on the case of *Thomas Lubanga Dyilo* does not permit drawing definite conclusions. Tendencies are nevertheless visible.

The analysis established that age as such is not referred to as exclusionary factor for child witness testimony. It has also been pointed out that child witness testimony is not necessarily limited to minors. Instead, one may also speak of 'child witnesses', when a young adult witness gives evidence about events that took place at a moment when the witness was a minor.

290 Witness 10 and 49 were older than eighteen years based on bone and dental-aging assessments. Witness 11 and 50 were the youngest. For all witnesses: there was no visible growth cartilage which made the experts conclude that they were at least 19 years of age. Witness 298 was between 15 and 16 years of age.

291 Art. 8(2)(b)(xxvi) Rome Statute.

292 Art. 8(2)(e)(vii) Rome Statute.

293 ICC-01/04-01/06-2773-red-teNg, paras. 92-44; ICC-01/04-01/06-2842, 176.

294 Kurth 2010, at 493-496.

In contrast to the actual appearance of child witnesses in the court room is the fact that child witness testimony is not extensively regulated in the Rome Statute and the respective rules. As a result, specific aspects relating to the legal status, such as children's ability to provide informed consent, the need to benefit from child specific protective measures, and the credibility of the child have not extensively been reflected in the procedural regulation. These aspects, however, appeared to be of particular relevance in the practice of the ICC. Based upon the analysis made, it is held that there is indeed a need to introduce a special regime which regulates child witness testimony in ICC proceedings. In particular because both the potential immaturity and the impact of conflict situations might bear negative implications for the credibility of the child.

In this regard, the immaturity of the witness and his or her (potential re-) traumatisation have been recognised by the procedural laws and the practice of the Court to require a particular child-sensitive response. At the same time, it has become clear that, bearing in mind the discussion on the maturity of the child witness and the risk of manipulation, children cannot generally be presumed to be indispensable witnesses even if crimes have been charged to which children had become direct victims.

It is to be noted in this regard that even if one third of the prosecution witnesses in the *Lubanga* case amounted to former child soldiers, the introductory hypothesis that child witnesses might be indispensable is disproven. The judgment of Trial Chamber I established that the calling of child witnesses, even if child-specific crimes such as the recruitment crime have been charged, cannot generally be considered a *conditio sine qua non* for a successful conviction. A conclusion which is supported by the Appeals Chamber Judgment of 1 December 2014 as also this judgment upheld the conviction of *Thomas Lubanga Dyilo*.[295]

In line with the foregoing, it is furthermore concluded, that even if the child is said to be generally capable of providing truthful testimony, measures to enhance the child's credibility might be necessary. This is because child-specific factors, such insufficient preparation for the testimony might have an impact on a child's ability to provide credible testimony. The decision takers are therefore invited to reassess whether an exception to the prohibition of witness proofing is called for when children give testimony.

In sum, it has become clear that the maturity of the child and the impact of conflict situations, in particular the likelihood of being traumatised, are to be examined when assessing whether child participation is in the best interests of the individual child. As exemplified by the unreliable testimony of young witnesses in the *Lubanga* case, giving testimony might not necessarily be in the best interests of the child. Being made subject to manipulation and subsequently being revealed as a lying and therefore unreliable witness cannot be considered to have a positive effect on the child. It stigmatises the child as being manipulative and a liar.

---

[295] ICC-01/04-01/06-312.

At least as far as the *Lubanga* case is concerned, the participation of child witnesses may even have negative implications for the image of former child soldiers. All child witness testimony has been unreliable. The perception that former child soldiers, or perhaps even children as such, are not to be considered as credible witnesses (and persons) could be reinforced. A perception which contravenes the research which has established that child testimony can, in principle, be used. The entire exclusion of the child witnesses' testimony could also give rise to further stigmatisation of former child soldiers and hinder their reintegration in post-conflict societies. Taking the *Lubanga* judgment into account, it is underlined that all parties involved have to assess the question whether the participation of child witnesses is still to be considered in their best interests if, in the end, their testimony is not considered to be reliable.

CHAPTER 3

THE CHILD VICTIM

3.1 INTRODUCTION

With the establishment of the ICC, for the first time in the history of international criminal law, victims can participate in international criminal proceedings.[296] The possibility of victim participation in criminal proceedings constitutes a novelty and special feature of ICC proceedings.[297] Children may also participate as victims. The participation as victim in ICC proceedings is not limited to the course of the criminal proceedings. As child claimant, children may also participate in the reparation proceedings. This capacity is further explored in *Chapter Five*. Instead of being limited to the role of beneficiary of substantive protection, the participation in the proceedings as victim participant and/or claimant, empowers the child to pursue his or her personal interest – this presupposes, however, that the investigator started investigations in a particular situation and that victims can prove, amongst others, a causal link between the harm suffered and the charges. In contrast to the procedural capacity of the child witness, the involvement of the child in these capacities is, without disregarding the two aforementioned potential constraints, less determined by a prosecutorial or defence strategy.

The first case concerned the recruitment of children as war crime. Children are the direct victims of this crime. It is no surprise, therefore, that children participated as victims in this case. This opportunity constituted a tool which enabled the child to express his or her personal views and concerns on matters that affect him/her.[298]

After a brief reflection on victim participation and an overview of actual child participation in ICC proceedings, this chapter examines three aspects of child participation in light of the first practice at the ICC: firstly, it examines the victim requirements as codified under the Rome Statute when applied to children; secondly, the chapter analyses constraints which may hinder children's effective

---

296 Art. 68(3) Rome Statute.

297 Moffet 2014, 94; Pena & Carayon 2013, at 2; de Brouwer, Heikkilä 2013, 1299-1374; McCarthy 2012, 48-51; Markus Funk 2010, 79; McGonigle 2009, 93-152; Chung 2007, 459-545; Greco 2007, 531-547; Trumbull 2007, 777-826; Doak 2007, 294-316; Stahn, Olàsolo & Gibson 2006, 219-238; Hemptinne & Rindi 2006, 342-350; Boyle 2006, 307-313.

298 Children are also eligible for participation as claimant in the reparation proceedings before the ICC (*Chapter Five*). Despite the different stages of the criminal and reparation proceedings, a number of aspects addressed in *Chapter Three* are also relevant for the child claimant and indicated as such.

access to the criminal proceedings; finally, it analyses to what extent the modalities of victim participation might require adjustment when children participate. Each of the forgoing aspects thereby analyses whether a distinct approach compared to adult participants is necessary when children participate in the course of the criminal proceedings.

The specific research questions addressed in this chapter read as follows: how are the victim requirements applied to children? To what extent is the application procedure child-sensitive, and does it take account of the evolving capacities of the child. When children succeed in applying for participation, the follow-up question is to what extent is the procedure governing the pre-trial and trial phase sufficiently child-sensitive? Finally, which modalities of victim participation are particularly (in)appropriate for children?

The previous chapter particularly addressed those legal aspects which should be taken into account when considering the question whether child witness participation in criminal proceedings is in the best interests of the child. The current chapter aims to focus more specifically on the question of whether and how child participation in criminal proceedings before the ICC is provided for in accordance with the evolving capacities of the child and whether a distinct procedural treatment is necessary for child participants compared to adult participants. As has been explained in *Chapter One*, the principle of the evolving capacities might provide guidance for answering the question whether participation in ICC proceedings can be considered to be in the best interests of the child.

3.2 Views on Victim Participation

Discussions concerning victim participation in the criminal proceedings before the International Criminal Court have been held since the drafting process of the Rome Statute.[299] Scholars who are in favour of victim participation argue in particular that victim participation in the course of international criminal proceedings strengthens the transparency of international criminal justice in relation to victims.[300] As a lesson to be learned from the lack of victim participation in the proceedings before the *ad hoc* tribunals, participation of victims in ICC proceedings brings victims' personal experiences and suffering into the court room setting.[301] The presence of victims thereby informs all parties involved and the Court, but also informs the

---

299 For general information, see, among many others, Chung 2008, at 460; Trumbull 2007; Biti & Friman 2001; Jorda & Hemptinne 1999.

300 Pena & Carayon 2013, at 6-8. See also, decision of Trial Chamber V ICC-01/09-01/11-460, para. 39.

301 Vasiliev 2015, at 4; Zappala 2010, at 137-138; McGonigle 2009, at 96; Jouet 2007, at 250; Trumbull 2007, at 786; Henzelin, Heiskanen & Mettraux 2006, at 341; Bassiouni 2006, at 241; Jorda & Hemptinne 2002, at 1388.

public of the harm they experienced.[302] In particular within the 'no peace without justice' debate it has been held that victim participation may contribute not only to the personal healing process of the individual victim but also to national reconciliation processes and the establishment of peace.[303] In sum, these voices welcome the possibility of victim participation in ICC proceedings. The participation of victims is recognised as a development which fills the gap of the earlier criminal courts and tribunals with regards to victims of international crimes.

In contrast to this applauding position, other scholars share the view that victim participation in the criminal proceedings is rather problematic.[304] It is argued that criminal proceedings before the ICC are not the right forum for victims of international crimes.[305] The lack of procedural clarity as regards the modalities of participation have been pointed out as constituting a particular risk for the fair trial of the accused.[306] In particular since the accusatorial nature of the criminal proceedings before the ICC does not leave room for the participation of a third protagonist in addition to the defence and prosecution. As a result of victim participation, the accused could be said to be confronted with a second prosecutor as allegations raised by victims also have to be counter argued. Furthermore, the critics point out that the potentially large number of victims is difficult to accommodate in the course of criminal proceedings without delaying the process as such. Victim participation might therefore put the expeditious administration of justice at risk.[307]

It can be concluded from the foregoing brief overview that the views concerning the added value of victim participation in the criminal proceedings before the ICC are divided. For the following discussion of child victim participation one should therefore keep in mind that the debate about victim, including child participation in the criminal proceedings before the ICC is still on-going. It is therefore that the present research, besides the aforementioned objectives of the current chapter, also aims to provide further ingredients as regards this academic exchange.

3.3 Child Victim Participation in ICC Practice

Including the *Lubanga* case, five out of the current eighteen cases (in eight situations) before the ICC include the war crime charge of the recruitment of children under the age of fifteen years.[308] The possible existence of child victim

302 Henry 2009, at 134; Trumbull 2007, at 802-803; Dembour & Haslam 2004, at 153-154; Goldstone 1996, at 489.
303 Keller 2009, at 275; Goldstone 1996, at 491.
304 Brants 2013, at 40; van den Wijngaert 2012; Guhr 2008, at 115.
305 Zappala 2010, at 144.
306 Ibid., at 141.
307 Ibid., at 138; Pena 2010, at 509; Blattman 2008, at 729; Jouet 2007, at 277; Bitti & Friman 2001, at 457.
308 http://www.icc-cpi.int/Menus/ICC/Situations+and+Cases/. Situation in Uganda; situation in the Democratic Republic of the Congo; situation in Darfur, Sudan; situation in the Central African

participants that may seek access to the ICC may, however, not be limited to these five cases. Instead, all cases pending before the Court charge crimes of which children could have become victims – such as charges of inhuman treatment, sexual slavery, rape, attacks against schools or direct attacks against the civilian population (see section 1.2, *Chapter One*).[309] The participation of children in the proceedings before the ICC might therefore not be limited to those individual cases that prosecute the recruitment of child soldiers. Thus far, child participation has in particular been addressed in the case of *Thomas Lubanga Dyilo* and in the proceedings against *Katanga & Ngudjolo Chui.*[310]

The overall number of child victim participants in the first case before the ICC, the proceedings against *Thomas Lubanga Dyilo*, amounts to 129 victims who successfully applied for participation.[311] Among these were approximately fifty child victims who were below the age of eighteen years when the application was filed.[312] The majority of the remaining victims that successfully applied for participation were former child soldiers that turned eighteen before filing their application, but were a child at the time they were victimised.[313] The high

---

Republic; situation in the Republic of Kenya; situation in Libya, situation in Côte d'Ivoire, situation in Mali.

309 Arts. 8(2)(b)(xxvi) and 8(2)(e)(vii) Rome Statute. For an overview of the charges see http://www.icc-cpi.int/Menus/ICC/Situations+and+Cases/.

310 See with regard to the proceedings against Germain Katanga and Mathieu Ngudjolo Chui the decision of trial Chamber II, ICC-01/04-01/07-1788, paras. 7-9. Approximately eight former child soldiers applied for participation.

311 ICC-01/04-01/06-2842, para. 15.

312 ICC-01/04-01/06-2842, para. 17. At least 49 child applicants either directly or through a third person acting on behalf of the minor, such as a parent or legal guardian, submitted an application for participation in the proceedings against *Thomas Lubanga Dyilo*. On the overall numbers of victims recognised, see Case Information Sheet of 15 October 2010, *The Prosecutor v. Thomas Lubanga Dyilo*, ICC-PIDS-CIS-DRC-01/004/10. With regard to the exact numbers of child applications, see ICC-01/04-01/-06-1556: nineteen applicants were children when the application was originally filed, paras. 74-79; twenty-two applicants were children for whom a third person other than the parent or legal guardian submitted the application but most of them had reached adulthood in the meanwhile, paras. 63-73; two applicants submitted an application without a person acting on their behalf while being under eighteen when filing the application, paras. 91-98; one application was submitted on behalf of a minor girl by her father, paras. 100-104. In the decision of 15 December 2008, the Chamber had to examine 118 applications. 92 applicants were granted victim status. Among the 92 applications, 45 applications were successfully filed by children themselves or on behalf of children. In the decision of 18 December 2008, Trial Chamber I granted another victim who was a minor at the time of application victim status, see in particular the Annex A 2. ICC-01/04-01/06-1562; ICC-01/04-01/06-1861 and ICC-01/04-01/06-1861-AnxA2. Another 3 child applicants successfully submitted an application for participation in the decision of 19 July 2009, ICC-01/04-01/06-2035, see in particular Annex A, ICC-01/04-01/06-2065 and ICC-01/04-01/06-2065-Anx2.

313 While the overall number of participants recognised in the proceedings against *Germain Katanga and Mathieu Ngudjolo Chui* is remarkably higher (363), fewer child applicants have, to date, filed applications for participation in the criminal proceedings (between 4-8 former child soldiers). For information regarding the overall number of participating victims, see Case Information Sheet of 15 October 2010, "The Prosecutor v. Germain Katanga and Mathieu Ngudjolo Chui", ICC-PIDS-CIS-DRC2-03-004/10. The lower number of child participants may be caused by the fact that the

percentage of child participants can be explained by the fact that the only crimes *Thomas Lubanga Dyilo* has been accused of concern the conscription, enlistment and active use of children below the age of fifteen years in hostilities.[314] The only direct victims of this crime are children.[315]

3.4 Application of Victim Requirements to the Child

To participate in proceedings, children as adults must meet the criteria of victimhood. Article 68(3) of the ICC Statute regulates the notion of victimhood.[316] This provision, by not distinguishing between different categories of victims, also includes children as potential participants. It states that,

> '[w]here the personal interests of the victims are affected, the Court shall permit their views and concerns to be presented and considered at stages of the proceedings determined to be appropriate by the Court and in a manner which is not prejudicial to or inconsistent with the rights of the accused and a fair and impartial trial. Such views and concerns may be presented by the legal representatives of the victims where the Court considers it appropriate, in accordance with the Rules of Procedure and Evidence.'[317]

In order to participate in ICC proceedings, individuals need to be recognised as victims. Rule 85(a) of the Rules of Procedure and Evidence of the International Criminal Court defines victims as,

> 'natural persons who have suffered harm as result of the commission of any crime within the jurisdiction of the Court [...].'[318]

The drafters of the ICC RPE gathered their inspiration for the victim definition from the UN General Assembly 1985 Declaration of Basic Principles of Justice of Victims of Crime and Abuse of Power. [319] Art. 1 of the Declaration states that,

---

two accused have not only been charged with the recruitment crime (as in *Thomas Lubanga Dyilo*) but are also allegedly responsibility for the commission of other crimes falling within the jurisdiction of the International Criminal Court. About eight former child soldiers participated in the criminal proceedings. At least four applications were submitted by minors, ICC-01/04-01/07-1491, para 97. The third decision on the applications for participation submitted by victims provides that eight former child soldiers have been recognised, see ICC-01/04-01/07-1788, paras. 7-9. For more applications submitted by children (about thirteen) in the *Situation in Uganda* see ICC-02/04-125, paras. 12, 13, 28, 36-38, 53, 107-108, 111, 150, 191.

314 ICC-01/04-01/06-2, at 4.

315 Arts 2006, at 6.

316 Similarly, the European Court of Justice and the European Court of Human Rights have concise criteria to determine which individuals may participate in proceedings. For further information on how to file a case and which criteria are to be met before the ECtHR, see Leach 2001.

317 See also, ICC-01/04-101-tEN-Corr, para. 61.

318 2002 Rules of Procedure and Evidence of the International Criminal Court.

319 UN General Assembly 1985 Declaration of Basic Principles of Justice of Victims of Crime and Abuse of Power, UN General Assembly, UN Doc. A/RES/40/34 (1985).

'"Victims" means persons who, individually or collectively, have suffered harm, including physical or mental injury, emotional suffering, economic loss or substantial impairment of their fundamental rights, through acts or omissions that are in violation of criminal laws operative within Member States [...].'

This Declaration formed the basis for the later 2005 Basic Principles and Guidelines on the Right to a Remedy and Reparations for Victims of Gross Violations of International Human Rights Law and Serious Violations of International Humanitarian Law.[320] As the RPE of the ICC, no distinction is made between adult and child victims. Principle no. 8 defines victims as

> 'persons who individually or collectively suffered harm, including physical or mental injury, emotional suffering, economic loss or substantial impairment of their fundamental rights, through acts or omissions that constitute gross violations of international human rights law, or serious violations of international humanitarian law. Where appropriate, and in accordance with domestic law, the term "victim" also includes the immediate family or dependants of the direct victim and persons who have suffered harm in intervening to assist victims in distress or to prevent victimization.'[321]

In the first decisions relating to these provisions, Pre-Trial Chamber I, whose practice has been followed broadly by other Pre-Trial and Trial Chambers, held that victims who seek participation must establish the following four requirements:

- The victim must be a natural person
- who has suffered harm
- as a result of a crime
- within the jurisdiction of the ICC. [322]

The procedural capacity of the victim participant does not exist as a matter of right. Instead, it constitutes a potential right (depending on the competent Chamber's

---

320 2005 Basic Principles and Guidelines on the Right to a Remedy and Reparations for Victims of Gross Violations of International Human Rights Law and Serious Violations of International Humanitarian Law, UN Doc. A/60/147 (2005).

321 See also, Van Boven 1999, 77, at 78-79. The drafters of the UN Basic Principles did not address the question of whether the victim definition included the broader concept of indirect victims. See also, the dissenting opinion of Judge Blattmann, ICC-01/04-01/06-1119, paras. 4-6. Organisations and institutions can also be considered as victims. Rule 85(b) states that '[v]ictims may include organizations or institutions that have sustained direct harm to any of their property which is dedicated to religion, education, art or science or charitable purposes, and to their historic monuments, hospitals and other places and objects for humanitarian purposes.'

322 ICC-01/04-01/06-925, para. 13; ICC-02/04-101, para. 12. ICC-01/04-101-tEN-Corr, para. 79. The Pre-Trial Chamber held that the following four questions must be answered when determining victim status under Rule 85(a): 'Are the Applicants natural persons? Have they suffered harm? Do the crimes alleged by the Applicants fall within the jurisdiction of the Court? Is there a causal link between these crimes and the harm suffered by the Applicants?' See also, e.g., ICC-01/04-01/06-228, at 7; ICC-02/04-01/05-282, para. 8. See, for instance, ICC-02/04-101, para. 12. For a critical assessment of the victim requirements, see, Trumbull 2007, 777, at 290-801.

approval (Article 68(3) Rome Statute)).[323] In case of recognition, victim participants, including children, do not become true parties to the criminal proceedings (such as the Defence or Prosecution).[324] Instead, the relevant Chamber decides not only upon the approval or rejection of the application, but also on the concrete modalities of victim participation when convinced that the personal interests of the victim are affected.[325]

3.4.1 Natural person

First of all, victims who wish to participate must be a natural person – a human being.[326] According to Pre-Trial Chamber I, anyone who is not considered to be a legal person is a natural person.[327] Rule 85 RPE does not distinguish between different age categories of victims. Thus, all children – irrespective of their age – are, in principle, eligible for the participant status.[328]

3.4.2 Harm

The person who wishes to participate must have suffered harm. This may be of a material, physical or psychological nature.[329] The notion of harm within the meaning of the ICC Statute and its RPE is considered as being direct or indirect in nature.[330] Direct harm constitutes harm that is the result of crimes charged. Indirect harm may be caused by a crime within the jurisdiction of the Court that is allegedly committed against one person (the direct victim) but at the same time causes harm to another person (the indirect victim).[331] While Rule 85 RPE does not stipulate that indirect victims are included in the victim definition, this aspect was ruled upon by Trial Chamber I in the decision of 18 January 2008 in the *Lubanga* case. The Chamber clearly stated that indirect victims are included in the victim definition and may therefore be recognised as participants.

323 Art. 68(3) Rome Statute provides that, 'Where the personal interests of the victims are affected, the Court shall permit their views and concerns to be presented and considered at stages of the proceedings determined to be appropriate by the Court [...].'

324 For an overview of the Court's jurisprudence, see ICC-01/09-02/11-498, para. 10. Greco 2007, at 535. See for similar criticism, Ferstman & Goetz 2009b, 324-333.

325 Art. 68(3) Rome Statute, Rule 89(2) RPE of the International Criminal Court.

326 See, e.g., Henzelin *et al.* 2006, 317, at 322.

327 ICC-01/04-101-tEN-Corr, para. 80.

328 See also, Heikkilä 2004, at 18.

329 ICC-01/04-01/06-1432, para. 32.

330 Ibid., para. 1.

331 An example of indirect harm is the harm suffered by parents due to the recruitment of their child as a child soldier or the loss of a family member that has been killed, ICC-01/04-01/06-1432, para. 32. Contrastingly, the *ad hoc* Tribunals limited the victim status to direct victims. This limitation was criticized as being too narrow, see, e.g., Donat-Cattin 1999, 252; Donat-Cattin 2008, Article 68, at 1294-1295. See for general criticism about the role of victims before the *ad hoc* Tribunals, Jorda & de Hemptienne 2002, 1387, at 1387-1398. More recently, Trumbull 2007, at 786-789. On the recognition of indirect victims in general see: ICC-01/04-01/06-1432, para. 32; ICC-01/04-177-tENG, at 9. Greco 2007, at 536.

The Chamber ruled that,

> '[i]n relation to the link between the harm allegedly suffered and the crime, whereas Rule 85(b) of the Rules provides that legal persons must have "sustained direct harm", Rule 85(a) of the Rules does not include that stipulation for natural persons, and applying a purposive interpretation, it follows that people can be the direct or indirect victims of a crime within the jurisdiction of the Court.'[332]

This particular issue was confirmed and further elaborated on by the Appeals Chamber, which stipulated that both, direct and indirect victims must establish that they have suffered 'personal' harm. The Appeals Chamber concluded that it,

> 'confirms the finding of the Trial Chamber to the extent that the Trial Chamber determined that harm suffered by victims does not necessarily have to be direct and amends the decision to include that harm suffered by a victim applicant for the purposes of rule 85(a) must be personal harm.'[333]

Next to the recognition of the child as a direct victim, the child participant may therefore also be recognised as an indirect victim. This is at issue when the harm suffered by the direct victim gives rise to harm suffered by the child. When, for instance, the parents of a child died and their death is the result of a crime within the jurisdiction of the Court, the child can be considered to be an indirect victim. Pre-Trial Chamber II in the *Bemba* case, established in this regard that due to the close relationship with their parents, children are indeed recognised as indirect victims.[334]

3.4.3 The jurisdiction criterion

The alleged crime must constitute a crime within the jurisdiction of the Court. Article 5 of the Rome Statute provides that the current jurisdiction of the Court covers the crime of genocide, crimes against humanity or war crimes (jurisdiction *ratione materiae*).[335] In addition, the application to participate in the criminal proceedings must establish that the victimisation took place within the jurisdiction *ratione temporis* (Article 11 Rome Statute) and the jurisdiction *ratione personae* or *loci* (Article 12 ICC Statute).

---

332 ICC-01/04-01/06-1119, para. 91. This decision was confirmed by the Appeals Chamber on 11 July 2008, ICC-01/04-01/06-1432, para. 33.

333 ICC-01/04-01/06-1432, para. 39. The Rome Statute does not elaborate on a certain minimum level of harm. For criticism see, Henzelin *et al* 2006, at. 325. See also, Drumbl 2012, at 159.

334 Children as indirect victims – being the immediate family member and dependent of a deceased person and suffering personal harm as a result of the death of a relative, see ICC-01/05-01/08-320, paras. 41-51.

335 Art. 5 Rome Statute.

One specific crime is limited to a particular group of direct child victims.[336] This is the war crime of child recruitment as enshrined in Articles 8(2)(b)(xxvi) and 8(2)(e)(vii) Rome Statute.[337] Both provisions and the corresponding Elements of Crimes request that the direct victims were under the age of fifteen years at the moment of conscription, enlistment or direct use in hostilities.[338]

Furthermore, children can – irrespective of their specific age at the moment of crime commission – also qualify as direct victims of various crimes under the jurisdiction of the ICC, such as torture, inhuman treatment or sexual slavery. This is because the elements of these crimes are not restricted to the particular age of the victim. As the *travaux préparatoires* do not refer to any age limitation with the exception of the war crime of child recruitment, it seems that the age of the child victim has not been recognised as being of particular relevance during the drafting process in relation to the elements of crime.

3.4.4 The causality criterion

Pre-Trial Chamber I elaborated in its decision of 17 January 2006 that causality between the harm suffered and the crime must be proven.[339] The Chamber held that applicants must establish at an investigative (situational) stage,

> 'that there are grounds to believe that *the harm suffered is the result of the commission of crimes falling within the jurisdiction of the Court*. However, the Chamber considers that it is not necessary to determine in any great detail at this stage the precise nature of the causal link and the identity of the persons responsible for the crimes' (emphasis added).[340]

Thereby, the Pre-Trial Chamber introduced a distinction between participation at the investigation (situational) stage and trial (case) stage.[341] Pre-Trial Chamber II, whose practice has also been followed by Pre-Trial Chamber III, underlined that,

336 The ICC refers to the Convention on the Rights of the Child standard, see, among others, ICC-02/04-01/05-252, para. 20. For further discussion on the impact of the extensive number of victims seeking to participate, see Heikkilä 2004, at 152-154.

337 See, among other decisions concerning child victims of the recruitment crime, ICC-01/04-505, paras. 91, 93, 95, 97, 99.

338 Arts. 8(2)(b)(xxvi) and 8(2)(e)(vii) of the 2002 Elements of Crime of the International Criminal Court. See for further information on this particular crime, Cottier & Zimmermann 2008, at 466-475 (paras. 227-234).

339 ICC-01/04-101-tEN-Corr, para. 94.

340 Ibid., para. 94 ; No. ICC-01/04-423-Corr, para. 4; ICC-01/04-01/06-601, at 9.

341 ICC-01/04-101-tEN-Corr, para. 65. The Chamber held that it 'considers that the Statute, the Rules of Procedure and Evidence and the Regulations of the Court draw a distinction between situations and cases in terms of the different kinds of proceedings, initiated by any organ of the Court, that they entail. Situations, which are generally defined in terms of temporal, territorial and in some cases personal parameters, such as the situation in the territory of the Democratic Republic of the Congo since 1 July 2002, entail the proceedings envisaged in the Statute to determine whether a particular situation should give rise to a criminal investigation as well as the investigation as such. Cases, which comprise specific incidents during which one or more crimes within the jurisdiction

> '[t]he Single Judge will therefore refrain from analyzing the various theories on causality and will instead adopt a pragmatic, strictly factual approach, whereby the alleged harm will be held as "resulting from" the alleged incident when the spatial and temporal circumstances surrounding the appearance of the harm and the occurrence of the incident seem to overlap, or at least to be compatible and not clearly inconsistent.'[342]

Accordingly, in this decision, Pre-Trial Chamber II suggested a pragmatic instead of a formalistic approach when considering causality.

At trial stage, thus when the accused is already identified, the Appeals Chamber held that victims wishing to participate in the trial proceedings against *Thomas Lubanga Dyilo* must establish that the harm suffered is linked with the charges against the accused.[343] The causal requirement at trial stage between the harm suffered and the charged crime has also, for instance, been restated in the proceedings against *Jean Pierre Bemba.*[344] Thus far, the ICC did not distinguish between children and adults when examining the causality requirement.

3.4.5 The evidentiary standard used

As the burden of proof rests on those who apply for participation, victims are requested to submit convincing pieces of evidence in order to prove their victimisation. Various Chambers addressed in their decisions the evidentiary standard to be complied with in the pre-trial and trial phase of the proceedings.

Pre-Trial Chamber I elaborated in the earlier addressed decision of 17 January 2006,

> 'that there are *grounds to believe* that the harm suffered is the result of the commission of crimes falling within the jurisdiction of the Court.[345]

At trial stage, a higher standard was chosen. Victims were requested to establish *reasonable grounds to believe* that they have become victims of a crime charged.[346] With regard to the standard at trial stage, Pre-Trial Chamber I held in its decision of 29 June 2006 that the evidentiary standard is stricter. The Chamber ruled that,

> 'the [a]pplicants must demonstrate that a sufficient causal link exists between the harm they have suffered and the crimes for which there are *reasonable grounds to*

---

of the Court seem to have been committed by one or more identified suspects, entail proceedings that take place after the issuance of a warrant of arrest or a summons to appear.'

342 ICC-02/04-101, paras. 12-15. See also, ICC-01/05-01/08-320, para. 31.

343 ICC-01/04-01/06-1432, para. 65; ICC-01/04-01/06-60, at 10; ICC-01/04-01/06-172, at 6-8.

344 ICC-01/05-01/08-1091; ICC-01/05-01/08-1017.

345 Ibid., para. 94 ; No. ICC-01/04-423-Corr, para. 4; ICC-01/04-01/06-601, at 9.

346 ICC-01/04-01-601, at 11-12, 13.

believe that Thomas Lubanga Dyilo bears criminal responsibility and for which the Chamber has issued an arrest warrant' (emphasis added).[347]

The *grounds to believe* and *reasonable grounds to believe* standards of proof have been introduced in very early decisions and were similarly – though not necessarily with the same terminology – applied by other Chambers.[348]

Pre-trial Chamber I ruled in *the Germain Katanga and Mathieu Ngudjolo Chui* case that *prima facie* evidence is sufficient in order to establish that those who applied for participation in the criminal proceedings, including children, are victims. The standard of *prima facie* permits a presumption in favour of the victim who applies for participation if convincing evidence is submitted.[349] It is for this reason that Pre-Trial Chamber I pointed out that an assessment of the credibility of the victim statement is not made at this early stage. Why this conclusion is particularly relevant for the child is addressed in more detail in turn. The Chamber held that,

> '[c]onsidering further that the applicants are only required to demonstrate that the four requirements established by rule 85 of the Rules are met *prima facie* and that therefore the Single Judge's analysis of the Applications "will not consist in assessing the credibility of the [applicants'] statement[s] or engaging in a process of corroboration *strictu sensu*", but will assess the applicants' statements first and foremost on the merits of their intrinsic coherence, as well as on the basis of the information otherwise available to the Single Judge […].'[350]

In the same tenor. Pre-Trial Chamber II, whose practice has also been followed by Pre-Trial Chamber III, underlined that,

> '[a]s regards the method of examination and the required standard of proof, the Statute does not set forth general rules on the basis of which the reliability of relevant elements is to be assessed […]. Accordingly, in the absence of any such rules, the Chamber has broad discretion in assessing the soundness of a given statement or other piece of evidence. Such an assessment has to comply with the general principle of law that the burden of proof of elements supporting a claim lies on the party making the claim. […].'[351]

---

347 ICC-01/04-01/06-601, at 10; ICC-01/04-01/06-172, at 6-8. The standard set by the Pre-Trial Chamber for applications to a situation are 'grounds to believe', which is a relatively low threshold, see also, de Hemptinne & Rindi 2006, 342, at 345. The determination of the stage of participation depends on the moment of submission. At an early stage of submission, the investigation phase might still be ongoing. Victims would then apply to participate at the investigation phase. If, however, the charges against the alleged accused were confirmed and trial proceedings had commenced, victims may still seek to participate during a case.

348 For an overview of the first decisions on victim participation and a comparison of the Chamber's practice see, Chung 2008, at 459-542.

349 Herlitz 1994, 391, at 397.

350 ICC-01/04-01/07-357, at 8-9. Applicant a/0333/07 was still a minor at the moment of decision taking, at 7. See also, ICC-01/04-01/07-579, para. 67. Applicant a/0110/08 was the only minor applicant in the decision at issue.

351 ICC-02/04-101, paras. 12-15. See also, ICC-01/05-01/08-320, para. 31.

Accordingly, the credibility of the child is assessed at the pre-trial phase of the proceedings, but alongside criteria which are not set forth in the statutory rules. Instead, the Chamber is of the view that it has a broad discretion in this regard.

As regards the evidentiary standard at trial stage, Trial Chamber I also adopted a pragmatic approach based on the *prima facie* standard at trial stage. It was found that this standard was met despite the fact that inconsistencies existed concerning the birth date of some victims as set out in the application form and the submitted documents. The decision of Trial Chamber I stipulated furthermore, that the credibility of the victim is assumed as long as the provided documents do not indicate another conclusion. The assessment of the Chamber is of a nature which is also known in civil proceedings, as it assumed compliance with the criteria of Rule 85 RPE unless it is disproved. Trial Chamber I underlined that,

> '[t]he Chamber has carefully weighed the inconsistencies in each case, but in all the circumstances the differences do not, *ipso facto,* undermine the credibility of the applicants' assertion as to his or her age in the application form, supported by documents that have been provided such as student identity card, election cards and birth certificates. In the view of the Chamber, the material when considered overall, proves, *prima facie*, the identity and age of the applicants in accordance with the Trial Chamber's Decision on victims' participation.'[352]

Hence, Trial Chamber I underlined that generally speaking, a *prima facie* standard of evidence is adopted in order to determine victim status.[353]

Following the practice at pre-trial stage, Trial Chamber I did not examine the credibility of the victim's statement. The same Chamber underlined that this assessment must be distinguished from a higher evidence test. It held that,

> '[it] needs to be stressed that this is a *prima facie* conclusion, rather than one that is reached on the basis of a higher test, such as beyond reasonable doubt.'[354]

Also noteworthy in this regard is that the Appeals Chamber held in the case of the *Prosecutor v. Joseph Kony, Vincent Otti, Okot Odhiambo and Dominic Ongwen* on

---

352 ICC-01/04-01/06-1556, para. 89.

353 Ibid.; ICC-01/04-01/06-1556, paras. 73, 101-102, 111. The Chamber ruled that, 'the applicants have given *sufficient evidence to establish, prima facie,* that they are victims under Rule 85(a) of the Rules.' ICC-01/04-01/06-1724-Anx3, at 2-3.

354 ICC-01/04-01/06-1556, para. 120. Pre-Trial Chamber I stated, '[c]onsidering that the Chamber considers that the causal link required by rule 85 of the Rules at the case stage, is substantiated when the victim, and where applicable close family or dependents provides sufficient evidence to allow it be established.' The Chamber does not agree with defense request that there must be 'reasonable grounds to believe that there is a causal link between the harm suffered and the crimes [...].' ICC-01/04-01/06-172, at 7-8.

23 February 2009 that, a case-by-case analysis is necessary in order to determine whether the victim status criteria as set out in Rule 85(a) RPE are met.[355]

3.5 CHILDREN APPLYING FOR PARTICIPATION

The procedure to be followed when a victim wishes to participate in the criminal proceedings before the ICC is elaborated in the RPE of the Court. Since the RPE do not distinguish between adult and child victims, children applying for participation have to comply with the procedural requirements as set out in Rules 89-91 of the Rules of Procedure and Evidence. It will be established in turn that when children apply for participation, additional procedural particularities arise.
Paragraphs 1 and 2 of Rule 89 provide that,

> '(i)n order to present their views and concerns, victims shall make written application to the Registrar, who shall transmit the application to the relevant Chamber. Subject to the provisions of the Statute, in particular article 68, paragraph 1, the Registrar shall provide a copy of the application to the Prosecutor and the defence, who shall be entitled to reply within a time limit to be set by the Chamber. Subject to the provisions of sub-rule 2, the Chamber shall then specify the proceedings and manner in which participation is considered appropriate, which may include making opening and closing statements.'
>
> The Chamber, on its own initiative or on the application of the Prosecutor or the defence, may reject the application if it considers that the person is not a victim or that the criteria set forth in article 68, paragraph 3, are not otherwise fulfilled. A victim whose application has been rejected may file a new application later in the proceedings.'

The use of the joint application form which is made available by the Court (and which has also been suggested to be used in order to request reparations) is not compulsory. It is sufficient that the victim who applies for participation provides the Court with the information in writing as pointed out in Regulation 86 of the Regulations of the Court and asked for in the 'Request for Participation in Proceedings and Reparations at the ICC' (hereinafter 'the application form').[356] In relation to the application form the Registry pointed out that,

> 'experience showed that these two forms (originally there were two separate application forms) were sometimes confusing for victims, who sometimes filled in one instead of the other, or believed that in completing an application for participation in proceedings they were also applying for reparations. It was therefore decided to merge the two forms under RoC 86(1) and RoC(1) into one

355 *Situation in Uganda in the case of the Prosecutor v. Joseph Kony, Vincent Otti, Okot Odhiambo, Dominic Ongwen*, ICC-02/04-179, 23 February 2009, para. 2.

356 Application Form for Individuals. The ICC published a *Guide for the Participation of Victims in the Proceedings of the Court* which explains in detail how victims have to proceed with their applications. See also, Regulation 86, of the 2004 Regulations of the International Criminal Court.

> common form, which was approved by the Presidency in 2010. The new forms were not used by the majority of applicants in the *Lubanga* case, since their applications, whether for participation of for reparations, predated the merging of forms.'[357]

In contrast to the other Trial Chambers of the Court, Trial Chamber V introduced a different application procedure. It held that the procedure contained in Rule 89 of the Rules of Procedure and Evidence is only to be complied with as regards

> 'victims who wish to present their views and concerns individually by appearing directly before the Chamber, [...] other victims, who wish to participate without appearing before the Chamber, should be permitted to present their views and concerns through a common legal representative without having to go through the procedure established by Rule 80 of the Rules. [...] Victims who do not wish to present their views and concerns individually and directly to the Chamber, but rather to express those views and concerns solely through common legal representation, will not be required to submit an application under Rule 89(1) of the Rules. However, these victims may, if they so wish, register with the Registry, indicating their names, contact details as well as information as to the harm suffered. The Registry shall enter these victim registrations into a database, which it will administer and make accessible to the Common Legal Representative. The purpose of this registration is threefold: first, to provide victims with a channel through which they can formalize their claim of victimhood; second, to establish a personal connection between the victim and the Common Legal Representative, enabling victims to provide their input and allowing the Common Legal Representative to give relevant feedback to the victims; third, to assist the Court in communicating with the victims and in preparing the periodic reports referred to in paragraph 54 below.'[358]

The standard application form contains eight parts (A-H) which are briefly addressed in turn. Part A of the application form requests personal information about the victim, such as name, birth date, or information about the person acting on behalf of the victim. Part B asks for information about the alleged crime(s) and Part C to do so in regard to injury, loss or harm suffered. Victims can choose under Parts D and E in which specific, or perhaps even all stages of the proceedings (criminal and/or reparation), they wish to participate. Part F requests information about the legal representation of the victim. Finally, Part G asks the victim whether he or she would be concerned if their identity were to be revealed to the Defence or the Prosecutor and Part H requests the signature of the person applying for participation and also, if applicable, the signature of a third person acting on their behalf. Victims may choose to be represented before the Court by a legal representative. Rule 90 RPE states that,

> '1. A victim shall be free to choose a legal representative. 2. Where there are a number of victims, the Chamber may, for the purposes of ensuring the effectiveness of the

---

357 See, ICC-01/04-01/06-2806, para. 174.
358 See ICC-01/09-02/11-498, paras. 24, 48-49.

> proceedings, request the victims or particular groups of victims, if necessary with the assistance of the Registry, to choose a common legal representative or representatives. In facilitating the coordination of victim representation, the Registry may provide assistance, *inter alia*, by referring the victims to a list of counsel, maintained by the Registry, or suggesting one or more common legal representatives. 3. If the victims are unable to choose a common legal representative or representatives within a time limit that the Chamber may decide, the Chamber may request the Registrar to choose one or more common legal representatives. 4. The Chamber and the Registry shall take all reasonable steps to ensure that in the selection of common legal representatives, the distinct interests of the victims, particularly as provided in article 68, paragraph 1, are represented and that any conflict of interest is avoided. 5. A victim or group of victims who lack the necessary means to pay for a common legal representative chosen by the Court may receive assistance from the Registry, including, as appropriate, financial assistance. 6. A legal representative of a victim or victims shall have the qualifications set forth in rule 22, sub-rule 1.'

Completed forms should be sent to the Victims Participation and Reparations Section (VPRS) or to one of the Field Offices of the ICC.[359] Victims, including children, are encouraged to fill in the application form as completely as possible. This implies that the competent Chambers nevertheless consider applications that are not fully completed.

3.5.1 Legal competence of the child to apply for participation[360]

Turning next to the technicalities of the procedure when children apply for participation in the criminal proceedings, it is noted that children have to comply with additional requirements compared to adults. Adults are *only* requested to comply with the four requirements of Rule 85 RPE when accessing the ICC. Children have to comply with two additional requirements that are not called for in the statutory rules. These requirements relate to the legal (in)competence of the child to file an application and the related condition that another person should act on behalf of the child. Both aspects have been introduced by various Chambers of the ICC and have also been included in the amended application form. Paragraph 3 of Rule 89 RPE states that,

> 'an application *may also* be made by a person acting with the consent of the victim, or acting on behalf of a victim' (*emphasis added*).

359 At the time of writing, four field offices of the ICC are established: Kinshasa (Democratic Republic of the Congo), Abeche (Chad), Kampala (Uganda) and Bangui (Central African Republic), http://www.icc-cpi.int/Menus/ICC/About+the+Court/Practical+Information/Field+Offices.htm.

360 An earlier version of section 3.4.2 has been published by this author, see Hamzei 2010, 113-122. The present section constitutes an update.

Neither the Statute nor the RPE require that applications of a child *shall* be made by a person acting on behalf of a child. It is the application form which requires that the child meets two additional conditions. Firstly, it states that,

> '[u]sually a victim will apply for him/herself. In *some cases this is not possible*, for example because the victim is a child or is disabled [...]. In such cases, *another person may be permitted to act on behalf of the victim*. The victim should consent to have another person act on his/her behalf if the victim is able to' (emphasis added).[361]

Secondly, a child's application must contain proof of relationship between the child and the person acting on his/her behalf.[362] The Booklet Guide explicitly states that failing to do this will mean that the application has been invalidly presented.[363] These requirements have been incorporated into the application form through the practice of various Chambers of the Court.[364]

Practice of the Pre-Trial Chambers

Applications submitted by a minor have been rejected by Pre-Trial Chambers I and II.[365] The Single Judge of Pre-Trial Chamber I held that,

> 'Applicant a/0332/07 is a minor who submits a complete application on his own behalf; a student card is submitted as proof of identity; the date and location of the alleged crime(s) are sufficiently indicated on the application [...]. As Applicant a/0332/07 is a minor, however, his application must be submitted by a person who has attained the age of majority. Since the present application was submitted by Applicant a/0332/07 himself, it must be considered incomplete.'[366]

Pre-Trial Chamber II in its decision of 10 March 2009 held that,

> 'the principle of ensuring the expediency of the proceedings makes it appropriate to reject *in limine* the nine applications submitted by a minor [...].'[367]

According to this Chamber, if minors themselves submit applications, they may be excluded for reasons of judicial economy.

Pre-Trial Chamber I established that applications submitted by persons who are neither the next-of-kin nor legal guardian of a minor

---

361 See explanatory note to question 13. http://www.icc-cpi.int/NR/rdonlyres/48A75CF0-E38E-48A7-A9E0-026ADD32553D/0/SAFIndividualEng.pdf.

362 Ibid., see question 15-16 of the application form and the respective explanatory note.

363 Guide for the Participation of Victims, at 21.

364 ICC-01/04-374, paras. 12-13; ICC-02/05-111-Corr, para. 26; ICC-01/04-505, para. 17, 31; ICC-01/04-423-Corr, para. 31.

365 ICC-01/04-545. See also, view of Pre-Trial Chamber II, ICC-02/04-125, para. 7.

366 ICC-01/04-545, paras. 32-33.

367 ICC-02/04-180, at 5.

'must contain the consent of the next-of-kin or legal guardian that an application has been made on the minor's behalf.'[368]

Practice of the Trial Chambers

Trial Chamber II applied a more relaxed and therefore preferable approach as minors succeeded in filing an application on their own behalf. This Chamber is not of the belief that minor applicants should be prohibited from filing an application under Rule 89(3) RPE. It pointed out that a case-by-case assessment, in particular taking into account the maturity and powers of discernment of the child was appropriate.[369] Age itself has not been referred to as an exclusionary factor. By taking into account the maturity and powers of discernment of the child, this Chamber evaluates the capacity of the individual child. The Chamber does not explain how, against which yardstick, it takes its conclusions as regards the capacity of the child. It can therefore not be concluded whether the principle of the evolving capacities of the child would have been used by the Chamber as a yardstick. This principle aims to ensure that the child's limited autonomy is gradually to be enlarged in order to increase his/her own participation in the decision-making process (*Chapter One*). Regardless of the lack of direct reference, this permissive approach indicates that the Chamber takes the individual circumstances of particular children into account when deciding upon their application for participation.

A similar permissive approach has been adopted by Trial Chamber I in the *Lubanga* case.[370] The Chamber pointed out that it is generally of the view that child applications should be submitted by a person acting on behalf of the child. It held at the same time that the Rome Statute does not request that child applicants who are close to eighteen years of age are obliged to have a person acting on their behalf who fulfils the next-of-kin or legal guardian requirement. It stressed that other persons may also act on behalf of the child. This has been argued alongside the example of former child soldiers who are often separated from their family. It has also been recognised that large-scale crises may prevent children from proving kinship or guardianship. Moreover, it stipulated that the concept of legal guardianship itself may not exist as, for example, is the case in Eastern Congo. Trial Chamber I therefore ruled that it determines on a case-by-case basis whether the person acting on behalf of the child can be considered as suitable.[371]

---

368 ICC-01/04-505, para. 31.

369 ICC-01/04-01/07-933, para. 39. Interestingly, Trial Chamber II adopted a more lenient approach; it held that, in the absence of documents that establish the legal guardianship, a statement of two credible witnesses can establish legal guardianship.

370 ICC-01/04-01/06-1556, paras. 67-73.

371 Ibid., para. 72.

The Chamber did not establish criteria for the suitability of a third person. As a result, the question is left unanswered as to whether, for instance, child rights NGOs are potentially organisations that can submit an application on behalf of the child. This specific discussion is currently being held with regard to collective communications submitted by NGOs under the optional protocol to the Convention on the Rights of the Child which establishes an individual complaint mechanism.[372] There might be a justified fear that child rights NGOs acting on behalf of the child might support children's applications in order to promote their own organisational objectives. For this reason, monitoring mechanisms could be installed in order to prevent such abuse. It is to be kept in mind, that such abuse is also not unlikely when individuals act on behalf of the child. Accordingly, a carful assessment is already indispensable in cases in which individuals act on behalf of the child. Monitoring when NGOs act on behalf of children can therefore be presumed not to be so different from the monitoring of individual persons acting on behalf of the child. The Committee on the Rights of the Child held in General Comment No. 6 that,

> '[r]eview mechanisms shall be introduced and implemented to monitor the quality of the exercise of guardianship in order to ensure the best interests of the child are being represented throughout the decision-making process and, in particular, to prevent abuse.'[373]

Trial Chamber I also introduced an exception to the condition that applications *must* be submitted by a person acting on behalf of the child. It held that applications from children above the age of fifteen and close to the age of adulthood should still be considered.[374]

The Chamber did not rule that children below the age of eighteen years are *generally* recognised as being competent to submit an application for participation without a person acting on their behalf if they are mature and capable of understanding the implications of their applications.

Evaluation

The approach taken by the Trial Chambers compared to the position adopted by the Pre-Trial Chambers is preferred by the author for the above mentioned reasons. This does not mean that all questions have been addressed. These decisions still raise the questions whether, firstly, the Chambers were entitled to introduce the

---

372 UN General Assembly, Human Rights Council, Second Session, Working Group on an optional protocol to the Convention on the Rights of the Child, Second session, Geneva, 6-10 December 2010, Proposal for a draft optional protocol prepared by the Chairperson-Rapporteur of the Open-ended Working Group on an optional protocol to the Convention on the Rights of the Child to provide a communication procedure, explanatory memorandum, UN Doc. A/HRC.WG.7/2/2 (2010), paras. 9-14.

373 General Comment No. 6, para. 35.

374 ICC-01/04-01/06-1556, paras. 92-97.

additional requirements that a person who has attained the age of majority and is the next-of-kin or legal guardian has to submit an application on behalf of a minor applicant. Secondly, is there a legal basis to restrict applications submitted by minors for reasons of judicial economy? Even if a justification could be found by, for instance, referring to the fact that an exclusion is justified because of the procedural differences at pre-trial and trial stage, an explicit argumentation is to be provided for by the Court. It is to be noted that, on the basis of Rule 89(2) RPE, rejected applicants are free to submit a new application for participation at a later stage in the proceedings. Furthermore, other Chambers of the Court are not bound by this practice in terms of precedents.[375]

As a result of this specific treatment, orphans or children separated from their families might have unequal access to the International Criminal Court, because they are unable to fulfil the guardianship requirement compared to other children and adults. The wording of Rule 85 RPE enables *all* individuals to potentially qualify as a victim. It seems that the specific treatment when children apply for participation falls short of providing for a child-sensitive examination of applications submitted by particular groups of children. It seems furthermore that the specific circumstances of the individual child applicant are not taken into account. Does the exclusion of child applicants for this particular reason therefore fail to adequately (or perhaps even not at all) address the evolving capacities of the individual child which could (depending on the particular case) make the request to establish guardianship dispensable?

Without further explanation and reference to a legal basis, a rigid exclusion based in particular upon the age of the child (younger than 18 years old), entails the risk that the Court does not sufficiently take into account the evolving capacities of the individual child which call for a growing involvement of the child in accordance with his/her capabilities (*Chapter One*). An illustrative example of such exclusion would exist in relation to child-headed households. A child who leads a child-headed household (a phenomenon which is not uncommon in conflict situations) would, in light of this approach, neither be able to submit an application on his/her own behalf nor on behalf of his/her siblings and other dependents. It is also to be remembered in this regard, that disadvantaged children who lost or have been separated from their parents and live in a country in which an armed conflict is ongoing often are unable to establish guardianship.[376]

The possibility that children thus can participate in criminal proceedings leads again to the question whether participation can be considered to be in the best interests of the child – bearing in mind in particular the above addressed disadvantages of victim participation. When discussing this question the following aspects are to be kept in mind from a legal perspective: Despite the lack of a clearly developed procedural legal status of the child in the course of international criminal

375 Art. 21 (2) Rome Statute; Ferdinandusse 2004, 1041, at 1051 – 1053; Nerlich 2009, 305.

376 The Committee on the Rights of the Child underlined in General Comment No. 6 that establishing legal guardianship during large-scale emergencies could be difficult. See, General Comment No. 6, para. 38.

(and equally reparation) proceedings, the possibility to be involved in such proceedings should not be underestimated for numerous reasons. Firstly, when the most fundamental rights of the child are violated, and the immediate caregivers or the State cannot protect the child,[377] the international procedural capability of remedying the violations constitutes the only available remedy in order to restore justice.[378] The restoration of justice is of outstanding relevance during or in the aftermath of armed conflict and large scale violence.[379] Moreover, restoration of justice is not a progress that is limited to adults. Within this phase, children's involvement constitutes an added value to the overall process of conflict resolution and is part and parcel to a sustainable peace.[380] The Special Representative of the Secretary-General for Children and Armed Conflict underlined in the 2010 report that,

> '[t]o attempt transitional justice processes without involving children not only fails to comply with the Convention on the Rights of the Child – the most universally ratified international instrument – it also compromises the outcome of those processes.
>
> The imperative of child participation in transitional justice has gained both credence and clarity in past years. The importance and potential of transitional justice for children is evident. At the same time, it is more widely recognized that their views and experience provide unique and critical constitutions to these processes and to national reconciliation.'[381]

The legal competence of the child to apply for participation is therefore also to be seen in light of the fact that the recognition of children as '*key stakeholders in rule of law initiatives*' is due, as clearly underlined by the United Nations Secretary-General who underlined in the *UN Approach to Justice for Children* that,

---

377 The Convention on the Rights of the Child underlines that the primary responsibility to care for children rests with the family of the child. See for example articles 5, 18 and 21 of the CRC.

378 An international mechanisms is often necessary since domestic remedies are not accessible or not effective during or in the aftermath of an armed conflict or large scale violence.

379 Johnstone 2004, 5, at 11. While the author lists the various reasons for advocating victim participation, he questions whether victim participation in criminal proceedings has restorative effects. Radosavljevic 2008, 235, at 239-240. Zehr & Toews 2004, at 59.

380 Office of the Special Representative of the Secretary-General for Children and Armed Conflict, Strategic Framework 2009-2012, 9, http://www.un.org/children/conflict/english/strategicplan.html; O'Kane *et al.* 2009, at 260; International Center for Transitional Justice 2009. See more generally on the added value of child participation, Wall 2008, 523, at 535-536.

381 UN General Assembly, Report of the Special Representative of the Secretary-General for Children and Armed Conflict, UN Doc. A/65/219 (2010), paras. 44-45.

> '[a]ccess to justice, though increasingly recognized as an important strategy for protecting the rights of vulnerable groups, and thus for fighting poverty, rarely takes children into account.'[382]

Bearing the aforementioned in mind it is also to be noted that recognising on the one side the legal competence of the child to file an application for participation introduces at the same time the possibility of various procedural difficulties and the potential to expose children to additional risks, such as abuse of their caregivers, representatives or lawyers and, last but not least, re-traumatisation. Risks, however, do not diminish the laudable effects of granting children the choice of whether to participate.[383] Moreover, the likelihood of procedural difficulties that exist, for instance with regard to age and ability to give informed consent do not constitute a justification for limiting the child's exercise of his/her human rights, in particular the right to a remedy. It is notable in this regard that the Convention on the Rights of the Child enables *all* children, regardless of their age, to exercise their rights.[384]

What has become clear from the aforementioned is that procedural regulation should be introduced under the Rome Statute in the near future in order to clarify under which circumstances and conditions children are to be recognised as being legally competent to file an application for participation in the criminal proceedings before the Court. The current lack of procedural regulation entails the risk that neither the child nor the legal representative can evaluate prior to the actual application whether a child at all will be recognised to be legally competent to file an application.

3.5.2 Child-specific evidence

Of particular relevance for the current chapter are the forms of evidence which children who wish to participate may submit in support of an application for participation in the criminal proceedings.[385] While the crime-related evidentiary standard of Rule 85 RPE applicable to all victims who apply for participation is briefly described above (section 3.4.5), this section examines in particular the practice of the Court which introduced the requirement that additional administrative evidence has to be submitted when children apply for participation.

Firstly, reading Rule 85 RPE together with Articles 8(2)(b)(xxvi) and 8(2)(e)(vii) of the Rome Statute and the application form, it becomes clear that the child is

382 UN Secretary General, *Guidance Note of the Secretary-General: UN Approach to Justice for Children* 2008, http://www.unhcr.org/refworld/docid/4a54bbf70.html, at 2.

383 Van Boven 2007, 1, at 9.

384 Article 2 of the CRC states, that 'States Parties shall respect and ensure the rights set forth in the present Convention *to each child* within their jurisdiction *without discrimination* of any kind [...]' (emphasis added). Karp 2008, 89, at 114.

385 An earlier version of section 3.4.3 has been published by this author, see Hamzei 2010, 113-122. The present section constitutes an update.

requested to identify him/herself and in particular needs to prove that he/she was below the age of fifteen years at the time of the alleged recruitment in order to qualify as a victim of the recruitment crime.[386] Secondly, the child is required to present evidence which ascertains kinship or legal guardianship between the child and the person acting on behalf of the child. While the requirement of proof of legal guardianship has also been introduced for applicants with disabilities, proof of kinship only exists with regard to the minor child applicant.[387]

The procedural rules of the International Criminal Court are silent with regard to this administrative evidence. Reference to the Chambers' practice is therefore, again, indispensable in order to determine (if possible) the approach of the ICC to the proof of identity and kinship or legal guardianship.[388]

Proof of identity in practice

The Court practice established that providing evidence to prove identity is a major difficulty for children.[389] The qualification as a direct victim of the recruitment crime, for example, presupposes that the child can provide sufficient evidence that he or she was below the age of fifteen at the time of recruitment.[390] The difficulty for victims in general, including children, to fulfil this requirement has been addressed by Pre-Trial Chamber II. It recognised that proof of identity might not be possible as illustrated by the Ugandan conflict. The Chamber stated that,

> 'in a country such as Uganda, where many areas have been (and, to some extent, still are) ravaged by an ongoing conflict and communication and travelling between different areas may be difficult, it would be inappropriate to expect applicants to be able to provide a proof of identity of the same type as would be required of individuals living in areas not experiencing the same kind of difficulties.'[391]

Also, the 2008 draft ICC Strategy in Relation to Victims acknowledges that even the making of a photocopy of identity documents in order to prove identity can be impossible.[392] From reading the application form it becomes clear that victims can establish their identity by submitting documents such as a passport, driver's license,

---

386 As the application form, Regulation 86 of the Regulations of the Court lists the information which victims are required to provide.

387 See among many others, ICC-01/04-374, para. 12. For disabled persons, see ICC-02/04-125, para. 7.

388 Parts of this and the following sub section have briefly been addressed in an earlier publication by the author An earlier version of section 3.4.2 has been published by this author, see Hamzei 2012, 399-422. The present sections constitutes an update.

389 ICC-02/04-01/05-252, paras. 16-17.

390 Arts. 8(2)(b)(xxiv) and 8(2)(e) (vii) Rome Statute.

391 ICC-02/04-01/05-252, para.16; ICC-02/04-125, paras. 4-6.

392 The draft ICC Strategy in Relation to Victims, http://www.vrwg.org/VRWG_DOC/2008_Nov_VRWG_Victims_strategy.pdf, at 24, 26-27. See for similar criticism, Ferstman & Goetz 2009b, at 323-324.

letter from a local authority or a tax document.[393] Children, in contrast to adults, are usually not likely to be in possession of these documents. It is interesting to examine in this regard the practice of Pre-Trial Chamber II in the *Situation of Uganda*.

The Chamber requested the Victims Participation and Reparation Section (VPRS) to examine carefully the availability of identification documents under Ugandan law.[394] VPRS concluded in a report that there was an overall lack of identification documents issued by the Ugandan legal and administrative system.[395] It furthermore stated that children do not usually obtain identification documents. Obtaining a passport requires that,

> 'an applicant must fill in an application form, seek endorsement from different prescribed offices, pay a processing fee of not less than 30 US Dollars and undergo a waiting period of not less than three months.'[396]

This is a procedure which a child, in particular younger children, cannot be expected to follow. This is because a child is not only confronted with a financial burden, but also the physical inability to travel on his/her own and the overall dependence on the person(s) taking care of him/her.[397] In contrast to the ability of adults to establish identity by relying on a range of documents as listed in the application form, the Ugandan example demonstrates that many children are not likely to be able to establish their identity by relying on any of the documents mentioned. The lower threshold for proving identity as introduced by this Chamber is therefore a welcome step. The Chamber recognised that a child can establish identity and age indirectly by submitting a document which establishes a link between the parent and the child. The Judge stipulated that,

> '[t]his report should also provide information about the existence and obtainability, in the Ugandan legal or administrative system, of documents establishing the link between a child and a member of his or her family, such as birth certificates or other types of documents.'[398]

Similarly, another Chamber explicitly provided for a lower threshold by accepting documents such as family registration booklets, pupil identity cards, school

393 Application Form for Individuals.

394 ICC-02/04-01/05-252, para. 20. Judge Politi paid particular attention to child applicants. He recognised that children are not likely to possess identification documents on their own. He therefore required that the Victims Participation and Reparation Section of the ICC carefully examine the availability of identification documents under Ugandan law.

395 ICC-02/04-125-Anx, para. 10.

396 Ibid., para. 10, 13.

397 Ibid., para.13.

398 ICC-02/04-01/05-252, para. 20. The Judge stipulated that, '[t]his report should also provide information about the existence and obtainability, in the Ugandan legal or administrative system, of documents establishing the link between a child and a member of his or her family, such as birth certificates or other types of documents.'

documents and documents issued in rehabilitation centres for children associated with armed groups in order to identify a minor applicant.[399] Also the statement by two witnesses is recognised as being reliable in order to establish a child's identity. It can be concluded from this practice that the Court is aware of the fact that children might encounter difficulties when trying to prove identity.

Proof of kinship or legal guardianship in practice

The previously addressed practice of the Chambers pointed out that children face particular difficulties when they have to prove kinship or legal guardianship. Armed conflict might render it impossible to obtain the relevant evidence. Furthermore, the Chambers recognised that there might be domestic systems which do not have a system of legal guardianship (be it a *de facto* or *de iure* shortcoming).
With regard to proof of kinship or legal guardianship, Pre-Trial I Chamber I, requested 'sufficient evidence'. The Chamber ruled that,

> '[c]onsidering that the Chamber is also of the opinion, in light of the statement by the applicant and, in particular, in light of the documents appended to this application, that it has sufficient evidence to establish a familial relationship between Applicant a/0105/06 and his minor son on whose behalf he is acting.'[400]

A further step in terms of transparency was taken by Pre-Trial Chamber II. This Chamber introduced in the *Situation in Uganda* a list of documents, which may be relied upon in order to *adequately prove* the link between the child and the person acting on the child's behalf. The Chamber clarified that it

> 'will accept as proof of such link any of the following documents: (i) "short" birth certificate or "long" birth certificate, (ii) birth notification card, (iii) baptism card, (iv) letter issued by a Rehabilitation Centre, (v) letter from a local Council, (vi) affidavit sworn before a Magistrate or Commissioner of Oaths.'[401][402][403]

A similar flexible approach based on the *prima facie* standard was implemented at trial stage. Trial Chamber I in the *Lubanga* case held that

> 'the overall material provided by these applicants provides a sufficiently reliable indication of their age and identity [...]. In particular, the Chamber accepts that the documents and the other material prove, *prima facie*, that the applicants were under

---

399 ICC-01/04-423-Corr, op. cit., para. 15; see also, ICC-01/04-505, para.18.
400 ICC-01/04-01/06-601, at 12.
401 See also, ICC-02/04-125, para. 7.
402 In a later decision, Pre-Trial Chamber II requested from a girl and boy applicant such 'adequate proof of the link between the applicants and the person acting on their behalf' without elaborating further on the standard of 'adequate proof'. See ICC-02/04-172, para. 201. See also, ICC-02/04-125, paras. 12-13, 28, 36-38.
403 ICC-02/04-125, para. 7.

the age of fifteen at the time of the relevant events, as well as the identity of those people acting on their behalf, and their relationship with the applicants, where applicable.'[404]

These approaches of the various chambers underline that the Court takes the child-specific particularities into account and is thus aware of the fact children wishing to participate are also in practical terms to be treated differently compared to adults in order to enable this particular group to participate.

3.5.3 Categories of child applicants

Trial Chamber I introduced a distinction between child who apply for participation and other applicants when deciding upon victim participant status. This Chamber distinguished between different groups of applicants before assessing the criteria of Rule 85 RPE. In the decision of 15 December 2008, in which the Chamber focused on victims' applications to participate in the proceedings against *Thomas Lubanga Dyilo*, it divided the applications into two major groups A and B before considering the individual applications.[405] The former referred to those applicants who were allowed to participate, while the latter were refused.[406] Subsequently, the Chamber made a distinction between various sub-groups by stating that such a division is indispensable since each group of victims shares specific features.[407] The Chamber held that,

> '[f]or the purposes of this Decision, the Chamber has divided the applicants into groups, reflecting particular features which individual victims share and which are of broad importance.'[408]

Without elaborating further on the need to distinguish between different categories of applicants, the Chamber moved on to introduce various sub-groups. With regard to those applicants that were allowed to participate, the Chamber distinguished in particular between adult (or other) applications and child applications.

Adult versus child applicants

At least four of the eight sub-groups directly or indirectly relate to applications submitted by children. Group 1(d) refers directly to applicants who were children when their application was originally filed, but who are now adults or almost adults. Group 1(e) particularly relates to those applications where the date of birth is

404 ICC-01/04-01/06-1556-Corr-Anx1, para. 61.
405 ICC-01/04-04/06-1556, para. 137.
406 Two other groups were introduced by Trial Chamber I: applications where a person who is acting on behalf of a victim also suffered harm and applications where the applicant alleges harm unrelated to the crimes included in the charges. See ICC-01/04-04/06-1556, paras. 117-120.
407 Ibid., para. 53.
408 Ibid..

uncertain or the demobilisation date is a cause of concern. This is an issue which, by definition, only arises with regard to children, since only the recruitment crime as enshrined in Article 8 of the Rome Statute introduces age as an element of crime. Finally, the Chamber created a separate group of applications, 1(g), that were submitted by children who at the moment of decision taking were still under eighteen and the application was not made by a person acting on their behalf. An indirect reference to child applicants can be found in relation to group 1(c) which relates to applications that were submitted on behalf of a victim and the person acting on behalf of the victim is not a relative or the legal guardian of the applicant – two aspects (kinship and legal guardianship) which are foremost relevant with regard to child applicants. An explanation for this differentiation by the Chamber was not provided for.

This categorisation of applications is remarkable for three reasons. Firstly, the Chamber clarified in this decision that the division of applications has neither an impact on other decisions of the same Chamber nor are other Chambers of the Court bound by it.[409] Consequently, it is not possible to anticipate whether this Chamber or other Chambers will, in the future, categorise applications alongside the criteria established in the present decision or not. Secondly, in the view of the Chamber, such separation was necessary. It held that such separation was indispensable in order to properly decide on the applications. Thirdly, the procedural rules of the ICC do not introduce a division into various categories of applicants. Practical reasons might have been the rationale for distinguishing between different categories of applications on the basis of 'common administrative issues', such as proof of kinship or legal guardianship.

The foregoing analysis establishes that the statutory provisions do not recognise children as a particular group of applicants. Children, as other victims, have to establish that they have suffered harm as a result of a crime that falls within the jurisdiction of the Court. The examination of the Court's practice, on the other side, has shown that children are recognised as a particular group of applicants who are generally understood to be unable to submit an application for participation without the support of a third person.

Boy and girl applicants

In line with the forgoing section, the statutory provisions as such do not distinguish between boy and girl child applicants. A closer look at the practice of the Court, however, establishes, that child applicants might be distinguished as a result of their gender. This is because the Rome Statute of the International Criminal Court provides for crimes which are gender specific. The gender of the child can therefore be decisive for qualification into a gender-specific group of applicants. While the gender of the child might bear implications for other capacities, such as the child witness, the most extensive court practice before the ICC can be found in relation to

[409] Art. 21 (2) Rome Statute; Ferdinandusse 2004, 1041, at 1051-1053; Don Taylor III 2010, at 7.

child participants. Crimes within the jurisdiction of the ICC which particularly, though not exclusively, relate to the female gender are crimes which constitute sexual violence, such as rape, sexual slavery, enforced prostitution, forced pregnancy, enforced sterilisation and other forms of sexual violence as both war crimes and crimes against humanity.[410]

In the first case before the ICC, the criminal proceedings against *Thomas Lubanga Dyilo*, who has been convicted for having recruited children below the age of fifteen years, Trial Chamber I was confronted with the question as to whether female children fall within the definition of the recruitment crime. The entire problematic is the result of the fact that sexual violence has not been charged separately in the proceedings against *Thomas Lubanga Dyilo*. The discussion arose when the United Nations Special Representative of the Secretary General for Children and Armed Conflict, Radhika Coomaraswamy, submitted an *amicus curiae* brief which addressed *inter alia* the issue of '[t]he interpretation, focusing particularly on the role of girls in armed forces, of the term "using them to participate actively in hostilities."'

The commentators of this crime state that *active use in hostilities* does not entail the same meaning as *direct participation in hostilities*. While the former is understood to be limited to specific hostile acts,[411] the active use in hostilities refers to a broader category of acts which is not limited to actual involvement in combat.[412]

The Special Representative testified at a later stage in the proceedings on the question as to whether girls may fall within the definition of the elements of a crime even if they have not been directly involved in hostilities, but served exclusively in non-combat related roles, such as sexual slaves or as commander's wives.[413]

The lack of a crime charged in the *Lubanga* case relating to sexual violence made the Special Representative underline that an interpretation of the recruitment crime limited to male children would exclude female children from essential protection with far-reaching consequences, not only at trial stage, but also in the reparation phase if not remedied in specific forms of reparations (*Chapter Five*). The Special Representative held that services provided by girls could constitute a form of criminalised behaviour within the meaning of the recruitment crime, because,

> '[the] "using" crime creates a broad category for criminal liability. It proscribes the acceptance of a child's participation to support conflict. Children's participation takes numerous and varied forms and includes tasks and roles that are typically fulfilled by girls.'[414]

---

410 Arts. 7(1)(g), 8(2)(b)(xxii), (e)(vi) Rome Statute.
411 Melzer 2009, at 45; Fleck 2008 at 261-262.
412 See Lee 2001, at 205-206.
413 ICC-01/04-01/06-1175, 18 February 2008, para. 11; ICC-01/04-01/06-1229-AnxA, para. 22.
414 ICC-01/04-01/06-1229-AnxA, para. 17.

According to the Special Representative, the direct participation of female children in hostilities is not a necessary precondition in order to fulfil the prescribed elements of crime – an interpretation which is in line with the United Nations policy for disarmament.[415] This policy explicitly points out that members of armed forces and groups include girls which have been used for sexual services. The policy states that,

> '[t]e majority of participants in DDR programmes are usually made up of members of armed forces and groups who served in combat and/or support roles. These members are usually *mostly* men, but there are often also women, boys and girls.
>
> Although most members will have been actively engaged as combatants, many will have carried out logistic tasks and worked as cooks, porters, messengers and administrators, or have been women and girls used for sexual exploitation. This is often the case for women and children. Those have been associated with armed forces and groups in the above roles shall be considered part of the armed force and/or group.'[416]

Subsequently, the Special Representative underlined that the recruitment of girls for sexual purposes is also restated in the Paris Principles which define the term 'child solider' as follows:[417]

> '"A child associated with an armed force or armed group" refers to any person below eighteen years of age who is or who has been recruited or used by an armed force or armed group in any capacity, including but not limited to children, boys and girls used as fighters, cooks, porters, messengers, spies or for *sexual purposes*. It does not only refer to a child who is taking or has taken a direct part in hostilities' (emphasis added).[418]

In her conclusion, the Special Representative called upon Trial Chamber I to explicitly interpret the recruitment crime as including female child soldiers who have not directly participated in hostilities.[419] In the view of the Special Representative, such interpretation is indispensable in order to ensure that female

---

415 Ibid., para. 18. United Nations, Operational Guide to the Integrated Disarmament, Demobilization and Reintegration Standards, http://www.unddr.org/iddrs/iddrs_guide.php, para. 5.30. It is stated that, '[n]o distinction should be made between combatants and non-combatants when [DDR] eligibility criteria are determined, as these roles are blurred in armed forces and groups, where children, and girls in particular, perform numerous combat support and non-combat roles that are essential to the functioning of the armed force or group.'

416 Ibid., para. 4.1.

417 ICC-01/04-01/06-1229-AnxA, para. 24.

418 UNICEF, The Paris Principles and Guidelines on Children Associated with Armed Forces or Armed Groups (2007), at 7, http://www.unicef.org/emerg/files/ParisPrinciples310107English.pdf.

419 ICC-01/04-01/06-1229-AnxA, para. 25.

children, who served as sexual slaves, are not excluded from the group of potential child victims of the recruitment crime.

After the submission of the *amicus curiae* brief, the testimony of the Special Representative and previous evidence provided by three witnesses at the trial, the legal representatives of victims participating in the trial requested Trial Chamber I to modify the legal characterisation of the facts within the meaning of Regulation 55 of the Regulation of the Court. The legal representatives argued that, *inter alia*, the crime of sexual slavery should be included in the charges against *Thomas Lubanga Dyilo*.[420] The attempt of the legal representative to include sexual slavery within the charges anticipates that the labelling of female sexual slaves as child soldiers might not constitute the proper label. The Appeals Chamber however clarified that Trial Chamber I erred in its interpretation of Regulation 55 and that under the circumstances of the present case the suggested modification of the legal characterisation of the facts is impermissible.[421]

The unsuccessful attempt by the legal representatives to modify the legal characterisation of the facts by including the crime of sexual slavery calls for the careful assessment of the consequences of limiting the case against *Lubanga* to the war crime of child soldiering. The discussion which results from not having modified the legal characterisation of the facts has also been reflected in the previously addressed *amicus curiae* brief and relates particularly to the question whether the labelling as child soldiers blurs the distinction between the war crimes of the recruitment of child soldiers and of sexual slavery. Michael Kurth argued in this regard that,

> '[a]lthough the ICC has not explicitly ruled on the matter yet, it seems that such conduct would indeed fall outside the reach of these crimes [Article 8(2)(b)(xxvi) and Article 8(2)(e)(vii)] and should be covered by the war crimes of sexual slavery, as provided for in Articles 8(2)(b)(xxii) and Article 8(2)(e)(vi) of the Rome Statute, instead. It is submitted that these provisions are eventually better equipped to match the trauma and brutality of such atrocities.'[422]

This conclusion was based on the argument that the active use of children in hostilities is to be understood to be limited to combat-related activities. The author referred in his argumentation to the drafting history of this crime. He pointed out that such restrictive understanding has also been reflected by the drafters. According to Kurth, the *travaux préparatoires* explicitly request that active

---

420 ICC-01/04-01/06-1891, para. 17; ICC-01/04-01/06-2049. Regulation 55 of the Regulations of the Court states that, [i]n its decision under article 74, the Chamber may change the legal characterization of facts to accord with the crimes under articles 6, 7 or 8, [...], without exceeding the facts and circumstances described in the charges and any amendments to the charges.'

421 ICC-01/04-01/06-2216, para. 13. The Appeals Chamber reversed the finding of Trial Chamber I which held that Regulation 55(2) and (3) do not prohibit the inclusion of additional facts and circumstances which have not been addressed in the document containing the charges against the accused. See ICC-01/04-01/06-2205, para. 112.

422 Kurth 2010, 475, at 491.

participation, while not being limited to acts of active fighting, does clearly not include acts which are evidently not related to combat.[423]

Despite this concern, the frequency of such use in present day combat situations supports the assumption that girls indeed are also – or even specifically – recruited for this specific purpose.[424] Claiming that one underlying reason of recruitment is sexual slavery therefore aims to address the reality of the various roles that girl child soldiers fulfil today.[425] The recent attention paid to the multiple roles of girls in combat could explain why sexual slavery as a purpose of recruitment has only occasionally been recognised. Abigail Leibig criticised in this regard that,

> '[t]he focus on children serving in combat positions overshadows the experiences of many children who are abducted or recruited into armed forces and then forced into serving as domestic and sexual slaves; in many cases, girl soldiers experience these other roles in addition to serving in armed combat.'[426]

Similarly, Susan Tiefenbrun is concerned that,

> '[t]he trafficking of child soldiers is directly connected to sexual violence and the sexual exploitation of children who are mainly, but not exclusively, young girls.'[427]

The lack of legal research has been pointed out by Alfredson:

> 'The theoretical consequence of the lack of research on this subject is a continuing lack of understanding of the internal environment of militaries - during conflict or peace - as a context for sexual exploitation. To date the small literature that is directly relevant to sexual exploitation occurring within militaries tends to discuss the phenomenon firstly as another horrific by-product of war accompanying the breakdown of moral and legal standards. While the chaos of the war context is undoubtedly part of the problem, it explains neither the logic of armed groups abusing their own members (potentially debilitating them from carrying out military-related tasks), nor why sexual exploitation also occurs in non-conflict contexts.'[428]

The United Nations High Commissioner for Refugees includes girls in the definition of child soldiers by defining child soldiers as.

> 'any person under eighteen years of age who forms part of an armed force in any capacity and those accompanying such groups other than purely as family members as well as *girls recruited for sexual purposes* and forced marriage' (emphasis added).[429]

---

423 Ibid., at 490-491. UN Doc. A/CONF.183/2/Add.1 (1998).
424 See Leibig 2005, Introduction.
425 Ibid., paras. 18-19, 54.
426 Ibid., Introduction.
427 Tiefenbrun 2008, at 4.
428 Alfredson 2001, at 6.
429 Guidelines for Prevention and Response (2003), at 72.

The Secretary General of the United Nations stated that,

> '[t]here is little awareness of the extreme suffering that armed conflict inflicts on girls or the many roles girls are often forced to play during conflict and long after. *Girls are often abducted for sexual and other purposes* by armed groups and forces' (emphasis added)[430]

In line with these positions Judge Odio Benito argues in her separate and dissenting opinion attached to Trial Chamber I's judgment in the *Lubanga* case that,

> '[a]lthough the Majority of the Chamber recognises that sexual violence has been referred to in this case, it seems to confuse the factual allegations of this case with the legal concept of the crime, which are independent. By failing to deliberately include within the legal concept of "use to participate actively in the hostilities" the sexual violence and other ill-treatment suffered by girls and boys, the Majority of the Chamber is making this critical aspect of the crime invisible. Invisibility of sexual violence in the legal concept leads to discrimination against the victims of enlistment, conscription and use who systematically suffer from this crime as an intrinsic part of the involvement with the armed group.'[431]

The recognition that sexual violence can constitute a consequence of child recruitment is not only favourable in order to adequately address the realities of combat situations, but also for another reason. This inclusion fills an impunity gap in international criminal justice as regards war crimes, such as sexual violence, committed against a specific group of child victims.

It is argued that, even if sexual violence had been charged separately in the case at issue, a group of child victims of sexual violence remains which would not have been able to qualify as victims of the war crime of sexual violence (Articles 8(2)(b)(xii) and 8 (2)(c)(vi) Rome Statute). In these cases, a legal *lacuna* would exist. This could prevent child victims from participating in the proceedings before the ICC and might also make way for impunity under international criminal law. It could prevent perpetrators from being convicted for acts of sexual violence when having recruited children for this particular purpose.

In order to support this argument it is necessary to ask who is considered to fall within the category of 'protected persons' under International Humanitarian Law. Michael Cottier held that,

---

430 UN General Assembly/Security Council, Report of the Secretary-General, Children and armed conflict, UN Doc. A/55/163-S/2000/712 (2000), para. 34. See furthermore, UNICEF, Guide to the Optional Protocol on the Involvement of Children in Armed Conflict (2003), http://www.unicef.org/publications/index_19025.html, at 3. The Guide states that, '[o]nce recruited or forced into service, they are used for a variety of purposes. While many children participate in combat, others are used for sexual purposes, as spies, messengers, porters, servants or to lay or clear landmines. Many children serve multiple roles.'

431 ICC-01/04-01/06-2842, Separate and Dissenting Opinion of Judge Odio Benito, para. 16.

> '[International Humanitarian Law] typically protects persons and objects belonging to one of the parties to the conflict from certain abusive or overly destructive conduct *by an adversary party to the conflict*.' [432] (*Emphasis added*)

Similarly, Frits Kalshoven and Liesbeth Zegveld state that International Humanitarian Law, in particular the Law of Geneva

> 'serves to protect persons who, as a consequence of an armed conflict, are in the power of a party to the conflict of which they are *not nationals*.' [433] (*Emphasis added*)

As a consequence of the forgoing, war crimes can *only* be committed against protected persons who belong to the population of the other party to the conflict.[434] A similar line of argumentation has been adopted by the Defence of *Bosco Ntaganda*. The Defence asserted that

> 'that the crimes committed by members of armed forces on members of the same armed force do not come within the jurisdiction of international humanitarian law nor within international criminal law. Customary international law applying to all armed conflicts, be it international or non-international , is made up of several principles that are intended to protect civilians and making a clear distinction between civilians and combatants. Such law also sets out rules relating to the ways in which war is waged. International humanitarian law is not intended to protect combatants from crimes committed by combatants within the same group. Such crimes come under national law and human rights law. Thus, the charges found in counts 6 and 9 cannot be confirmed in accordance with the principle of legality.' [435]

It is helpful in this regard to remember that the criminalisation of breaches of International Humanitarian Law by the codification of war crimes in the respective statutes paved the way for individual criminal responsibility. [436] International criminal responsibility may not exist for *any* act committed during armed conflict, but is limited to those acts which have been criminalised under international criminal law, such as war crimes under the Rome Statute. Moreover, only acts committed against 'protected persons' can be considered as breaches of International Humanitarian Law. Crimes committed against persons who do not belong to the adversary party per definition fall outside the group of potential victims of an international crime. It can be presupposed, that the majority of child victims, who have been recruited solely for sexual purposes will – in many cases –

---

432 Cottier & Zimmermann 2008, at 284.

433 Kalshoven & Zegveld 2011, at 45.

434 Werle 2005, at 299. http://werle.rewi.hu-berlin.de/05_War%20Crimes-Summary.pdf. Werle pointed out in this regard that, '[w]ar crimes based in the law of Geneva, that is the four Geneva Conventions and the Additional Protocols, can generally be committed only against persons who are not, or are no longer, participating in hostilities.'

435 ICC-01/04-02/06-T-10-Red-ENG WT 13 February 2014, at 27.

436 Cryer *et al.* 2010, at 225-227.

not belong to the adversary. This has also been the case in the proceedings against *Thomas Lubanga Dyilo*. The Registry pointed out that,

> '[t]here are a number of other important features of the *Lubanga* case which should also be noted at the outset. The first concerns the ethnic character of the conflict in the region. The *Union des Patriotes Congolais* being mostly comprised of members of the Hema ethnic community, is alleged to have drawn child soldiers predominately from this ethnic group with the result that, should reparations be awarded in the case, the majority of victims will be from one side of an ethnic conflict in which both sides suffered harm.'[437]

Accordingly, sexual violence committed against children belonging to the same conflict party can never constitute the war crime of sexual violence, since these children fall outside the concept of 'protected persons' under International Humanitarian Law within the meaning of the war crime of sexual violence.

In contrast to the aforementioned interpretation, Prosecutor Fatou Bensouda pointed out in the proceedings against *Bosco Ntaganda* that due to the particular position of child soldiers under international humanitarian law, child soldiers, in particular recruited girls, can also become victims of the war crime of sexual violence – be it not simultaneously when directly participating in hostilities. The Chief Prosecutor argued that,

> '[w]hile it is generally the case that IHL regulates conduct directed towards those external to a military force rather than to those internal to a military force, this general proposition does not constitute an irrebuttable presumption. Indeed, the prohibition on conscripting or enlisting child soldiers or allowing children to directly participate in hostilities is an exception to the general proposition precisely in order to provide non-derogable protections for children as a particularly vulnerable group. Critically, these war crimes can only be perpetrated by members of a military force against victims which are from the same military force. The protections attached to children contitue to apply during armed conflict: while soldiers may forfeit protection from attack by directly participating in hostilities, this does not impact on their other legal protections. This includes their protection against being subjected to sexual violence – a position supported by customary practice.'[438]

Pre-Trial Chamber III confirmed on 9 June 2014 the charges against *Bosco Ntaganda* including the war crime of sexual violence allegedly committed against child soldiers. The Chamber held in this regard that,

> 'children under the age of 15 years lose the protection afforded by IHL only during their direct/active participation in hostilities. That said, the Chamber clarifies that

---

437 ICC-01/04-01/06-2806, para. 7.
438 ICC-01/04-02/06-276-Red, paras. 187-188.

> those subject to rape and/or sexual enslavement cannot be considered to have taken active part in hostilities during the specific time when they were subject to acts of sexual nature, including rape, as defined in the relevant Elements of Crimes. The sexual character of these crimes, which involve elements of force/coercion or the exercise of rights of ownership, logically preclude active participation in hostilities at the same time. Accordingly, the Chamber finds that UPC/FPLC child soldiers under the age of 15 years continue to enjoy protection under IHL from acts of rape and sexual slavery, as reflected in article 8(2)(e)(vi) of the Statute. The Chamber is, therefore, not barred from exercising jurisdiction over the crimes in counts 6 and 9.'[439]

While at first sight, this position clearly constitutes a child-sensitive approach as it enables in particular recruited girls, who have not been directly involved in acts of hostilities to qualify as victims of sexual violence, a few critical notes are necessary. The inherent legal problem according to the present author in relation to this interpretation relates to aspects of evidence in procedural practice and a blurry application of the principles of protected persons and distinction under international humanitarian law – despite the child-sensitive aim of providing children below the age of fifteen years a wider range of protection.

It might not constitute a difficulty to distinguish theoretically between the moment of direct participation in hostilities and the moment of victimisation as a result of sexual violence from the victims or even perpetrators position. In practice, however, this might not be such an easy exercise, in particular when evidence is to be submitted in the course of criminal proceedings which usually take place after a certain period of time has passed. Furthermore, does this interpretation *a contrario* imply that at the moment of crime commission these victims regain their protected persons status also in relation to hostile acts from the other party? In other words, are these children at the moment of crime commission not any longer legitimate targets because of having regained their civilian status despite, for instance being at a place which qualifies as a military objective and being dressed as a combatant? If so, does this mean that a hostile attack from the other party to the conflict being performed at the same moment when sexual violence against a young recruit is committed (for instance a surprise attack during night), constitute an attack against a protected person and thus qualifies as a war crime under the Rome Statute? Finally, when exactly do these victims of sexual violence regain their status as combatant? Again an important aspect in particular for the perceptive of the other party to the conflict.

Without further qualification, the possibility to switch from the status of a legitimate target as a child soldier to a protected person when becoming the victim of sexual violence constitutes a vague interpretation of the principles of protection and distinction under international humanitarian law – a departure which, without

439 ICC-01/04-02/06-309, 9 June 2014, paras. 79-80.

further explanation and clear delimitation leads to legal uncertainty and lack of transparency not only under international humanitarian law but also under international criminal law.

Despite losing sight of the general need to provide children with sufficient protection also in terms of international criminal law, the author suggests that a transparent and legally convincing alternative is suggested by Cottier who argues that the only exception within international criminal law that criminalises certain acts committed against persons belonging to the same conflict party is the crime of recruitment. Cottier addressed this particularity of this crime. He stated that,

> '[t]he two offenses defined under article 8 para. 2(b)(xxvi) Rome Statute comprise two particularities distinguishing them from most other war crimes. First, they primarily *protect children against their own authorities* as is clear from the essence of article 8 para. 2(b)(xxvi). Perpetrator and victims of these war crimes thus may belong to the same party to the conflict. This criminalization of acts committed against or 'vis-à-vis' persons belonging to the same party to the conflict deviates fundamentally from the general thrust of international humanitarian law and the law of war crimes, which typically regulate acts committed against persons belonging to an adversary party to the conflict. Relations between a State and its own nationals are more characteristically the subject of human rights law. [...]
>
> However, the wording of the provision in no way excludes its application to the use enlistment or conscription of *children belonging to another party to the conflict* or indeed of *any other child*. It would not make sense to protect children belonging to the same party to the conflict but not those not belonging to that party. These considerations apply to both the use of children to participate actively in hostilities as well as to their enlistment or conscription into armed forces.'[440]

The war crime of child recruitment is thus not limited to the narrow interpretation of 'protected persons' under International Humanitarian Law. It has become clear why the concept of this crime should encompass children recruited for the particular purpose of sexual slavery. In case of non-inclusion, children who have solely been recruited for purposes of sexual slavery are at risk that their suffering falls outside the jurisdiction of the International Criminal Court. It is therefore argued that the inclusion of this particular group of child victims serves to close the legal *lacuna* in relation to children solely recruited for sexual purposes.

It needs to be noted at the same time, that if these children qualify as child soldiers they might – as a consequence of their combatant status – constitute legitimate military targets under International Humanitarian Law.[441] The inclusion of children which have solely been used for sexual purposes therefore provides on

---

440 Cottier & Zimmermann 2008, at 470. See similarly, ICRC Commentary to article 77 para. 2 Add. Protocol I. Comfort women – which crime was charged by Tokyo Tribunal, Indonesia.

441 Kalshoven & Zegveld 2011, at 101-102.

the one side for additional protection, but on the other side entails the risk of being lawfully targeted.

It can be concluded that, as pointed out by the United Nations Special Representative of the Secretary-General for Children and Armed Conflict, the interpretation of the recruitment crime as enshrined in the Rome Statute is to be interpreted broadly in order to cover today's tasks and roles of female child soldiers, but also to prevent impunity of perpetrators. The ICC should generally recognise that numerous tasks carried out by girls which do not directly relate to combat activities fall within the ambit of this particular crime. Limiting the crime of child recruitment to combat related purposes disregards the realities of today's armed conflicts and the multiple functions of female child soldiers. An interpretation of the 'using crime' which is restricted to combat-related, messenger or porter activities therefore neglects the experiences of many female children during combat.[442] Instead, a broad interpretation reflects that the ICC does take into account the realities of combat as described by the former Secretary-General of the United Nations:

> 'For many, however, entry into an armed group meant being subjected to sexual abuse. A number of accounts indicate that the sexual abuse started in the training camps, with instructors being responsible, and persisted throughout the training. [...] In some cases, sexual abuse, when it did occur, was of limited duration or was carried out in a sporadic manner, with different perpetrators depending on the situation at hand. Other girls were subjected to a more regular pattern of sexual abuse, effectively repeated rape, over longer periods, assigned to one military officer for example. These girls are commonly referred to as "war wives". In many ways the girls suffer a double jeopardy, many reportedly serving both as fighting elements in active combat and concomitantly being used to satisfy the sexual appetites of their commanders. Some, however, were reportedly abducted solely for use as sexual slaves.'[443]

The practice of Trial Chamber I with regard to female child witnesses who testified on their experiences as child soldiers establishes its awareness of today's combat realities.[444] The SCSL by contrast, has only questioned one young female witness on this particular crime since its establishment.[445] The Sierra Leonean and Liberian Truth and Reconciliation Commission, on the other hand, collected the statements

---

442 UN Report of the Preparatory Committee on the Establishment of an International Criminal Court, Draft Statue & Draft Final Act, UN Doc. A/Conf.183/2/Add.1 (1995), at 21, footnote. 12.

443 UN Security Council, Special report on the events in Ituri, January 2002 - December 2003 of 16 July 2003, UN Doc. S/2004/573 (2004), para. 152.

444 To date, three former female child soldiers have given testimony. In addition, applications for participation submitted on behalf of female child claimants have also been accepted.

445 Until December 2005 only one young female witness gave testimony on her experiences as a child soldier. See Sanin & Stirnemann 2008, at 15.

of numerous female child victims not only on sexual violence but also on their recruitment as child soldiers.[446]

Whether other ICC Chambers will explicitly include sexual violence within the recruitment remains to be seen. The elements of the crime of recruitment, in any case, do leave sufficient room for such an interpretation.

3.6 General Modalities of Participation

Pursuant to Article 68(3) of the Rome Statute, victims may present their views and concerns. In order to participate at a particular moment, the victim must establish that his or her 'personal interests' have been affected.[447] It has earlier been explained that the Court distinguishes between participation at situational and case level.[448] The modalities of participation can therefore also be addressed by distinguishing between the possibility of participating in the different stages of the proceedings before the ICC. In turn, an overview of the core modalities of participation is provided for.

The Rome Statute and the respective procedural rules do not provide extensive explanation on how victims may participate. The specific modalities of child participation are neither addressed. The case law of the Court is therefore mainly assessed in order to shed light on the concrete modalities of participation. It will be seen that child specific modalities of participation have neither been reflected upon in the respective practice.

Participation at situational/investigational level

The decision of Pre-trial Chamber I of 17 January 2006 addressed the modalities of victim participation at investigational level in more detail. The Chamber held that in line with Article 68(3) of the Rome Statute, victims may in particular present their views and concerns and file documents.[449] In this regard, they may participate in public hearings.[450] Similar approaches as regards the modalities of participation at situational level can be found in the situation of Uganda and Darfur (Sudan).[451] Pre-Trial Chamber I ruled in particular that,

---

446 TRC Sierra Leone, Report, Volume 2, http://www.sierra-leone.org/Other-Conflict/TRCVolume2.pdf, at 14, 273-293. Republic of Liberia, Truth and Reconciliation Commission, Volume Three: Appendices Title II: Children, the Conflict and the TRC Children Agenda, at 30-31, http://www.trcofliberia.org/reports/final.

447 Art. 68(3) Rome Statute provides that '[w]here the personal interests of the victims are affected, the Court shall permit their views and concerns to be presented and considered [...].' See also, Trial Chamber I Decision on Victims' Participation of 18 January 2008 and Appeals Chamber Decision in which the Appeals Chamber clarified that victims must establish a link between the personal interests and the charges. ICC-01/04-01/06-1432, para. 65.

448 ICC-01/04-101-tEN-Corr, paras. 23 ff., 57.

449 Ibid., para. 71.

450 Ibid., paras. 71ff.

451 Decision on Victims' Applications for Participation a/0010/06, a/0064/06 to a/0070/06, a/0081/06 to 1/0104/06 and a/0111/06 to a/0127/06 (Public Redacted Version) Situation in Uganda (ICC-

'victims' guaranteed right of access to the Court entails a positive obligation for the Court to enable them to exercise that right concretely and effectively."[452]

Related to Article 68(3) is the possibility of participation based upon Article 19(3) of the Rome Statute. This provision entails the possibility for victims to participate in proceedings on challenges of the jurisdiction of the Court and admissibility of the Court.[453]

Participation at pre-trial stage

At pre-trial stage, participation in particular takes place within the context of confirmation of charges hearings. The legal representative may participate in the hearing, and upon the discretion of the Chamber, even during *in camera* or *ex parte* hearings.[454] Important to note is that, in contrast to victim participation at the trial stage, victims are not allowed to introduce evidence into the court record at pre-trial stage.[455] At the confirmation of charges hearing, the possibility to make opening and closing statements and the request for leave to intervene during the hearing are of particular importance in this regard.[456] In accordance with Rule 91(2) the victims' representative may be present and participate at the hearing. The competent

---

02/04-101) Pre-Trial Chamber II, 10 Aug. 2007. Decision on the Requests of the OPCD on the Production of Relevant Supporting Documentation Pursuant to Regulation
86(2)(e) of the Regulations of the Court and on the Disclosure of Exculpatory Materials by the Prosecutor, Darfur Situation(ICC-02105-110), Pre-Trial Chamber I, 3 Dec. 2007.

452 Ibid., para. 71.

453 As regards the challenges on jurisdiction, see, Observations of Victims a/0001/06, a/0002/06 and a/0003/06 Regarding the Challenge to Jurisdiction Raised by the Defence in the Application of 23 May 2006,Lubanga(ICC-01/04-01/06-349), Pre-Trial Chamber I,24 Aug. 2006; Observations on behalf of victims on the Defence Challenge to the Jurisdiction of the Court, Mbarushimana(ICC-01/04-01/10-417), Pre-Trial Chamber I, 12 Sept. 2011. Challenges of admissibility, see in the Ruto case, victims, through the OPCV, were invited to participate in the proceedings on the admissibility challenge by the Government of the Republic of Kenya. See, Decision on the Application by the Government of Kenya Challenging the Admissibility of the Case Pursuant to Article 19(2)(b) of the Statute, Ruto, Kosgey & Sang (ICC-01/09-01/11-101), Pre-Trial Chamber II, 30 May 2011.

454 See for detailed information, Representing Victims Before the International Criminal Court 2010, 87.

455 Decision on the Set of Procedural Rights Attached to Procedural Status of Victim at the Pre-Trial Stage of the Case, Katanga & Ngudjolo (ICC-01/04-01/07-474), Pre-Trial Chamber I,13 May2008;See also, Corrigendum to the Decision on Evidentiary Scope of the Confirmation Hearing, Preventive Relocation and Disclosure under Article 67(2) of the Statute and Rule 77 of the Rules, Katanga & Ngudjolo (ICC-01/04-01/07-428-Corr), Pre-Trial Chamber I, 25 April 2008, para 6, in which the Chamber found that the "confirmation hearing has a limited scope and by no means can it be seen as an end in itself" and the Prosecutor should carefully analyse the evidence on which it intends to rely so as to limit it to "the very core evidence of the case Decision on the Set of Procedural Rights Attached to Procedural Status of Victim at the Pre-Trial Stage of the Case, Katanga & Ngudjolo (ICC-01/04-01/07-474), Pre-Trial Chamber I, 13 May 2008, para. 17.

456 ICC-01/04-01/06-462, 6-7; ICC-01/05-01/08-320, paras. 101-108.

Chamber may, however, be of the view that the intervention where necessary should be limited to written observations and submissions.

Participation at trial stage

Explicit reference to the modalities of participation at trial stage can be found in Rule 89(1) RPE which provides for the possibility of opening and closing statements.[457] A particular opportunity constitutes the possibility to participate in person. In this matter, the case law established that victims may testify under oath.[458] In addition to the possibility that victims' legal representatives attend and participate in the hearings, written submissions may be filed by the representatives.[459] Furthermore, victims have access to the case index and may introduce evidence if the Chamber is of the view that this will assist in the determination of the truth.[460] Also important to note, is the possibility that the legal representative of the victims may question witnesses.[461] This procedural opportunity enables victims, through their legal representative, to ask questions which might provide supportive evidence which could, for instance, also be referred to at a later stage during the reparation proceedings. Victims are thus able, by providing their legal representative with the necessary information, to raise questions which are important to them while being less relevant for the other parties.

Participation at interlocutory appeals

The participation of victims at interlocutory appeals is limited to presenting their views and concerns if their personal interests are affected on those matters which are raised on appeal by the Prosecution or Defence.[462]

As the specific modalities of child participation are not at all explicitly addressed in the procedural regulation it seems that the drafters of the Rome Statute and the entire ICC system did not expect that, as far as the modalities of participation are concerned, there is a need to draw particular attention to child participation. This may be because the drafters did not at all expect that children would ever participate.

Having addressed the general modalities of participation during the various stages of the criminal proceedings which are relevant for all victims and bearing in mind the silence of the law as regards child specific aspects, one may raise in particular the question whether there should be child-specific modalities when

457 See also, ICC-01/04-01/06-119, para. 117; ICC-01/04-01/07-1665, 9.
458 ICC-01/04-01/07-1665, paras. 19-30.
459 Rule 91(2) of the Rules of Procedure and Evidence; ICC-01/04-01/07-1788-tENG.
460 With regard to the case index, see, ICC-01/04-01/06-1119, paras. 108-109, 138.
461 ICC-01/04-01/06-2340; ICC-01/05-01/08-1729, para. 15.
462 ICC-01/04-503, para. 101; ICC-02/05-138, paras. 60-62; ICC-01/04-01/06-1335, para. 50.

children participate. In order to answer this question, one needs to address how child victims participated thus far.

3.7 CHILD-SPECIFIC MODALITIES OF PARTICIPATION: THE REPRESENTATION OF THE CHILD

Thus far, child victims participated in ICC proceedings through their legal representative. Generally speaking, the legal representation of the victim participant in international criminal proceedings constitutes a novelty. Only through the establishment of the International Criminal Court has light been shed on this unique opportunity for victims of crimes within the jurisdiction of the Court.[463] The uniqueness is based on the fact that prior to the establishment of the ICC, victim participation in international criminal proceedings was not only very limited but furthermore did not enable victims on a statutory basis to have a legal representative at their disposal. The procedural rules of the International Criminal Court do not separately address the representation of child participants. This section proceeds in two steps: firstly, it describes the general rules applicable to the legal representation of victim participants; secondly, it analyses the specific question concerning the representation of the child. It is examined in particular whether there is a need to child-specific representation which is to be distinguished from the representation of adult participants.

3.7.1 General rules governing the representation of victims

In order to facilitate their participation, participants can freely choose – thus, not being obliged – to hand over their legal representation.[464] Rule 89 of the Rules of Procedure and Evidence provides that,

> '[a] victim shall be free to choose a legal representative.'[465]

The second possibility of representation before the ICC is common legal representation. This particular form of representation is an option for the competent Chamber when victims participate in large numbers, which could negatively impact the effectiveness of the proceedings.[466] While victims themselves can make the decision on individual representation by a particular legal representative, common

463 UN General Assembly, Report of the International Criminal Court, UN Doc. A/65/313 (2010), para. 3. Bitti & Friman 2001, at 456; Jorda & de Hemptienne 2002, 1387, at 1388.

464 ICC-02/04-105, at 4-5. Vasiliev 2015, at 51.

465 In a more recent decision, Trial Chamber V decided that 'there is no unqualified right on behalf of victims to participate individually in the proceedings'. See, ICC-01/09-02/11-498, para. 20.

466 Regulation 80(1) Regulations of the Court. See No. ICC-02/04-105, at.4-5. See ICC-02/04-01/05-252, paras. 80, 162. See also, ICC-02/04-125, para. 192 and ICC-02/04-01/05-282, para. 192. See also in this regard, the different approach of Trial Chamber V. This Chamber ruled that common legal representation is clearly to be preferred when large numbers of victims participate, ICC-01/09-02/11-498, paras. 26-28.

legal representation constitutes a discretionary power of the Chamber. In accordance with paragraph 2 of Rule 90, the Chamber may

> 'request the victims or particular groups of victims, […] to choose a common legal representative or representatives.'

When selecting common legal representatives, the Chamber is called upon to ensure that,

> 'the distinct interests of the victims, particularly as provided in article 68, paragraph 1, are represented and that any conflict of interests is avoided.'[467]

A common language of the representative and the victims and a common country of origin are – as suggested by various Chambers, such as Pre-Trial Chamber III and Trial Chamber I – decisive for the selection of common legal representatives.[468] Factors such as geographical closeness of victims, common crimes allegedly committed against a particular group of victims and the existence of common interests among the victims form a common denominator for the common legal representation of victims.[469]

While all victims, if accepted for participation, may participate in the proceedings by presenting their views and concerns in accordance with Article 68(3) Rome Statute, particular forms of participation, such as the questioning of witnesses and the accused, are reserved for those participants who appointed a legal representative.[470]

The specific moment of the commencement of legal representation has been interpreted broadly by various Chambers of the Court. Pre-Trial Chamber II in the *Bemba case*, for instance, underlined that,

> '[w]ith a view to providing as soon as possible legal representation to victims applying to participate in the proceedings, the Single Judge requests the Registry to provide the victims with assistance pursuant to rule 90(2) of the Rules. Where no legal representative has been appointed by the victims, the Office of Public Counsel for Victims *shall*, as assigned by the Registry, act as legal representative of the victims from the time they submit their applications for participation, until a legal representative has been appointed' (*emphasis added*).[471]

Accordingly, the Office of Public Counsel for Victims (OPCV) is to be appointed as legal representative for those victims who are not legally represented when filing

467 Rule 90(4) RPE. See also, ICC-01/04-01/07-660, 3 July 2008, at 9.

468 ICC-01/05-01/08-322, para. 14; ICC-01/05-01/08-1005, para. 11.

469 ICC-01/04-01/06-1119, paras. 123-126; See No. ICC-01/05-01/08-322, paras. 7-15; ICC-01/05-01/08-1005, paras. 18-21.

470 Rule 91 RPE.

471 ICC-01/05-01/08-103-tENG-Corr, para. 10. See also, ICC-01/04-374, paras. 41-44, 49-50; ICC-01/04-01/06-1211, para. 34; ICC-01/04-395, at 3-4; ICC-01/05-01/08-699, para. 23.

their application for participation. This implies that even before being recognised as victims within the meaning of Rule 85 RPE, participants may benefit from legal representation even if they do not appoint a legal representative out of their own motion. The foregoing practice illustrates that the Chambers encourage, if not even request as indicated by the use of the verb '*shall'* in relation to the appointment of the OPCV, participants to engage with the Court through a legal representative.

Thus, in principle, victims participate – when recognised as participant – through their legal representative.[472] It has been explained before that, in order to participate at a particular moment, the legal representative must establish that the 'personal interests' of his/her clients are affected.[473] The statutory rules do not provide guidance on whether individuals may appear *in person*, without a legal representative in the courtroom. During a status conference in the *Lubanga* case, however, Trial Chamber I clarified that,

> '[i]t needs to be remembered that this is a court of law and, in particular, this is the criminal trial of an accused, and the presumption is that those who participate in the proceedings will be lawyers, lawyers acting for individuals or for bodies, for entities.
>
> If individuals are to be allowed to participate in person, there would have to be cogent, indeed powerful, reasons for that exceptional course to be waived, because it doesn't need for us to say that the people without legal training coming to talk about very difficult things that have happened to them could have a real capacity for destabilising these court proceedings. So if proposals of this kind are to be made, they need to be made in writing, they need to be made fully, and they need to set out very clearly why it is both necessary and appropriate for individuals to be asking the Chamber to appear in person, to participate in person, rather than through the legal representatives who have been made available to them. At the end of the day, this is not a truth and reconciliation commission or a body of that kind.
>
> So we're not saying no, but we're saying exceptional and for good reason.'[474]

Victims' participation in the courtroom is therefore in principle limited. Victims' interests can be represented during the course of the criminal (and/or reparation) proceedings of the ICC in two ways: through single or joint/common legal representation. Trial Chamber I ruled a few days later that,

> '[t]he Chamber is aware, however, that the personal appearance of a large number of victims could affect the expeditiousness and fairness of the proceedings, and

---

472 In addition to the participation moments in the criminal proceedings, child claimants are eligible for participation in reparation proceeding which are addressed in *Chapter Five*.

473 Art. 68(3) Rome Statute provides that '[w]here the personal interests of the victims are affected, the Court shall permit their views and concerns to be presented and considered [...].' See also, Trial Chamber I Decision on Victims' Participation of 18 January 2008 and Appeals Chamber Decision in which the Appeals Chamber clarified that victims must establish a link between the personal interests and the charges. ICC-01/04-01/06-1432, para. 65.

474 ICC-01/04-01/06-T-101-ENG, 12 January 2009, at 43-44.

> given that the victims' common views and concerns may sometimes be better presented by a common legal representative (i.e. for reasons of language, security or expediency), the Trial Chamber will decide either *proprio motu*, or at the request of a party or participant, whether or not there should be joint representation of views and concerns by legal representatives at any particular stage in the proceedings.'[475]

Large numbers of participants might, therefore, explain why the Court prefers common legal representation.[476] The wording of the aforementioned decision shows in particular that the Chamber does not only prefer but may even see the necessity to impose common legal representation.

3.7.2 Representation of the child

In its practice, as has been established in section 3.5.3, the Court has considered children as a separate group of participants. In the *Katanga* case, Trial Chamber II ordered the common legal representation of children and, in particular, the common representation of former child soldiers.[477]

The practice of Trial Chamber I and II introduced the idea of common legal representation of participants. Before Trial Chamber I, 120 or so participating victims in the *Lubanga* case were divided into three groups and accordingly represented by three teams of legal representatives. The Chamber justified its division by referring to the earlier mentioned general aspects (such as language, time, place and circumstances, crimes etc.).[478] Two individual teams of legal representatives and the Office of Public Counsel for Victims (as a third team) represented the participating victims.[479] Child participants in the *Lubanga* case, however, were not explicitly ordered to be separately represented. A possible explanation can be found in the crimes charged. Since the indictment of *Thomas Lubanga Dyilo* only charges the recruitment of children below the age of fifteen years (Article 8(2)(b)(xxvi), Article 8(2)(e)(vii) Rome Statute), the direct and indirect victims of the crimes are less likely to have conflicting interests when represented by one common legal representative. As previously underlined, the direct victims of this particular crime are those children who were below the age of fifteen years at the time of recruitment; indirect victims are those who suffer harm as a result of the victimisation of the direct victim, such as the parents of recruited children. Both direct and indirect victims thus share an interest in the prosecution of this particular crime and are likely to speak the same language and originate from the same country or even region.

A need for separate legal representation would therefore have exist if additional crimes, which introduce conflicting interests among victims, were also charged.

475 ICC-01/04-01/06-1119, para. 116.
476 See also, Olásolo & Kiss 2010, at 157.
477 ICC-01/04-01/07-1328, paras. 9-11.
478 ICC-01/04-01/06-1119, para. 124.
479 Walleyn *et al.* 2009, at 2.

This is the case before Trial Chamber II. It – following the proposal of all legal representatives involved – ordered in the *Prosecutor v. Germain Katanga and Mathieu Ngudjolo Chui* case the common legal representation of former child soldiers.[480] The Chamber held that,

> '[t]he proposal was said to be based on a 'compromise' between the legal representatives and consisted of three different 'teams' of legal representatives. The reason for having three different 'teams' was said to be the necessity of avoiding any conflict of interest. In particular, the group of victims who were identified as giving rise to a potential conflict of interest were the victims of the enlistment of child soldiers, who took an active part in the attack and may therefore also be seen as perpetrators. In its observations on the legal representatives' proposal, the Registry subscribed to the view that there exists a potential conflict of interest between those victims who participated in the attack (the victims of the crime of conscription and enlistment of children under fifteen years of age and the fact that they were used to participate actively in hostilities) and the other victims. [...] Falling outside of this large group (*of the other victims*), there is a small number of applicants who are former child soldiers, who allege to have participated in the attack of 24 February 2003. They may thus have perpetrated some of the crimes that victimised the other applicants.'[481]

The possibility of conflicting interests between various groups of victims was therefore the rationale behind the introduction of separate legal representation. Two individual teams of legal representatives and the OPCV were appointed as legal representative.[482] The OPCV served, in particular, as legal representative of those victims who were not represented otherwise. Trial Chamber II summarised and followed the practice of various Chambers by stating that,

> 'three Chambers have thus far deemed it necessary to request the Registry to appoint the Office of Public Counsel for Victims as the legal representative of the victims, pending a decision of the Chamber on their victim status, or until a legal representative is appointed.'[483]

The appointment of the OPCV as legal representative may, however, lead to a conflict of interests. In proceedings, such as those against *Katanga and Ngudjolo Chui*, where other crimes are charged besides the recruitment of children, the

---

480 See also, ICC-01/04-01/07-1788, para. 7-9.

481 ICC-01/04-01/07-1328, paras. 5-6, 12c.

482 ICC-01/04-01/07-876. The Chamber was not convinced to establish a third group, see ICC-01/04-01/07-1328, para. 12. See also, ICC-01/04-01/07-1788, para. 7. The decision states that, '[o]n 22 July 2009, the Chamber ordered that the Registry, after consulting the Legal Representatives, assist the victims in the case in choosing a common legal representative. The Chamber also considered it necessary to divide the victims into two groups, the first group consisting of former child soldiers alleged to have participated in the attack on Bogoro on 24 February 2003, and the second consisting of all the other victims.' ICC-01/04-01/07-1788, paras. 7-9. ICC-01/04-01/07-1491, para. 27.

483 ICC-01/04-01/07-933, paras. 44-45.

OPCV is likely to not only represent former child soldiers (as in the *Lubanga* case). The OPCV might also represent the alleged victims of these child soldiers as the OPCV is the office which will be appointed by the relevant chamber as legal representative of those victims who are not represented otherwise. Representing former child soldiers and their victims at the same time may cause conflicting interests despite the efforts of the OPCV to underline that this scenario is not likely since,

> '[t]he Principal Counsel allocates staff members of the Office to each situation and case taking into account, *inter alia*, [...] the need to avoid conflicts of interests. [...] In this respect, the Principal Counsel respectfully suggest that one counsel should represent victims of different attacks, while another one should represent former child soldiers. Indeed, the appointment of these two counsel prevents any conflict of interests from arising amongst the victims. It also enables a legal representation taking into account the specificities of the two different categories of victims. [...] The Principal Counsel informs the Single Judge that the resources of the Office at this point in time allow the OPCV to represent both categories of victims.'[484]

Attempts to avoid conflicting interests, by, for instance, establishing a Chinese wall within the OPCV are not promising. The small number of staff members available and the immense workload of the OPCV give rise to question of the effectiveness of such a construction. In its manual for legal representatives, the OPCV states that since its establishment in September 2009,

> 'the office has, as of July 2010, represented approximately 2000 victims and has submitted approximately 300 submissions in the various proceedings before the Court. The Office has also assisted 30 external representatives in all situations and cases and provided close to 600 legal advices/researches to them.'[485]

Moreover, since all OPCV staff are situated in closely connected and shared offices at the premises of the ICC, the sustainability of a Chinese wall construction is even more likely to be unsuccessful. Secondly, for the same reasons mentioned in the previous paragraph, conflicts of interest could also arise between participants represented by the OPCV and those who are represented by individual legal representatives, who rely on the legal research and advice provided by the OPCV in accordance with Regulation 81(4)(a).[486]

Irrespective of the fact that the OPCV held before Trial Chamber I that,

---

484 ICC-02/04-01/05-358, paras. 13-17. See also, ICC-02/04-173.

485 Representing Victims Before the International Criminal Court, at 34.

486 Regulation 81(4)(a) provides that, '[t]he Office of Public Counsel for victims shall provide support and assistance to the legal representative for victims and to victims, including, where appropriate: (a) Legal research and advice [...].'2004 Regulations of the International Criminal Court, Official Journal Publication ICC-BD/01-01-04.

> '[t]he Office tries to avoid conflicts of interest by ensuring that the teams representing particular individuals or groups of victims are not responsible for providing advice to the legal representatives of other victims.'[487]

The Defence team and external legal representatives addressed this issue before the same Chamber and pointed out that the representation of victims by the OPCV constitutes a potential conflict of interests between those two categories of represented participants.[488] Considering the large amount of victims participating in the current proceedings, entrusting the relevant Chambers with the task of avoiding a conflict of interests by deciding on a case-by-case basis when calling the OPCV to represent victims – as suggested by the OPCV – is difficult. This difficulty also remains when the Chambers are supported by the Victims Participation and Reparation Section.[489] Conflicting interests may not always be visible at first sight.

Instead, as stated by various legal representatives, the Office of the Prosecutor and also the Defence in the *Lubanga* case, the task of the OPCV should be largely limited to legal research and providing advice to external legal representatives.[490]

Both the common legal representation of children and a potential of conflict of interests when representing this particular group of child participants is likely to reoccur before the International Criminal Court. Various pending cases before the ICC charge, besides the war crime of recruitment of children below the age of fifteen years, crimes which may be committed by the recruited child soldiers. As an alternative to the exclusion of the OPCV from all forms of legal representation (e.g. for those victims who do not have a legal representative), a practical solution would be to prevent the OPCV from acting as the legal representative of former child soldiers.

As regards the question of whether the common legal representation of former child soldiers (but also child victim participants in general) is in the best interests of the individual child, it is pointed out that such representation could bear a number of advantages for the participants. It is noted, however, that the actual advantage, bearing in mind the limited practice, cannot yet be established. The primary advantage of such representation could stem from the fact that the common interests of those children are bundled together – interests which reflect their common needs by virtue of being children. The legal representative could thus place the individual interests of, for instance, former child soldiers into the bigger picture of the criminal proceedings. The representative thereby draws the Court's attention to the overall dimensions of child soldering (or being a child victim). Bundling the representation of children should furthermore be preferred, since such representation may enable the legal representative to collect information more easily due to his or her access to a wide range of information provided by the participants. Having better access

487 ICC-01/04-01/06-T-67-ENG, 9 January 2008, at 3, lines 2-16. ICC-01/04-01/06-1211, para. 14.
488 ICC- 01/04-01/06-1211, paras. 20-22.
489 ICC- 01/04-01/06-1211, paras. 31-32.
490 Walleyn *et al.* 2009, at 2. ICC-01/04-01/06-1211, paras. 18-24.

might be of particular importance when claiming reparations at a later stage (*Chapter Five*).

Furthermore, the common legal representation of former child soldiers, but also of children in general if not giving rise to inter-child conflicts of interests, is also preferable due to the limited financial sources available to children. As established below, the provision of legal aid for child participants is not *ipso facto* guaranteed. The common legal representation of children could, however, pave the way for *pro bono* representation of children. Free legal representation of children has also been called for in the *Guidelines of the Committee of Ministers of the Council of Europe on child friendly justice*.[491]

On the other hand, the common legal representation of children constitutes a setback for the possibility to be individually represented in the proceedings as individual representation does not request the legal representative to look for a common denominator as regards the interests to be represented. Instead, the entire strategy of representation can then be based on the individual interest of the victim being represented. But as the Court is empowered to order common legal representation for reasons of judicial economy, exercising this particular right on an individual basis might anyway be excluded.

In any case, child-focused common legal representation largely depends on the experience of the appointed lawyer. Sufficient training and practice on child rights issues is therefore indispensable and should be assessed by the relevant Chamber before appointing a legal representative to children.[492] Such assessment could, for instance, be made by requiring years of practice experience of legal representatives particularly in representing minor clients. A similar request has also been manifested in the *Guidelines of the Council of Europe on child friendly justice*, which state that,

> '[l]awyers representing children should be trained in and knowledgeable on children's rights and related issues, receive ongoing and in-depth training and be capable of communicating with children at their level of understanding.'[493]

The awareness of the Court to ensure that qualified legal representatives represent the interests of children has been restated in a report on the legal representation of victims of the Victims Participation and Reparation Section in the *Situation in the Republic of Kenya*. VPRS underlined in its report that,

> '[it] regrets that it was not ultimately able to identify appropriate representatives to speak specifically on behalf of victims who are children or young people. Of course,

491 Council of Europe Guidelines 2010, IV. Child-friendly justice before, during and after judicial proceedings, A. General elements of child-friendly justice, para. 39.
492 www.vrwg.org/downloads/publications/DraftGuidelinesIntermediaries_Lawyers.pdf.
493 Council of Europe Guidelines 2010, IV. Child-friendly justice before, during and after judicial proceedings, A. General elements of child-friendly justice, para. 39.

> many if not all of the victim communities represented include children and youth, but in so far as the views of younger victims might vary from those of their older community leaders, these were not made visible in this process. This was due in large part to the short time period available which constrained efforts by the VPRS to identify appropriate representatives.'[494]

Accordingly, the need to have separate legal representation of children and ensuring that the search for legal representatives for them is not suffering from time constraints, has also been recognised in the aforementioned situation before the Court. The recognition of VPRS that the search for legal representatives who are experienced in child rights issues was mainly unsuccessful due to time constraints indicates that the ICC is advised to have child rights specialised legal representatives either within the OPCV or, as an alternative, have a short-list of potential external child rights lawyers at hand in order to ensure that children's interests are from the outset of their involvement with the ICC properly represented. As neither the *ad hoc* Tribunals nor other international judicial institutions have been confronted with the need for legal representatives who are specialised in child rights issues, guidance on this child specific modality of participation is not provided for in the law and practice of the other international criminal proceedings. National experience in representing children could (in addition to the experience in representing victims in general) in this regard be a condition for being appointed as a legal representative of child victims. An additional or alternative requirement for appointment could be the completion of trainings and/or universal programs on the representation of children. It could be, on the other side, that lawyers who are experienced in representing children or having completed courses on this very specific field of law rarely exist. In such a case, the ICC is therefore encouraged to not only provide trainings for legal representatives in general (as is already the case), but also trainings which specifically address the representation of the child victim.

Bearing the aforementioned aspects in mind, it is concluded that the need for child adequate representation is not limited to cases such as the proceedings against *Katanga and Ngudjolo Chui* in which the recruitment of child soldiers is charged. Instead, it also extends to cases in which children have become victimised as a result of other crimes within the jurisdiction of the Court. In other words, the representation of children by legal representatives who are properly trained in this field is to be achieved in the proceedings before the ICC. If this is not the case, child participants might be at risk of not being represented in a manner which sufficiently focusses on those aspects which are inherent to be a child.

3.7.3 Children expressing their views and concerns in the courtroom

A request by victims to personally appear in the courtroom and give evidence was submitted by a legal representative of three participants on 2 April 2009.[495] Among

494 ICC-01/09-17-Corr-Red, para. 49.
495 ICC-01/04-01/06-2032-Anx, 26 June 2009.

these were two child participants who claimed to be former child soldiers.[496] Despite the arguments raised by the Prosecution and Defence teams against such participation, Trial Chamber I allowed these three victims to personally give evidence while adjourning their request to present their views and concerns *in person*.[497] The Trial Chamber underlined that the selection of specific victims to participate in person is to be based on facts. The Chamber held that,

> '[f]act-specific decisions will be required, taking into account the circumstances of the trial as a whole. For instance, the personal contributions of a few victims are unlikely to have the same impact on the proceedings as when a large number of victims individually wish to express their views and concerns. To take an extreme example, if all the participating victims in this case (94) sought to present their views and concerns, depending always on the circumstances of their discrete interventions, that course may be antithetical to the fair trial of the accused. Accordingly, it will be necessary for the Chamber to consider these applications on their individual merits, balancing a wide variety of factors that will include the requirements and circumstances of the trial as a whole.'[498]

The children testified on their alleged recruitment and harm suffered. In contrast to the testimony provided by children in the witness capacity which was addressed in the previous chapter, the current witnesses' testimony was not determined by question strategies of the defence and prosecution teams and thus provided for more extensive elaboration of their personal experiences. While most of the testimony was given in closed session to protect the identity of the witnesses (whether the closed session was also ordered because they were children cannot be concluded from the decision), parts of the questioning by their legal representative show that the opportunity to testify in the course of the criminal proceedings before the ICC was used by the legal representative to enable the participants to anticipate on their personal expectations. The possibility to express his/her expectations is especially relevant in regard to possible future reparation awards ordered by the Court. When asked about his expectations for his future, bearing in mind the harm suffered as a former child soldier, the witness stated that,

---

496 ICC-01/04-01/06-2032-Anx, paras. 31-32.

497 Arguments raised by the Defense and Prosecution, ICC-01/04-01/06-2032-Anx, 26 June 2009, paras. 3-4, 5-7. In order to prevent unnecessary repetition, the Chamber held in the same decision that '[o]nce the three participating victims have completed their evidence, they will be in the best position, at that stage, to determine whether they wish to express their views and concerns personally on issues such as the harm they individually experienced and the approach to be taken to reparations, if they have chosen to give evidence on all relevant matters within their knowledge and experience, it may be more appropriate for any additional submissions (which may involve complex legal issues) to be advanced by their legal representatives. However, the Chamber will deal with the position of each victim following their evidence, once the individual circumstances of, and the detail of the requests from, each of these three participating victims are clear. At that stage the Chamber will determine, if relevant, when and by whom any views and concerns are to be presented, bearing in mind the situation of the victims and the need to ensure that the trial of the accused is fair' (para. 40).

498 ICC-01/04-01/06-2032-Anx, para. 27.

> '[w]ell, I am a pupil today. My parents did not tell me to go – or show me how to go and finish. We were not fishers. And when I was a youngster, I was not given the time to go and wander around, so the only direction I was given was that of going to school. So what I mean by this is that I would like to study as I am studying today.'[499]

The desire to continue his studies draws Trial Chamber I's attention to the personal wish of this participant at a stage in which reparation claims are not considered in detail. One may question whether such elaboration is, bearing the criminal nature and objectives of the proceedings in mind, adequate in the course of the criminal proceedings as the participation of the child in the criminal proceedings per definition does not enable the child to ever come into consideration for any form of reparations. Instead, the provision of reparations is limited to the reparation proceedings before the ICC (*Chapter Five*). On the other side, enabling the individual to address his/her personal claims in the course of the criminal proceedings constitutes an opportunity which lacks precedents in international criminal proceedings. It is noteworthy to remember that the form of reparation proceedings and the order of reparation awards by the ICC is, to date, still unclear and not yet put into practice (*Chapter Five*). Accordingly, the possibility to personally give evidence at this stage of the proceedings constitutes a particular opportunity for child victims to recall the harm done to them. Testifying at this early stage could constitute a form of satisfaction for the individual. The participation of former child soldiers in the capacity of participant in the course of criminal proceedings may draw the Court's attention to those needs and experiences which have not been addressed during the questioning of witnesses who were called by the Prosecution or Defence.

Allowing and enabling children to participate in international mechanisms during or in the aftermath of conflict situations can have a positive effect on the overall well-being of traumatised children. The Committee on the Rights of the Child held that participation of children in judicial proceedings has particular positive effects:

> 'Children's participation helps them to regain control over their lives, contributes to rehabilitation, develops organizational skills and strengthens a sense of identity.'[500]

The positive effects of child participation are, as underlined by the Committee on the Rights of the Child, not limited to procedures under national law. Accordingly, the Committee promotes a comprehensive participation of children which includes participation

> 'at the grass-roots, community, and national *or international levels'* (emphasis added).[501]

---

499 ICC-01/04-01/06-T-227-Red-ENG, 14 January 2010, at 71-72.

500 General Comment No. 12, para. 125.

UNICEF underlined with regard to children's involvement in truth and reconciliation commissions that,

> '[c]hildren's statements to a truth commission can foster intergenerational dialogue about what happened during the conflict and what can be done to prevent further violence and victimization of children. This exchange can bring families together in the effort to restore peace and reconstruct the social fabric. While adult testimony about child rights violations helps paint a picture of the range and types of violations suffered, children's voices are necessary for understanding their perspectives.'[502]

A similar, perhaps even the same, argumentation is applicable when the child is involved in judicial proceedings before the ICC as the statements provided by children unavoidably draw the Court's, but also the parents' and most likely also communities' attention to the particular experience, needs and expectations of the child. Such statements could thus constitute a platform for further dialogue not only *about* the child but also *with* the child victim concerned. In line with the aforementioned and from a more general perspective, international law, especially the law of procedure, should therefore enable (without any coercion) and not prevent the child from participation in international procedures since a restrictive or even prohibitive approach neglects the recognition of the child as bearer of human rights and in particular as a bearer of the right to a remedy which includes the right to access to justice, receive reparations and access to information.[503] International mechanisms are of particular importance due to often ineffective or non-existent national mechanisms during or in the aftermath of conflict situations. This omission was also underlined in the report of the United Nations open-ended working group that explored the possibility of an optional protocol to the Convention on the Right of the Child to provide a communications procedure:

> 'In many countries, children did not have access to effective remedies for the violations of their rights and domestic remedies were often inadequate or non-existent.'[504]

---

501 Ibid., para. 13.

502 UNICEF 2010a, at 7.

503 UN General Assembly, Basic Principles and Guidelines on the Right to a Remedy and Reparations for Victims of Gross Violations of International Human Rights Law and Serious Violations of International Humanitarian Law, UN Doc. A/60/147 (2005). Van Boven 2007, 1 at 8; Karp 2008, 89, at 114. The Committee on the Rights of the Child held in this regard that '[t]he Convention requires that children, including the very youngest children, be respected as persons in their own right. Young children should be recognized as active members of families, communities and societies, with their own concerns, interests and pints of view', General Comment No. 7, para. 5.

504 UN General Assembly, Human Rights Council, Report of the open-ended working group to explore the possibility of elaborating an optional protocol to the Convention on the Rights of the Child to provide a communications procedure, UN Doc. A/HRC/13/43 (2010), para. 18.

However, it should be kept in mind that, as was elaborated upon in *Chapter One*, it is still being debated whether criminal proceedings as such are the right forum for this opportunity, in particular when considering the participation of children. After all, the participation of children in the criminal proceedings does not lead to an actual award of reparations. Purely being limited to story-telling might from a child perspective be not as satisfactory as actually benefitting from concrete forms of reparations. This is because the reflection on the benefits of storytelling might, depending in particular on the specific evolving capacities of the participating child, be difficult to conceive for a child participant.

The statement of the second former child soldier suggests the conclusion that participation at this stage enables them to elaborate on the consequences of their recruitment and their future expectations:

> Q: Mr Witness [...] what are the consequences of your time doing military service within the UPC?
> A: Well, it wasn't my – I wasn't – I didn't enroll of my own volition.
> Q: Mr Witness.
> A: Yes?
> Q: Are you satisfied with the time that you spent within the UPC armed group?
> A: No, not at all.
> Q: Since you're not happy, what would you like for today and for the future for yourself?
> A: Well, what I'm asking for is for help in resuming my education.
> Q: Now, when you say that you're not satisfied with the time that you spent within the UPC, why is that so?
> A: No. I'm not happy. Why? Because they found me and I was a school child and I did not want to become a soldier. It was not of my volition.[505]

At the same time, the statement of this alleged former child soldier establishes that it cannot generally be assumed that all child participants are capable of formulating their expectations on the ICC proceedings. While the third (adult) participant who was invited to give evidence could clearly formulate his expectations from the proceedings before the Court, the second former child soldier replied when asked what he expected from this trial and his participation,

> '[w]ell, I don't have an answer.'[506]

---

505 ICC-01/04-01/06-T-230-Red-ENG, 21 January 2010, at 45-46.

506 Ibid., at 46. For the statement of the third claimant, a former Head of School, see ICC-01/04-01/06-T-225-Red-ENG, 12 January 2010, at 31. When being asked by the legal representative why he decided to give evidence *in person* and what his expectations were, he replied that, 'I considered it appropriate to come and testify before this high International Court to be able to speak about the situation which occurred in the Mahagi territory. You know, your Honour, the territory of Mahagi was forgotten. It was – it did not constitute the subject of a serious investigation by the International Court, while this was a territory which was victim of a lot of abuses. And if we have taken a few examples of pupils that were enlisted, this is only a small sample of what really had happened. [...] This was an opportunity for us to be able to say to the

Clearly, the young witness did not know how to address his expectations. This reply demonstrates that there is reason to question whether the participation of child victims in criminal proceedings can generally be considered the right forum for children bearing in mind the principles of the best interests and evolving capacities. This doubt is furthermore strengthened when considering the recent judgment in the *Lubanga* case. With regard to the former child soldiers who were allowed to give evidence as requested by their legal representative, the majority of the Chamber held that,

> '[t]he evidence of a/0225/06, a/0229/06 [...] contains internal inconsistencies which undermine their credibility. a/0225/06's recollection of his abduction and military service lacked clarity, and he demonstrated uncertainty when questioned about the details of those events. [...] a/0225/06 gave significantly unhelpful answers on occasion when questioned about the gaps and inconsistencies in his testimony. [...] a/0229/06 was inconsistent in his account of his abduction and military service. [...] He was often vague in his answers and he tended to respond by stating that he was unable to answer the questions.'[507]

This excerpt shows that the credibility of the child victim participants was examined in detail before coming to the conclusion that,

> 'it accepts that there is a real possibility that victims a/0229/06 and a/0225/06 [...] stole the identities of Thonifwa Uroci Dieudonné (D-0032) and Jean-Paul Bedijo Tschonga (D-0033) in order to obtain the benefits they expected to receive as victims participating in these proceedings. The Chamber is persuaded there is significant weaknesses as regards the evidence of a/0225/06, a/0229/06, [...] to the extent that their accounts are unreliable. Given the material doubts that exist as to the identities of a/0229/06 and a/0225/06 [...], the permission originally granted to a/0229/06 [and] a/0225/06 [...] to participate as victims is withdrawn. In general terms, if the Chamber, on investigation, concludes that its original *prima facie* evaluation was incorrect, it should amend any earlier order as to participation, to the extent necessary. It would be unsustainable to allow victims to continue participating if a more detailed understanding of the evidence has demonstrated they no longer meet the relevant criteria.'[508]

Only after having examined the former child soldiers in person, the Chamber came to the conclusion that their statements are not only unreliable, but also that due to the significant inconsistencies in their statements, they were excluded from further participation in the proceedings. The Chamber was no longer convinced that the

---

world what happened in Mahagi territory and to ask for reparations, if possible, such that this reparation be linked – perhaps some people might doubt this – they could carry out an investigation to be able to establish guilt in this regard because, in our humble opinion, we consider that the charges which are put in terms of conscription and enlistment are insignificant when you consider what we have experienced in Mahagi territory.'

507 ICC-01/04-01/06-2842, paras. 499-500.

508 Ibid., para. 502.

participants were victims of the charged crime. For the same reasons, Trial Chamber I ruled that also the child witnesses with dual status, thus those children who gave evidence as witnesses in the criminal proceedings while participating as victims at the same time, were also to be excluded from further participation.[509] The majority of the Chamber held in particular that,

> 'given the Chamber's present conclusion as to the reliability and accuracy of these witnesses, it is necessary to withdraw their right to participate'.[510]

While this decision was taken in the course of the criminal proceedings, the general formulation of the Chamber as regards the right to participate might have implications for these child victims participation in reparation proceedings. The dissenting judge Odio Benito pointed out in her opinion in relation to the child victim witnesses with dual status that,

> '32. [t]hese witnesses were subject to multiple interviews and strenuous examination and cross-examination, which took place on numerous occasions, during a period of time ranging from 2005 to 2009-2010. In all of these interviews and interrogatories they were asked to recall events that occurred between 2002 and 2003. Although there is doubt as to the exact age of these individuals at the time of the events, it has been proven that all of them certainly children or adolescents at the time of their interviews with OTP investigators in 2005. Some of them could have also been under the age of 18 when they gave testimony in court in 2009-2010. These witnesses (and anyone under those circumstances) could explicably and logically have difficulties in recollecting events [...]. In fact, with such elapses of time it would be suspicious if the accounts would remain perfectly alike and unchanged. Memory is faulty. This is more the case for children and adults having suffered any traumatic events.
>
> 34. [...] although I agree with the Majority of the Trial Chamber that the testimonies of these young individuals should not be used for the purposes of determining the individual criminal responsibility of Mr Lubanga, their victims' status should remain unaffected.
> 35. Additionally and critically, it is unfair and discriminatory to impose on individuals with dual status a higher evidentiary threshold (beyond reasonable doubt) as regards their victims' status, while all other victims participating in the proceedings have not been subject to thorough examination by the parties and the Chamber, as these young persons have been. When reparations are evaluated, it will be up to the Trial Chamber to determine the criteria utilized in determining their final status. Consequently, I consider they should maintain their status as victims for the remaining proceedings in this trial.'[511]

---

509 Ibid., paras. 478-484.
510 Ibid., para. 484.
511 ICC-01/04-01/06-2842, Separate and Dissenting Opinion of Judge Odio Benito, paras. 32-35.

Child victim participants might therefore be better advised to limit their participation by not giving evidence in person and thus *only* being represented by a legal representative. It remains to be seen, however, how the Chamber in the *Lubanga* case, but also other Chambers in future reparation proceedings, will examine the reliability of victims' claims. It goes without saying that the fairness of the proceedings against the (alleged) perpetrators requests an assessment of the reliability of children claims – the exact standard, however, is still to be developed.

If however, the examination of children's claims is not made subject to such a thorough examination at reparation stage compared to the questioning of child participants within the course of the criminal proceedings, it could be assumed that child participation at the reparation stage is to be considered to be more in the best interests of the child than his or her participation during the criminal proceedings. Whether participation in the course of the reparation proceedings will indeed be of a less intensive nature remains to be seen.

It has become clear that the lack of procedural regulation in any case leads to an unclear procedural status of the child participant when giving evidence in the course of the criminal proceedings. In particular, potential risks, such as the risk of being excluded from further participation cannot, under the current system, be anticipated upon as illustrated by the *Lubanga* case. It is therefore argued that a streamlined practice and regulation is necessary in order to enable the child participant and the legal representative to evaluate prior to an actual involvement in person whether child participation should be applied for already during the criminal proceedings or whether it is advisable to participate in the reparation proceedings.

3.7.4 Legal aid for the representation of the child

Closely related to the legal representation of the child participant is the legal aid regime of the International Criminal Court. Rule 90(5) RPE states that,

> '[a] victim or group of victims who lack the necessary means to pay for a common legal representative chosen by the Court may receive assistance from the Registry, including, as appropriate, financial assistance.'[512]

The Registrar determines whether a victim is indigent and whether full or partial payment should be granted.[513] Despite the lack of a victim indigence form, the

---

[512] See also, Regulation 113 of the 2006 Regulations of the Registry of the International Criminal Court, Official Journal of Publication ICC-BD/03-01-06 states:
'1. For the purpose of participation in the proceedings, the Registry shall inform victims that they may apply for legal assistance paid by the Court, and shall supply them with the relevant form(s).
2. in determining whether to grant such assistance, the Registrar shall take into account, inter alia, the factors mentioned in article 68, paragraph 1, any special needs of the victims, the complexity of the case, the possibility of asking the Office of Public Counsel for Victims to act, and the availability of pro bono legal advice and assistance.
3. Regulations 130-139 shall apply mutatis mutandis.'

practice of the Court stipulates a child-sensitive attitude regarding the provision of legal aid.[514] The very first granting of legal aid by the Registrar to a victim was to a child participant in the proceedings against *Thomas Lubanga Dyilo*. In the decision of 3 November 2006 the Registrar decided to provide the minor claimant legal aid, considering that,

> 'la victime étant mineure, elle doit être présumée ne pas disposer des resources pour prendre en charge tout ou partie des coûts lies à sa representation légale devant la Cour et qu'au surplus, l'examen préliminaire les informations qu'elle a fournies relativement à ses bien mobiliers, immobiliers et autres confirme qu'elle ne dispose pas de resources pour prendre en charge tout ou partie de ces coûts; [...].'[515]

Similarly, in the proceedings against *Germain Katanga and Mathieu Ngudjolo Chui*, the Registrar held in the case of one of the applicants that,

> 'it can reasonably be assumed that he does not have the means to pay for all or any of the costs associated with his legal representation.'[516]

Citing the facts that the victim was unemployed, did not have a house or home and was only supported by his family, in a preliminary review of the situation of the victim the Registrar came to the conclusion that the minor could not pay for his legal representation.[517]

In a more recent decision, Pre-Trial Chamber I in the case of *The Prosecutor v. Bahar Idress Abu Garda* in the Situation in Darfur, Sudan, also recognised the indigence of minor child participants.[518] The Registry assumed the indigence of the minor siblings in the decision at issue.[519]

---

513 In accordance with Regulation 84(1) and 113(2) of the 2006 Regulations of the Registry of the International Criminal Court, Official Journal of Publication ICC-BD/03-01-06.

514 It needs to be noted that due to the lack of an indigence form for victims, victims continue to use the indigence form that is available to suspects. See ICC-01/04-494, 14 April 2008, para. 9. Since the prosecutorial jurisdiction of the Court is limited to persons over eighteen (art. 26 Rome Statute), the form does not address the assessment of indigence of persons, and in particular victims that are under eighteen.

515 ICC-01/04-01/06-650.

516 ICC-01/04-01/07-562, at 4-6. The Registrar considers 'that since the Applicant is a minor, it can be reasonably presumed that he has no resources to cover costs for his legal representation,' and therefore decides to temporarily consider the applicant to be wholly indigent pursuant to regulation 85(1) of the Regulations of the Court while the decision remains subject to investigation over the applicant's financial resources. The Registrar adds that the amount of the legal aid to be granted to the applicant will be determined on a case-by-case basis. See also, ICC-01/04-01/07-652.

517 See ICC-01/04-01/07-562, at 4-5.

518 Applicant a/0192/09 successfully submitted an application on her own behalf and on behalf of her minor siblings claiming that they have suffered harm as a result of their father's death. ICC-02/05-02/09-121, paras. 63-64.

519 ICC-02/05-02/09-172, at 4. See also, ICC-02/05-02/09-195, at 4; ICC-02/05-02/09-197, 20 October 2009, at 4-5.

This leniency only constitutes a preliminary provision of legal aid. It cannot be concluded from the practice whether the indigence of children is treated as equally as the indigence of adults. Accordingly, if a child-specific approach to indigence is not visible, this does not permit the conclusion that the Registry generally provides children with legal aid by virtue of them being children. It cannot be determined with certainty whether or not the Registry is of the view that all children should benefit from free legal aid as requested in the *Guidelines of the Committee of Ministers of the Council of Europe on child friendly justice.*[520] The provision of legal aid is only considered on the basis of a preliminary preview of the situation of the child.

The importance of free legal aid to children is recognised not only on the European continent, but also in Africa. In Europe, Finland and Italy, for instance, grant child victims of certain crimes free legal aid without taking into account the possessions of the child victim or its caretakers.[521] Moreover, the South African Constitution establishes that such practice constitutes a constitutional right of children.[522]

3.8 CONCLUSION

It has become clear that the procedural rules of the International Criminal Court do not prohibit a child from participating in the criminal proceedings. Practice has established that particular requirements have been introduced by various Chambers when children apply for participation – requirements which are not required to be fulfilled by other victims in order for them to be recognised as a victim within the meaning of Rule 85 RPE. Accordingly, a distinction between children and other categories of victim participants, especially adult participants, exists in the practice of the Court. By distinguishing children from other participants, various Chambers stated that children face particular difficulties such as, for instance, being required to provide proof of their identity. Those Chambers thereby recognised that difficulties exist not only as a result of the consequences of an armed conflict, but also because of child-specific aspects such as age.

In any case, large numbers of victims and a lack of procedural clarity should not immediately be used as arguments leading to the conclusion that child victim participation in criminal proceedings is not the correct forum for victims of crimes within the jurisdiction of the court. Neither should the risk of endangering the fairness, impartiality and expeditiousness be seen as a reason for exclusion from the

---

520 Council of Europe Guidelines 2010, IV. Child-friendly justice before, during and after judicial proceedings, A. General elements of child-friendly justice, para. 39.

521 CURE, *Child victims in the Union – Right and Empowerment – A report of the CURE project* 2009-2010, The Crime Victim Compensation and Support Authority Sweden (2010), http://www.brottsoffermyndigheten.se/default.asp?id=3251, at 82. See for further analysis of domestic systems which provide for free legal aid UNICEF 2009b, at 54.

522 1996 Constitution of the Republic of South Africa Act, Schedule 28(1)(h), http://www.info.gov.za/documents/constitution/1996/.

outset. After all, as long as the Rome Statute provides for the possibility of victim participation on the basis of Article 68(3) of the Rome Statute without explicitly excluding minor victims from this procedural avenue, children should not be prohibited from applying for participation without a justification which is provided for in law. If children are to be excluded from participation in the criminal proceedings, such a decision should in particular mirror a case-by-case assessment of the situation of the individual child.

It has at the same time become clear that the participation of children in criminal proceedings may not generally be considered to be in the best interests of a child, in particular when children give evidence in person and are subjected to a thorough examination. The lack of maturity is one factor which could constitute a reason why this kind of participation is not adequate for minor participants. In this regard, if they are questioned about their alleged suffering it might also, as is the case with child witnesses, entail the risk of re-traumatisation. At the same time, it has also become clear that child victim participation can have positive implications for a child – be it from a personal perspective of the individual child or with regard to the broader objectives of transitional justice processes.

The procedural particularities which arise when children participate thus seem to suggest that the best interests of the child are to be considered on a case-by-case basis prior to their participation. It cannot generally be assumed that child participation is in the best interest of the minor. Instead, the evolving capacities of the individual child are to be carefully assessed. In addition to an assessment of the individual child, the Court, including all actors involved in the course of the criminal proceedings, should take sufficiently into account that child participation requests a sensitive response in practice which, thus far, is rarely addressed in the procedural regulation of victim participation. Experience and where necessary trainings on the procedural implications of child participation, in particular trainings on how to involve, address and protect the child in the course of the criminal proceedings thereby constitute an avenue which could ensure that children participate in a manner which is child-sensitive. Experience in representing children in domestic proceedings and special trainings aim to ensure that children are approached by all actors in a child-sensitive way as long as there is no corresponding procedural regulation under the Rome Statute and the respective rules which explicitly provides for procedural treatment of child participants in relation to the those aspects that require a treatment which differs from adult participation.

CHAPTER 4

THE CHILD PERPETRATOR AND THE CHILD OF A(N) (ALLEGED) PERPETRATOR

4.1 INTRODUCTION

The current chapter focusses in more detail on the fact that children themselves can qualify as perpetrators of international crimes and the possibility to prosecute child perpetrators internationally. In addition, the chapter examines the procedural implications when a child of a(n) (alleged) perpetrator is involved in the course of the criminal proceedings before the International Criminal Court.

Children participate as soldiers in hostilities.[523] The phenomenon of child soldiers and their involvement in conflict situations is a continuing reality. Today's estimated number of child soldiers amounts to more than 300,000 children.[524] As a consequence of their recruitment, children have committed and continue to commit the most atrocious acts amounting to international crimes, such as war crimes and crimes against humanity.[525] The procedural capacity of the child perpetrator under international criminal law, to date, only concerns children between the age of fifteen and eighteen years at the moment of crime commission. The question raised with regard to this procedural capacity reads as follows: Are the best interests of the child taken into account when considering the international criminal prosecution of (alleged) child perpetrators?

The capacity of the child of a(n) (alleged) perpetrator is not a strictly legal one. This is because it is derived from the child's parent who is charged with or convicted for international crimes. Being the child of a(n) (alleged) perpetrator might bear numerous and far reaching consequences. The child is likely to be confronted with the factual and often lengthy separation from his/her parent considering that institutions, such as the *ad hoc* Tribunals or the ICC in The Hague, are situated far away from their home and proceedings (including detention) tend to last for several years. The parent's involvement in criminal proceedings may also lead to stigmatisation and exclusion of the child in his/her community. In addition to these non-legal consequences, a number of issues arose in the practice of the ICC which anticipate that certain decisions taken by the Court may have particular consequences for the child and may therefore require that the Court sufficiently takes into account that decisions addressed at the (alleged) perpetrator may have implications for the child. It is for this reason that this derived capacity – despite its

523 Mann 1987, 32, at 50; The Redress Trust 2006, at 5-22. See generally, Cohn & Goodwin-Gill 1994.
524 UNICEF, fact sheet, http://www.unicef.org/emerg/files/childsoldiers.pdf.
525 Ibid..

limited procedural value – is nevertheless assessed as a procedural capacity within this research since it may give rise to questions concerning the best interests of the child.

4.2 Recruitment of Child Soldiers

The participation of children in hostilities can be traced back in history, but it has particularly increased during the past decades.[526] The *Cape Town Principles and Best Practices* of 1997 propose actions to be taken by States and communities in order to prevent child recruitment, demobilise child soldiers and reintegrate these children into family and community life.[527] The Coalition to Stop the Use of Child Soldiers underlined once more in its *Global Report 2008* that 'where armed conflict does exist, child soldiers will almost certainly be involved.'[528]

Forced or voluntary recruitment is the result of different causes and is led by varying motivations.[529] Children, particularly orphans, the unaccompanied, the less-wealthy or those that come from a disadvantaged background who do not participate in an education system and who spend their free time on the streets, are at particular risk of becoming child soldiers because they do not benefit from the shelter that is provided by educational institutions, family networks or other bodies.[530]

Furthermore, a child may not be able to oversee the consequences of signing up for voluntary recruitment. Above and beyond, recruiters prefer to use children because they can be easily influenced, coerced and controlled.[531] One witness of the

526 Mann 1987, at 50-52; Honwana 2006, at 1. Revaz & Todres 2006, at 303. See generally, Abbott 2000, 499-537; Harvey 2003. See with regard to the Democratic Republic of the Congo, UN General Assembly/Security Council, Children and armed conflict, Report of the Secretary-General, UN Doc. A/59/695-S/2005/72 (2005), para. 18; UN Security Council, Report of the Secretary-General on children and armed conflict in the Democratic Republic of the Congo, UN Doc. S/2006/389 (2006), paras. 18-27.

527 Cape Town Principles 1997. The Principles define a child soldier as 'any person under eighteen years of age who is part of any kind of regular or irregular armed force or armed group in any capacity, including but not limited to cooks, porters, messengers and anyone accompanying such as groups, other than family members. The definition includes girls recruited for sexual purposes and for forced marriage. It does not, therefore, only refer to a child who is carrying or has carried arms.'

528 Soldiers - Global Report 2008, at 12. See also, Child Soldiers - Global Report 2004, at 12. Children have been recruited throughout history, see, for example, Singer 2005, at 9-15. Armed forces or opposition groups in developing countries, in particular, are well-known for recruiting children and using them actively in hostilities, see, UN General Assembly/Security Council, Report of the UN Secretary-General, Children and armed Conflict, UN Doc. A/62/609-S/2007/757 (2007), paras. 19-136. See also, Hingorani 1989,133-138; Breen 2003, 453, at 468-470.

529 See generally, Happold 2005; Tiefenbrun 2008, 415, at 426-434; Francis 2007, 207, at 211-214; Brett 1999, 875, at 859-862; Cohn & Goodwin-Gill 1994, at 37-43.

530 Cahn 2006, 413, at 421; Van Bueren 1994, at 813; De Berry 2001, 92, at 94-105. See also, Cape Town Principles 1997, 2-3.

531 UNICEF 2005c, at 44; Wessells 2006, at 33-37; Udombana 2006, 57, at 61-67; Gustaffson 1999, 328, at 332; Becker 2010.

Prosecution in the *Case of the Prosecutor v. Germain Katanga and Nathieu Ngudjolo Chui* stated that,

> '[il] préférait étre escortée [sic] par les enfants soldats ages de moins de 16 ans parce qu'ils exécutaient sans oppositions.'[532]

The existence of and trade in light weapons (predominantly AK 47s) enables recruiters to effectively use children in combat, since the light weight of such weapons means that they can be easily carried and handled by children.[533] Additionally, the large number of children among combatants can also be explained by the majority of children among the overall population.[534]

4.3 PROSECUTING THE CHILD

Child perpetrators of crimes under international law were never charged with such crimes in international (judicial) proceedings. The first and only international mechanism that explicitly entails the jurisdictional mandate for the prosecution of alleged child perpetrators was the Special Court for Sierra Leone. Article 7 of the Statute stipulates that the Court has jurisdiction over minors who were between fifteen and eighteen years of age when the alleged crime was committed.[535] Consequently, on the one hand, the SCSL Statute recognises that children may be perpetrators but, on the other hand, lacks jurisdiction over child perpetrators below the age of fifteen years.

As regards those children who were between fifteen and eighteen years at the moment of crime commission, it was extensively discussed whether they should be held criminally responsible under international law.[536] Numerous arguments were

[532] See, ICC Case Information Sheet 'The Prosecutor v. Germain Katanga & Mathieu Ngudjolo Chui', http://www.haguejusticeportal.net/Docs/Fact%20Sheets/Katanga_Chui_EN.pdf. Statement of W-28 at DRC-OTP-0155-0106 at 0113, para. 37.

[533] Gallagher 2001, 310, at 329. UNICEF 2005c, at 44. UN General Assembly/Security Council, Report of the UN Secretary General on Children and Armed Conflict, UN Doc. A/58/546-S/2003/1053 (2003), paras. 42-44; Rosen 2005, at 14-16; Wessells 2006, at 18-19.

[534] Gallagher 2001, at 325; Bledsoe 1993, at 5.

[535] Paragraph 1 of art. 7 of the 2002 Statute of the Special Court for Sierra Leone states: 'The Special Court shall have no jurisdiction over any person who was under the age of fifteen at the time of the alleged commission of the crime. Should any person who was at the time of the alleged commission of the crime between fifteen and eighteen years of age come before the Court, he or she shall be treated with dignity and a sense of worth, taking into account his or her young age and the desirability of promoting his or her rehabilitation, reintegration into and assumption of a constructive role in society, and in accordance with international human rights standards, in particular the rights of the child.'

[536] See for example, Happold 2006, 69-84. See in particular UN, Security Council, Report of the Secretary-General on the establishment of a Special Court for Sierra Leone, UN Doc. S/2009/915 (2000). The Secretary-General underlined that, 'The question of child prosecution was discussed at length with the Government of Sierra Leone both in New York and in Freetown. It was raised with all the interlocutors of the United Nations team, the members of the judiciary, members of the legal profession and the Ombudsman, and was vigorously debated with members of civil

raised in favour of and against the criminal prosecution of minors.[537] The Prosecutor of the SCSL proclaimed in this context that he does not intend to start proceedings against minors regardless of his jurisdictional mandate, but instead – as is the case for the other international criminal tribunals – focuses on the ones who bear the greatest responsibility, while children, in principle, did not bear such responsibility in the Sierra Leonean conflict.[538] He underlined that children who committed crimes are instead to be recognised as victims.[539]

At the time of writing, the last case before the Special Court for Sierra Leone – the trial of the former Liberian president *Charles Taylor* – reached the appeals stage.[540] None of the cases brought has involved children in the capacity of a child perpetrator being charged with crimes within the Special Court's jurisdiction.

The subsequent inclusion of Article 26 in the Rome Statute brought the discussion concerning the international criminal responsibility of the child before the ICC to an end by excluding persons below the age of eighteen from the ICC's jurisdiction.[541] The international criminal prosecution of minors has thus been rejected. Considering the practice of the SCSL and the drafting history of this particular provision, it is also unlikely that children will be prosecuted at an international level for having committed international crimes before a future international court or tribunal.[542] Excluding minors from the jurisdiction of the ICC does, however, not imply that minors can principally not be prosecuted before national courts.[543] It has been underlined by Clark and Triffterer that,

---

society, non-governmental organizations and institutions actively engaged in child-care and rehabilitation programmes', para. 34.

537 *The Prosecutor of the Tribunal v. Naser Orić* (IT-03-068-T), Judgment, 30 June 2006, para. 400. In this decision Trial Chamber II of the ICTY ruled that, 'the Defence submits that even if the beating by the youth was considered to have caused Milisav Milovanović's death, there can be no criminal liability for a war crime committed by an individual below the age of eighteen. The Trial Chamber considers this submission as completely unfounded in law, as no such rule exists in conventional or customary international law.' For a critical assessment of the exclusion of minors from the Court's jurisdiction, see, Frulli 2002, 527-541. For an overview of the legal framework see, Bakker 2010.

538 Press release SCSL, 2 November 2002, http://www.sc-sl.org/LinkClick.aspx?fileticket=XRwCUe%2BaVhw%3D&tabid=196. Art. 1(1) of the 2002 Special Court Statute states: 'The Special Court shall [...] have the power to prosecute persons who bear the greatest responsibility for serious violations of international humanitarian law and Sierra Leonean law committed in the territory of Sierra Leone since 30 Nov.1996 [...].' Kendall & Staggs 2005, at 7.

539 Press release SCSL, 24 June 2004, http://www.sc-sl.org/LinkClick.aspx?fileticket=TazwrTR%2bT7Q%3d&tabid=196.

540 See, http://www.sc-sl.org/CASES/ProsecutorvsCharlesTaylor/tabid/107/Default.aspx.

541 Art. 26 Rome Statute states that, '[t]he Court shall have no jurisdiction over any person who was under the age of eighteen at the time of the alleged commission of a crime.' See also, Parmar et al. 2010, Introduction, xv, at xxv.

542 For a brief historical overview, see Roger & Triffterer 2008, at 771-775.

543 Without referring to domestic practice, W. Schabas argues that ''[j]uveniles my be prosecuted for international crimes, just as they may be prosecuted for ordinary crimes, subject to national legislation governing the minimum age of responsibility and the applicable norms of international human rights law.' Schabas 2010, at 445.

> 'taking into consideration that complementarity and thereby the priority of national criminal jurisdiction prevails anyhow, it appears not only justifiable but also preferable to leave the group under eighteen to the national courts. They are much better equipped to take care of the specific situation in which children have been committing crimes under international criminal law.'[544]

International justice mechanisms have not been used and recognised as a forum to hold child perpetrators responsible. One may therefore conclude that the international criminal prosecution is not considered to be in the best interests of the child.

Instead, a limited number of national cases has been initiated against minor perpetrators. One of the few national examples of a case against an alleged child soldier exists in the practice of the United States in relation to Guantánamo Bay.[545] In 2007 a United States military commission charged Omar Ahmed Khadr, a Canadian citizen who was detained in 2002, with war crimes that were committed at the age of fifteen.[546] Due to a plea deal, judicial proceedings were never held.[547] The Rwandan '1994 minors' that have been detained for crimes committed during the Rwandan genocide constitute another example of national cases against child perpetrators.[548] Compared to the overall number of perpetrators convicted for the Rwandan genocide, minor perpetrators constitute a very small group.[549] The lack of a broadly established practice to prosecute minors for the commission of international crimes before domestic courts underlines that also under national law, child perpetrators are rather seen as victims of conflict situations instead of being seen as perpetrators.

---

544 Ibid., at 775.

545 Another case that involved an alleged child perpetrator in Guantánamo Bay constitutes the case of Mohammed Jawad, who was detained on the Cuban island as an alleged 'child enemy combatant', Amnesty International, *United States of America – From ill-treatment to unfair trial. The case of Mohammed Jawad, child 'enemy combatant'*, 13 August 2008, AI Index: AMR 51/091/2008, http://www.amnesty.org/en/library/asset/AMR51/091/2008/en/d47d414f-693e-11dd-8e5e-43ea85d15a69/amr510912008eng.pdf. His release was ordered on 30 July 2009, Amnesty International, *USA: Judge orders Mohammed Jawad's release from Guantánamo, Administration still mulling trial*, http://www.amnesty.org/en/library/info/AMR51/088/2009/en/refresh. See also, Human Rights Watch, Releasing Jawad: A Boys life at Guantanamo (2010), http://www.hrw.org/en/news/2010/01/11/releasing-jawad-boy-s-life-guantanamo.

546 UNICEF, *UNICEF concerned over possible prosecution of child soldier* (2008), http://www.un.org/apps/news/story.asp?NewsID=25496&Cr=child&Cr1=soldier. For an overview of the background of the case, see Human Rights First, *The Case of Omar Ahmed Khadr, Canada* (2008), https://secure.humanrightsfirst.org/us_law/detainees/cases/khadr.htm; Amnesty International, *USA: Military Commission proceedings against Omar Khadr resume, as USA disregards its international human rights obligations*, 26 April 2010, AI Index: AMR 51/029/201, http://www.amnesty.org/en/library/asset/AMR51/029/2010/en/23618d64-1d1b-4af0-a9b5-04df1ceaddb2/amr510292010en.html.

547 Omar Ahmed Khadr, Human Rights Watch, http://www.hrw.org/news/2012/10/25/omar-ahmed-khadr.

548 Morrill 2005, 103, at 106.

549 Human Rights Watch, Lasting Wounds, Consequences of Genocide and War on Rwanda's Children (2003), at 33, http://www.hrw.org/reports/2003/rwanda0403/rwanda0403-05.htm.

Notwithstanding the non-existence of international judicial proceedings against children in the capacity of child perpetrators, the fact that children committed the most heinous crimes of concern to the international community was recognised during children's participation in non-judicial procedures of truth and reconciliation commissions like for instance in the TRCs of Sierra Leone and Liberia.[550] Remarkably, the mandate of the Sierra Leonean TRC points out that the Commission is vested with the task of implementing special procedures when children who committed international crimes participate.[551] Cook and Heykoop pointed out that in order

> '[t]o make sure that all children were treated equally as victims and witnesses before the TRC, the statement-taking forms for children omitted the section designated for perpetrators so that children were identified in the database only as victims or witnesses. This made it clear that the policy and approach of the TRC was to include children's experiences in the findings of the Commission, but not to hold children accountable for the atrocities that took place.'[552]

For the first time in the history of TRCs', the Sierra Leonean TRC explicitly referred to children who committed international crimes in its regulation and final report.[553] The TRC Act of 2000 addressed the needs of child victims and introduced special procedures and measures for the protection of children who have committed these crimes.[554] In its final report of 2004, the Commission pointed out that most children who have been found to have committed international crimes are also child victims.[555] In addition to the general findings on this particular group of children, the TRC's final report includes an entire chapter on children in armed conflict in which the substantive particularities regarding this specific group are addressed.[556] The Commission underlined that it does not aim to determine the guilt of former child soldiers. Instead, it does attempt to assess children's role as "victim-

550 TRC Sierra Leone Vol. 3B, Chapter 4 Children and the Armed Conflict in Sierra Leone. Siegrist 2006, 53-65. With regard to the TRC of Liberia, see Volume III, Title II, 'Children, the Conflict and the TRC Children Agenda', www.http://trcofLiberia.org/, at 65. The appropriateness of accountability of child perpetrators through alternative to judicial proceedings is also restated in the Key Principles for Children and Transitional Justice which provide that, '[a]ccountability measures for alleged child perpetrators should be in the best interests of the child and should be conducted in a manner that takes into account their age at the time of the alleged commission of the crime, promotes reintegration and potential to assume a constructive role in society. In determining which process of accountability is in the best interests of the child, alternatives to judicial proceedings should be considered wherever appropriate.' UNICEF 2010b, 407-411, at 3.6.

551 Section 7(1)(4) of the Truth and Reconciliation Commission Act 2000, Being an Act to establish the Truth and Reconciliation Commission in line with art. XXVI of the Lome Peace Agreement and to provide for related matters; http://www.sierra-leone.org/Laws/2000-4.pdf.

552 Cook & Heykoop 2010, 159, at 171.

553 Ibid., at 164.

554 See for example sections 6(2), 7 (2) and 7(4) of the 2000 TRC Act.

555 TRC Sierra Leone Vol. 1, Chapter 5, Methodology and Process, at 190.

556 Ibid., at 286.

perpetrators" and thereby addresses the non-judicial accountability of the child.[557] In this regard, the TRC published statistical information on children who committed crimes during the Sierra Leonean conflict.[558] The recognition of the fact that children have committed international crimes in the course of the conflict is thereby established in the TRC's regulation and also reflected in its findings. Similarly, the Truth and Reconciliation Commission for Liberia paid particular attention to these children. It recognised that the international prosecution of this particular group of children has not been recognised by the international community. Instead, the Commission invited former child soldiers to give a statement before the TRC. The criminal prosecution of children was advised to be regulated under national law or alternative justice mechanisms, such as in the Rwandan Gaçacça system.[559]

4.4 Being the Child of a(n) (Alleged) Perpetrator

Decisions taken by the Court and its organs may indirectly affect the child of a(n) (alleged) perpetrator and give rise to consequences which particularly affect the child. While qualifying such consequences as a victimisation of the child is considered a step too far, the Court should nevertheless be aware of the potential negative implications for the child.

In this regard, it needs to be noted that the term *child* in this context is understood as referring to the biological (or 'legally' recognised) minor child of the (alleged) perpetrator.[560] This derived procedural capacity differs from the other procedural capacities of the child in the sense that it does not enable children to participate in the proceedings, but rather exists due to their parent's procedural capacity as a(n) (alleged) perpetrator and detainee.

This capacity is of particular relevance concerning two issues. Firstly, being the child of a(n) (alleged) perpetrator bears consequences for the child and family life at home. Enforcement measures, such as the freezing of assets, of course have implications for the family of the accused.[561] If applied without sufficiently taking into account the particular needs of the child in his/her daily life such as the payment of school fees and other family allowances, the child is at risk of being negatively affected. Secondly, another issue which underlines that particular consequences arise for the child is mirrored in the organisation of family visits. The various institutions grant the accused and convicted parent the right to family

---

557 TRC Sierra Leone Vol. 3B, Chapter 4, Reparations, at 286, 439.

558 Appendix 1, Statistical Appendix to the Report of the Truth and Reconciliation Commission of Sierra Leone, A Report by the Benetech Human Rights Data Analysis Group of the Truth and Reconciliation Commission (2004), http://www.sierra-leone.org/TRCDocuments.html, at 19.

559 See TRC Liberia, Volume Three: Appendix, at 91-93. The 2005 TRC Act recognised that children may be victims and perpetrators, art. VIII, section 26 (n). The Act underlined the need to adopt in this regard specific measures of protection and procedures. For general information on the involvement of children in the Liberian TRC, see, Sowa 2010, 193-230.

560 With regard to the age of the child, the Convention on the Rights of the Child's standard of eighteen years could constitute a benchmark.

561 Article 93(1)(k) Rome Statute; Rules 45, 61(D) of the ICTY and ICTR RPE.

visits.[562] This right aims to serve the wellbeing of the detainee and enables the child to keep contact with the parent despite the detention of his/her parent.[563] The Convention on the Rights of the Child stipulates in this regard that,

> '[n]o child shall be subjected to arbitrary or unlawful interference with his or her privacy, family, home or correspondence [...].'[564]

Article 9 paragraph 2 states furthermore that,

> 'States Parties shall respect the right of the child who is separated from one or both parents to maintain personal relations and direct contact with both parents on a regular basis, except if it is contrary to the child's best interests.'[565]

In practice, the organisation of family visits leads to various difficulties that might constrain the ability of the child to visit his/her parent – as illustrated by the various decisions made concerning family visits of the accused *Thomas Lubanga Dyilo*, *Germain Katanga* and *Mathieu Ngudjolo Chui*. These decisions addressed *inter alia* the number of family visits and the amount of members eligible for visiting their relative.[566] The latter, for instance, is a father of six children. He argued that the

> 'decision on family visits adopted by the Registrar contradicts her obligations in that it only allows for occasional family contact.'

---

562 Rule 58-64bis of the 1994 Rules of the International Criminal Tribunal for the Former Yugoslavia Governing the Detention of Persons awaiting Trial or Appeal before the Tribunal or otherwise Detained on the Authority of the Tribunal, UN Doc. IT/38Rev. 9 (2005), (as amended on 21 July 2005). The application form for visits is online available http://www.icty.org/x/file/Legal%20Library/Detention/permission_visit_detainee_en.doc. Rule 41 of the 2003 Rules Governing the Detention of Persons Awaiting Trial or Appeal before the Special Court for Sierra Leone or Otherwise Detained on the Authority of the Special Court for Sierra Leone ("Rules of Detention"), (as amended on 14 May 2005), http://www.sc-sl.org/LinkClick.aspx?fileticket=sSNS1UL5T3w%3D&tabid=176.

563 The Preamble of the Convention on the Rights of the Child recognises 'that the child, for the full and harmonious development of his or her personality, should grow up in a family environment, in an atmosphere of happiness, love and understanding [...].'

564 Art. 16 CRC. Art. 9(4) states in this regard that, '[w]here such separation results from any action initiated by the State Party, such as the detention, imprisonment, exile, deportation or death [...] of one or both parents of the child, that State shall, upon request, provide the parents, the child or, if appropriate, another member of the family with the essential information concerning the whereabouts of the absent member(s) of the family [...].'

565 See similarly, art. 24(3) of the European Charter of Fundamental Rights.

566 For general discussion of their family visits and size of family, see Report of the Court on the financial aspects of enforcing the Court's obligation to fund family visits to indigent detained persons, ICC-ASP/8/9, 6 May 2009. *Germain Katanga* is married and is the father of two children. See ICC-01/04-01/07-6, at 2. ICC- Request to lift freezing order to enable Jean-Pierre Bemba to meet his family's expenses, 01/05-01/08-567-Red, at 18. With regard to the organisation of family visits, see ICC-01/04-01/07-733 and International Criminal Court, Assembly of State Parties, Report of the Court on family visits to indigent detained persons, ICC-ASP/7/24, 5 November 2008.

The Presidency of the ICC underlined in this regard that a

> 'detained person's right correlates with the interests of other affected individuals such as those of his children of minority age who wish to have contact with their detained parent. [...] the Presidency finds that, in the instant case, a positive obligation to fund family visits must be implied in order to give effect to a right which would otherwise be ineffective in the particular circumstances of the detainee.'[567]

This decision illustrates that some difficulties have been observed.[568] The questions which, to date, have not been addressed relate to the concept of a family and whether children of all spouses are eligible for family visits. Furthermore, visa issues still exist for children who wish to visit their parent. The introductory assumption that decisions taken by the Court and its organs may indirectly affect the child of a(n) (alleged) perpetrator and give rise to consequences which particularly affect the child is thus supported by the first decisions relating to family visits.

The ICC is also likely to be confronted with requests concerning the frequency and costs of family visits, in particular when the prisoner is indigent.[569] These questions all have in common that they request child sensitivity by procedural awareness and regulation in order to ensure that the negative implications for the child can be limited or even prevented. For this reason when deciding on issues concerning the (alleged) perpetrator, it is indispensable to also take into account the best interests of the child and his/her rights as contained in the Convention on the Rights of the Child, in particular the child's right to family life. The recognition of the right of the child to visit his/her imprisoned parents (when being in the best interests of the child) has been addressed particularly within the European context by child rights organisations.[570] It has been pointed out by the *European Network for Children of Imprisoned Parents* (Eurochips), an organisational network which monitors the treatment of children with imprisoned parents in Europe that,

> '[a]cross the EU, good practice examples have been observed regarding support with family contact both on a regular basis, and in cases of an emergency with many examples of flexibility being offered by prison regimes in relation to visits to prisons. For example, in Poland, prisoners who have custody of children below 15 years of

567 ICC-ROR217/02/08-8, paras. 1, 35, 37. Regulation 179(1) of the Regulations of the Registry provides that, '[t]he Registrar shall give specific attention to visits by family of the detained persons with a view to maintaining such links'. See also, for instance, ICC-01/05/01/08-310.

568 Article 16(1) CRC.

569 ICTY and ICTR seem to refuse to financially support family visits of indigent prisoners. See in this regard, *The Prosecutor v. Momcilo Krajisnik* (IT-00-39-T), Decision on the Defence's Request for an Order Setting Aside, in part, the Deputy Registrar's Decision of 3 February 2004. This is problematic, considering that the ECtHR (see for instance, *Trosin v. Urkaine*, Judgment of 23 February 2012, Application no. 39758/05; *Messina v. Italy* (No. 2), Judgment of 28 September 2000, Application no. 25498/94) considered family visits to be a fundamental right of the prisoner.

570 Eurochips 2011.

age can request one additional visit per month. In Poland and Denmark, it is also possible to combine a number of visits a month into longer ones – this means the visits will be rarer but may have a better quality, especially for families that have to travel considerable distances to visit their relative in prison. In many countries (including Italy, the UK, France, Poland, Sweden, Norway, Belgium), some prisons organize special visits for children with their imprisoned parent where they are able to spend quality time together; however these are sometimes linked to the prisoner's good conduct as opposed to being prioritised to meet the needs of the child.'[571]

In light of this national practice, the ICC is advised to facilitate regular contact between imprisoned parents and their children. In addition, the Court should provide for the organisation of family contacts and visits in the respective rules. This codification aims in particular to ensure legal transparency for detained persons about the possibility to see and stay in contact with their families.

It is also to be kept in mind that visiting parents in the detention facilities of the ICC in the Netherlands is likely to be expensive, if not even unaffordable for children. The *European Network for Children of Imprisoned Parents* examined the payment of such visits in the European area. It held illustratively held that,

'[t]he high cost and inconvenience of travelling to prisons (especially if using public transport), which are often a long way from where the family live and located some distance from public transport stops, deter many families from visiting. In the UK, the government's Assisted Prison Visits Scheme provides a right to financial support for families on low income. In Sweden, the *kommuns* (municipalities) cover the travel costs of children visiting imprisoned parents. In Poland, financial support is discretionary and can depend on the area the family is living.'[572]

While imprisonment during the course of ICC proceedings can be expected to be arranged in the majority of the cases in The Hague, Netherlands, imprisonment following a conviction could be taken over by any State Party which is willing to take care of convicted persons. This means, that convicted parents will not necessarily be imprisoned in the country of their origin. The regular arrangement of family visits therefore gives rise to certain costs (in addition to the practical difficulties of arranging family visits abroad). The ICC is thus called upon to also provide for adequate regulation of the particular challenges relating to family visits abroad.

In general terms, the Committee on the Rights of the Child recommended in particular that,

'States parties ensure that the rights of children with a parent in prison are taken into account from the moment of the arrest of their parent(s) and by all actors involved in

571 Ibid., at 11-12.
572 Ibid., at 12.

> the process and at all its stages, including law enforcement, prison service professionals, and the judiciary.'[573]

Thus, domestic practice relating to family visits can provide guidance for the ICC when deciding upon family visits and should therefore be taken into account. Considering the financial aspects of family visits, it might, for instance, be appropriate to reserve a separate chapter within the budget of the ICC for children visiting their detained parent. It can be concluded that the arrangement of family visits is only one example which shows that contact in general is to be established by taking into account the rights of the child to be in contact with his/her parent. Accordingly, the ICC organs which are involved in decisions concerning family visits are called upon to ensure that during pre-trial and trial detention of the accused, child rights aspects are not forgotten. The case-by-case examination of the best interests of the child requires furthermore that such decisions are not limited to an assessment of the prisoner's interest to see his/her family but also take into account whether such visits are in the best interests of the child

4.5 Conclusion

Children commit international crimes. The international criminal prosecution of minor perpetrators has, however, clearly been rejected under the Rome Statute of the International Criminal Court. The question which remains is how to deal with these child perpetrators at an international level while at the same time bearing in mind the best interests of the child. The practice of TRCs established that children's commission of international crimes can be dealt with at an international level without a judicial forum. This practice has been pointed out to be of particular relevance within the post-conflict, reconstruction and reconciliation period. The exclusion of prosecuting minors under the Rome Statute of the International Criminal Court left at the same time no room for doubt that the international prosecution of children when having committed war crimes, crimes against humanity or the crime of genocide, is not accepted to be the proper forum for the adjudication of child perpetrators.

With regard to the procedural capacity of the child of a(n) (alleged) perpetrator it can be concluded that it is crucial that international criminal courts and tribunals recognise that the child may be negatively affected by decisions taken against his/her parent in the course of international criminal proceedings. Although the freezing of assets and restrictions to family life may be justified within the context of criminal proceedings, the limited understanding of the particularities of the child limits or even prevents the child from visiting his/her parent or living in child-adequate circumstances by, for example not being able to attend school due to a parent's involvement in international criminal proceedings. In conclusion, this procedural capacity requests child sensitive awareness as regards the possible

573 Committee on the Rights of the Child, "Children of Incarcerated Parents" 2011, para. 31.

implications for children from the judges and the Registry of the ICC; but equally from defence lawyers representing the interests of their clients in relation to their family life. Finally, while this procedural capacity might be considered less relevant from a criminal law perspective, particular importance is derived from the perspective of child rights. The fact that the child may indeed fall within this procedural capacity requests an adequate legal response which sufficiently takes into account the particular impact of the parent's involvement in international criminal proceedings on the rights of the child.

PART II

THE CHILD IN INTERNATIONAL REPARATION PRACTICE

CHAPTER 5

THE CHILD CLAIMANT

5.1 INTRODUCTION

On the basis of Article 75 of the Rome Statute, a child who has become the victim of international crimes that fall within the jurisdiction of the Rome Statute can, like adults, claim reparations in order to remedy the harm suffered.[574] The opportunity to not only participate in the course of the criminal proceedings (*Chapter Three*) but also claim reparations, constitutes an additional opportunity for children to be involved in ICC proceedings by pursuing their personal interests.

Reparations for international crimes claimed by a child constitute, in principle though, a twofold novelty: firstly, as with all victims of international crimes, until the establishment of the ICC, victims were unable to claim reparations before an international court or tribunal specifically mandated to adjudicate claims of this nature; secondly, children in particular have only occasionally been involved in other existing international or regional complaint mechanisms pursuing claims on their own behalf. Whether, however, the ICC will indeed be able to implement these two novelties in practice, remains to be seen.

This chapter examines the participation of children in reparation proceedings before the ICC bearing in particular in mind that prior to the establishment of the ICC, victim participation was largely limited to the participation of adult victims. It has been established in the foregoing chapters that child participation in criminal proceedings may require procedural treatment which takes into account the evolving capacities of the individual child. A similar need, which requests child specific treatment from a procedural and substantive perspective, might also exist in relation to child participation in reparation proceedings.

The first case before the ICC, the proceedings against *Thomas Lubanga Dyilo* draws particular attention to child soldiers. The recruitment of children below the age of fifteen years is the only war crime being charged in this case. In light of this uniqueness, also addressed in the course of the previous chapters, the current chapter will scrutinise once more this specific case.[575] The child sensitivity of the

574 A brief overview of the procedural particularities in relation to the child claimant have earlier been published by this author, see Beckmann-Hamzei 2012. The present chapter constitutes an update.

575 ICC-01/04-01/06-2904. See in particular para. 181. The Chamber held that, '[a]lthough in this decision the Trial Chamber has established certain principles relating to reparations and the

law and practice is thus specifically addressed in light of the possibility for children to claim reparations. The analysis also aims to establish to what extent the principles (from a procedural and substantive perspective), which have been developed in this specific case, are also relevant and can be applied more generally to children claiming reparations for harm suffered as a result of an international crime.

The central questions which are examined in this chapter read as follows: how is the right to reparation applied to children in the proceedings before the International Criminal Court? The analysis examines to what extent is or should there be a child claimants participation which constitutes a modified or distinct approach to adult participation. It will be considered in particular whether it is necessary to adjust the procedures regulating reparation claims but also the substantive aspects of reparations specifically for child claimants. Moreover, it will scrutinise to what extent the participation of children in reparation proceedings is in the best interests of the child. Or, whether the participation of children as claimants can be considered not worthwhile because of not providing child victims with a meaningful international remedy?

The chapter commences with a brief overview of the right to reparation – a right which finds its origin in human rights law and which in particular has been implemented by human rights institutions. Specific attention is paid to the question whether and if so how the human rights approach as regards the right to reparation is relevant for child participation in the ICC context. The discussion is followed by a brief analysis of the legal framework of ICC reparation proceedings. Afterwards the research focusses on the specific procedural aspects which played a role in the ICC's practice in relation to child claimants. Taking the different civil nature of reparation proceedings as a starting point, the chapter zeroes in on those features that are of particular relevance to the child. In this regard, the chapter examines the child-specific forms of reparations from a procedural and substantive perspective (5.4.1). Then, the chapter focusses on the child and young adult's eligibility as regards child-specific forms of reparations (5.4.2). Finally, selected issues concerning the implementation of reparation awards in relation to the child claimant are analysed (5.4.3).

Based on earlier findings on the possible transfer of the approaches adopted by human rights institutions to ICC reparation proceedings, the practice of the ICC towards the child claimant is examined in particular in light of the practice of those institutions and in particular Truth and Reconciliation Commissions which are experienced in child rights matters.

---

approach to be taken to their implementation, these are limited to the circumstances of the present case. This decision is not intended to affect the rights of victims to reparations in other cases, whether before the ICC or national, regional or other international bodies.'

5.2 The Child as Beneficiary of the Right to Reparations

The right to reparations

The right to reparation is a general principle of international law. In 1928 the Permanent Court of International Justice ruled that,

> 'it is a principle, even a general conception of law, that any breach of engagement involves an obligation to make reparation.'[576]

Accordingly, damage which is the result of a violation of a rule must be compensated. While this ruling concerned a inter-state dispute and the obligation of a state to compensate the other state in case of a violation, further analysis is necessary in order to determine whether and how individuals can rely on a right to reparations.

The right to reparations has indeed been codified in international and regional human rights law.[577] The first comprehensive and more general international legal document addressing the right to reparations for victims of gross violations of international human rights law and serious violations of international humanitarian law has been agreed upon by the General Assembly only in 2005.[578] In Resolution 60/147 the United Nations' General Assembly adopted and proclaimed the *Basic Principles and Guidelines on the Right to a Remedy and Reparation for Victims of Gross Violations of International Human Rights Law and Serious Violations of International Humanitarian Law*.[579] Principle 11 defines victims' right to remedies as follows:

> '[r]emedies for gross violations of international human rights law and serious violations of international humanitarian law included the victim's right to the following as provided under international law:
>
> (a) Equal and effective access to justice;
> (b) Adequate, effective and prompt reparation for harm suffered;
> (c) Access to relevant information concerning violations and reparation mechanisms.'

576 Permanent Court of International Justice, Case concerning the Factory at Chorzów (Claim for Indemnity) (Merits), Series A, No. 17 (1928), at 29.

577 See, among others, art. 8 of the Universal Declaration of Human Rights, art. 2(3) International Covenant on Civil and Political Rights, art. 39 of the Convention on the Rights of the Child, art. 41 European Convention on Human Rights.

578 Capone 2013,50-57.

579 Basic Principles and Guidelines on the Right to a Remedy and Reparations for Victims of Gross Violations of International Human Rights Law and Serious Violations of International Humanitarian Law, UN Doc. A/60/147 (2005).

The right to reparation is thus part of the right to an effective remedy.[580] Principle 15 provides specifically in relation to reparations that,

> '[a]dequate, effective and prompt reparation is intended to promote justice by redressing gross violations of international human rights law or serious violations of international humanitarian law. Reparation should be proportional to the gravity of the violations and the harm suffered. (…) In cases where a person, a legal person, or other entity is found liable for reparation to a victim, such party should provide reparation to the victim or compensate the State if the State has already provided reparation to the victim.'[581]

Despite the fact that, to date, the right of individuals to reparations has been codified in human rights law, the question remains how victims of violations of international humanitarian law – a distinct branch of international law which applies to parties to an armed conflict – can claim reparations.[582] It has repeatedly been pointed out that international humanitarian law does not provide a procedural right to claim reparations.[583] A major step in order to provide victims of international humanitarian law with such a right has been taken with the UN Basic Principles. These are not limited to victims of violations of human rights law but include victims of serious violations of international humanitarian law.[584] Another step further has been taken with the coming into force of the Rome Statute. Article 75 of the Rome Statute explicitly enables individuals (at the discretion of the Court) to claim reparations for having suffered harm as a result of international crimes within the jurisdiction of the Court. The procedural possibility for individuals to claim reparations for having become victims of breaches of international humanitarian law has thereby entered the field of international criminal law.[585] The earlier addressed gap of a procedural possibility to claim reparations for having suffered harm as a result of a violation of international humanitarian law has thereby been closed to a certain extent, namely in relation to those violations which qualify as victims of an international crime within the jurisdiction of the ICC.

Bearing in mind the aforementioned, the United Nations' General Assembly Basic Principles, despite their non-binding legal force, enjoy broad recognition. This recognition is, for instance, reflected in the fact that the ICC also refers to almost identical formulations in the Rome Statute and the respective rules as regards reparation and in particular the available forms of reparation (5.3, 5.4.3).[586] Further,

580 Donat-Cattin 2008, Article 75, at 1400.
581 See similarly, art. 1 of the Declaration of International Law Principles on Reparation for Victims of Armed Conflict (The Hague, Resolution 2/2010).
582 Droege 2007, at 348.
583 Zegveld 2003, at 487. Kleffner 2002, at 238.
584 Zegveld 2003, at 499.
585 Droege 2007, at 354.
586 For a brief overview of the drafting history on victims' right to reparation before the International Criminal Court, see Donat-Cattin 2008, Article 75, at 1400-1402.

the Court explicitly recognised the relevance of the UN Basic Principles in its case law. In the decision of 18 January 2008, Trial Chamber I ruled that,

> '[i]n light of Article 21(3) of the [Rome] Statute, and taking into consideration the decision of the Appeals Chamber that it "makes the interpretation as well as the application of the law applicable under the Statute subject to internationally recognised human rights", the Trial Chamber has considered the Basic Principles and Guidelines on the Right to a Remedy and Reparation for Victims of Gross Violations of International Human Rights Law and Serious Violations of International Humanitarian Law ("Basic Principles") [...].'[587]

Principles 19 to 23 of the UN Basic Principles refer to the following forms of reparation: restitution, compensation, rehabilitation, satisfaction and guarantees of non-repetition. The available forms of reparations under the ICC reparation framework, in particular with regard to child claimants, will be addressed in detail below (5.4.1).

The child as a beneficiary of the right to reparations

Bearing in mind the aforementioned aspects of the right to reparations one may raise the question whether the right to reparation is also a right of the child. It can indeed be assumed that the child is a beneficiary of the right to reparation.[588] This assumption can be made as the UN Basic Principles do not distinguish between adults and children. Furthermore, in support of this assumption, it is noted that the Preamble of the UN Basic Principles also refers to Article 39 of the UN Convention on the Rights of the Child. Article 39 states that,

> 'States Parties shall take all appropriate measures to promote physical and psychological recovery and social reintegration of a child victim of: any form of neglect, exploitation or abuse; torture or any other form of cruel, inhuman or degrading treatment or punishment; or armed conflicts.'

---

587 ICC-01/04-01/06-1119, para. 35.

588 The other components of the right to a remedy are the right to access justice and the right to know the truth. For a brief overview of the right to a remedy, see Donat-Cattin 2008, Article 68, at 1279; Donat-Cattin 2008, Article 75, at 1400. See, for example, art. 8 of the 1948 Universal Declaration of Human Rights, adopted and proclaimed by General Assembly resolution 217 A (III) (1948), UN Doc. A/810 (1948), at 71; art. 2(3) of the 1966 International Covenant on Civil and Political Rights, 993 UNTS 171; art. 39 of the 1989 Convention on the Rights of the Child, 1577 UNTS 3. See also, Principles 15-18 of the 2005 Basic Principles and Guidelines on the Right to a Remedy and Reparations for Victims of Gross Violations of International Human Rights Law and Serious Violations of International Humanitarian Law, UN Doc. A/60/147 (2005). For further information on the right to reparation for violations of international humanitarian law, see, Gillard 2003, at 529-553. Reparations within the context of international criminal proceedings, see, Zegveld 2010, at 77-111; UNICEF 2010a, at 51; UNICEF 2009b, at 96.

The reference in the Preamble of the UN Basic Principles to Article 39 of the UN Convention on the Rights of the Child underlines that children are also to be seen as beneficiaries of the right to a remedy and thereby also the right to reparation.

Furthermore, the International Law Association also took position to this particular aspect. The Reparation for Victims of Armed Conflict Committee adopted a declaration which specifically addresses the right to reparation for victims of armed conflict. Article 4 (2) of the *Declaration of International Law Principles on Reparation for Victims of Armed Conflict* (The Hague, Resolution 2/210) also states that children are also to be seen as beneficiaries of the right to reparation. The Commentary on this paragraph underlines that,

> 'due account [is] to be taken of situations where victims are in no position to claim themselves, as for example when the victim is incapacitated or a minor child. In these situations, third persons might be legally entitled to claim on behalf of the victim. However, reparation has to be awarded to the victim.'

In the same tenor, the non-governmental organisation *International Center for Transitional Justice* held in a 2011 report that,

> '[t]he right to reparations extends to all victims of gross human rights violations, including children. Few reparations programs have explicitly recognized children as beneficiaries, however, and others have struggled with effectively designing and administering child-sensitive reparations. Child-specific reparations are crucial because they reaffirm the rights of children in face of past violations, attempts to remedy lost opportunities and provide for their futures.'[589]

In similar words, the ICC Trust Fund for Victims pointed out that child victims' right to a remedy and reparation is undeniable.[590]

Specifically in relation to victims of armed conflict, the Reparation for Victims of Armed Conflict Committee of the International Law Association underlined in 2010 that,

> '[i]n view of the relevant state practice and taking note of a strong majority among scholars, the Committee came to the conclusion that until most recently, international law did not provide for any right to reparation for victims of armed conflicts.'[591]

---

[589] Aptel & Ladisch 2011, at 4.

[590] ICC-01/04-01/06-2872, para. 39. See generally on the right to an effective remedy, van Boven 2009, at 22-25. ICC-01/04-01/06-2872, para. 39.

[591] Reparation for victims of armed conflict Committee of the International Law Association, Introduction, Draft Declaration of International Law Principles on Reparation for Victims of Armed Conflict (Substantive Issues) (2010), at 2.

Thus, the International Criminal Court, as the institution which is mandated to rule on reparations for the commission of international crimes, is the first and moreover the only permanent international criminal court, specifically mandated to rule on reparation claims of this nature.[592]

Having established that the child is indeed a beneficiary of the right to reparation one may turn to the second aspect of this paragraph, namely the possibility to transfer a human rights approach to ICC proceedings. Bearing in mind that the roots of this concept lie in general public international law and thus not as such in international criminal or international humanitarian law, the branches of law which are predominantly applied in the context of ICC proceedings, it is necessary to consider whether the findings of human rights institutions (as the institutions being most experienced in ruling on reparation claims which have been filed by individuals) can be referred to as a yardstick for the interpretation of the ICC reparation scheme. The ICC reparation scheme is, after all, in need of such a yardstick as a guiding procedural regulation and practice is almost non-existent. As the regional human rights courts are the judicial institutions with the most experience in applying the right to reparation, this chapter will refer to the practice of the European Court of Human Rights as one example of an experienced judicial institution in this matter.

Article 34 of the ECHR, entitled 'Individual applications' provides that,

> '[t] the Court may receive applications from any person, non-governmental organization or group of individuals claiming to be the victim of a violation by one of the High Contracting Parties of the rights set forth in the Convention or the Protocols thereto.'[593]

Article 41 ECHR states that,

> '[i]f the Court finds that there has been a violation of the Convention or the Protocols thereto, and if the internal law of the High Contracting Party concerned allows only partial reparation to be made, the Court shall, if necessary, afford just satisfaction to the injured party.'

Individuals may thus apply for reparations before the European Court of Human Rights, a possibility in relation to which the Court is well known for having established extensive practice.

592 Donat-Cattin 2008, Article 75, at 1401; Mazzeschi 2003, at 343. For further information on the right to reparation for violations of international humanitarian law, see Gillard 2003, at 529-553. Reparations within the context of international criminal proceedings, see Zegveld 2010, at 77-111; UNICEF 2010a, at 51; UNICEF 2009b, at 96.

593 See also, art. 61(1) of the American Convention on Human Rights.

The possibility to transfer human rights concepts, as for instance established in the case law of the European Court of Human Rights or the Inter-American Court of Human Rights, to ICC proceedings has been elaborated upon in *Chapter One*. It has been argued that based upon Article 21(1)(b) and (3) of the Rome Statute, the ICC is invited to interpret the Rome Statute and its Rules of Procedure and Evidence in light of other international treaties. The Court may therefore not only rule upon child participation in light of the internationally recognised interpretation of the Convention on the Rights of the Child but also in light of other relevant human rights treaties, such as the European Convention on Human Rights. The ICC is therefore advised to carefully assess those mechanisms, which are experienced in child participation.

Trial Chamber I, indeed, seems to follow such an approach in the *Lubanga* case by explicitly stating that,

> 'given the substantial contribution by regional human rights bodies in furthering the right of individuals to an effective remedy and to reparations, the Chamber has taken into account the jurisprudence of the regional human rights courts and the national and international mechanisms and practices that have been developed in this field.'[594]

Seeking guidance in the law and practice of the experienced institutions may, however, only be interesting for the ICC when these institutions have indeed been confronted with cases in which children claim reparations.

One may or may not be surprised that only a small percentage of claims have been brought by children. As a preliminary note, it therefore seems that children have not invoked their right to reparation frequently. Furthermore, neither the procedural nor the substantive aspects of reparation claims submitted by minor claimants are explicitly addressed and regulated in great detail.

The Council of Europe published data on cases before the European Court of Human Rights which deal(t) with child rights issues. The Council points out that at the ECtHR, 303 cases dealt with issues that were relevant to children between 1968 and March 2014.[595] Considering that at the end of 2011 more than 46,000

---

594 ICC-01/04-01/06-2904, para. 186.

595 The Council of Europe provides for an overview of all cases http://www.coe.int/t/dg3/children/caselaw/CaseLawChild_en.asp. Most applications were submitted by parents, see among many others, *Eriksson v. Sweden*, Judgment (Merits and Just Satisfaction) of 22 June 1989, Application no. 11373/85, para. 1; *Mubilanzila Mayeka and Kaniki Mitunga v. Belgium*, Judgment (Merits and Just Satisfaction) of 12 October 2006, Application no. 13178/03. Only in a few cases children applied on their own behalf. See Commission decision, *X. and Y. v. The Netherlands*, Admissibility Decision of 19 December 1974, Application no. 6753/74, at 118-119; Court judgment, *Tyrer v. United Kingdom*, Judgment (Merits) of 25 April 1978, Application no. 5856/72; V. *v. United Kingdom*, Judgment (Merits and Just Satisfaction) of 16

applications have been ruled upon by the ECtHR, the number of cases involving children constitutes a small percentage.[596] Taking a closer look at these cases, it becomes clear that the majority dealt with the substantive protection of children under the ECHR, such as protection under Article 8 ECHR – the right to family life.[597] Most of these cases have been lodged by parents who argued that their conventional right regarding separation from parents or the medical treatment of their children have been violated. Children themselves did not submit a complaint on their own behalf in the vast majority of the cases. This means that children were rather the object of the dispute before the ECtHR instead of taking a more active role as a claimant.

The American alternative at regional level is manifested in the American Convention on Human Rights.[598] As before the Human Rights Committee and the ECtHR, child victims are not excluded from submitting a complaint to the Inter-American Commission of Human Rights.[599] Complaints may be submitted for a violation of their rights committed by Member States of the Organization of American States.[600] Thus far, child victims themselves did not submit a complaint. The Inter-American Court was confronted with cases which were submitted as

December 1999, Application no. 24888/94; *T. v. United Kingdom*, Judgment (Merits and Just Satisfaction) of 16 December 1999, Application no. 24724/94; *S.C. v. United Kingdom*, Judgment (Merits and Just Satisfaction) of 15 June 2004, Application no. 60958/00; *Costello-Roberts v. UK*, Judgment of 25 March 1993, Application no. 13134/87; *D., H. and others v. Czech Republic*, Judgment of 7 February 2006, Application no. 57325/00; *A. v. The United Kingdom*, Judgment (Merits and Just Satisfaction) of 23 September 1998, Application no. 25599/94, para. 7; *A. and B. v. The United Kingdom*, Admissibility Decision of 9 September 1996, Application no. 25599/94.

596 For statistical information see, European Court of Human Rights, pending and decided Applications Allocated to a Judicial Formation, http://www.echr.coe.int/NR/rdonlyres/92D2D024-6F05-495E-A714-4729DEE6462C/0/Pending_applications_chart.pdf; http://www.echr.coe.int/NR/rdonlyres/7B68F865-2B15-4DFC-85E5-DEDD8C160AC1/0/Stats_EN_112011.pdf.

597 Art. 8(1) of the 1953 Convention for the Protection of Human Rights and Fundamental Freedoms states that, '[e]veryone has the right to respect for his private and family life, his home and his correspondence.' *Tyrer v. the United Kingdom*, Judgment (Merits) of 25 April 1978, Application no. 5856/72; *Marckx v Belgium*, Judgment (Merits and Just Satisfaction) of 13 June 1979, Application no. 6833/74; *Johnston and Others v. Ireland*, Judgment (Merits and Just Satisfaction) of 18 December 1986, Application no. 9697/82; *Vermeire v. Belgium*, Judgment (Merits) of 29 November 1991, Application no. 12849/87.

598 1978 American Convention on Human Rights, 1144 UNTS 123.

599 Article 23 in conjunction with 27 Rules of Procedure IACHR. The Inter-American system distinguishes between petitioners and victims. Article 1 of the Rules of Procedure of the IACtHR defines a 'victim' as a 'person whose rights have been violated according to a judgment pronounced by the Court,' while an 'alleged victim' is defined as a 'person whose rights under the Convention are alleged to have been violated.' A 'petitioner' not necessarily the victim itself but the person who actually fills the complaint.

600 Art. 44 American Convention on Human Rights in conjunction with art. 27 of the Rules of Procedure of the IACHR.

representatives of the minor victims either by the parents of the children or NGOs.[601]

It is interesting to also briefly look at the UN human rights mechanism in order to see whether complaints have been submitted by children. To date, just one complaint has been submitted to the UN Human Rights Committee by a 16-year-old boy, while other complaints relevant to children were, as in the case of the ECtHR, submitted by parents or close family members of the child in their own right.[602] The new Protocol under the Convention on the Rights of the Child is likely to be the first complaint mechanism which is specifically designed to provide access to an international complaint procedure for the child. The recently adopted complaint procedure (December 2011) is likely to be the only human rights mechanism which will receive more complaints submitted by minors than adults. Moreover, in contrast to the other human rights treaties, this mechanism (once entered into force) is the only mechanism, which is mandated to address human rights violations *and* selected violations of international humanitarian law.[603] It thereby constitutes the only existing human rights mechanism which will be mandated to rule upon the recruitment of child soldiers. It is important to note that decisions of the Committee on claims submitted by children are legally not binding for the State concerned.

It can be concluded that the child is a beneficiary of the right to reparation. It has also been established that the law and practice of experienced institutions, such as

---

601 *"Street Children" (Villagrán-Morales et al.) v. Guatemala*, 19 November 1999 (Merits), at para. 5; *Yean and Bosico Children v. The Dominican Republic*, 8 September 2005, at para. 5; *Vargas-Areco v. Paraguay*, 26 September 2006, at para. 6. See for further information, Capone 2013, at 190-196.

602 As of 9 April 2008, the Human Rights Committee registered 1777 communications with respect to 82 countries. Statistical survey of individual complaints dealt with by the Human Rights Committee under the Optional Protocol to the International Covenant on Civil and Political Rights (9 April 2008), http://www2.ohchr.org/english/bodies/hrc/stat2.htm. *S.H.B. v. Canada*, Communication No. 192/1985, *S.H.B. v. Canada*, UN Doc. CCPR/C/29/D/192/1985 (1987); *A. and S.N. v. Norway*, Communication No. 224/1987, *A. and S.N. v. Norway*, UN Doc. CCPR/C/33/D/224/1987 (1988); *Darwinia Rosa Mónaco de Gallicchio v. Argentina*, Communication No. 400/1990, *Darwinia Rosa Mónaco de Gallicchio v. Argentina*, UN Doc. CCPR/C/53/D/400/1990 (1995); *Baban et al. v. Australia*, Communication No. 1014/2001, *Baban et al. v. Australia*, UN Doc. CCPR/C/78/D/1014/2001 (2003); *Derksen v. The Netherlands*, Communication No. 976/2001, *Derksen v. The Netherlands*, UN Doc. CCPR/C/80/D/976/2001 (2004).

603 UN General Assembly, Rights of the Child, UN Doc. A/RES/66/141, A/66/PV.89 (2011). Arts. 38-39 of the 1989 Convention on the Rights of the Child, 1577 UNTS 3 and 2000 Optional Protocol to the Convention on the Rights of the Child on the Involvement of Children in Armed Conflict, 2173 UNTS 222. In 2011, an open-ended working group drafted an Optional Protocol to the Convention on the Rights of the Child to provide a complaint procedure against State Parties. General Assembly, Human Rights Council, Seventeenth session, Agenda item 5, Human rights bodies and mechanisms, Report of the Open-ended Working Group on an optional protocol to the Convention on the Rights of the Child to provide a communications procedure, UN Doc. A/HRC/17/36 (2011). See for recent update www.crin.org.

the European Court of Human Rights, can indeed be referred to as yardstick in the context of ICC proceedings. It is, however, also shown that children have not frequently applied for reparations in their own right before the aforementioned human rights institutions.

5.3 Rules and Practice Governing Reparation Proceedings

The few rules and early practice governing reparation proceedings before the International Criminal Court serve as the point of departure for an analysis of the legal status of the child claimant. In turn, the legal framework of child claimant participation is addressed in light of both the general rules applying to reparation proceedings and specific aspects which arise for the child claimant. This approach is chosen in order to examine whether and to what extent the ICC is already or should be encouraged to adopt a child sensitive approach which is to be distinguished from the approach to be taken when adult victims participate.

The analysis is in particular based on the first case and judgment of Trial Chamber I in the proceedings against *Thomas Lubanga Dyilo*. It is noted that procedural details of reparation proceedings, such as the application of eligibility criteria, are left unregulated.[604] Neither do the *travaux preparatoires* serve as a guiding yardstick in relation to the procedural details of reparation proceedings. Instead, the Court itself is vested with the task of developing principles which regulate the award of reparations.[605]

It is due to the major lack of procedural regulation that this chapter immediately includes the first practice of the Court in relation to reparation proceedings in order to provide an overview of the ICC's reparation scheme. The procedural implications of the existing regulation in light of the addressed practice are therefore, in contrast to the approach of the previous chapters, a major part of the current section.

General aspects of reparation proceedings

Pursuant to Regulation 86 of the Regulations of the Court, applications for participation in reparation proceedings have to be submitted to the Registrar. A joint application form for criminal and reparation proceedings has been made available on the website of the Court.[606] The existence of the joint form alludes that the technical matters as regards the information and documents which are to be

[604] ICC-01/04-01/06-2863, para. 10.
[605] Art. 75 Rome Statute.
[606] The joint application form is online available, http://www.icc-cpi.int/menus/icc/structure%20of%20the%20court/victims/forms?lan=en-GB. For further discussion about the information to be provided in the form, see *Chapter Three*.

provided are very similar, if not even the same, as the procedure to be followed when applying for participation in criminal proceedings.[607]

With regard to the additional common administrative aspects of the application procedure, further information can be found in *Chapter Three* (sections 3.4-3.5). The administrative similarity does not imply that participation in the reparation proceedings is dependent on participation in the criminal proceedings. Instead, the Rome Statute and the respective rules do not require that participation in the reparation proceedings necessitates previous participation in the criminal proceedings. Neither is the submission of reparation claims dependent on the conclusion of the criminal proceedings or the commencement of reparation proceedings. Accordingly, victim participation in the criminal and reparation proceedings are in principle two distinctive possibilities of victim participation before the ICC.

Irrespective of the general independence of reparation proceedings, in one aspect, the successful claiming of reparations is definitely interrelated with criminal proceedings. As will be established in greater detail below, individual reparation awards ordered against the accused can only be implemented after a successful conviction of the perpetrator.[608] This, once more, does not imply that victims have to participate in criminal proceedings, but means that criminal proceedings have successfully been concluded before reparation awards can be implemented against a convicted person.

In substantive terms, article 75 of the Rome Statute constitutes the heart of the reparation scheme of the ICC. It states that,

> '[t]he Court shall establish principles relating to reparations to, or in respect of, victims, including restitution, compensation and rehabilitation. On this basis, in its decision the Court may, either upon request or on its own motion in exceptional circumstances, determine the scope and extent of any damage, loss and injury to, or in respect of, victims and will state the principles on which it is acting.'

This provision clearly leaves the Court with a wide discretion as regards reparation procedures and, in particular, the form and implementation of reparation awards. Limited guidance can be found in this provision in relation to the forms of reparations which are addressed in more detail below (5.4.1).

Particular attention is to be paid to the practical handling of requests for reparations. Remarkably, the Trust Fund for Victims, and not the judicial institution of an ICC Chamber, has been mandated by Trial Chamber I to decide upon access or denial of

---

607 See, Rule 94-99 RPE.
608 Rule 98(1) RPE.

the potential beneficiaries.[609] An approach which can be criticised for introducing a procedure which is no longer under judicial scrutiny – while the establishment of the ICC was particularly welcomed for providing victims of international crime with a judicial remedy. Such practice implies that the right to claim reparations right loses its judicial dimension and thereby renders, in fact, the codification of Article 75 of the Rome Statute – to claim remedies - meaningless as regards the right to claim remedies before a judicial institution. As the right to a remedy encompasses the right to access justice, the availability to judicial reparation proceedings is thereby included.[610]

Trial Chamber I's decision in the *Lubanga* case to delegate the substantive processing of reparation claims mainly to the TFV constitutes a development which therefore gives rise to concern. The Chamber itself pointed out that,

> '[it] agrees with the observation of Pre-Trial Chamber I when it stated: The reparation scheme provided for in the Statute is not only one of the Statute's unique features. It is also a key feature. In the Chamber's opinion, the success of the Court is, to some extent, linked to the success of its reparation system. [...]'[611]

The delegation to a non-judicial institution, such as the TFV, which is not an organ of the Court, entails the risk that the success or failure of the reparation proceedings is largely decided outside the ICC.[612] Such a development cannot be said to mirror and accomplish the groundbreaking step that the International Criminal Court is the first permanent international criminal court which does not only aim to combat impunity but also to provide victims of international crimes with an opportunity to claim judicial remedies for the harm suffered. As the judicial remedies before the ICC for victims of international crimes, to date, constitute the only international avenue which might enable victims to enforce their legal right to a remedy, the transferal of this task to a non-judicial institution, not bound by the rule of law, is to be questioned.

Delegation of the task to decide upon the substantive details of reparations to a non-judicial institution means in particular that victims', including children's, legal right to reparation is assessed by an institution, which is not experienced and equipped to address the legal components of the right to a remedy. It may thus be questioned

---

609 Ibid., para. 284.

610 See in this regard, Principle VII 11(1) 2005 Basic Principles and Guidelines on the Right to a Remedy and Reparations for Victims of Gross Violations of International Human Rights Law and Serious Violations of International Humanitarian Law, UN Doc. A/60/147 (2005). Principle IX 17 also refers to reparation judgments, which underlines once more that the right to reparation entails a judicial reparation mechanism when the liability of individuals or institutions has been established.

611 ICC-01/04-01/06-2904, para. 178.

612 Trial Chamber I also delegated the decision taking on the legal representation of victims to the Registry. See, see ICC-01/04-01/06-2904, para. 268.

what the added value of the newly introduced reparation procedure before the International Criminal Court is, if in the end, it is not the Court who decides upon reparation claims. One may even argue that, while the Rome Statute creates the impression that victims, including children, may legally claim reparations, the transfer to the Trust Fund for Victims constitutes a delegation of a judicial task which has not been intended by the drafters of the Rome Statute and thus constitutes a delegation which is not in accordance with the overall idea and objective of victim participation in the proceedings before the ICC. Even if the author of this thesis is of the view that the determination of the legal components of the right to claim reparations should be dealt with within the ICC, it does not take away that one may validly question whether a chamber composed of dominantly criminal law judges is sufficiently experienced in deciding upon on applications of a rather civil law nature. The Court might therefore re-think whether a specialised chamber should be vested with this specific task.

The conclusion that the Court's delegation of a judicial task and mandate as regards reparation claims to the Trust Fund for Victims is criticised in particular in light of the practice of Trial Chamber I. According to Trial Chamber I, the task of the Court is mainly minimised to 'monitoring and oversight functions', instead of pursuing its mandate as provided for in the Rome Statute of the International Criminal Court.[613]

The importance of a procedurally regulated assessment has also been pointed out by the Reparation for Victims of Armed Conflicts Committee of the International Law Association. In 2012, the Committee concluded in its final report to the Sofia Conference that,

> '[a] substantive right to reparation includes a procedural right to access to an effective mechanism to which victims may submit their claims.'

As the current procedural rules of the Trust Fund for Victims do not provide for such procedure for claimants, including child claimants, it may indeed be questioned whether this delegation constitutes a referral to an effective mechanism.

A step further in the course of reparation proceedings relates to the actual award of reparations. As regards the award of reparations, the Trust Fund for Victims has an important role. Rule 98 of the RPE states that,

> '[t]he Court may order that an award for reparations against a convicted person be deposited with the Trust Fund where at the time of making the order it is impossible or impracticable to make individual awards directly to each victims.'

613 Ibid., para. 286.

According to the Rules of Procedure and Evidence, the Trust Fund for Victims may thus be approached and involved upon a Court order when, for instance, the indigence of the convicted person or the large number of claimants prevent an effective award of reparations.

Furthermore, as conflict situations might make it impossible for a child to access the ICC due to ongoing fighting, for instance, children themselves might not at all be in the position to access the Court in order to claim reparations. There is, however, an opportunity that even without submitting a reparation claim, children may nevertheless become beneficiaries of reparation awards. This is because the International Criminal Court may also award reparations on its own motion (*proprio motu*).[614] The OPCV indicated in this regard that Trial Chamber I should indeed make use of this statutory possibility in the reparation proceedings in the *Lubanga* case.[615] This empowerment of the Court could constitute another opportunity for children be beneficiaries of reparation awards. Particular importance may be underlined in relation to child claimants as this possibility may indeed enable children in a more child-sensitive manner to successfully benefit from reparations without having to comply with all the technical and practical difficulties of the application procedure. It still needs to be seen, however, whether at all and to what extent if at all the ICC will make use of this possibility in relation to children. While TRC practice in relation to the forms of reparations will show that children have been singled out as regards the particular forms of reparations, it may be said that a reparation award made by the ICC on the basis of the *proprio motu* power only towards child victims is less likely to ever be taken as the exercise of this competence as such can be expected to occur not frequently. If ever being relied upon by the ICC, it is then rather unlikely that the Court will give an reparation award which is limited to one specific group of victims. As far as the Lubanga case is concerned (the only case which have reached the reparation stage at the time of writing), such approach is not yet feasible.

Child-specific aspects of reparation proceedings

The information which the child is required to submit (irrespective of applying for reparation during trial proceedings or afterwards), amongst others, relates to the child's identity and must contain a rather detailed description and proof of the alleged crime and harm suffered. Similar to when applying for participation in criminal proceedings, a child can be expected to encounter difficulties in providing the administrative and crime-related evidence (*Chapter Three*). Decisive for filling out the application form are, for instance, not only the capacities of the individual child and the available support of adults when filling out the form, but also the

614 Rule 95 of the 2002 Rules of Procedure and Evidence of the International Criminal Court. For a detailed analysis of the ICC reparation regime, see Dwertmann 2010.

615 ICC-01/04-01/06-2904, para. 53.

existence of birth registration administration. After all, when conflict situations separate a child from his/her family and identification documents are not at the disposal of the child, the official registration of a child can be crucial for successfully proving identity. It is therefore that Trial Chamber I ruled that,

> '[i]n the reparations proceedings, victims may use official or unofficial identification documents, or any other means of demonstrating their identities that are recognised by the Chamber. In the absence of acceptable documentation, the Court may accept a statement signed by two credible witnesses establishing the identity of the applicant and describing the relationship between the victim and any individual acting on his or her behalf.'[616]

It is to be remembered that if, irrespective of the subsequent need that the eligibility criteria, form and implementation of reparations need to be child-sensitive, the reparation proceedings themselves, in particular access requirements, do not sufficiently take into account the constraints a child might be confronted with, the aforementioned right of the child to an effective remedy may become meaningless.[617] In this regard, UNICEF research underlines that in order to ensure that children in fact receive repairing benefits, it needs to be taken into account that,

> '[a]ccess may be impeded by a lack of information, information provided in an inappropriate format or a lack of necessary documents, or by fear of reprisal, stigma and violence. For example, children are even more likely than adults to be illiterate and to lack financial resources that might be necessary (such as for travel, photocopying of documents, etc.) to be aware of, find out about or realize their rights. Additional challenges are that children often are not perceived as independent actors entitled to seek or receive reparations in their own right. [...] Addressing such challenges requires meaningful participation by children and their communities and by children's rights organizations.'[618]

Similarly, the *United Nations Guidelines on Justice in Matters involving Child Victims and Witnesses of Crime* suggest that,

> '35. Child victims should, wherever possible, receive reparation in order to achieve full redress, reintegration and recovery. Procedures for obtaining and enforcing reparation should be readily accessible and child-sensitive [...].'[619]

---

616 ICC-01/04-01/06-2904, para. 198.

617 See generally on the right to an effective remedy, van Boven 2009, at 22-25. The ICC Trust Fund for Victims pointed out in similar words that child victims' right to a remedy and reparation is undeniable, see ICC-01/04-01/06-2872, para. 39.

618 UNICEF 2010a, at 56.

619 ECOSOC Guidelines 2005. See also, '36. Provided the proceedings are child-sensitive and respect these Guidelines, combined criminal and reparations proceedings should be encouraged, together with informal and community justice procedures such as restorative justice [...].'

Without going into the details of the application procedure itself, Trial Child I explicitly pointed out that a number of requirements which were also requested when applying for participation in the criminal proceedings, are still to be provided for. As for children applying for participation in criminal proceedings, Trial Chamber I stipulated that,

> '[p]ursuant to Rule 85 of the Rules, reparations may be granted to direct and indirect victims, including the family members of direct victims [...]. In order to determine whether a suggested "indirect victim" is to be included in the reparations scheme, the Court should determine whether there was a close personal relationship between the indirect and direct victim, for instance as exists between a child soldier and his or her parents. It is to be recognised that the concept of "family" may have many cultural variations, and the Court ought to have regard to the applicable social and familial structures. In this context, the Court should take into account the widely accepted presumption that an individual is succeeded by his/her spouse and children.'[620]

While the general distinction between direct and indirect victims was also applied in the course of criminal proceedings, the explicit application of a broad concept of a family and the recognition that children might also qualify as victims through succession constitutes a new development which (thus far) has not been applied in the course of criminal proceedings. Such an interpretation may allow for a wider circle of child claimants to come into consideration for reparations.

Another note needs to be made in relation to the violations for which child victims may seek access to the ICC. As has been elaborated throughout the book, the commission of international crimes leads to high numbers of child victims. Those crimes are, however, not the only violations which occur during conflict situations. Many other violations of the fundamental rights of the child occur simultaneously, such as violations of the right to education and to the enjoyment of the highest standard of health.[621] The *International Center for Transitional Justice* underlined in this regard that,

> '[i]n many cases, the conflict or rights violations disrupt a child's education and destroy her or his family support structure, thus creating a situation where children as young as eight years are left to care and provide for their younger siblings. Adults may already have benefited from education and job training before the conflict and may be in a better position to find a sustainable livelihood. In contrast, in many cases children have nothing to go back to; thus one of the serious consequences of massive human rights violations are the lost opportunities.'[622]

Beneficiaries of ICC reparation awards are, however, only those children who have suffered harm as a result of a crime within the criminal jurisdiction of the Court.

---

620 Ibid., paras. 194-195.
621 Arts. 24 and 28 of the Convention on the Rights of the Child, 1577 UNTS 3.
622 Aptel & Ladisch 2011, at 27.

The judicial mandate of the Court, as in the course of the criminal proceedings, covers war crimes, crimes against humanity and genocide.[623] Accordingly, a child who is the victim of any other violation is not entitled to access the Court in order to request reparations from a convicted perpetrator or to come into consideration for collective reparations.[624] A child can therefore not claim reparations before the ICC, for instance, when it was unable to attend school or suffered from insufficient health care due to conflict situations – rights, which have been provided for under the Convention on the Rights of the Child. This limitation could be considered to lead to an arbitrary situation. This is because child victims of international crimes might, for instance, be eligible for reparations in forms of educational training while children who were not able to attend school as a result of the conflict situation are not eligible for these forms within a ICC context. It is noted that this limitation could be said to find its justification in the determination of the jurisdiction of the ICC, the focus of the Court on individual criminal responsibility and the need to guarantee a fair trial for the accused. Reparation claims from victims of violations beyond the ICC Statute could thereby constitute a threat to the fairness of the proceedings and in particular lack a legal basis under the Rome Statute.

With regard to the potential limitation of beneficiaries to victims of the charged crimes in a particular case, in the same decision Trial Chamber I briefly referred to qualification criteria by limiting the group of potentially entitled beneficiaries to those victims who have suffered harm as a 'result from the crimes of enlisting and conscripting children under the age of 15 and using them to participate actively in the hostilities.'[625] It can be deluded from this practice that, as anticipated above, victims of other child rights violations which have not been charged, are indeed not entitled to claim reparations in the respective case.

It is also noteworthy, that Trial Chamber I in the decision establishing the principles and procedures to be applied to reparations, elaborated upon the standard of proof claimants have to comply with when accessing the ICC. The Chamber explicitly held that,

> '[a]t trial, the prosecution must establish the relevant facts to the criminal standard, namely beyond reasonable doubt. Given the fundamentally different nature of these

623 Art. 5 Rome Statute, Rule 85 of the 2002 Rules of Procedure and Evidence of the International Criminal Court.

624 Rule 94 of the 2002 Rules of Procedure and Evidence of the International Criminal Court state that, '[a] victim's request for reparations under article 75 shall be made in writing and filed with the Registrar.' The procedural particularities, which accompany children when filing an application for reparations are similar to the access related particularities of children in the criminal proceedings and are therefore not repeatedly addressed in the current Chapter. Until 30 September 2011 the Court received 743 applications for reparations from victims, see Registry Facts and Figures - facts up to date as of 30 September 2010, http://www.icc-cpi.int/NR/rdonlyres/F67584DE-F045-45E2-9503-8F4D16B3DEAA/282642/RegistryFactsandFiguresEN.pdf.

625 ICC-01/04-01/06-2904, para. 247.

> reparations proceedings, a less exacting standard should apply. Several factors are of significance in determining the appropriate standard of proof at this stage, including the difficulty victims may face in obtaining evidence in support of their claim due to the destruction or unavailability of evidence. This particular problem has been recognised by a number of sources, including Rule 94(1) of the Rules, which provides that victims' requests for reparations shall contain, to the extent possible, any relevant supporting documentation, including names and addresses of witnesses. Given the Article 74 stage of the trial has concluded, the standard of "a balance of probabilities" is sufficient and proportionate to establish the facts that are relevant to an order for reparations when it is directed against the convicted person. When reparations are awarded from the resources of the Trust Fund for Victims or any other source, a wholly flexible approach to determining factual matters is appropriate, taking into account the extensive and systematic nature of the crimes and the number of victims involved.'[626]

Trial Chamber I introduced as a principle rule in the reparation proceedings in the *Lubanga* case not only a lower evidentiary threshold compared to the standard applied in the course of criminal proceedings, but it also distinguished between reparations awarded directly from the accused and an even lower standard when reparations are awarded through the Trust Fund or another source. Considering the surrounding circumstances, victims of international crimes in general, but also child victims in particular, finding themselves in such a lower standard clearly constitutes a welcome attitude by Trial Chamber I in the *Lubanga* case – even if this is not specifically addressed at child claimants.

At the same time, it seems that it might also encourage victims to apply for participation in the reparation proceedings instead of aiming to participate in the criminal proceedings. As a result of the more lenient evidentiary threshold in the reparation proceedings, it seems that the Court thereby indirectly tries to limit interest and the actual number of victim participants in the criminal process.

5.4 Children Claiming Reparations before the ICC: Current and Future Challenges

It will be established in turn that children indeed claim reparations in the proceedings before the ICC for having suffered as a result of international crimes. The ICC is an institution which (in contrast to human rights institutions) is specifically mandated to adjudicate claims which are based on the commission on international crimes.[627] Prior to the establishment of the ICC, victims of the most

626 ICC-01/04-01/06-2904, paras. 251-254.

627 What remains is international humanitarian law. Despite being the branch of international law which provides for the most specific protection of children during armed conflict, it still fails to provide for a complaint procedure. See among others, Bassiouni 2006, at 204-205; Kleffner 2002, at 238. For further information, see Heintze 2007, 91, at 101; Kleffner & Zegveld 2000, at 384-401.

serious crimes under international law were unable to claim reparations before an international criminal court or tribunal with the exception of the Statutes of the *ad hoc* tribunals. These allow for the restitution of property.[628] Reparation proceedings before the ICC therefore constitute – next to the possibility to apply for participation in the criminal proceedings (*Chapter Three*) – a novelty in international (criminal) justice.[629]

In the case of Cambodia, individuals can also claim reparations before the Extraordinary Chambers in the Courts of Cambodia (ECCC). Due to the primary reliance of the ECCC on national law and the very limited practical relevance of these Chambers' practice in relation to children, the possibility to claim reparations before this judicial institution is not addressed in greater detail in the current research.[630]

Despite the lack of extensive practice with regard to children claiming reparations before the ICC, the permissible practice of various Chambers regarding children's participation in criminal proceedings (*Chapter Three*) provides some insight into a likely reparation approach of the Court.[631] Furthermore, first

---

628 See arts. 24(3) ICTY Statute, art. 23(3) ICTR Statute. Zegveld 2010, at 77-111; Bassiouni 2006, at 241; Bachrach 2000, 7, at 16; Walleyn 2002, 51, at 57; Trumbull 2007, at 786-789.

629 Art. 75 Rome Statute in conjunction with Rule 94 of the 2002 Rules of Procedure and Evidence of the International Criminal Court, Regulation 88 of the 2004 Regulations of the International Criminal Court and Regulation 104 of the 2006 Regulations of the Registry of the International Criminal Court. Gillard 2003, at 545; Dwertmann 2010, at 15-16; Gray 1996, at 77; Ferstman, Goetz & Stephens 2009; Trumbull 2007, at 789. Plenty of legal research has been carried out on reparations in general. See among many others, Bank & Schwager 2007, 367-412; Bílková 2007, 1-11; de Brouwer 2007, 207-237; Bassiouni 2006, at 203-279; Kalshoven 1991, 827-858; Keller 2007, 189-218; Roth-Arriaza 2004, 157-219; Zappala 2010, 137-164; Zegveld 2003, at 497-526; van Boven 1996, 339-355; van Boven 2009, 19-40; Correa, Guillerot & L. Magarrell 2009, 385-414. Zegveld 2010, 77, at 88. In the case of Cambodia, besides the ICC, individuals can also claim reparations before the Extraordinary Chambers in the Courts of Cambodia (ECCC). Due to the primary reliance of the ECCC on national law and the very limited practical relevance of these Chambers' practice in relation to children, the possibility to claim reparations before this judicial institution falls outside the scope of this research. See generally on victim participation before the ECCC, Mohan 2009, 733-775; Bair 2008, 507-552. The Statutes of the *ad hoc* Tribunals only provided for the restitution of property as a form of reparation, see arts. 24(3) ICTY Statute and 23(3) ICTR Statute. For a brief overview of the drafting history on victims' right to reparation before the International Criminal Court, see Donat-Cattin 2008, Article 75, at 1400-1402.

630 Zegveld 2010, 77, at 88. See generally on victim participation before the ECCC, Mohan 2009, 733-775; Bair 2008, 507-552. The Statutes of the *ad hoc* Tribunals only provided for the restitution of property as a form of reparation, see arts. 24(3) ICTY Statute and 23(3) ICTR Statute. For a brief overview of the drafting history on victims' right to reparation before the International Criminal Court, see Donat-Cattin 2008, Art. 75, at 1400-1402.

631 With regard to child participants, see among other decisions concerning child victims of the recruitment crime, ICC-01/04-505, paras. 91, 93, 95, 97, 99. Children as indirect victims - being the immediate family member and dependent of a deceased person often results in personal harm as a result of the death, see ICC-01/05-01/08-320, paras. 41-51. The ICC Registry only provides for general statistical information on the number of applications for reparations. Registry Facts and Figures - facts up to date as of 30 September 2010, http://www.icc-cpi.int/NR/rdonlyres/F67584DE-F045-45E2-9503-8F4D16B3DEAA/282642/RegistryFactsandFiguresEN.pdf.

conclusions can be drawn from the practice of Trial Chamber I as regards reparation claims submitted by children against *Thomas Lubanga Dyilo*. In this case, the Registry informed Trial Chamber I that of the 85 applications which have been submitted in total, 77 applications for participation in reparation proceedings have been submitted by victims or on behalf of victims who argue they were below the age of 15 years at the time of their recruitment as a child soldier.[632] On 28 March 2012, the Registry of the ICC reported to Trial Chamber I that,

> '[o]f the 85 applications, 53 have been introduced by women and 32 by men; 77 applications have been submitted by or on behalf of persons claiming to be under the age of 15 at the time of the events, seven by parents of such persons and one school Director.'[633]

It is noteworthy in this regard that Trial Chamber I, in the decision of 7 August 2012, underlined the importance of ensuring the *accessibility* of the proceedings by not only providing proper information, but also by taking into account the views of the child. The Chamber pointed out that,

> '[t]he victims of the crimes, together with their families and communities should be able to participate throughout the reparations process and they should receive adequate support in order to make their participation substantive and effective. [...]. The Court shall provide information to child victims, their parents, guardians and legal representatives about the procedures and programmes that are to be applied to reparations, in a form that is comprehensible for the victims and those acting on their behalf. The views of the child are to be considered when decisions are made about individual or collective reparations that concern them, bearing in mind their circumstances, age and level of maturity.'[634]

Child victims thus indeed managed to file their applications. The large majority of victims that filed applications for reparations concerns the direct victims of *Thomas Lubanga Dyilo*, namely child victims who were recruited when below the age of fifteen years.

Noteworthy in this regard is that Trial Chamber I unmistakably pointed out that not only those victims who had already participated in the criminal proceedings against *Thomas Lubanga Dyilo* or who had applied for reparations through the application form could participate. Instead, the Chamber held that,

> '[a]ll victims are to be treated fairly and equally as regards reparations, irrespective of whether they participated in the trial proceedings. Notwithstanding the submissions of the defence and the legal representatives of victims, it would be inappropriate to limit

632 ICC-01/04-01/06-2847, para. 9. Until 17 August 2012, 86 applications have been submitted. See, ICC-01/04-01/06-2906.
633 ICC-01/04-01/06-2847, para. 9.
634 ICC-01/04-01/06-2904, paras. 203, 214-215.

> reparations to the relatively small group of victims that participated in the trial and those who applied for reparations.'[635]

It seems that the Court encourages far more victims to participate in the reparation process than limiting the participation to the small group who already successfully applied. It is laudable that the Chamber did not limit the potential group of beneficiaries of reparations in the *Lubanga* case to those victims who were participating in the proceedings at the time of the decision but invites all victims qualifying as direct and indirect victims of the charged crimes.[636] As a result of this positive attitude of the Chamber as regards those victims who have not already participated in the course of the criminal proceedings, the potential group of beneficiaries of reparations is clearly not limited to those victims who participated in the course of the criminal proceedings.

The child claimant can expect to be confronted with similar, if not the same, constraints as in criminal proceedings (*Chapter Three*) when seeking access to reparation proceedings. This assumption can be made since in principle the child has to communicate his/her request for reparations to the Court through the earlier addressed joint application form.[637]

The Chamber pointed out in the same decision that,

> '[t]he victims of the crimes, together with their families and communities should be able to participate throughout the reparations process and they should receive adequate support in order to make their participation substantive and effective.'[638]

Such a victim-centred approach seems to minimise the potential advantage of having already participated during the criminal proceedings. This also means that the added value of child participation in the course of the criminal proceedings. may be questioned even more, since, as was established in *Chapter Three*, participation in the criminal proceedings cannot be considered to be generally in the best interests of the child.

On the other hand, the potential advantage of prior participation may, amongst others, be seen in the fact that in cases which do not lead to a conviction of the alleged perpetrator, further participation and thus hearing of victim's voices is impossible. Waiting until the commencement of reparation proceedings to convince

---

635 ICC-01/04-01/06-2904, para. 187.

636 ICC-01/04-01/06-2904, para. 194.

637 Similarly, aspects related to child victims' representation and the provision of legal aid can also be expected to reoccur. Since this issue has been analysed in relation to the child participant in *Chapter Three*, the following sections are foremost limited to those child-specific particularities that have not been addressed within the context of the criminal proceedings.

638 ICC-01/04-01/06-2904, para. 203.

the Court of victim's alleged suffering entails therefore the risk of never being heard by the International Criminal Court. Furthermore, participation during the criminal proceedings might, which has, however, not yet been proven, pave the way for a stronger position in the course of reparation proceedings. After all, as a result of their successful prior participation, victim's allegations and claims have already been raised and thereby drew the Court's attention to their individual harm suffered.

Moreover, considering that Trial Chamber I ruled that it is not at all examining those requests for reparations which have been submitted to the Registry prior to this decision, it seems that waiting for the public debate which is held at local level constitutes an opportunity for victims to claim remedies which is a lot easier than applying for reparations prior to the local activities (section 5.4.3 Implementation).[639] As the localities should be those which have been mentioned by Trial Chamber I in the judgment and where the crimes for which *Thomas Lubanga Dyilo* has been convicted were committed, the ICC and the potential benefit of reparation are brought close to the victims.[640] In particular for children, the closeness might constitute an opportunity to submit reparation claims which is far more realistic than trying to apply for reparation proceedings via the formalistic avenue and far away in The Hague.

The aforementioned decision of Trial Chamber I dated 7 August 2012 on the principles and procedures to be applied to reparations, as will be shown throughout this chapter, does, in addition to the major silence of the procedural regulation as regards reparations and in particular child specific aspects, not provide for extensive insight into child-specific challenges the child is and can be expected to be confronted with. Those issues, which might arise with regard to the child in the course of reparation proceedings, have therefore (thus far) not been mirrored extensively in the practice of the relevant Chambers. The analysis of the ICC's reparation scheme (to a large extent) can, as a consequence of the aforementioned gaps in law and in practice, only attempt to anticipate on the current and future challenges the child is likely to be confronted with when requesting reparations.[641]

The following sections examine under which conditions, whether and in which form child victims may claim child-specific reparations before the ICC and to what extent a modified approach is required for children in contrast to adults. The section concludes with an examination of the issues concerning the implementation of reparation awards.

Aspects addressed include the child-specific forms of repartions (5.4.1), the eligibility to these (5.4.2) and difficulties in relation to the implementation of

639 The Chamber instructed the TFV to consider these applications, see ICC-01/04-01/06-2904, para. 284. With regard to the public debates at local level, see, para. 282.

640 Ibid., para. 282.

641 Similarly, Ferstman & Goetz 2009b, at 324-333.

reparation awards (5.4.3). The following sections therefore examine whether the ICC, first of all, is the ICC advised to provide different forms of reparations to children compared to other categories of victims? Secondly, should the ICC introduce eligibility criteria for child claimants in order to benefit from child-specific reparations. Finally, is it also necessary to adjust the procedures regulating the implementation of reparation when children are the beneficiaries? This analysis thereby aims to provide insights into the underlying question whether at all or to what extent child participation in reparation proceedings before the ICC is in the best interests of the child or perhaps dispensable for providing child victims with an international remedy?

5.4.1 Forms of reparations

As the Rome Statute and the related procedural rules do not provide for extensive guidance on the forms of reparations - especially not in relation to the child claimant – selected legal documents, the practice of various TRCs and the Inter-American Court of Human Rights is referred to as a yardstick for an evaluation of the ICC reparation scheme as far as the child claimant is concerned. While limited guidance is provided in the final report of the Liberian TRC, the final report of the Sierra Leonean TRC constitutes, up till now, the only TRC report which addresses in more detail children as beneficiaries of specific forms of reparations.[642]

Reparations share the same purposes for both adult and child victims of international crimes, such as undoing injustice, the restoration of justice and annihilating the consequences of the wrongful act(s). It will be established in turn that in addition to the commonly shared objectives, reparations awarded to children are to be made in a child-sensitive form in order to constitute an effective remedy for children from a substantive perspective.[643] This means that while the award of reparations shares a common objective for adult and child victims, the nature of reparations to be provided, as will be seen, differs between adult and child victims.

General aspects concerning the forms of reparations

The central provision concerning reparations, which is applicable to all claimants, can be found in the Rome Statute. Article 75 of the Rome Statute states that,

> '[t]he Court shall establish principles relating to reparations to, or in respect of, victims, including restitution, compensation and rehabilitation.'

---

642 Children also seem to participate in the statements sessions of the Kenyan Truth and Reconciliation Commission, http://www.tjrckenya.org/. For general information on the establishment, mandate and criticism of the Kenyan TRC see, Reliefweb Kenya; Amnesty International Kenya 2008.

643 Ferstman, Goetz & Stephens 2009, at 24-25. See for example Principles 14-15 of the 2005 UN Basic Principles. For a more detailed overview of the purposes of reparations, see Dwertmann 2010, at 37-43; Magarrell 2009, 2; Shelton 2006, at 6-10.

The wording of Article 75 Rome Statute stipulates that the forms of reparations are not limited to restitution, compensation and rehabilitation, which have primarily been developed in the course of State Responsibility and explicitly defined in the UN Basic Principles.[644]

As regards a definition of these forms of reparation, the 2005 UN Basic Principles are useful to refer to. The Basic Principles define restitution, compensation, rehabilitation and satisfaction as follows:

> '19. *Restitution* should, whenever possible, restore the victim to the original situation before the gross violations of international human rights law or serious violations of international humanitarian law occurred. Restitution includes, as appropriate: restoration of liberty, enjoyment of human rights, identity, family life and citizenship, return to one's place of residence, restoration of employment and return of property.
> 20. *Compensation* should be provided for any economically assessable damage, as appropriate and proportional to the gravity of the violation and the circumstances of each case, resulting from gross violations of international human rights law and serious violations of international humanitarian law [...].
> 21. *Rehabilitation* should include medical and psychological care as well as legal and social services.'

Article 75(2) prescribes furthermore that a conviction constitutes the necessary pre-condition for a reparation award. Accordingly, after the conviction of an alleged perpetrator, the Court may order individual awards directly against the convicted person or deposit a(n) (individual or) collective award with the Trust Fund which has been established for the benefit of victims and mandated to assist the Court in reparation issues.[645]

---

644 General Assembly Resolution 60/147 of 16 December 2005, para. 19-22. For further discussion of the types of restitution, rehabilitation and compensation, see, Donat-Cattin 2008, Article 75, at 1403-1404. Dwertmann 2010, at 15-16, 51-56. For further information on the doctrine of State Responsibility, see Bassiouni 2006, at 205-231. As the forms of reparations before the ECCC are mainly to be suggested by the lawyers representing civil parties in the proceedings, the current research does not address the details of this specific reparation scheme. For further information see, FIDH 2011.

645 As the ECCC do not have a trust fund for victims and considering that most of the (alleged) perpetrators are indigent and bearing in mind the fact that the ECCC are not mandated to award individual reparations (being limited to collective and moral reparations, ECCC Internal Ruler 23(1)(a) and (b)), the reparation scheme and the potential forms of reparations to be awarded by the ECCC are not addressed within the ambit of this research. Arts. 75(2) and 79 Rome Statute; Rules 97 and 98 of the 2002 Rules of Procedure and Evidence of the International Criminal Court. Rule 98 states that, '1. Individual awards for reparations shall be made directly against a convicted person. 2. The Court may order that an award for reparations against a convicted person be deposited with the Trust Fund where at the time of making the order it is impossible or impracticable to make individual awards directly to each victim. [...]. 3. The Court may order that an award for reparations against a convicted person be made through the Trust Fund where the number of victims and the scope, forms and modalities of reparations makes a collective award more appropriate.' Assembly of State Parties, Establishment of a fund for the benefit of victims of crimes within the jurisdiction of the Court, and of the families of such victims, Resolution ICC-

Considering that most of the alleged perpetrators in the pending criminal proceedings before the ICC have provisionally been found wholly indigent, with the exception of *Jean-Pierre Bemba Gombo*, reparations in the form of compensation - if restitution is at all possible (which is rather unlikely bearing in mind the underlying crimes) - is in the majority of cases not feasible.[646] Neither is it conceivable that those persons are able to provide for rehabilitation – a form of reparations which is more suitable in cases of State Responsibility, which is a type of responsibility not at issue in ICC proceedings which is limited to the prosecution of individuals.[647] Individual awards for reparations which are made directly against a future convicted person are, therefore, most likely to be ordered in other forms of reparations such as satisfaction.[648]

Bearing the forgoing in mind, it is understandable why Trial Chamber I came to the conclusion that collective reparations, which are to be provided through the Trust Fund for Victims, are to be preferred in the *Lubanga* case. The Chamber ruled that,

> '[g]iven the uncertainty as to the number of victims of the crimes in this case – save that a considerable number of people were affected – and the limited number of individuals who have applied for reparations, the Court should ensure there is a collective approach that ensures reparations reach those victims who are currently unidentified. [...] The convicted person has been declared indigent and not assets or property have been identified that can be used for the purposes of reparations. The Chamber is, therefore, of the view that Mr Lubanga is only able to contribute to non-monetary reparations. Any participation on his part in symbolic reparations, such as public or private apology to the victims, is only appropriate with his agreement'[649]

The Trust Fund for Victims (TFV) may indeed be more suitable and capable of providing for collective awards and the other forms of reparation when, for instance,

---

ASP/1/Res.6, adopted at the 3rd plenary meeting, on 9 September 2002. The mandate of the Trust Fund also provides for the disbursement of reparations to individuals, see, Regulation 59-68 of the 2005 Regulations of the Trust Fund for Victims, ICC-Asp/4/Res.3 See for further information, Shelton 2006, at 230-238.

646 ICC-01/04-01/06-63; ICC-01/04-01/07-79; ICC-01/04-01/07-298; ICC-01/05-01/08-76. ICC-01/04-01/06-2806, para. 10. Trial Chamber I also ruled that restitution is not very likely to be an achievable form of reparations in the *Lubanga* case, see ICC-01/04-01/06-2904, paras. 223-225.

647 Art. 25(1) in conjunction with art. 26 Rome Statute. The forms of reparations as defined in the UN Basic Principles are considered to be forms of reparations which are available in cases of state responsibility, see Gillard 2003, at 535. Dwertmann 2010, at 129-149.

648 Art. 75(2) Rome Statute in conjunction with Rule 94(1)(f) of the 2002 Rules of Procedure and Evidence of the International Criminal Court. Dwertmann 2010, at 150-159. The 2005 UN Basic Principles define satisfaction as follows: '22. *Satisfaction* should include [measures such as] (a) Effective measures aimed at the cessation of continuing violations; (b) Verification of the facts and full and public disclosure of the truth [...]; (c) The search for the whereabouts of the disappeared, for the identities of the children abducted, and for the bodies of those killed, [...]; (e) Public apology, including acknowledgement of the facts and acceptance of responsibility; [...]', para. 22.

649 ICC-01/04-01/06-2904, paras. 219, 269. See also, para. 274.

the number of victims render individual awards inappropriate.[650] Noteworthy in this regard is that in cases where the ICC orders that a reparation award against a convicted person is to be deposited with the Trust Fund, the Board of Directors may decide to complement its 'resources collected through awards for reparations with "other resources of the Trust Fund."'[651] At the beginning of 2011, the total sum of those 'other resources' which are comprised of voluntary contributions from governments, international organisations or individuals, amounted to € 5.8 million. A further increase of voluntary contributions has been pointed out in the Draft Strategic Plan of the Trust Fund in 2013.[652] The largest amount of these resources (€ 4.45 million) has been allocated to activities in the Democratic Republic of the Congo, Northern Uganda and the Central African Republic and may be spent within the ambit of the second mandate of the Trust Fund.

Regulation 50 of the Regulations of the Trust Fund state that the Trust Fund is also mandated to provide

> 'physical or psychological rehabilitation or material support for the benefit of victims and their families.'[653]

In contrast to the Trust Fund's mandate in relation to reparation orders of the Court, this mandate may be implemented irrespective of a prior conviction and reparation award.[654] In addition to the abovementioned amount of resources allocated to particular situations pending before the ICC, currently € 1.5 million has specifically been allocated for the award of future reparations – an increase compared to 2010 where the resources for reparations amounted to € 750.000.[655] It needs to be

---

650 Regulation 69 Regulations of the 2005 Regulations of the Trust Fund for Victims.

651 Regulations 54 and 56 Regulations of the 2005 Regulations of the Trust Fund for Victims.

652 http://www.trustfundforvictims.org/news/tfv-board-directors-approves-draft-strategic-plan-raises-reparations-reserve-€-1-million.

653 For an overview of the Trust Fund's assistance to children and youth, see The Trust Fund for Victims, *Assistance to children and youth*, http://www.trustfundforvictims.org/projects#Assistance%20to%20children%20and%20youth. As stated in the Fall 2010 Programme Progress Report of the Trust Fund for Victims, '[t]he dual mandate of the TFV envisions the possibility for victims and their families to receive assistance separate from and prior to a conviction by the Court, using resources the TFV has raised through voluntary contributions. While this support is distinct from awards for reparations, in that it is not linked to a conviction, it is key in helping repair the harm that victims have suffered […]. [T]he TFV can provide assistance to victims in a more timely manner than may be allowed by the judicial process. Secondly, assistance is targeted to victims of the broader situations before the ICC, regardless of whether the harm they suffered stems from particular crimes charged by the Prosecutor in a specific case.' Trust Fund for Victims, Programme Progress Report, *Learning from the TFV's second mandate: From implementing rehabilitation assistance to reparations* (2010), http://www.trustfundforvictims.org/, at 47. For a more recent overview of the activities of the Trust Fund, see Trust Fund for Victims, Programme Progress Report Summer 2012.

654 Regulations 50 (a) and (b) of the 2005 Regulations of the Trust Fund for Victims. 2010 Trust Fund for Victims, Programme Progress Report, at 40.

655 Regulations 21 and 47, 48 of the 2005 Regulations of the Trust Fund for Victims. 2010 Trust Fund for Victims, Programme Progress Report, at 40, http://www.trustfundforvictims.org/financial-info.

underlined that this amount constitutes the available Trust Fund resources for reparation awards at a specific moment for all cases before the ICC – while an exact number of all potential cases before the ICC cannot be given in advance. Bearing in mind the indigence of most alleged perpetrators, this limited amount is unlikely to be sufficient to finance the entirety of potential (individual or collective) reparation claims of large numbers of claimants if, in particular, compensation is requested. As a result, the need to complement the reparation allocated resources with 'other resources' of the Trust Fund for Victims does not only seem to be expectable, but has also been suggested by Trial Chamber I in the *Lubanga* case.[656]

Child specific aspects concerning the forms of reparations

With regard to the forms of reparations which could be considered to be adequate for child victims of international crimes, it is noted at the outset that due to children's steady psychological and physical developmental status (as reflected in the principle of the evolving capacities), reparations for children should take sufficiently into account the particular needs of children as reflected in the

> 'interdependence of children's political, civil, economic and social rights [...] and consider children who have experienced violations of a broad set of rights [...].'[657]

The *Key Principles for Children and Transitional Justice* request in particular that,

> '[r]eparations programmes should be based on a careful assessment of the harms suffered by girls and boys during armed conflict and political violence to determine their individual and collective needs. [...] In determining reparations for children, due account should be taken of the relevant provisions and principles of the CRC, such as the right to health care and education and the rights of children with disabilities to special care.'[658]

The Registry of the ICC pointed out in the *Second Report on Reparations* in the *Lubanga* case that,

> '[f]or children who lose their childhoods through conscription, and the opportunities and possibilities it affords, loss of social, education and familial opportunities are a key form of harm inflicted through conscription. Such forms of harm have been widely recognized in international jurisprudence.'[659]

Accordingly, wiping out the consequences of the wrongful act(s), for instance, requests that reparations awarded to children are to be targeted in the sense that their particular needs are accommodated. It thereby needs to be taken into account

---

656 ICC-01/04-01/06-2904, paras. 271-274.
657 UNICEF 2010a, at 55.
658 UNICEF 2010b, at 415. Shelton 2006, at 298.
659 01/04-01/06-2806, para. 21.

that full reparation of the harm suffered by the child during armed conflict cannot easily be imagined; moreover it may not even be possible.[660] Repairing the loss of family members, irrecoverable bodily harm and foremost the loss of a person's (entire) childhood are in itself not eligible for recovery.[661]

The *International Center for Transitional Justice* held in this regard in a 2011 report that,

> '[t]he right to reparations extends to all victims of gross human rights violations, including children. Few reparations programs have explicitly recognized children as beneficiaries, however, and others have struggled with effectively designing and administering child-sensitive reparations. Child-specific reparations are crucial because they reaffirm the rights of children in face of past violations, attempts to remedy lost opportunities and provide for their futures.'[662]

It is therefore argued in this research that the distinguishing factors between adult and child specific forms of reparations concern in particular the following three aspects, namely, access to and provision of child specific health care, education and family live/shelter. While all victims of international crimes might be in need of health care, access to health care is to be provided in a manner which also enables children to benefit from health care measures. This is because a large group of children, depending on the individual evolving capacities, is likely to be dependent on adults when seeking access to health care. In other words, in situations in which support persons are not at hand, a particular group of child victims of international crimes might face difficulties in accessing health care measures. Furthermore, not being in the position to benefit from health care measures which also aim to provide assistance as regards the harm which requests an immediate response exposes children to the risk to suffer even further from neglect as one of the potential consequences of situations in which international crimes are committed.[663]

The second aspect which calls for child specific forms of reparations relates to children's need to benefit from educational training. While education is usually delayed if not even provided at all during and as a result of conflict situations, children who are for these reasons prevented from participating in educational programs are particularly disadvantaged. This is, for instance, because sufficient educational training is, *inter alia*, crucial for enabling the child to build up a stable future in particular in economic terms.[664] Considering the before mentioned, the more important it is that children are entitled to receive forms of reparations which aim to fill the gaps of educational training in order to enable the child to build up a stable future on the basis of those skills which are taught during educational trainings. In contrast to children, adults (generally speaking though) face not the

660 UNICEF 2010a, at 51. Mazurana & Carlson 2010, at 25.
661 Mazurana & Carlson 2009, 162-214.
662 Aptel & Ladisch 2011, at 4.
663 Tyler, Allison and Winsler 2006, 3.
664 Hammarberg 1990, 100.

difficulty of having missed educational training when having reached adulthood prior to the commencement of the conflict situation. As a result, they are in principle capable to rebuild their economic existence based on the educational and vocational training they have benefitted from when peace is re-established. Child specific forms of reparations should therefore include educational training which addresses the individual needs of the victims, taking in particular into account the particular educational phase the child claimant has not been able to benefit from as a result of having suffered from international crimes. This also means, that young adults who have been victims of a crime within the jurisdiction of the ICC and who have been prevented from participating in educational programs during childhood as a consequence of the conflict situation should also be able to come into consideration for educational programs being award despite having reached majority in the meanwhile.

The third distinguishing core factor relates to children's need to be provided with sufficient shelter as a measure which could be provided for by reparation awards. While family live cannot per definition be expected to be re-established after the course of conflict situations, providing children with shelter in terms of a safe environment constitutes the core condition in addition to essential health care measures. Without a safe environment, the healthy development of the child in accordance with their evolving capacities is not easy to be ensured if not even impossible.

The aforementioned pillars of forms of reparations to children complements the approach developed by the inter-American Court, the so called 'damage to a life plan' concept, which also calls for a holistic view as regards the forms of reparations to be provided to child victims.[665]

Turning next to the characteristics of ICC reparation proceedings, when considering potential forms of reparations, huge numbers of victims, including child victims, are to be expected to claim reparations before the ICC. Reparations in the form of compensation, in particular individual cash payments, are less likely to be awarded to (individual) children. While the example of Germany shows that a large number of victims as such does not prevent cash payments to be awarded, as illustrated by the reparation agreement which was concluded between Israel and the Federal Republic of Germany in 1952 but also the 772 million Euros which Germany agreed in 2013 to award to Holocaust survivors, such approach, at least to date, seems less likely in the context of ICC proceedings.[666] This is because the currently amount of financial resources which are at the disposal for victims in the course of ICC proceedings, make it simply not likely that individual cash payments constitute a realistic form of reparation to be awarded.[667] In addition, considering the

---

665 See in this regard, Chamberlain 2014, at 212.

666 Honig 1954, 564; Spiegel 2013 http://www.spiegel.de/international/germany/germany-to-pay-772-million-euros-in-reparations-to-holocaust-survivors-a-902528.html.

667 The final report of the Sierra Leonean TRC underlined that reparations in the form of cash payments are not generally considered to be appropriate bearing in mind the large number of

importance of health care, education and shelter as forms of reparation for children, it may generally be questioned whether cash payments are adequate for young claimants.

Considering furthermore the indigence of the majority of the (alleged) perpetrators currently facing judicial proceedings before the ICC, it is neither likely that the ICC will award reparations in the form of restitution and rehabilitation if not being deposited from the Trust Fund for Victims.

Alternatively, reparations in the form of satisfaction and/or guarantees of non-repetition could constitute forms of reparations directly ordered against the convicted person since these forms of reparations can be offered independently of the financial constraints of the convicted person. The Registry of the ICC suggested in its Second Report on Reparations that collective awards could even be provided to a group of victims "as a Whole". It underlined that,

> '[i]n the context of the Lubanga case specifically, collective award to a group of victims as a whole would for instance be appropriate in a situation where a large number of children had been abducted for purposes of child conscription from a particular locality resulting in enduring harm to the social fabric of the community.'[668]

Legal research and international practice on how a child's needs could be reflected in child-specific forms of reparations is, to date, available to a very limited extent. The thus far available guidance on child-specific forms of reparations is addressed in turn. Particular attention has been granted to child beneficiaries within a few international documents. More extensive guidance can be found in the final report of the Sierra Leonean Truth and Reconciliation Commission.[669] The form of reparation awards to child claimants therefore confronts the ICC with the difficulty that major guidance, in particular within the context of judicial proceedings, is non-existent. This omission, however, constitutes at the same time a challenge for the ICC to promote that children, for the first time in international criminal justice, will benefit from child-specific and therefore child-sensitive reparation awards.

---

victims and, in particular, the expressed preference of individual victims to receive reparations in the form of social services, see TRC Sierra Leone Vol. 2, Chapter 4, Reparations, at 245.

668 ICC-01/04-01/06-2863, para. 73. See also, Trial Chamber I's elaboration, see ICC-01/04-01/06-2904, paras. 226-231.

669 Mazurana & Carlson 2010, at 1-2. In addition, the following truth commissions also mentioned children as particular beneficiaries of reparations: South Africa, Guatemala (Commission for Historical Clarification and Recovery of Historical Memory Project), Peru, Timor-Leste and Liberia, UNICEF 2010a, at 88. The Sierra Leonean TRC, however provided for the widest range of crimes, including sexual and gender-based crimes, that qualify children to benefit from reparation programmes (individual reparation awards have, however, not yet been implemented). For further information see, Mazurana & Carlson 2010, at 12-14. For an overview of the mandates of the various TRCs, see Parmar 2010.

Little guidance as to the forms of reparations can be found, for instance, in the Convention on the Rights of the Child. Article 39 of the Convention on the Rights of the Child points out that,

> 'States Parties shall take all appropriate measures to promote physical and psychological recovery and social reintegration of a child victim of: any form of neglect, exploitation, or abuse; torture or any other form of cruel, inhuman or degrading treatment or punishment; or armed conflicts. Such recovery and reintegration shall take place in an environment which fosters the health, self-respect and dignity of the child.'

Article 6(3) of the Optional Protocol to the Convention on the Rights of the Child on the involvement of children in armed conflict reflects a similar request that children are in need of targeted reparations by requesting States Parties to

> 'take all feasible measures to ensure that persons within their jurisdiction recruited or used in hostilities contrary to the present Protocol are demobilized or otherwise released from service. States Parties shall, when necessary, accord to such persons all appropriate assistance for their physical and psychological recovery and their social reintegration.'[670]

Similarly, the *United Nations Guidelines on Justice in Matters involving Child Victims and Witnesses of Crime* suggest that,

> 'reparation may include restitution from the offender ordered in the criminal court, aid from victim compensation programmes administered by the State and damages ordered to be paid in civil proceedings. Where possible, costs of social and educational reintegration, medical treatment, mental health care and legal services should be addressed.'[671]

These international documents establish that reparations to children ought to be ordered in the form of rehabilitation measures if restitution or financial compensation is not conceivable. The Registry of the ICC, however, critically pointed out that it is to be taken into account that,

> '[i]n the specific context of the Lubanga case a number of factors are significant as regards the practicability or feasibility of individual or social rehabilitation as a form of reparation. The first is cost. While the provision of medical rehabilitee, including measures such as prosthetic treatment, undoubtedly has the potential to substantially alleviate the harm suffered by child soldiers, some of whom have been grievously injured in the course of hostilities, it is also a resource intensive form of reparation. For instance, the establishment and operation of some form of medical service capable of providing various forms of assistance to an appropriate category of

670 2000 Optional Protocol to the Convention on the Rights of the Child on the Involvement of Children in Armed Conflict, 2173 UNTS 222.

671 ECOSOC Guidelines 2005, para. 37.

victims would require trained and skilled professional staff, certain forms of specialized equipment might also be necessary depending on the help the programme was established to provide and such a programme could also be expected to attract significant operational costs. Moreover, the greater the number of victims such a programme sought to assist the greater these costs could be expected to be. Given the resource intensive nature of rehabilitation programmes, it should therefore be born in mind that the establishment of such a programme may have implications for the other forms of reparation that it would be possible to award and, more generally, for the number of victims whom it would be possible to assist.'[672]

Clearly, the Registry underlines the financial limitations which have implications for the forms of reparations to be awarded. Compared to the reparation which Germany agreed upon to award from 2014 onwards to Holocaust survivors, which, *i.a.*, explicitly covers the medical treatment of the victims, the provision of medical treatment in the case of former child soldiers confronts the ICC with serious difficulties.[673] A failure to provide adequate medical treatment, in particular the treatment of those child victims who are in need of prosthetic treatment might, if not being provided, lead to meaningless reparation from a child perspective. This may be assumed, because it is a fact that the physical recovery constitutes the *condition sine qua non* for benefitting from any other form of reparation. Deciding upon the forms of reparation to be awarded in light of the most immediate needs of child victims therefore seems to be a necessity if reparation are to be effective from the victim's perspective. In other words, educational training as a form of reparation, despite being of crucial importance for child victims, can be expected to not be of use for the beneficiaries if physical constraints which are the result of the victimisation hinder the victim to access the training.

Rehabilitation, as was explained before, is furthermore not realistically a form of reparation which convicted perpetrators are frequently able to provide. Notwithstanding the lack of guidance of these documents in terms of reparations ordered directly against a convicted person, they nevertheless underline the importance of rehabilitation and reintegration measures for child victims, which has, indeed also been recognised by Trial Chamber I in the *Lubanga* case.[674]

In addition to the international legal documents that explicitly refer to the child in terms of reparation, the final report of the Sierra Leonean Truth and Reconciliation Commission provides for further guidance by recommending particular forms of reparations to child claimants.[675] While selective forms of reparations which have

672 ICC-01/04-01/06-2863, para. 96.
673 Spiegel 2013.
674 ICC-01/04-01/06-2904, paras. 232-236.
675 It needs to be noted that the recommended reparations in the final report of the Sierra Leonean TRC still have to be implemented by the government of Sierra Leone. Most TRCs failed to specifically address the issue of reparations to be awarded to children. See in this regard, Mazurana & Carlson 2010, at 9. The Commission was mandated to recommend reparations. See

been recommended by the TRC to the Government of Sierra Leone could also be directly ordered against convicted persons in the context of ICC reparation proceedings, the majority of reparations recommended by the Sierra Leone TRC are, due to the collective character and financial complexity, more suitable to be deposited with the Trust Fund for Victims if similarly applied within ICC reparation proceedings.

Depositing reparation orders with the Trust Fund constitutes an option, which would enable the Court to address the needs of large groups of victims, including particular measures for children. It is to be noted, that the mandate of the Trust Fund in this particular context constitutes a welcome possibility in order to provide targeted reparations to the victims. This position is to be distinguished from the earlier made general criticism (section 5.3) as regards the approach of Trial Chamber I taken in the *Lubanga* case by transferring the decision on reparation awards as such to the TFV. While the Trial Chamber's approach taken is criticised for transferring judicial responsibilities to a non-judicial organ, the decision on the actual forms of reparation is seen as a task which requests especially insights into the substantive needs of the victims and not the question whether the victim fulfils the legal requirements for coming at all into consideration for reparation. A decision by the TFV on the forms of reparation which reflect most adequately the needs of the victim therefore constitutes a decision which the TFV could be equipped and mandated to take.

An appropriate form of reparation awards ordered directly against a convicted person could, for instance, be of symbolic nature. The TRC of Sierra Leone suggested that individuals could be ordered by the ICC to acknowledge their crime(s) committed against children and publicly apologise.[676] The value of such apology is, however, prior to such an order to be assessed on a case-by-case basis. This is because a forced apology, which does not reflect that the perpetrator means to honestly apologise is of any value to the victims.

The majority of recommendations made by the Sierra Leonean Commission relate to health or education benefits and are therefore suitable to provide the ICC with guidance if reparation orders are deposited with the Trust Fund for Victims.[677] The Sierra Leonean TRC recommended measures such as:

- assistance to children branded with scars
- health care for amputees or other war-wounded children
- health care for child victims of sexual violence

Article XXVI of the 1999 Lomé Peace Agreement (Ratification) Act and section 7(6) of the 2000 Act to establish the Truth and Reconciliation Commission in line with Article XXVI of the Lomé Peace Agreement and to provide for related matters (2000 TRC Act).

676 TRC Sierra Leone Vol. 2, Chapter 4, Reparations, at 263.

677 Ibid., at 250. See also, for the particular need of war-affected children to receive reparations in the form of educational training, Capone 2010, 98-110.

- free counselling and psychological support
- free education at a basic level for all children
- free education until senior secondary school level for particular groups of children, including war-wounded children, orphans, abducted children and former child soldiers.[678]

By recommending specific reparations for children, the Commission recognised that children constitute a particular group of beneficiaries which are in 'dire need of urgent care […] and specific measures of reparations'.[679] The Sierra Leonean TRC concluded that it is also necessary to distinguish among children themselves and called for specific forms of reparations for particular groups of children. The final report points out in this regard that,

> '[w]hereas many of the recommendations of the Commission refer to all the children in Sierra Leone, the Commission is nevertheless convinced that some specific reparations measures need to be taken in respect of those categories of children who suffered during the war or that still suffer from the consequences of the war such as abducted children, forcibly conscripted children and orphans. The Commission places particular focus on restoring lost educational opportunities for children.'[680]

Likewise the final report of the Liberian TRC recommended particular forms of reparations to be awarded to specific groups of children. The Commission pointed out that,

> '[w]hile reparations generally should avoid targeting specific categories of children, certain groups of victims might need special attention. In particular, reparations should include specific provisions for those victims who have been falling through the cracks of specific post-conflict programs targeted at children, notably former CAFF [children associated with the fighting forces] who have not gone though the DDRR process, girls who have been victims of sexual violence, rape, and sexual slavery, children separated from their parents and family members, children with severe psychosocial trauma and children with social adaption and reintegration problems.'[681]

In line with the above, the Sierra Leonean and Liberian TRCs, in contrast to other TRCs, also recommended particular reparations for child victims of sexual and gender-based violence, such as reparations which provide treatment to the harm suffered as a result of maltreatment of the reproductive system of girls and young

678 TRC Sierra Leone Vol. 2, Chapter 4, Reparations, at 258-259, 261.

679 Ibid., at 242-243.

680 Ibid., at 243.

681 Republic of Liberia Truth and Reconciliation Commission, Volume Three: Appendices, Title II: Children, the Conflict and the TRC Children Agenda (2009), http://trcofliberia.org/reports/final-report, at 108.

women, including HIV-testing as victims of gender-based violence are more likely to be HIV positive.[682]

The ICC could be particularly inspired by the final report of the Sierra Leonean TRC when ordering future reparation awards for a variety of reasons: Firstly, the ICC is likely to be confronted with similarly large numbers of claimants - reparation orders beyond the form of satisfaction or guarantees of non-repetition when ordered directly against the convicted persons are therefore not likely to constitute suitable forms of reparations.

Secondly, the focus of the Sierra Leonean TRC could encourage the ICC to deposit reparation awards with the Trust Fund in order to encourage a collective approach towards children by, for instance, ordering measures relating to the particular health and educational needs of child claimants. Such a need has not only been explicitly referred to the Registry of the ICC, but also by the OPCV which represents child claimants in the proceedings against *Thomas Lubanga Dyilo.*[683] Thirdly, as in the case of the Sierra Leonean TRC, the ICC might also be advised to distinguish between the needs of particular groups of children. In other words, the ICC is likely to be confronted not only with child claimants who have perpetrated themselves international crimes as former child soldiers – being thus perpetrator and victim at the same time - but also child victims or (victim) witnesses of other crimes within the jurisdiction. Forms of reparations will therefore need to reflect the differences which flow from the various procedural capacities. While there might be a large number of child victims who are in need of medical treatment – irrespective of their procedural capacity – former child soldiers might be in need to benefit in particular from demobilisation, disarmament and reintegration measures. They are thus not only likely to be in need of health and educational measures. This particular group of child victims may therefore be said to be in need of a broader variety of reparations compared to child victims of other international crimes. Children who are victims of other international crimes, such as sexual violence might be in need of particular psychological treatment instead. Consequently, the particular form of reparation for child victims is to be assessed on a case-by-case basis and should in particular focus on the immediate needs of the victim in order enable the victim to benefit from the awarded reparation.

The importance of child-specific measures and the effectiveness of addressing children's needs on a collective basis is also reflected in the current projects of the Trust Fund for Victims. These focus not only on counselling, vocational training and the reintegration of former child soldiers and/or abductees, but also on the measures to be taken for children orphaned by war, in particular the counselling and material support for family members who care for children who lost their parents

---

682 See similar request, UNICEF 2010a, at 56. Mazurana & Carlson 2010, at 15. TRC Liberia, Volume Three: Appendix, at 108-109.

683 ICC-01/04-01/06-2863, paras. 47-61, 98-105.

during war.[684] The Fall 2010 Programme Progress Report of the Trust Fund underlines that ensuring that large numbers of children benefit from the Trust Fund's projects does not entail that targeted, thus child-specific, measures cannot be provided at the same time. The Trust Fund describes its approach, namely 'targeting both specific categories and specific needs' using an example from one of its projects in Ituri, Eastern Congo:

> 'Many of these children were abducted into fighting forces, but others were made vulnerable by war in other ways: some lost their parents, some lost their entire families. In designing the project so that all of these children impacted by conflict are supported together, former child combatants can avoid the label of "child-soldier". This is especially important as one of the primary goals of reintegration programmes is to help young people escape stigma and discrimination from their families and communities.'[685]

With regard to the reintegration of former child combatants and abducted children, the TFV implemented particular projects which

> 'utilize a combination of individual and collective approaches whereby each youth is (1) provided with a kit containing most of the supplies needed for his or her livelihood rehabilitation activity of choice (such as a sewing machine for tailoring or goats for breeding), and (2) is integrated into a group with other youth implementing similar activities.'[686]

The Trust Fund decided to implement projects for child soldiers and/or abductees by combining individual approaches and programmes offered to communities after doing a survey among this particular group of victims.[687] In Northern Uganda, on the other hand, the same group of victims indicated a preference for individual benefits.[688] Thus, depending on the perception of former child soldiers in the specific post-conflict community - which is often determined by the role of family, communities and cultural aspects of a particular society - children benefited from individualised reparation projects. If considered more suitable, a combination with community projects were also implemented by the Trust Fund.[689]

This practice underlines, that generalised forms of child-specific reparations do not necessarily reflect the needs of children belonging to a particular post-conflict society. ICC awarded reparations targeting the needs of child claimants are

---

684 The Trust Fund for Victims, *Assistance to children and youth.*

685 Trust Fund for Victims, Programme Progress Report, *Learning from the TFV's second mandate: From implementing rehabilitation assistance to reparations* (2010), http://www.trustfundforvictims.org/, at 6.

686 Ibid., at 13.

687 Ibid., at 13. See similarly the request of the OPCV to implement a combination of individual and collective reparations in the *Lubanga* case, ICC-01/04-01/06-2863, para. 14.

688 Ibid., at 14.

689 See with regard to the need to take sufficiently into account the role of family, community and culture when awarding reparations to children, Mazurana & Carlson 2010, at 19-21.

therefore also to be ordered in light of the specific needs of child claimants within particular conflict societies.

Taking a closer look at the decision of Trial Chamber I in the *Lubanga* case on the principles and procedure to be applied to reparations, it can be concluded that as a first step, the Chamber's approach is promising. Though only very briefly, the Chamber did explicitly state that the age of a child victim constitutes a crucial factor when deciding upon forms of reparations. The Chamber held that,

> '[p]ursuant to Article 68(1) of the Statute, one of the relevant factors – which is of high importance in the present case – is the age of the victims. Pursuant to Rule 86 of the Rules, the Court shall take account of the age-related harm experienced by, along with the needs of, the victims of the present crimes. Furthermore, any differential impact of these crimes on boys and girls is to be taken into account. In reparations decisions concerning children, the Court should be guided, *inter alia*, by the Convention on the Rights of the Child and the fundamental principle of the "best interests of the child" that is enshrined therein.'[690]

Unfortunately, the Chamber did not elaborate in detail to what extent the Convention on the Rights of the Child and the principle of the best interests of the child are to be taken into account. Furthermore, the Chamber did not only underline the importance of reparations which adequately accommodate the suffering of victims of sexual and gender-based violence, but also called for a 'specialist, integrated and multidisciplinary approach.'[691] Also a case-by-case approach has been indicated as being appropriate – without elaborating, however, on potential difficulties in achieving such an approach.[692] Forms, such as rehabilitation and reintegration programmes for former child soldiers, medical services and assistance with housing and education have – as was the case in the mechanisms addressed before – been suggested by Trial Chamber I as constituting adequate forms of reparations.[693]

5.4.2 Eligibility

As a preliminary note it is to be pointed out that the decision of Trial Chamber I of 7 August 2012 establishing the principles and procedures to be applied to reparations in the *Lubanga* case did not address any aspect relating to eligibility.[694] One may therefore wonder whether eligibility is indeed to be expected to be an issue when child claimants participate in reparation proceedings. It is established in turn that this is indeed the case.

The silence of Trial Chamber I as regards eligibility criteria in this specific decision might be explained by the fact that parties and participants themselves did

690 ICC-01/04-01/06-2904, paras. 210-211.
691 Ibid., para. 207.
692 Ibid., para. 213.
693 Ibid., paras. 216, 221.
694 ICC-01/04-01/06-2904.

not raise issues relating to the eligibility to child-specific forms of reparations. It might also be simply unconsciously that the Chamber did not rule on this aspect.

Based on the experience of the Sierra Leonean Truth and Reconciliation Commission, which is addressed in more detail in the previous section dealing with the forms of reparations, it can be argued that the eligibility for child specific-reparations constitutes an issue which also might arise in future ICC reparation proceedings. Considering in particular the large number of potential child claimants, the ICC might simply be compelled to introduce eligibility criteria in order to be able to adequately divide the available but limited sources among child claimants. Considering furthermore, that child claimants will usually, with the exception of the *Lubanga* case, will not constitute the only group of victims which is potentially entitled to receive reparations the Court can be said to be in even greater need to introduce eligibility criteria. This is because the simultaneous prosecution of other crimes besides the recruitment crime automatically widens the categories of potential claimants beyond the group of child claimants. In other words, in order to ensure that those child claimants who are in greatest need of child-specific reparation measures as a consequence of the harm suffered from an international crime will indeed receive such reparations, might deem it indispensable to introduce eligibility criteria.

At the same time, the application of eligibility criteria will most likely limit the group of potential beneficiaries. Such limitation will then also confront the Court with the difficulty to decide upon the question who can be considered to be in greatest need to benefit from child-specific forms of reparation. In line with the aforementioned, the Court can also be expected to be confronted with the question of whether child-targeted reparations are limited to the group of claimants below the age of eighteen or whether young adults might also be potential beneficiaries of child-targeted reparations. These questions, irrespective of the fact that it is not of a legal nature, unavoidably requests the ICC again, to look at a holistic approach when dealing with children in the course of the proceedings in order to implement a child-sensitive approach as regards the child claimant. As it has been established throughout this research, such child-sensitive approach is indispensable in order to adequately accommodate the child in the proceedings – be it as participant in the criminal proceedings or as claimant in reparation proceedings.

In contrast to the previous lack of child-specific regulation, selected TRC practice offers some reference on eligibility criteria. In addition to the limited guidance provided in the final report of the Liberian TRC, the final report of the Sierra Leonean TRC constitutes, up till now, the only TRC report which addresses in more detail children as beneficiaries of specific forms of reparations and provides guidance on the application of eligibility criteria.[695] Truth and Reconciliation

695 Children also seem to participate in the statements sessions of the Kenyan Truth and Reconciliation Commission, http://www.tjrckenya.org/. For general information on the

Commissions, such as the TRC for South Africa, Peru or Timor-Leste mention children as beneficiaries, but do not provide guidance with regard to the particular aspect of eligibility.[696]

The Sierra Leonean TRC limited the group of child beneficiaries to particular groups of child victims, such as war-wounded victims, victims of sexual violence, children who were orphaned as a consequence of any abuse or violation within the TRC's mandate. In addition, the TRC set an eligibility condition as regards the age of child claimants. The Sierra Leonean TRC ruled that, firstly, the crime causing harm to the child victim should have occurred between 23 March 1991 (beginning of the conflict) and 1 March 2002 (lifting of state of emergency); secondly, only those children who were eighteen years of age or younger on 1 March 2002 were eligible for reparations for children.[697] As a consequence, young adults who suffered from violations during their childhood but reached majority before 1 March 2002, were not considered to be eligible for those reparations which were particularly designed to address the needs of children.

The final report of the Liberian TRC, on the other hand, established that children *and* young adults should be eligible for child-specific forms of reparations. It stated that,

> '[r]eparations should aim at repairing the consequences of violations borne by children during the Liberian conflict. There should be symbolic and material reparations for Liberia's children *and* young adults' (emphasis added).[698]

Having reached majority, therefore, in view of the Liberian TRC, should not prevent young adults from being eligible to receive reparations which aim to repair the consequences of the wrongful acts committed against young adults during childhood. The TRC recommended in particular that lost educational opportunities should in particular be covered by reparations by providing additional schooling for those in need. The final report indeed underlines that such measures provided to young adults indeed bear positive consequences for the victims.[699] Bearing in mind that young adults might still have child-specific needs and should therefore also be eligible for child-specific forms of reparations therefore requests that eligibility criteria do not prevent this particular group of victims from benefitting from child-specific forms of reparations.

The ICC might also be confronted with the need, in order to ensure the practicability of the reparation proceedings, to introduce eligibility criteria for

establishment, mandate and criticism of the Kenyan TRC see, Reliefweb Kenya; Amnesty International Kenya 2008.

696 UNICEF 2010a, at 88.

697 TRC Sierra Leone Vol. 2, Chapter 4, Reparations, at 248, 250. For an overview of the conflict, see TRC Sierra Leone Vol. 1, Chapter 1, Mandate, at 21-46.

698 TRC Liberia, Vol. 3: Appendix, at 107.

699 TRC Liberia, Vol. 3, Title II, at 100.

specifying the group of victims, including children, who are entitled to specific forms of reparations. A requirement which is based on a temporal element could be helpful in this regard. The period which has been determined to constitute the time frame in which the prosecutor investigated the charged crimes, as contained in the confirmation of charges decision, could for this purpose be referred to as the time slot. Eligibility for child-specific forms of reparations could thus be said to require that claimants have been a child at the moment of crime commission, which simultaneously falls within the period of the confirmation of charges decision. This solution would lead to the result that victims, despite having reached majority in the course of the proceedings, might nevertheless be entitled to request child specific forms of reparation. While Rule 85 RPE does not explicitly provide for such limitation, it could be argued that this limitation is within the object and purpose of this provision and victim participation as such, as it still enables all potential direct and indirect victims to claim reparations. Claiming reparations as such is thus not limited, only the entitlement to a particular form of reparations, namely those who are child-specific, is made dependent on this temporal requirement. That the overall group of victims is automatically limited by specific period stated in the confirmation of charges decision is a practical consequence which exists regardless of the nature of the proceedings (criminal or reparation proceedings). This is because participation in a specific case requires as such that victims comply with the temporal element as stated in the confirmation of charges decision as they would otherwise not qualify as victims of a crime within the jurisdiction of the ICC which is charged against an (alleged) perpetrator.

An upper age limit as introduced by the Sierra Leonean TRC with regard to claimants eligibility to request child-specific reparations, on the other hand, bears far-reaching consequences for children who have reached majority in the meantime but are nevertheless in need of reparations which target the particular needs attacked during childhood, and should therefore be avoided by the ICC. This is because, as has been elaborated in the previous section, victims, who have reached majority in the meanwhile might nevertheless be in need of child specific forms of reparations, such as educational training or particular medical treatment. Being limited to forms of reparation which do not address the particular needs of child claimants (independent of the fact that they might have reached majority in the meanwhile), and especially lost opportunities due to their suffering during childhood, entails the risk to not adequately enable these victims to effectively benefit from reparation awards. Such reparation awards would then not mirror a child-sensitive approach of the ICC.

In the reparation proceedings against *Thomas Lubanga Dyilo*, the competent Chamber should therefore hold that entitlement to child-specific forms of reparations is dependent on the specific age of a claimant at the moment of crime commission (which is also included in the confirmation of charges decision). Thereby, the Court will not exclude those victims from child-specific forms of reparations who have reached majority during the time frame charged or within the course of the proceedings.

In conclusion, based on the practice of more experienced mechanisms it is argued that child claimants may in the future indeed be expected to be confronted with child-specific eligibility criteria in order to come into consideration for forms of reparations which address the particular needs of this group of victims. Examining carefully the practice of experienced mechanisms might therefore provide useful guidance for the ICC when determining who is to receive child-specific forms of reparations.

5.4.3 Implementation

General aspects of implementation

Concerning the previously examined aspects, the statutory provisions of the International Criminal Court largely remain silent on the implementation of reparation orders. If reparation orders are made against a convicted person or deposited with the Trust Fund for Victims, limited guidance on the modalities for the disbursement of reparations awards can be found in the Rome Statute or the Regulations for the Trust Fund For Victims.[700] In addition, Trial Chamber I's decision of 7 August 2012 in the *Lubanga* case does set out a five-step implementation plan. According to this plan, the TFV, in conjunction with the Registry, the OPCV and appointed experts, determine which localities are to be addressed in the reparation process. Second, these actors consult with the localities selected. Third, the appointed experts determine the harm suffered within the localities. Subsequently, the principles and procedures of reparation proceedings are to be publicly explained in the localities. During the public debates, victims are invited to express their expectations. Finally, proposals for collective reparations are collected in order to forward them for approval to a competent Chamber of the ICC.[701] Accordingly, the Chamber mainly delegates the substantive parts of the reparation proceedings to the Trust Fund for Victims. The Chamber explicitly held that,

> '[it] is satisfied that, in the circumstances of this case, the identification of the victims and beneficiaries (Regulations 60 to 65 of the Regulations of the TFV) should be carried out by the TFV. [...] The Chamber accordingly: [...] [r]emains seized of the reparations proceedings, in order to exercise any necessary monitoring and oversight functions in accordance with Article 64(2) and (3)(a) of the Statute (including considering the proposals for collective reparations that are to be

700 Regulation 66-68 of the 2005 Regulations of the Trust Fund for Victims.
701 ICC-01/04-01/06-2904, para. 282.

developed in each locality, which are to be presented to the Chamber for its approval) [...].'[702]

Despite the attempt of Trial Chamber I to provide more clarity as regards reparation proceedings by setting out the reparation proceedings in a five-step implementation plan, numerous questions remain unanswered. As a consequence, the reparation proceedings in the *Lubanga* case, but equally the implementation of other reparation awards trigger numerous questions.[703]

Child-specific aspects of implementation

Bearing in mind the procedural particularities which arose thus far in criminal proceedings, the following two questions, among others, are likely to occur in reparation proceedings in relation to the child claimant: Firstly, how should the Court determine what is considered to be in the best interests of the child? Will the individual child (need to) have a say? Secondly, bearing in mind the urgency of children's needs, are child claimants' reparation requests to be treated with priority compared to adult or other claimants' reparation claims? In turn, guidance on these two questions is sought in the remaining provisions, the practice of the ICC within the criminal proceedings and, again, the involvement of children in the Sierra Leonean TRC.

5.4.3.1 Best Interests

The assessment of the best interest of the child has been examined within the ambit of *Chapter One*. Similar, if not even greater relevance of the principle of the best interests compared to the previous chapters exists when reparation awards are to be implemented. Article 3 of the Convention on the Rights of the Child, which has been recognised by various Chambers as applicable law in the pending criminal proceedings before the Court states that,

> '[i]n all actions concerning children, whether undertaken by public or private social welfare institutions, courts of law, administrative authorities or legislative bodies, the best interests of the child shall be a primary consideration.'[704]

Considering that various Chambers recognised the applicability of the Convention on the Rights of the Child, in particular Article 3, the extent to which the determination of the best interests of the child could play a role in reparation proceedings, in particular whether children themselves have a say in what is in their

---

702 ICC-01/04-01/06-2904, paras. 283, 289.

703 Less child-specific questions, such as the potential implication of appeal proceedings and the general time frame of reparation proceedings are interesting but outside the ambit of this research.

704 1989 Convention on the Rights of the Child, 1577 UNTS 3.

best interests when expressing their preference for particular forms of reparations needs to be examined.[705]

Chapter One underlined that an assessment of the best interests of the child is to be made in light of the evolving capacities of the individual child. Such consideration should further take into account that a universal standard for the best interests of the child does not exist.[706] The earlier mentioned *Guidelines* of the Council of Europe are restated as a yardstick for an assessment of the best interests of the child as regards the implementation of reparation awards. The *Guidelines* request that,

> 'their views and opinions shall be given due weight; all other rights of the child, such as the right to dignity, liberty and equal treatment shall be respected at all times; a comprehensive approach shall be adopted by all relevant authorities so as to take due account of all interests at stake, including psychological and physical well-being and legal, social and economic interests of the child.'[707]

Accordingly, as pointed out in *Chapter One*, the best interests of the child can be assessed through a three-fold test which goes beyond a purely legal assessment: Firstly, the child needs to express his or her views which are to be taken into account; secondly, the best interests of the child in a particular situation need to be examined in light of the other rights of the child. Thirdly an interdisciplinary approach is to be applied in order to scrutinise the non-legal fields of interests, such as the psycho-social constitution of the individual child. As underlined by the Committee on the Rights of the Child, the ICC is encouraged to consider that,

> 'according to their evolving capacities, [children] can progressively exercise their rights.'[708]

Also within the context of reparation proceedings, the Court is advised to enable children to progressively exercise their right to reparation and allow their individual participation, by, for instance, inviting them to express their personal views and concerns on the forms of reparations.

Despite the major lack of procedural rules regulating the implementation of reparation awards, Article 75(3) Rome Statute, indeed, enables the Court to 'invite [...] representations from or on behalf of [...] victims' which the Court shall take into account before making a reparation order. This provision, therefore, empowers the Court to also invite child claimants and/or their legal representatives to bring

705 For further analysis on the question of whether children are capable of express their views, see, *Chapter One*.

706 Ibid..

707 Council of Europe Guidelines 2010.

708 Committee on the Rights of the Child, 33rd session, 19 May-6 June 2003, General Comment No. 4 (2003) Adolescent health and development in the context of the Convention on the Rights of the Child, UN Doc. CRC/GC/2003/4, 1.

their views and concerns to the attention of the Court before reparation awards are made.

It is noteworthy to repeat in this regard that two former child soldiers (child participants) were invited by Trial Chamber I to give evidence in the courtroom in the criminal proceedings against *Thomas Lubanga Dy*ilo (*Chapter Three*). During their testimony, both young adults also expressed their wish to receive educational training as a form of reparation to be awarded by the Court.[709] Their testimony therefore provided the Court with valuable insights into the personal views and expectations of the young adults. After the conviction of *Thomas Lubanga Dyilo*, Trial Chamber I invited legal representatives and the Office of Public Council for Victims to file submissions in which the expectations of victims were also expressed.[710]

In addition, the Court can also assess the personal views and expectations of child claimants by studying their respective application forms. Question 34 of the standard form invites claimants to describe what they expect to receive. On the other side, as the use of the application form is not compulsory for child claimants, one may generally question whether the form will be used to a great extent in the future. If this will not be the case, the Court will be in need to receive information as regards the preferred forms of reparation from other sources, such as the earlier addressed meetings at community level. Next to the potential usefulness of the application form for the Court, it may also be noted at this point that, bearing in mind the limited forms of reparations the Court will be able to order directly against a convicted person, the explanatory note, which states that victims can also expect reparations in the form of compensation or restitution, might be confusing for child claimants (but also adult claimants). It might in particular create wrong expectations concerning what kind of reparations can be expected from the Court.[711]

The relevance of the possibility for children to express their personal expectations through the one or the other means depends, however, on the promotion of this option in a child sensitive manner. Particularly important in this regard is the earlier addressed right of the child to be adequately informed (*Chapter One*). Children are accordingly in specific need of being properly informed and supported in order to formulate their expectations within the possible forms of reparations which could be awarded by the ICC. Since the number of claimants is likely to be of such size that individual hearings are less feasible, the written statement in any case invites claimants, including children, to formulate their personal needs, expectations and preferences. The extent to which the ICC and in particular the Trust Fund for Victims will take the child-specific wishes into account remains to be seen.

709 See for further discussion, http://www.katangatrial.org/2011/03/judges-in-katanga-and-ngudjolo-trial-hear-testimony-from-participating-victims/.
710 ICC-01/04-01/06-2869; ICC-01/04-01/06-2864.
711 International Criminal Court, A guide for the Participation of Victims, at 11-12.

In line with the foregoing, the practice of various TRCs also underlines that victims, including children, have personally been invited for statement sessions.[712] In addition to the possibility for children to express their individual views on reparation in person, the Sierra Leonean TRC cooperated with the Children's Forum Network. The Commission stated in its final report that,

> '[t]he children of Sierra Leone have not had a meaningful role and voice in the social, political and economic life of Sierra Leone despite the fact that they were compelled to adopt adult roles during the conflict. The establishment of the Children's Forum Network (CFN), an advocacy group run by children, enabled the Commission to hear and listen to the voices of Sierra Leone's children telling about their experiences in the civil war.'[713]

Increasing the role of child rights NGOs in the context of ICC reparation proceedings could therefore constitute another option in order to fully assess the best interests of the child in respect of reparations to be received. Bearing in mind that many potential child claimants have been permanently or are temporarily separated from their parents due to international crimes, strengthening the position of the child claimant by relying on the support of child rights NGOs potentially constitutes a meaningful tool to enable the Court to fully understand the broad variety of children's needs and wishes. Such need has been pointed out by the Registry. It held that,

> '[t]he information in the possession of these groups [NGOs such as UNCIEF but also local child rights organisations] may be of great assistance to the Court in determining matters of reparations.'[714]

UNICEF submitted in March 2012 a request to participate in the reparation proceedings in the *Lubanga* case in order to assist the Court on matters in relation to child victims.[715] In April 2012, Trial Chamber I, indeed granted leave to UNICEF and a number of other organisations to submit written representations.[716]

5.4.3.2 Prioritisation

Another aspect which relates to the implementation of reparations concerns the question of the potential priority of claims submitted by child claimants. The ICC

---

712 UNICEF 2010a, at 88. See with regard to the Sierra Leonean TRC, TRC Sierra Leone Vol. 2, Chapter 4, Reparations, at 235. Children also seem to have been invited to statement sessions before the Kenyan TRC, Children also seem to participate in the statements sessions of the Kenyan Truth and Reconciliation Commission.

713 Ibid., at 18.

714 ICC-01/04-01/06-2863, para. 200.

715 ICC-01/04-01/06-2855-Anx3.

716 ICC-01/04-01/06-2870, para. 22. Trial Chamber I provides an overview of all submissions, see, ICC-01/04-01/06-2904.

Statute, again, does not provide guidance on the issue. Regulation 65 of the Trust Fund, on the other hand, establishes that

> '[t]aking into account the urgent situation of the beneficiaries, the Board of Directors may decide to institute phased or priority verification and disbursement procedures. In such cases, the Board of Directors may prioritize a certain sub-group of victims for verification and disbursement.'[717]

Accordingly, if the Trust Fund may generally decide to prioritise between certain sub-groups of victims, the prioritisation of the implementation of child claimants' reparations is not excluded at the outset.

Previous practice with regard to the priority of children's reparations was, again, established by the Sierra Leonean TRC. By recommending specific reparations for children, the TRC of Sierra Leone recognised that children constitute a particular group of beneficiaries which is in 'dire need of urgent care.'[718] Despite the fact that the conflict in Sierra Leone resulted in a large amount of victims, the Commission saw a need to give priority to the needs of children. The Commission concluded that reparations to children should be

> 'prioritised as victims in need of particular care and assistance given the enduring effects of the violations they suffered.'[719]

A prioritised implementation of reparation requests of child claimants therefore does not lack precedence and could also be adopted by the ICC. Furthermore, the prioritisation of reparation awards was also suggested to Trial Chamber I in the *Lubanga* case. The Registry pointed out in its Second Report on Reparation in this case that,

> 'the Chamber may consider something [...], by which resources for redress are prioritized in favour of some victims but not others on the basis of equitable criteria in those many cases where the resources at its disposal for redress are insufficient to provide meaningful redress to all victims potentially eligible. In these circumstances it may make more sense to prioritize resources so that certain groups of victims, such as those most in need or those most seriously affected by the crime in question, can receive some meaningful form of redress through Court-ordered reparations.'[720]

It is therefore a welcome step, that Trial Chamber I ruled that children may indeed benefit from prioritised treatment. The Chamber held that,

> '[it] recognises that priority may need to be given to certain victims who are in particularly vulnerable situations or who require urgent assistance. These may

717 Regulation 65 of the 2005 Regulations of the Trust Fund for Victims.

718 TRC Sierra Leone Vol. 2, Chapter 4, Reparations, at 242-243.

719 Ibid..

720 ICC-01/04-01/06-2806, para. 31.

> include, *inter alia*, the victims of sexual or gender-based violence, individuals who require immediate medical care (especially when plastic surgery or treatment for HIV is necessary), as well as severely traumatized children, for instance following the loss of family members.'[721]

Does this mean that a child's claim is generally to be prioritised compared to claims from adult victims? One may indeed assume that, bearing in mind the psychological and physical developmental progression of the child that claims which request medical treatment are to be prioritised – a position which also appears to be adopted before the Sierra Leonean TRC and by Trial Chamber I of the ICC. This may be explained by the fact that (further) delay in medical treatment might cause more disproportionate negative implications for the child compared to adult victims. One may even argue that also victims who have reached majority in the meanwhile are entitled to such prioritised treatment when having suffered harm as a result of an international crime during childhood. Whether a priority of claims beyond a medical necessity, such as claims requesting educational training, will be introduced remains to be seen. In any case, it needs to be remembered that since other Chambers have not yet ruled on reparations, it remains to be seen whether a prioritised treatment for children will generally be provided for.

5.5 Conclusion

It has become clear, that, without having yet been extensively confronted with specific questions concerning the forms, eligibility and implementation of reparation awards in relation to the child claimant in the young practice of the Court, the ICC can be expected to be confronted with these aspects in the future. Each of these issues requires that child-sensitive awareness is present in order to ensure that children and young adults can benefit from reparation awards which adequately address the particular needs that are inherent to childhood. It has also been pointed out that these needs are not limited to immediate reparation measures which aim to support the child victim in terms of medical recovery. Instead, a holistic view is to be applied when considering not only who is eligible for child-specific reparations, but also when determining the precise forms of reparations and a potential prioritisation of claims submitted by child victims when implementing reparation awards.

The material scale of an effective remedy requires that reparations to children and young adults reflect their particular needs in order to constitute meaningful reparations. The fact that the procedural framework of reparation proceedings before the ICC is not provided for in the statutory rules, constitutes a complicating factor in this regard.

As regards the decision of Trial Chamber I to not examine individual applications but to forward all to the TFV raises the particular questions of what the

---

[721] ICC-01/04-01/06-2904, para. 208.

added value of early reparation requests is, and whether individual requests for reparations being transmitted to the Court prior to the commencement of reparations proceedings is at all in the best interests of the child – bearing in mind the possibility of joining the proceedings at a later stage by participating in the public debates at local level.

In any case, as long as the Rome Statute and the respective procedural rules create the impression that reparations are awarded by the judicial institution of the ICC, a delegation to the Trust Fund cannot be applauded. Instead, the Court should himself fulfil this task, be it with, for example the establishment of specific reparation chambers, including chambers whose members are experts in child rights issues.

As was pointed out previously, the examination of the evolving capacities of the child requires a complex assessment (*Chapter One*). The lack of an explicit analysis of the evolving capacities of child participants in the *Lubanga* case might be caused by the fact that the criminal proceedings simply prevent the ICC from a detailed inquiry. The conclusion of these proceedings may therefore invite but also enable the Court to change perspective. From being a fair trial watchdog, the Court may now also (without losing sight of the fact that the convicted person also has the right to a fair trial in reparation proceedings) act as a protector of the various facets of the best interests of the child. Furthermore, the judges could pay particular attention to the need that a child is invited to participate in accordance with his or her evolving capacities. In addition to the responsibility of judges to take the child-specific particularities into account, explicit awareness of the other actors involved, in particular the Registry, the Trust Fund and the legal representatives has been established as being indispensable for child-sensitive participation in reparation proceedings before the ICC.

In conclusion, if the ICC aims to ensure that children and young adults can remedy the harm suffered during childhood as a result of a crime within the jurisdiction of the Court, the Court is encouraged to bear in mind that not only the procedure itself needs to be child-sensitive but also the material component of the proceedings relating to the forms of reparations. In addition, child-sensitivity should not be limited to those who are minors when claiming reparations. Instead, an adequate response in the law of procedure and practice is necessary in order to also enable young adults who have suffered from violations of rights during childhood to remedy these violation(s) and be in particular eligible for child-specific forms of reparations. Such a response could provide an effective remedy for child victims (being children and young adults in the course of reparation proceedings) in procedural and substantive terms which goes further than only providing *effective access*.

Part III

Concluding and Comparative Evaluation

CHAPTER 6
EVALUATION AND FUTURE PERSPECTIVES

6.1 INTRODUCTION

Each of the foregoing chapters draws conclusions as to the child-specific particularities before the ICC pursuing two research aims:

- *to analyse whether and to what extent the proceedings are child sensitive;*
- *to establish whether additional child-specific regulation and awareness is necessary in order to accommodate the particular needs of the child.*

It has been established, where necessary, whether additional child-specific regulation and awareness is necessary in order to adequately accommodate the particular needs of the child.[722] The research thereby also assessed whether it is possible at all that ICC proceedings are sufficiently child sensitive. If not, it might be necessary to reconsider the possibility that children participate. Summarising the foregoing, the concrete objective this research focused on has been formulated as follows:

> *The research aims to provide informed insights into whether participation in ICC proceedings is in the best interests of the child.*

When addressing these aims, it has been kept in mind that, even if victims, including children, participate in the proceedings before the Court and claim reparations, I agree with the perspective that the ICC has as its primary objective to ensure a fair trial for alleged perpetrators. Accordingly, throughout the entire research, the punitive nature has been of foremost importance when balancing the best interests of the child against the core objective of international criminal justice. Bearing in mind the objective of the ICC, the fight against impunity, an individual examination of a child (and in particular the individual child's best interests) could be considered to be beyond the capacities of a criminal court whose core task is to safeguard that alleged perpetrators receive a fair trial. One may therefore as such still question the principal relevance of child participation in ICC proceedings.

---

722 See also in this regard, Doek 1992, at 632.

The various chapters point out that child participation in ICC proceedings (but also other international criminal and reparation proceedings), indeed, requires a child-specific response in law and in practice. This response aims to ensure that children's involvement in various capacities can be considered to be in their best interests and in accordance with their evolving capacities.

The current chapter aims to develop a concluding comparison of only a few procedural aspects: namely those which are (or are likely to be) commonly shared among the various procedural capacities of the child.

The following evaluation therefore focuses on an assessment of the ICC's position towards the same procedural particularities within different procedural capacities of the child. It will address three questions, namely, whether, and if so, to what extent and why did the various Chambers of the Court approach the same particularity differently? This comparative approach at the end of this research aims to add another perspective on child participation in ICC proceedings – a perspective which constitutes an additional incentive for the evaluation of the legal aspects of child participation. Subsequently, based on the examined regulation and practice in this research, the chapter draws final conclusions as regards the principal relevance of child participation in international judicial proceedings. Finally, alongside ten final recommendations, this chapter calls for further research in light of the procedural dimension of child participation in the criminal and reparation proceedings before the ICC (while not being limited to the latter).

6.2 Evaluation

The numerous procedural particularities which arose in the ICC's practice in relation to the child witness, victim and claimant point out that these three procedural capacities can be considered to play a dominant role in the existing practice of the ICC. Selected peculiarities are commonly shared. The individual criminal responsibility of a child perpetrator or being the child of a(n) (alleged) perpetrator have either been excluded from the jurisdictional mandate of the ICC or played (thus far) a minor role. Accordingly, particular attention is awarded to a comparative evaluation of the commonly shared particularities relating to the child witness, victim and claimant.

6.2.1 Legal capacity of the child

The legal capacity of the child constitutes a procedural particularity which arose especially in relation to the child witness (*Chapter Two*) and victim (*Chapter Three*)

– a particularity which is likely to also arise in future reparation proceedings (*Chapter Five*).

The legal capacity is the requirement which is to be examined prior to children's participation in ICC proceedings. This is because, in principle, only those children who possess legal capacity are eligible for participation. The minor age of the child has, however, been found to be a potential constraint to children's participation as minors are frequently seen as lacking full legal capacity.

Various Chambers established that a child victim is, in principle, not recognised as being legally competent to submit an application for participation on his/her own behalf. Thus, while adult applicants are *only* requested to comply with the four requirements of Rule 85 RPE when accessing the ICC, children have to comply with two additional requirements that are not called for in the statutory rules. These requirements relate to the legal (in)competence of the child to file an application and the related condition that another person should act on behalf of the child. Both aspects have been introduced by various Chambers of the ICC and have also been included in the amended application form. This implies that these Chambers held that only next-of-kin or the legal guardian of the child victim are seen as competent third persons who may submit an application for participation on behalf of the child (*Chapter Three*). The exclusion has been based on the fact that the respective victims were minors.

The minor age of the child has also been a procedural particularity which received specific attention when children were invited to testify in the witness capacity. The limited legal capacity of children has been reflected in the need to be provided with the consent of another person when a minor is called into the witness stand. The adult consent was deemed indispensable as the child was not deemed to be able to provide informed consent to testify.

In contrast to the approach of the Chambers as regards the child victim, the limited legal capacity of the child witness has been dealt with differently. The competent Chambers ruled in this regard that the appearance of the child witness is not conditional on the consent of the next-of-kin or legal guardian. At first hand, it is surprising (bearing in mind the potential risk of re-traumatisation during testimony) that the procedural rules on the questioning of children are broader by establishing that other adults who are *relevant* (thus not being limited to kinship or legal guardianship as is the case for child victim participants) may also provide the necessary consent to call a child as a witness (*Chapter Two*).

Despite a further explanation of what is to be understood under *relevant adult*, this addition bears particular consequences for the Prosecution. It enables the Prosecution, regardless of the fact that a potential child witness may not be in contact with his/her parents or legal guardian, to question children, because of being allowed to obtain consent from a wider range of persons. This opportunity is of particular interest for the Prosecution when questioning former child soldiers or refugee children who stay in disarmament, demobilisation and reintegration or refugee camps. These children may not yet have re-established contacts with their families due to the consequences of their recruitment and flight. The re-unification may be further complicated by a possibly still ongoing armed conflict such as the conflict in the Democratic Republic of the Congo.

While both, child victims and witnesses are not automatically recognised as always having full legal capacity before the ICC, the possibility of relying on a *relevant adult* in relation to child witnesses raises the question why the Court, thus far, followed a stricter approach with regard to child applications for participation in criminal proceedings despite the fact that this group of children faces the same practical constraints as child witnesses. In light of the lack of explanation for the stricter approach, it seems that the Court, depending on the competent Chamber, thereby aims to indirectly limit the number of participating child victims.

Bearing in mind the examined difficulties for child victims of international crimes to access the ICC (*Chapter Three*), enabling child victims or claimants to also rely on *relevant adults* (not fulfilling the kinship or legal guardian requirement) when submitting the joint application form, would allow children to access more easily the criminal and/or reparation proceedings of the International Criminal Court. This is particularly the case when conflicting interests between the child and his or her parents, but also the separation from and the loss of parents and the non-existence of a system of legal guardianship are at issue.

The addressed practice of various Chambers, however, introduced the condition that if neither parent(s) nor the legal guardian submit an application on the child's behalf, child victims have to provide the consent of next-of-kin or a legal guardian that someone else submits an application on behalf of the child. Such a requirement has, however, far-reaching consequences since it restricts the child in accessing the criminal and/or reparation proceedings before the ICC. UNICEF clarified in this regard that,

> '[a] common constraint on the child's right to express views and concerns is the requirement that his or her parent give prior authorization. Such a constraint is not compatible with the recognition of children's full right to express their views and concerns [...].'[723]

Accordingly, the Court should depart from the strict requirement that the child's limited legal capacity can only be bypassed with the consent of next-of-kin or a legal guardian. Instead, the Court should assess whether another person's consent is to be requested and if so, under which conditions child rights NGOs or other care-takers, for instance, could be considered as being suitable to provide such consent.

---

[723] UNICEF 2009b, at 44.

Furthermore, a case-by-case assessment should be relied upon when deciding on whether a child's request for participation should be accompanied at all with the consent of another (relevant) person. Such a decision should, however, not be made in light of the age of the child, but be based on an assessment of the capability of the individual child to communicate and express his or her views, in other words the decision should be taken in light of the evolving capacities of the individual child (*Chapter One*). A competence of the judges to examine the capability of a individual child to communicate and express his or her views cannot automatically be assumed as such decision requests expertise beyond the law. Instead, transparent proof of expertise and, if necessary, the support of qualified and trained experts when taking this decision is suggested in this context.

What is clear from this practice in relation to the legal status of the child witness, victim and claimant is that there is a strong need for transparency in the Court's practice. Questions of a possible limitation of the child's legal capacity are of such an essential nature as they are decisive for the legal status of the child participant that they should be answered in line with (as long as there is no procedural regulation) a publicly available Court strategy and coherent Court practice in order to enable children, their care takers and legal representatives to anticipate on their legal (potential) legal status before the International Criminal Court.

6.2.2 Informed consent of the child

Closely related to the legal capacity of the child is his/her ability to provide informed consent - an issue which also arose in the criminal proceedings with regard to the child witness and victim. The doctrine of informed consent generally plays an important role in three situations: when a child is called to the witness stand, when the Court intends to use confidential medical information concerning the child during the trial or when a child participant or claimant is represented by a legal representative. Five components have been held to be the elements of informed consent: information, competency, understanding, voluntariness and decision.[724] The second element, the competency of the child to provide informed consent, has received particular attention in the ICC's practice.

While it is argued in this research that age itself should not be a factor which determines the legal capacity of a child, it has been relied upon in practice in particular when assessing whether a child is able to provide informed consent. Though the ICC does not draw a sharp distinction based on age when assessing the vulnerability of a witness and his/her need for specific protection (see below), the international standard of eighteen (Article 1 CRC), by contrast, is strictly applied in

724 Meisel & Roth 1983, 265, at 271-272.

so far as the consent of an adult is requested before calling a child to the witness stand.[725] Thus, while in terms of protection it is not decisive whether the young witness is older or younger than eighteen years of age, requesting the consent of a third person before calling a child to the witness stand establishes that in this regard, child witnesses are strictly seen as children below the age of eighteen and unable to provide an informed consent on whether testifying in the witness stand.

Whereas the need to recognise that the child himself or herself is capable of providing informed consent in relation to acting as a witness may be questioned, child victims and claimants, on the other side, should generally be seen as being competent to provide such consent.

The request to recognise child participants and claimants competency to provide informed consent becomes particularly clear when assessing the possibility to be represented by a legal representative. *Chapter Three* established that being represented by a legal representative in the proceedings before the Court, requires that an informed decision is made. If the child, however, is seen as not being competent to provide informed consent, he/she cannot come into consideration for such representation without the support of others. Participation without a legal representative, as underlined in *Chapter Three*, reduces the modalities of participation. This is because participation through a legal representative entails more extensive participation options. Accordingly, child victims and claimants should in principle be recognised as being legally competent to formulate an informed decision on their legal representation in ICC proceedings.

The same assumption can, however, not generally be made with regard to child witnesses' ability to provide informed consent. This is particularly the case when a child cannot be expected to be able to oversee the possible negative implications of witnessing – such as re-traumatisation and the risk of self-incrimination (*Chapter Two*). Not presuming generally that the child can give an informed consent with regard to testimony, does not take away the possibility that individual children are capable of doing so. Thus, while the child should be presumed to be capable of providing an informed consent in relation to participation in the criminal and/or reparation proceedings, this capability should be carefully examined before calling a child to the witness stand. This examination should not be limited to the competent judges prior to actually calling a child into the witness stand. Instead, a preliminary examination should also be undertaken by those actors who intend to call child witnesses, namely, the prosecution and defence teams. This preliminary examination aims to, firstly, ensure that children's involvement with the ICC is critically assessed from the outset and, secondly, to ensure that children's best interests are constantly respected and examined by all actors involved. Such preliminary assessment could be achieved by introducing the respective provisions

[725] ICC-01/04-01/07-692, 16-18; interesting practice before the SCSL where child protection agency gave consent in cases where parents were not at the disposal, see, Sanin & Strirnemann 2008, 22.

in the relevant code of conducts, but more effectively by a regulation under the Rome Statute.

As far as the reparation proceedings in the *Lubanga* case are concerned, Trial Chamber I seems to be of the view that children are indeed seen as being legally competent to provide informed consent, at least when being entitled to receiving reparations.[726]

6.2.3 Age of the child

The determination of the age of the child has crystallised to become a central issue for the child witness, victim and most likely also for the child claimant. The determination of the age of a child witness or participant is particularly relevant when they are called to testify on their recruitment as a child soldier (victim witness, *Chapter Two*) or when filing an application for participation as an alleged victim of this crime (*Chapter Three*). Obviously, only those witnesses who were below the age of fifteen years at the time of recruitment are able to provide evidence on the alleged crime as a direct victim. Equally, only those child victims who were recruited when they were below the age of fifteen years are eligible for the victim status of the recruitment crime.

Chapter Three established that various Chambers of the International Criminal Court adopted a pragmatic approach with regard to the age determination of a child victim by applying a *prima facie* standard at pre-trial and trial stage, notwithstanding the fact that inconsistencies existed with regard to the date of birth of some applicants.[727] A range of documents but also the statement of two witnesses, were accepted as establishing the identity and age of the applicant.[728] Efforts by the Defence counsel of *Thomas Lubanga Dyilo*, who argued that the exact age of participants at the time of crime commission had not been established, were mainly only successful when the participant failed to submit *any* identification document which could establish his or her age.[729] The majority of child victims seeking access succeeded, despite the doubts raised by the Defence, in sufficiently establishing, *prima facie*, their age.[730]

---

726 ICC-01/04-01/06-2904, para. 204.

727 ICC-01/04-01/07-357, 8-9. Applicant a/0333/07 was still a minor at the moment of decision taking, see ICC-01/04-01/07-357, 7. See also, ICC-01/04-01/07-579, 67. Applicant a/0110/08 was the only minor applicant in the decision at issue. ICC-01/04-01/06-1556, 89. ICC-01/04-01/06-1556, 73, 101-102, 111. The Chamber ruled that, 'the applicants have given *sufficient evidence to establish, prima facie,* that they are victims under Rule 85(a) of the Rules.' ICC-01/04-01/06-1724-Anx3.

728 ICC-01/04/423-Corr, p. 15; see also, ICC-01/04-505, p. 18.

729 See for example, ICC-01/04-01/06-186AnxA1, 235-246.

730 Ibid., 3-228.

While this *prima facie* standard approach could be said to contravene the earlier statement that the ICC indirectly aims to limit child participation by restricting children's legal capacity to apply for participation on their own behalf and not automatically recognising children's capacity to provide informed consent, one needs to be aware of the exact moment when the decision on the child's capability is taken and when age is to be proven. The former decision is taken prior to an actual examination of the application for participation. Children are thus potentially excluded already before the merits of their application (including an assessment of proof of age) have been touched upon. It is therefore argued, that the approach taken by the Court, thus far, in relation to the child's capability constitutes an constraint which constitutes a general entrance hurdle to child participation in ICC proceedings. The less restrictive approach of a *prima facie* standard, which is adopted at a later stage, can therefore not be said to mirror a generally child oriented attitude of the Court.

Bearing the aforementioned in mind, I therefore still critically view the fact that, as *Chapter Five* established, an even more lenient approach was adopted by Trial Chamber I in the reparation proceedings against *Thomas Lubanga Dyilo* before the Court with regard to the child claimant.

In contrast to the *lenient* approach in relation to child victim participation in the criminal and reparation proceedings, remarkably higher efforts were taken in order to prove the age of a child witness who is called to the witness stand to testify on his/her recruitment as child soldier.

The Prosecution invited two expert witnesses on age determination in order to establish the age of the child witness called in the case against *Thomas Lubanga Dyilo*. The Prosecution thereby aimed to achieve that Trial Chamber I was convinced *beyond reasonable* doubt about the allegation that the accused committed the war crime of enlistment and recruitment of children below the age of fifteen years (*Chapter Two*).

The higher evidentiary threshold of proving *beyond reasonable doubt* mirrors that, depending on the procedural capacity of the child in combination with the crimes charged, the Court will apply different standards of proof. From an institutional perspective, such an approach mirrors that criminal proceedings request a higher burden of proof in order to safeguard that alleged perpetrators receive a fair trial.

From a child rights perspective, this is a logical and welcoming approach which does not render child participation unfeasible for reasons of age determination since (thus far) the higher threshold is applied in relation to child witnesses and not victims and claimants. This positive conclusion does, however, not diminish the earlier raised criticism that the Court (on a general basis) indirectly seems to restrict child participation. The welcoming approach in relation to age determination of child victims is therefore only a partial success from a child rights perspective as the overall approach remains to be rather restrictive.

6.2.4 Protection of the child

Another aspect which arises in relation to the child witness, victim and claimant concerns the child's need to specific protection. The need to provide child witnesses and victims with sufficient protection has been recognised. With regard to child victims' need to receive protective measures in order to prevent re-traumatisation, Trial Chamber I ruled, for instance, that,

> 'protective and special measures for victims are often the legal means by which the Court can secure the participation of victims in the proceedings, because they are a necessary step I order to safeguard their safety, physical and psychological well-being, dignity and private life in accordance with Article 68(2) of the Statute.'[731]

The legal representatives of the participating victims in the *Lubanga* case underlined that many victims are children coming from the ethnic group of the accused.[732] The application of protective measures may therefore be an indispensable tool in order to protect the integrity of victims and ensure meaningful participation.[733]

In line with the argumentation of the legal representatives, Trial Chamber I also recognised the particular vulnerability and need of specific procedural protection of child witnesses.[734] In addition, various Chambers of the International Criminal Court developed a child-focussed practice in order to prevent that children's participation in the one or the other procedural capacity does not contravene the best interests of the child. The appearance of the first child witness in the *Lubanga* case, at the same time, illustrates that the Court still needs to further develop the protection of the child and in particular apply a case-by-case assessment on whether sufficient measures have been adopted. An assessment of the concrete needs should include an examination of the psychological needs of the child by experts, such as psychologists. Furthermore, a case-by-case assessment should also address the child's need for support and advise concerning the legal aspects and (potential) legal implications – an assessment which is not necessarily limited to the competent judges, but may also involve prosecution and defence teams as well as legal representatives.

6.2.5 Credibility of the child

The question whether a child is a credible statement provider has been raised in particular in relation to the child witness and child victim.

---

[731] ICC-01/04-01/06-1119, 128.
[732] Ibid., 38.
[733] Ibid., 46.
[734] Ibid., 127.

Child witness testimony is accompanied by a number of factors which could be assumed to be decisive for the child's credibility to provide truthful testimony in international criminal proceedings. The immaturity of the young witness and the likelihood that the child has been traumatised in the course of the conflict are important in this regard. *Chapter Two* established in more detail that a child-sensitive approach is necessary in order to ensure that a child is able to provide truthful testimony.

Questions concerning children's trustworthiness were, however, also raised in relation to the child victim in the Court's practice. As far as the credibility of the child as statement provider is concerned, it needs to be pointed out that the trustworthiness of the two former child soldiers, who were called by Trial Chamber I to testify in the victim capacity, was indeed challenged by the Defence (*Chapter Two* and *Three*). Uncertainty as to their truthfulness was not only raised during their testimony, but in particular in the aftermath when the Defence of *Thomas Lubanga Dyilo* (successfully) argued that the two witnesses lied about their identity.[735]

Trial Chamber I seems to adopt a strict approach since it ordered the disclosure of confidential identifying information within the application form in order to enable the Defence to clarify whether the doubts raised were justified and to guarantee the fairness of the proceedings and the right of the accused to receive a fair trial.[736]

Doubts were furthermore raised by the Defence in relation to the credibility of child victims due to contractions within their application form for participation.[737] Contrastingly, the same Chamber, but also Pre-Trial Chamber I, did *not* deem it necessary to examine the credibility of child victim participants at the respective stages of the proceedings as far as children have 'only' submitted an application for participation and did not participate in another procedural capacity before the ICC. Pre-trial Chamber I held that,

> '[co]nsidering further that the applicants are only required to demonstrate that the four requirements established by rule 85 of the Rules are met *prima facie* and that

735 Challenges as to the credibility during the testimony, see, for instance, testimony witness 0225 transcript of 15 January, ICC-01/04-01/06-T-228-Red-ENG WT 15-01-2010 1-63 NB T, p. 34. Challenges which have been raised after their testimony and the testimony of Defense witness 32, see, ICC-01/04-01/06-2586-Red, 4 February 2011, 3. Trial Chamber I pointed out that, witness 32 'alleges that although he is the "real" victim (having filled out the relevant forms), he has been supplanted by participating victim a/0225/06.'

736 ICC-01/04-01/06-2586-Red, 32, 42.

737 ICC-01/04-01/06-1861-AnxA1. The Defense argued, for instance, in relation to application a/0078/06 that 'there are contradictions between the two applications, [...]. [...] these contradictions cast serious doubts over the honesty and precision of the applicant's claims', 18. In response to the application for participation of applicant a/0229/06 the Defense held that, 'the application includes significant contradictions which indicate that the credibility of the applicant and reliability of his application are in doubt', 43. See furthermore, for example, with regard to applicant a/0234/06, 21; a/0238/06, 23; a/0156/07, 33, a/0230/06, 46, a/0049/06, 64; a/0221/06, 214; a/0162/07, 228.

> therefore the Single Judge's analysis of the Applications "will not consist in assessing the credibility of the [applicants'] statement[s] or engaging in a process of corroboration strictu *sensu*", but will assess the applicants' statements first and foremost on the merits of their intrinsic coherence, as well as on the basis of the information otherwise available to the Single Judge [...].'[738]

Likewise, Trial Chamber I underlined that the credibility of the statement is assumed as long as the provided documents do not indicate another conclusion, despite the fact that inconsistencies existed with regard to some applicants' birth date as set out in the application form and the submitted documents.[739]

The Chamber thereby established that it distinguishes between child witnesses and child victims in its assessment of credibility. While the latter is assumed on a *prima facie* basis, challenges of the Defence have been successful in examining child witnesses credibility in more detail. As a result of such careful assessment, all former child soldiers who were called by the Prosecution to give testimony in the *Lubanga* case have been dismissed by Trial Chamber I (*Chapter Two*). In addition to these child witnesses, the Defence also succeeded in convincing that those child victims who gave testimony before Trial Chamber I in person had to be declared as being unreliable due to serious contradictions in their testimony.

Such practice indicates that the Chamber thereby introduces a balanced approach (bearing in mind the above mentioned critical remarks) between on the one side, the right of the accused to a fair trial, which requires a detailed assessment of the child's statement and, on the other side, the possibility for child victims to participate.

6.3 Principal Relevance of Child Participation

It is pointed out throughout the entire research that, to date, the International Criminal Court constitutes the only international avenue to justice which enables victims of international crimes, including children, to be involved to such a remarkable degree. Victim participation before the Cambodia and Lebanon tribunals, on the other side, is provided for, but to a lesser degree.

---

738 ICC-01/04-01/07-357, 8-9. Applicant a/0333/07 was still a minor at the moment of decision taking, see ICC-01/04-01/07-357,7. See also, ICC-01/04-01/07-579, 67. Applicant a/0110/08 was the only minor applicant in the decision at issue.

739 ICC-01/04-01/06-1556, 89. Trial Chamber I held that, '[t]he Chamber has carefully weighed the inconsistencies in each case, but in all the circumstances the differences do not, *ipso facto,* undermine the credibility of the applicants' assertion as to his or her age in the application form, supported by documents that have been provided such as student identity card, election cards and birth certificates. In the view of the Chamber, the material when considered overall, proves, *prima facie*, the identity and age of the applicants in accordance with the Trial Chamber's Decision on victims' participation.'

A child can participate by not only being called to the witness stand as part of a prosecutorial or defence strategy, but also by submitting an application for participation in criminal and/or reparation proceedings. This specific possibility, for the first time in the history of international criminal law, enables children to directly enforce violations of their rights to the extent they have been criminalised under the Rome Statute. The recognition of the child as a procedural actor with procedural rights and the need for procedurally regulated protection constitutes a tremendous and welcome step in international (criminal) law. It contributes to the humanisation of international law.

It nevertheless needs to be taken into account that the ICC, in its early practice, has been confronted with a serious omission in procedural regulation and struggled in various instances when children were involved. It furthermore needs to be borne in mind that the Court is likely to be confronted with similar but also other procedural particularities in the future when children participate. A particular filed of attention could, for instance, be the regulation of family visits – an aspect which thus far has not received much attention as the Court struggled with numerous other issues relating more directly to the course of the criminal proceedings. Furthermore, the concretisation of reparation orders can also be expected to confront the ICC with child-specific questions which have, to date, not been (comprehensively) addressed. The analysis establishes that the participation of the child in the proceedings before the ICC is not a straightforward exercise. Instead, the major lack of procedural child-specific regulation, but also fair trial constraints, prevent the Court from being obliged to comprehensively take into account the particular needs of the child which often request a case-by-case assessment.

Despite the forgoing doubts as regards child participation in ICC proceedings, it needs to be underlined that certain forms of child participation are not likely to disappear from ICC practice. Ensuring, for instance, the well-being of child witnesses was a recurring issue which requested all actors involved to adapt the procedures and behaviour to the particular needs of young human beings in order to, for instance, prevent re-traumatisation. Considering the importance of children who can provide insider information, especially with regard to the recruitment crime, it is unfeasible that this procedural capacity will disappear in the future. Similarly, the consequences which children of (alleged) perpetrators are facing and the legal issues which arise due to the involvement of their parents in ICC proceedings, such as family visits and allowances are neither likely to disappear from the list of the challenges facing the ICC.

With regard to these aspects, the ICC is therefore called upon to not only develop guidelines and include procedural rules, but in particular to streamline its practice in order to promote the protection of children and the foreseeability of the Court's decision-taking. This is not only important from a child rights perspective, but equally relevant from a defence point of view.

6.4 FINAL RECOMMENDATIONS AND NEED FOR FURTHER RESEARCH ON CHILD PARTICIPATION IN INTERNATIONAL CRIMINAL AND REPARATION PROCEEDINGS

The introductory chapter underlined that the present research aims to determine child specific procedural particularities as reflected in the laws and practice of international criminal and reparation proceedings with a particular focus on the ICC. Accordingly, the research is not intended to provide an exhaustive analysis of the child-specific procedural issues, but only seeks to provide a major step and incentive for a comprehensively researched legal status of the child when participating in the proceedings before the International Criminal Court. The need for further research is supported by numerous arguments. These are addressed in the light of ten final recommendations which are based on the findings made in the various chapters of this research. The examination of the procedural particularities concerning the child establishes that the ICC and all actors involved should especially adhere to the following recommendations:

1. *A presumption of the child's capability to participation should generally prevail. This presupposes respect for the evolving capacities which is indispensable in order to enable the individual child to participate to the greatest extent possible.*[740]
2. *Critical monitoring is required in order to ensure that the child is recognised as a holder of independent rights.*[741]
3. *ICC proceedings should be more accessible to those children who wish to participate in criminal and/or reparation proceedings.*[742]
4. *The ICC should publish child participation statistics in order to promote transparency. In addition, the child-specific benefits/outcomes of participation should also be publicly pronounced.*[743]
5. *Child participation in ICC proceedings should not be limited to consultation of the child but include active participation of the child participant.*[744]
6. *The legal status of the child should be recognised as not being a static concept, but constantly influenced by the evolving capacities of the individual child.*[745]

---

740 See in this regard Chapter 1, section 1.3.4 & 1.3.5., Chapter 3, section 3.5.1; Chapter 5, section 5.2.

741 See in this regard; Chapter 2, section 2.4.2; Chapter 3, section 3.2 & 3.5.1; Chapter 5, section 5.2.

742 See in this regard, Chapter 1, section 1.1; Chapter 3, section 3.2; Chapter 5, section 5.2 & 5.4.

743 See in this regard; Chapter 2, section 2.2; Chapter 3, section 3.3; Chapter 5, section 5.4.

744 See in this regard, Chapter 1, section 1.3.5; Chapter 2, section 2.4; Chapter 3, section 3.5.1 & 3.7.3; Chapter 5, section 5.4.

745 See in this regard, Chapter 1, section 1.3.5; Chapter 2, section 2.4.1; Chapter 3, section 3.5.1; Chapter 5, section 5.2.

7. *The capacity of the individual child should be the triggering aspect for child participation and not age.*[746]
8. *The ICC and actors involved shall seek guidance from the Committee on the Rights of the Child when interpreting the principles of the best interests and evolving capacities.*[747]
9. *A legal aid scheme needs to be developed providing for pro bono legal aid for minors.*[748]
10. *The limitation of access for children to the ICC cannot be justified on the basis of judicial economy if not equally applied towards adults.*[749]

Recommendation 1
A presumption of the child's capability to participation should generally prevail. This presupposes respect for the evolving capacities which is indispensable in order to enable the individual child to participate to the greatest extent possible.

Recommendation 2
Critical monitoring is required in order to ensure that the child is recognised as a holder of independent rights.

In light of the first and second recommendation it is to be remembered that child participation before the ICC has only recently commenced. Future ICC proceedings can be expected to also involve children, in particular as long as there is no international judicial alternative for the child who wants to participate in criminal proceedings or claim reparations for harm suffered as a result of an international crime. In order to ensure that child participation does not contravene the best interests and evolving capacities of the child, a comprehensive assessment of procedural particularities, in particular potential risks but also benefits of child participation, are to be defined. This comprehensive overview aims to enable all persons involved, including the child, to assess the advantages and disadvantages prior to their participation. A presumption of the child's capability to participate thereby aims to ensure that the child is not overlooked as a potential participant in international proceedings. Critical monitoring mechanisms should hereby carry the task of ensuring that the child is recognised as a holder of independent rights. Failure to do so should be spotted and made public. Research should therefore examine whether, for instance, monitoring mechanisms are available under the existing institutions, such as the Committee on the Rights of the Child or whether there is a need to set up a distinct institution which may also operate independent from ICC proceedings and being mandated to monitor child participation also in

[746] See in this regard Chapter 1, section 1.3.4 & 1.3.5., Chapter 3, section 3.5.1; Chapter 5, section 5.2.
[747] See in this regard Chapter 1, section 1.3.4 & 1.3.5.
[748] See in this regard Chapter 3, section 3.7.4.
[749] See in this regard Chapter 3, section 3.5.1.

other than the criminal and reparation proceedings before the International Criminal Court.

Various chapters also underline that the participation of children can give rise to conflicts of interests between the child and his or her parent(s). While there might be instances in which a child indeed wishes and is entitled to participate, even without the consent or against the will of next-of-kin, research should analyse how and to what extent international proceedings need to take into account that the child, while recognised as having an independent legal status from adults, is (usually) also part of a family. Despite the fact that the legal status of the child is complex and challenging and inherent to this status are tensions between the rights of parents and children but also the rights of defenders, research should examine how these tensions and challenges, which are likely to remain, can be balanced without negatively affecting the interests of the parties involved.

Recommendation 3
ICC proceedings should be more accessible to those children who wish to participate in criminal and/or reparation proceedings.

Recommendation 4
The ICC should publish child participation statistics in order to promote transparency. In addition, the child-specific benefits/outcomes of participation should also be publicly pronounced.

As regards the third recommendation, it is stated that accessibility for child participants presupposes *inter alia* that clarity exists as regards how the ICC proceedings are accessible. While selected documents, such as the UN *Handbook for Professionals and Policymakers on Justice in matters involving child victims and witnesses of crime* or the Council of Europe *Guidelines on Justice in Matters involving Child Victims and Witnesses of Crime* provide useful guidance in determining some of the procedural particularities, the overall use of these documents is limited due to their primary focus on domestic proceedings, and in particular judicial proceedings which are accessible during peacetime.

The need therefore remains to establish a guiding document on child participation in international criminal/reparation proceedings which are held during or in the aftermath of an armed conflict or large-scale violence. This guiding document should in particular be accessible to all stakeholders and provide transparent guidance on child participation. These guidelines should specifically address the implications of conflict situations on the procedural status of the child. As long as the ICC itself does not include a transparent child focus in its procedural regulations, such an international guiding document should be referred to as the minimum standard for child participation in order to promote and ensure transparency in decision making.

In relation to the fourth recommendation it is stated that, as long as the current machinery of child participation in ICC proceedings remains in the *status quo*, the ICC should publish child participation statistics in order to promote transparency to the greatest extent possible. Such statistics should not be limited to the actual amount of children who participate or whose applications for participation have been rejected. The statistics should also make information available on the practical difficulties children face when seeking access or participate. Furthermore, additional statistics which provide sufficient research material is needed on what children as beneficiaries of reparation awards expect to receive and what their specific needs are during or in the aftermath of conflict situations. While educational training, health care and shelter might be the most predominant needs of children, future research should establish more precisely and in particular context related which forms of reparations could adequately remedy the suffering of the child. Knowing the particular impacts of conflict situations, research should therefore establish how children as international legal actors can gain redress in a child-friendly manner.

Based upon the statistics it can then be seen whether, in relation to which procedural aspects and to what extent a response in law and practice is necessary in order to accommodate child participation when children seek access and participate in the course of the proceedings. In addition, the child-specific benefits/outcomes of participation should also be publicly pronounced. Such practice could, at least to a certain extent, bring clarity into the thus far rather unpredictable flow and implications of child participation.

Recommendation 5
Child participation in ICC proceedings should not be limited to consultation of the child but include active participation of the child participant.

The fifth recommendation aims to stimulate research which provides further justification for an active participation of the child. This active participation may take place in different forms, taking the individual developmental status of the child into account. Furthermore, the implications of different cultural backgrounds might also be an important factor when establishing the adequate modalities for active participation. Future research should therefore, amongst other things, also address the implications of different cultural backgrounds of the child on his/her needs, but also the child's capabilities when involved in a procedural capacity. Different cultural backgrounds might, for instance, need to be taken into account when a particular hierarchical relationship exists between children and adults. After all, such relationships might also have implications for children's ability to provide truthful testimony. Raising allegations against an adult and providing testimony on alleged crimes might, for instance, be particularly difficult for minor witnesses when their cultural background does not allow them to raise their voices against adults or make accusations against adults. In addition to the research focusing on the particular needs of children, it should also be examined to what extent the parties involved (such as judges, prosecutors, defence lawyers, legal representatives and psycho-social staff) could benefit from more child-tailored training in order to be properly prepared to address the child in a child-sensitive manner in the court room.

The aim of active participation is, however, at the same time to be viewed critically. It is repeatedly pointed out throughout the research that the participation of the child might give rise to tension between child protection and the rights of defendants. Research should therefore also examine how to balance these two seemingly conflicting interests and propose procedural modalities on how to properly address the need of the child for protection, his/her limited autonomy, the right to participation and the evolving capacities of the child on the one side, and the right of the accused to receive a fair trial on the other side.

Recommendation 6
The legal status of the child should be recognised as not being a static concept, but constantly influenced by the evolving capacities of the individual child.

Recommendation 7
The capacity of the individual child should be the triggering aspect for child participation and not age.

The sixth recommendation aims to remind all actors who engage with children in the course of the proceedings that the legal status of the child is inextricable linked with the evolving capacities of the child. The practice of the ICC, as mirrored in the first decisions before the ICC, established that the Court's understanding of, in particular, the principles of the best interests and the evolving capacities of the child – the core principles relating to children's participation – reflects a rather restrictive approach of the Court and limited recognition of the child as a legal subject with evolving legal autonomy. This practice thereby established that the Court, including the various organs next to the competent Chambers, needs guidance on how to involve children in a child-sensitive manner in order to fill the current omissions and lack of child-specific understanding.

The practical difficulties of many children being supported by their parents or legal guardians in the proceedings before the International Criminal Court gave rise to the question whether others should be recognised as being competent to act on behalf of the child. Research is therefore needed to examine *inter alia* under which conditions and to what extent national and/or international human rights institutions, including non-governmental organisations, such as *Save the Children* or *War Child,* should be recognised as being appropriate and legally competent to act on behalf of a child.

As regards the seventh recommendation, it is underlined once more that age itself should not be decisive for including or excluding children from participation in ICC proceedings. Research is therefore needed which focusses in detail on the overall criteria which should be applied when deciding upon the capability of the child to participate in international criminal and/or reparation proceedings. While guidance on these aspects could have been expected to be available under the Optional Protocol to the Convention on the Rights of the Child on a Communications Procedure, one will rather be disappointed. Even if Article 2 of the Optional Protocol explicitly refers to the best interests, age and maturity of the child, it is not further explained how these factors are taken into account in order to ensure that child participation is in accordance with the evolving capacities of the individual child. Aside from the focus of this research, it is noted that the effectiveness of a complaint procedure under the CRC is expected to be limited due to the lack of a sufficiently child-focused Optional Protocol. Such criticism is based on the fact that the provisions are rather generally formulated and constitute mainly copies of the provisions of the existing UN complaint mechanisms – mechanisms which have, to date, mostly been relied upon by adult complainants and not children.

Moreover, even if coming into force, the Committee on the Rights of the Child will – like the Committees under the other UN Human Rights Treaty mechanisms – be limited in addressing and if necessary criticising the legal status of the child under national law. If however, national proceedings fail to recognise children's legal status and the accompanying procedural rights and need for protection – a scenario which is not unlikely in particular in conflict regions – the Committee will be limited to assess the respective shortcomings but cannot provide children with an international avenue to justice where their rights could be enforced. Against this background it is the more important that not age itself but the capacity of the individual child constitutes the triggering aspect for child participation.

Recommendation 8
The ICC and actors involved shall seek guidance from the Committee on the Rights of the Child when interpreting the principles of the best interests and evolving capacities.

The entire research has stipulated that the assessment of the individual child's best interests and evolving capacities should be decisive in enabling or preventing the child from participating in ICC proceedings. This implies per definition that the participation of the child may, indeed, be limited. What, however, is to be understood under the child's capacity to be capable of participating has not yet been fully researched. Transparent reasoning on whether or not allowing the child to participate therefore needs to be supported with research that enables decision takers to argue whether and in particular why a child is capable or incapable of participating.

Accordingly, as long as a more transparent understanding and assessment of the best interests and evolving capacities principles is not available, the eight recommendation aims to encourage the ICC and actors involved to seek guidance from the Committee on the Rights of the Child when interpreting the principles of the best interests and evolving capacities. Bearing in mind the lack of a clearly established standard of interpretation concerning these two core principles of child participation, further research is not only indispensable in order to promote the development of child-sensitive ICC proceedings, but also to strengthen children being universally recognised as not being human beings of the future but as human beings entitled to immediately benefit from their child- specific rights and protection – not only in a substantive dimension but also from a procedural perspective.

Recommendation 9
A legal aid scheme needs to be developed providing for pro bono legal aid for minors.

The request of the ninth recommendation finds it justification in the fact that a child, being usually financially dependent on adults, may simply be prevented from relying on the right to a remedy when pro bono legal aid is not available. As the right to a remedy constitutes a human right, and since human rights are inclusive of all human beings, children should be viewed as having unlimited legal capacity with regard to the enforcement of this right in the case of rights violations during conflict situations without being prevented from relying on this right due to financial shortcomings. Accordingly, international law should promote equal justice with regard to the recognition of the legal status and legal capacity of all human beings with the additional ingredient of pro bono legal aid for minor participants. Research should therefore analyse how, for instance, funding mechanisms could be introduced in order to ensure a sufficiently equipped financial budget to represent children on a pro bono basis.

Recommendation 10
The limitation of access for children to the ICC cannot be justified on the basis of judicial economy if not equally applied towards adults.

The *status quo* of the international legal status of the child – as far as children's substantive protection is concerned – can be characterised as a decently established legal status with a broad range of legal protection provided for under international law. The *status quo* of the international procedural legal status of the child, on the other side, remains at an early stage which requests further research and more extensive regulation under international law.

When further developing the procedural legal status of the child, it is indispensable to underpin that childhood should be seen as an independent legal status – instead of a phase which prepares children for adulthood. The latter perspective prevents focusing on the procedural rights of children during childhood. Accordingly, future research should ensure that children should not be seen as *mini adults* but as independent legal subjects of law. In light of the foregoing, the tenth recommendation aims to underline that grounds for exclusion of child participation, such as judicial economy, do not constitute a valid justification if not being equally applied to adults. Instead, such a rigid exclusion of only children discriminates children and prevents them from participation in ICC proceedings.

SUMMARY
THE CHILD IN ICC PROCEEDINGS

A child who has been victimised during an armed conflict or large-scale violence does not only face the challenge to heal from the immediate suffering caused to his or her physical or psychological well-being. Instead, the child also has to cope with the often traumatising experiences of conflict situations in the long term. Separation from family or even the loss of family members are just two instances which are likely to have consequences that a child will be confronted with during and in the aftermath of the armed conflict or large-scale violence.

International law, in particular the protection of children during and in the aftermath of armed conflict, is reflected in numerous child-specific international legal documents. In addition to children's substantive protection, the status of children seems to have gained another component: the child as procedural player. This is because children have increasingly participated not only in criminal proceedings before the Special Court for Sierra Leone, but also in proceedings before the International Criminal Court. Whether the child is also in need of particular procedural protection as a result of being a child, has not yet been comprehensively addressed under international law and is therefore the subject of this research.

Taking into account the serious lack of international regulation concerning the procedural status of the child in international criminal proceedings, the research aim is twofold: Firstly, it analyses whether and to what extent the proceedings are sufficiently child-sensitive. Secondly, a lack of child sensitivity might lead to child participation which cannot be considered to be in the best interests of the child. Consequently, where necessary, this research aims to establish whether additional child-specific regulation and awareness is necessary in order to adequately accommodate the particular needs of the child. It thereby also aims to assess whether it is at all possible that ICC proceedings are sufficiently child-sensitive. If not, it might be necessary to reconsider the possibility that children participate. To summarise the above, the concrete objective of this research reads as follows:

The research aims to provide informed insights into whether and to what extent participation in ICC proceedings is in the best interests of the child.

In light of this research aim, the problem statement reads as follows:

To what extent is the ICC procedural framework child-sensitive taking account of the evolving capacities of the child?

With a view to shedding light on this problem statement, some concrete research questions have been formulated that guide the evaluation of the different capacities in which children participate. In sum, this research addresses child participation in the following five procedural capacities: the child witness, the child participant, the child perpetrator, the child of an (alleged) perpetrator and the child claimant.

While Article 1 of the Convention on the Rights of the Child defines children as human beings below the age of eighteen years, this research is not led by an explicit age limitation of young adults as the author is of the view that a case-by-case analysis is necessary in order to determine whether a participant can be considered a child participant. Based on the above, the term child participant is neither understood to be limited to infants and young children, nor does the current understanding of the term exclude young persons above the age of eighteen years who are in their early twenties but who suffered harm as a child. Both adolescents in their teenager years and young persons who have reached majority at the time of their involvement in ICC proceedings, might indeed qualify as child participants within the ambit of this research.

Also important to note, is that the assessment of the best interests of the child is not limited to a legal assessment and should generally be made on a case-by-case basis. This research, however, does not aim to provide a definite answer to the overreaching question of whether child participation in the proceedings is in the best interests of the child. It is limited to providing an assessment as far as the legal aspects are concerned concerning all actors involved, in particular the judges, when deciding on whether or not children should participate. The limitation to an examination of the child sensitivity from a legal perspective also explains why this research does not try to give a final and definite conclusion on whether child participation should generally be encouraged or not.

The substantive part of the book is divided into three parts. Pursuant to the primary aim of this research (the examination of the child-specific procedural particularities and the child-sensitivity of the ICC procedure), Part I (criminal proceedings) and Part II (reparation proceedings) address the procedural particularities of the child participant. Both parts focus on the question of whether and to what extent ICC proceedings are child-sensitive. The analysis of the law and practice focusses in particular on the question: to what extent procedural insensitivities exist when children access and are involved in ICC proceedings. Pursuant to the second research aim (to determine whether there is a need for child-specific regulation), the examination of the procedural status of the child within each capacity seeks to provide not only an overview of the procedural rights and protection of the child, but also to scrutinise those fields in which additional procedural regulation, child-focused awareness and practice is needed. As the procedural particularities might vary depending on the specific procedural capacity in which children are involved, each capacity is addressed in a separate chapter.

Chapter Two analyses the law and practice with regard to the child witness. Particular attention is paid to the law and practice of the SCSL and the ICC. The child, as bystander, victim, or even perpetrator of international crimes, may qualify as an important witness in international criminal proceedings. Due to the usually huge numbers of witnesses of international crimes, the child is more likely to be called to the witness stand only when crimes were committed directly towards him/her. Two issues which received particular attention at the ICC concern the difficulties associated with age determination of children when called in particular as victim witness of the war crime of recruiting children below the age of fifteen years, and the impact of trauma on the credibility of the child witness. Another aspect which is addressed in relation to the child witness concerns the ability of the child to provide informed consent for his or her participation as a witness in criminal proceedings. It is shown that, compared to the following procedural capacities of the child, the child witness capacity constitutes the only one which has also played a role in other international criminal proceedings, namely those before the ICTY and the SCSL. Consequently, in contrast to the remaining analysis, only the research on the child witness capacity could rely on more extensive previous international court practice. Remarkably, while the other capacities clearly restrict the qualification of the child to the age of the individual child, this is not the case with regard to the child witness. This capacity rather includes all young people who were witness to international crimes. As a consequence, the procedural protection granted is neither limited to those below the age of eighteen, nor to children above a certain minimum age. Instead, protection is also applied to witnesses above the internationally recognised standard of eighteen years of age as codified in article 1 of the Convention on the Rights of the Child – thus, protection is not dependent on the child status.

Chapter Three focuses on the child as victim participant. For the first time in the history of international criminal law, victims, including children, are allowed to participate in criminal proceedings at the International Criminal Court. Children can thereby pursue their personal interests, independent of a prosecutorial or defence strategy. The chapter examines child-specific procedural particularities which are above all the result of the child's limited legal capacity. Questions are pursued relating to the ability to file an application on his/her own behalf or the possibility of being represented by a legal representative in the course of the proceedings.

This chapter presents the procedural requirements the child has to comply with in order to be recognised as a victim participant in criminal proceedings. Court practice has established that the ICC distinguishes between children and other applicants - a distinction which is not provided for in the Rome Statute or its Rules of Procedure and Evidence. Alongside this distinction, various Chambers introduced that child applicants have to comply with requirements in addition to the ones provided for in Rule 85 of the Court's Rules of Procedure and Evidence in order to be considered for the status of victim participant. Furthermore, in contrast to the procedural capacity of the child witness, the age of the child applicant has repeatedly been relied upon by various Chambers (with no mention in the Rome Statute and the Rules of Procedure and Evidence) when deciding upon the legal capacity of the child to file an application for participation on his or her own behalf. A coherent established practice in relation to the legal capacity of the child to file an application for participation is, however, still absent. Subsequently, attention is paid to the practical difficulties faced by the child applicant which arise when filing an application for participation, such as proof of identity and kinship or legal guardianship.

Once acknowledged as victim participants in proceedings, the participation of children can take place in various forms. The analysis therefore also discusses the possibility that a child appears *in person* before the Court.

Another aspect analysed in light of the practice of the ICC concerning child participants is gender. The practice of various Chambers alludes that whether a child is a boy or a girl can give rise to procedural implications based on gender. After all, not recognising that girls who have been recruited solely for the purpose of sexual violence can qualify as child soldiers within the sense of the recruitment crime entails the risk of impunity as regards the crimes perpetrated against these victims. This is because these crimes are likely to fall outside the scope of the war crime of sexual violence as codified in the Rome Statute.

Two additional interrelated aspects are the representation of the child and the provision of legal aid. While the Court seems to prefer the common legal representation of children, such a generalised approach cannot be found in relation to the provision of legal aid to children.

Chapter Four looks at the possibility of the procedural capacity of the child perpetrator and the procedural capacity of the child of a(n) (alleged) perpetrator. It addresses the international practice in regard to these two capacities. The participation of child soldiers in hostilities is a well-known and continuing reality. Despite the existence of child perpetrators, their international prosecution has only been possible - though limited to those children aged between fifteen and eighteen years at the time of alleged crime commission - without ever having been initiated, before the SCSL. By excluding the jurisdiction on persons below the age of eighteen from the mandate of the ICC (Article 26 Rome Statute), the establishment of the International Criminal Court brought the discussion on whether prosecuting minors before the ICC to an end.

Chapter Four also highlights selected procedural particularities in relation to the implications for the child of a parent being prosecuted by the Court. In contrast to the previous procedural capacities, the age of the child is a less decisive factor. When a parent is involved as an alleged perpetrator or has been convicted by the ICC, the detention and imprisonment can give rise to not only financial and social implications for a child, but is also likely to bring up questions regarding the amount of and entitlement to family visits – aspects which have not been dealt with in the Rome Statute or its Rules of Procedure and Evidence.

Subsequently, *Part II* addresses the child in international reparatory justice mechanisms. *Chapter Five* discusses the law and practice of the ICC regarding the child claimant who is a victim of the crimes falling within the jurisdictional mandate of the ICC.

The first decisions of the Court in relation to the child participant already anticipate various procedural aspects in relation to the access of the child claimant. In addition, one can allude from the practice of the European Court of Human Rights, which is experienced in reparation claims, that the ICC is also likely to be confronted with the question of whether, and to what extent, statutory limitations should be applied when a child files a reparation request? Considering that reparations for gross human rights violations and serious violations of international humanitarian law were not provided for on a statutory basis prior to the establishment of the ICC, it is not surprising that the Court is also faced with the question of which forms of reparations are to be awarded to the child? Bearing in mind the huge numbers of potential child claimants (which have already confronted the Court in the *Lubanga* case with practical difficulties prior to awarding reparations), it is also feasible that the Court will need to establish eligibility criteria.

The last challenge addressed in this chapter - perhaps even the biggest challenge for the ICC - relates to the fact that the Court will need to develop an effective implementation mechanism in order to ensure that the child, in the end, benefits from reparation awards.

Finally, *Part III* provides a concluding and comparative evaluation of the procedural capacities of the child in the proceedings before the ICC. *Chapter Six* connects and assesses the core conclusions reached within each chapter and offers some overreaching reflections on the position of the child as a procedural actor in the criminal and reparation proceedings before the International Criminal Court. The research concludes with a view to the future, and in particular calls for further research and procedural regulation of the procedural particularities in relation to child participation in ICC proceedings.

Samenvatting
Participatie van kinderen in de procedure voor het Internationaal Strafhof (Summary in Dutch)

Een kind dat slachtoffer is geworden ten tijde van een gewapende strijd of grootschalig geweld wordt niet alleen geconfronteerd met de uitdaging om van het directe psychologische en fysieke leed te helen. Tegelijkertijd dient het kind gedurende het hele leven te leren omgaan met de vaak traumatiserende ervaringen. Scheiding van de familie of het verlies van familieleden zijn slechts twee voorbeelden van mogelijk consequenties van een gewapende strijd of grootschalig geweld voor het kind.

Het internationale recht, in het bijzonder de bescherming van kinderen ten tijde van of na afloop van een gewapende conflict omvat talrijke kind-specifieke regelingen. In aanvulling op de materieel rechtelijke bescherming van het kind schijnt de rechtsstatus van het kind een verdere component verkregen te hebben: het kind als procedurele deelnemer. De reden hiervoor is dat het kind steeds meer deelneemt in internationale juridische procedures. Niet alleen in de context van de internationaal strafrechtelijke procedure voor het Speciale Hof voor Sierra Leone, maar tevens in de procedures bij het Internationaal Strafhof. De vraag of het kind in aanvulling op zijn materieel rechtelijke bescherming tevens behoefte heeft aan een kind-specifieke procedurele bescherming omdat het een kind is, is tot heden niet omvattend beantwoord binnen het internationale recht. Deze vraag staat centraal in het voorliggend onderzoek.

Rekening houdend met het feit dat er een ernstig gebrek is aan internationale regelgeving betreffende de procedurele status van het kind in een internationale strafprocedure, omvat dit onderzoek twee centrale doelstellingen: ten eerste wordt er geanalyseerd of en in welke omvang internationale strafprocedures voldoende kind-specifiek zijn. Ten tweede, een gebrek aan kind-specificiteit kan leiden tot deelname van het kind, welke niet in het belang van het kind is. Dit onderzoek heeft tot doel vast te stellen of additionele kind-specifieke regelgeving en bewustzijn noodzakelijk is om de behoeften van het kind in de procedure adequaat te accommoderen. Hierbij beoordeelt het onderzoek tevens of het überhaupt mogelijk is dat de procedures bij het Internationaal Strafhof voldoende kind-specifiek kunnen zijn. Indien dit niet het geval is, is het wellicht noodzakelijk om de mogelijkheid kinderen deel te laten nemen te heroverwegen. Samenvattend kan de concrete doelstelling van dit onderzoek als volgt worden geformuleerd:

> *Het onderzoek heeft tot doel een weloverwogen inzicht te geven ten aanzien van de vraag of en in welke* omvang *deelname aan de procedures bij het Internationaal Strafhof in het belang van het kind is.*

Indachtig deze doelstelling van het onderzoek, luidt de probleemstelling als volgt:

> *In welke mate is het procedurele raamwerk van het Internationaal Strafhof voldoende kind-specifiek bij het in acht nemen van de zich ontwikkelende vermogens van het kind?*

Om nader toelichting te geven ten aanzien van deze probleemstelling werden concrete onderzoeksvragen geformuleerd, welke als richtlijn dienen voor een beoordeling van de verschillende capaciteiten waarin het kind participeert. Samenvattend kan worden vastgesteld, dat dit onderzoek de deelname van het kind in de volgende vijf procedurele capaciteiten analyseert: het kind als getuige, het kind als deelnemer, het kind als dader, het kind van een (vermeende) dader en het kind als eiser.

Artikel 1 van het Kinderrechtenverdrag bepaalt dat ieder mens onder de achttien jaar een kind is. Dit onderzoek daarentegen, is niet gebaseerd op een dusdanig strikte leeftijdsbeperking. De auteur is van mening dat een case-by-base analyse noodzakelijk is om te bepalen of een procedurele deelnemer ook als kind deelnemer erkend mag worden. Uit het bovengenoemde volgt dat de term kind deelnemer binnen het kader van dit onderzoek zich niet beperkt tot kinderen onder de achttien jaar. De uitleg van de term in dit onderzoek sluit ook jonge volwassenen boven de achttien jaar, die schade hebben geleden tijdens hun jeugd, niet uit als kind deelnemer. Dit heeft tot gevolg dat zowel minderjarige pubers, maar ook jonge volwassenen die ten tijde van hun deelname aan de procedures bij het Internationaal Strafhof achttien jaar of ouder zijn zich kunnen kwalificeren als kind deelnemer binnen het kader van dit onderzoek.

Tevens is het van belang te vermelden dat de beoordeling van het belang van het kind niet beperkt is tot een juridische analyse en op case-by-case basis dient uitgevoerd te worden. Dit onderzoek beoogt geen definitief antwoord op de vraag te formuleren of deelname van kinderen in de strafrechtelijke procedure bij het Internationaal Strafhof in het belang van het kind is. Het beperkt zich echter tot een analyse van de juridische aspecten welke van belang zijn voor alle betrokken partijen in de procedure, in het bijzonder rechters, die een beslissing dienen te nemen betreffende de vraag of kinderen wel of niet zouden moeten deelnemen. De beperking van onderzoek van de kind specificiteit vanuit een juridisch perspectief, verklaart in het bijzonder waarom het onderzoek niet tot doel heeft een definitief antwoord te geven ten aanzien van de vraag of participatie van kinderen in het algemeen wel of niet aan te moedigen is.

Het boek is ingedeeld in drie delen. Overeenkomstig het primaire onderzoeksdoel (de analyse van de kind-specifieke procedurele bijzonderheden en de kind gevoeligheid van de procedure bij het Internationaal Strafhof), beschouwen Deel I (strafprocedure) en Deel II (schadevergoedingsprocedure) de procedurele bijzonderheden ten aanzien van de participatie van kinderen. Beide leggen de nadruk op de vraag of en in welke mate de procedures bij het Internationaal Strafhof kind-specifiek zijn. De analyse van de regelgeving en praktijk richt zich in het bijzonder op de volgende vraag: in welke mate bestaan er procedurele onachtzaamheden wanneer kinderen toegang tot het Hof zoeken of betrokken zijn bij een lopende procedure bij het Internationaal Strafhof. Op grond van de tweede onderzoeksdoelstelling (het bepalen of er een noodzaak is voor een kind-specifieke regelgeving), heeft de beschouwing van de procedurele status van het kind binnen iedere procesrechtelijke capaciteit, niet alleen tot doel een overzicht te bieden van de procedurele rechten en bescherming van het kind. Tevens wordt beoogt zorgvuldig te onderzoeken binnen welke gebieden aanvullende procedurele regelgeving, een kind georiënteerde bewustzijn en praktijk noodzakelijk is. Aangezien de procedurele bijzonderheden per specifieke procedurele capaciteit van elkaar kunnen afwijken, wordt ieder procesrechtelijke capaciteit in een afzonderlijke hoofdstuk nader onderzocht.

Hoofdstuk Twee analyseert de regelgeving en praktijk ten aanzien van de kind getuige. In het bijzonder wordt aandacht besteed aan de regelgeving en praktijk van het Sierra Leone Tribunaal en het Internationaal Strafhof. Het kind als omstander, slachtoffer of zelfs dader van internationale misdrijven kan een belangrijke getuige zijn in internationale strafprocedures. Gezien de normaalgesproken grote aantallen van getuigen in internationale misdrijven, is men eerder geneigd het kind als getuige op te roepen indien het rechtstreeks slachtoffer is geworden van een internationaal misdrijf. Twee aspecten die binnen het Internationaal Strafhof bijzonder aandacht hebben ontvangen, hebben betrekking op het bepalen van de leeftijd van het kind in gevallen waar kinderen als getuigen werden opgeroepen (omdat zij tevens slachtoffer zijn van het oorlogsmisdrijf van het rekruteren van kinderen onder de vijftien jaar) en op de gevolgen van trauma op de geloofwaardigheid van de kind getuige. Een ander aspect van groot belang betreft het vermogen van het kind om een bewuste toestemming ten aanzien van zijn deelname als getuige in de strafprocedure te geven. Het is aangetoond dat vergeleken met andere procedurele capaciteiten van het kind, de capaciteit van de kind getuige de enige is welke tevens van belang was in andere internationale strafprocedures, namelijk de procedures bij het Joegoslavië Tribunaal en Sierra Leone Tribunaal. Derhalve, in tegenstelling tot bestaand onderzoek, kan slechts de analyse van het kind in de capaciteit van getuige rekenen op de praktijk van vroegere uitgebreide internationale straftribunalen. Het valt in deze samenhang op, dat de capaciteit van de kind getuige in tegenstelling tot de andere procedurele capaciteiten, niet is beperkt tot een bepaalde leeftijdsgrens. De procedurele capaciteit van de kind getuige omvat alle jonge mensen welke getuige zijn van een internationaal misdrijf. Dit heeft tot gevolg dat de procedurele bescherming niet is beperkt tot getuigen onder de achttien jaar of boven een minimum leeftijd, op het moment van getuigenis. In tegendeel, procedurele bescherming werd ook getuigen geboden, die ouder dan achttien jaar (standaard van artikel 1 van het Kinderrechtenverdrag) waren op moment van getuigenis. Bescherming voor deze categorie van getuigen is derhalve niet afhankelijk van de kind status zoals genoemd in de zin van artikel 1 van het Kinderrechtenverdrag.

In *Hoofdstuk Drie* staat het kind als participerend slachtoffer centraal. Voor de eerste keer in de geschiedenis van het internationaal strafrecht mogen slachtoffers, waaronder ook kinderen, deelnemen in de strafrechtelijke procedure bij het Internationaal Strafhof. Kinderen kunnen hierdoor hun eigen belangen nastreven, onafhankelijk van de strategie van de aanklager of verdediging. Het hoofdstuk onderzoekt de kind-specifieke procedurele bijzonderheden welke bovenal het gevolg zijn van de beperkte rechtsbekwaamheid van het kind. Centraal staan vragen ten aanzien van de bekwaamheid van het kind om zelfstandig een aanvraag tot participatie in te dienen en de mogelijkheid om tijdens de procedure vertegenwoordigd te worden door een advocaat.

Dit hoofdstuk legt de procedurele vereisten voor waaraan het kind dient te voldoen om erkend te worden als een participerend slachtoffer in de strafprocedure. Uit de praktijk van het Internationaal Strafhof blijkt dat het Hof onderscheid maakt tussen kinderen en andere aanvragers – een onderscheid dat niet is bepaald in het Statuut van Rome of in de procedure en bewijsregels van het Hof. Naast dit onderscheid hebben verschillende kamers van het hof extra vereisten waaraan kinderen dienen te voldoen ingevoerd, boven de reeds in Regel 85 van de procedure en bewijsregels van het Hof, om in aanmerking te komen voor de status van een participerend slachtoffer. Bovendien werd, in tegenstelling tot de procedurele capaciteit van de kind getuige, de leeftijd van de minderjarige aanvrager door verschillende kamers als reden genoemd om een beslissing te geven op de rechtsbekwaamheid van de minderjarige ten aanzien van zijn capaciteit om een aanvraag in te dienen in zijn eigen naam. Vermeld moet worden dat deze praktijk niet is voorgeschreven of geregeld door het Statuut van Rome en de procedure en bewijsregels van het Hof. Een coherente gevestigde praktijk ten aanzien van de rechtsbekwaamheid van het kind om zelfstandig een aanvraag tot participatie in te dienen, ontbreekt tot op heden. In aanvulling op de voorafgaande procedurele bijzonderheden onderzoekt dit hoofdstuk tevens de praktische problemen die zich voordoen wanneer het kind een aanvraag tot participatie wil indienen. Hieronder vallen bijvoorbeeld de noodzaak van het bewijzen van zijn identiteit en verwantschap, of wettelijke voogdijschap.

De participatie van kinderen kan plaatsvinden in verschillende vormen zodra het kind erkend wordt als deelnemend slachtoffer in de procedure bij het Internationaal Strafhof. Dit onderzoek behandelt derhalve ook de mogelijkheid dat het kind *in personam* optreed bij het Hof.

Een ander aspect dat nader onderzocht wordt indachtig de praktijk van het Internationaal Strafhof betreft het geslacht van het kind. Uit de praktijk van verschillende kamers blijk dat het geslacht van de minderjarige participant implicaties kan voortbrengen voor de procedure. Per slot van rekening, het niet erkennen van het feit dat ook meisjes, die uitsluitend werden gerekruteerd voor seksuele doeleinden of diensten, ook gekwalificeerd kunnen worden als kindsoldaten, binnen het kader van de misdaad van rekruteren, kan verregaande gevolgen hebben. Het gevaar van straffeloosheid van de dader is hier van bijzonder belang. Dit is omdat deze daad niet binnen de categorie van het oorlogsmisdrijf van seksuele geweld valt, zoals gecodificeerd in het Statuut van Rome.

Twee andere onderling samenhangende aspecten die nader onderzocht worden, zijn de vertegenwoordiging van het kind door een advocaat en het genieten van rechtsbijstand. Terwijl het Internationaal Strafhof een voorkeur schijnt te hebben voor de procedurele vertegenwoordiging van het kind door een advocaat, is een dergelijk algemene aanpak niet zichtbaar ten aanzien van het garanderen van rechtsbijstand voor de minderjarige.

Hoofdstuk Vier beschouwt de mogelijkheid van de procedurele capaciteit van de kinddader en de procedurele capaciteit van het kind van een verdachte of dader. In het bijzonder gaat dit hoofdstuk in op de bestaande internationale praktijk van deze twee procedurele capaciteiten. De deelname van kindsoldaten in gevechtshandelingen is algemeen erkend en een dagelijkse realiteit. Ondanks het bestaan van kind daders, bestond de mogelijkheid tot een internationale strafrechtelijke vervolging uitsluitend bij het Sierra Leone Tribunaal. Alleen het Statuut van het Sierra Leone Tribunaal biedt de mogelijkheid minderjarigen welke ten tijde van de vermeende daad tussen de vijftien en de achttien jaar waren, strafrechtelijk te vervolgen. In de praktijk van het Sierra Leone Tribunaal werd echter nooit gebruik gemaakt van deze procedurele mogelijkheid. In tegenstelling tot deze procedurele mogelijkheid sluit Artikel 26 van het Statuut van Rome de strafrechtelijke vervolging van minderjarigen bij het Internationaal Strafhof uit. De discussie of minderjarigen door dit Hof vervolgd zouden kunnen worden, is hiermee tot een einde gebracht.

Het vierde hoofdstuk vestigt tevens de aandacht op de procedurele bijzonderheden ten aanzien van de gevolgen voor kinderen wier ouders strafrechtelijk vervolgd worden door het Internationaal Strafhof. In tegenstelling tot de voorgaande procedurele capaciteiten, is de leeftijd van het kind hier van minder groot belang. De vervolging van maar ook veroordeling en aansluitende gevangenisstraf voor een ouder kan zowel financiële als ook sociale gevolgen voor de minderjarige hebben. Tevens kunnen er vragen opkomen ten aanzien van het recht op en aantal van familiebezoeken. De regeling van familiebezoeken wordt echter niet behandeld binnen het Statuut van Rome of binnen de procedure en bewijsregels van het Internationaal Strafhof.

Aansluitend aan de voorafgaande analyse betracht het onderzoek de status van de minderjarige binnen schadevergoedingsprocedures van internationale aard. *Hoofdstuk Vijf* stelt de regelgeving en praktijk van het Internationaal Strafhof ten aanzien van de minderjarige eiser die slachtoffer is geworden van een misdrijf binnen de jurisdictie van het Hof, ter discussie.

Reeds de eerste beslissingen van het Hof met betrekking tot de minderjarige deelnemer anticiperen dat er een aantal procedurele aspecten in verband met de toegang tot het Hof bestaan voor de minderjarige die aanspraak wil maken op schadevergoeding. Men dient verder in gedachten te houden dat het niet eerder mogelijk was om als individu een schadevergoedingsklacht in te dienen indien schade werd geleden door internationale misdrijven. Derhalve zal het Internationaal Strafhof zich tevens moeten buigen over rechtsvragen ten aanzien van de vorm van schadevergoedingen en in het bijzonder de vraag of de minderjarige een bijzondere vorm van schadevergoeding behoeft. Bovendien is te verwachten dat gezien het groot aantal potentiële minderjarige eisers (het Hof heeft reeds kennis gemaakt met de praktische moeilijkheden voorafgaande het toekennen van schadevergoeding in de *Lubanga* zaak) ertoe zal leiden dat het Hof eisen zal introduceren om in aanmerking te komen voor kind-specifieke vormen van schadevergoeding.

De laatste uitdaging, wellicht de grootste voor het internationaal Strafhof, betreft het feit dat het Internationaal Strafhof een effectief implementatie mechanisme zou moeten ontwikkelen om te kunnen bewerkstelligen dat het kind op den duur daadwerkelijk profijt heeft van de toegekende schadevergoeding.

Ten slotte omvat Deel III een concluderende en vergelijkende beoordeling van de procedurele capaciteiten van het kind binnen de procedures bij het Internationaal Strafhof. *Hoofdstuk Zes* verbindt en evalueert de belangrijkste conclusies van ieder hoofdstuk en biedt een overkoepelende reflectie op de rechtsstatus van de minderjarige als procedurele deelnemer in de straf- en schadevergoedingsprocedure bij het Internationaal Strafhof. Het onderzoek sluit af met een zicht op de toekomst en vraagt in het bijzonder om verder onderzoek en procedurele regelgeving van de procedurele bijzonderheden ten aanzien van participatie van minderjarigen in de procedures bij het Internationaal Strafhof.

SELECTED BIBLIOGRAPHY

Abott 2000
A. Abbott, 'Child soldiers: the use of children as instruments of war', (2000) 23 *Suffolk Transnational Law Review* 499-537.

Abresch 2005
W. Abresch, 'A Human Rights Law of Internal Armed Conflict: The European Court of Human Rights in Chechnya,' (2005) 16 *European Journal of International Law* 741-767.

Abu Hein *et al.* 1993
F. Abu Hein *et al.*, 'Trauma and mental health of children in Gaza', (1993) 306 *British Medical Journal* 1130.

Akhavan 2001
P. Akhavan, 'Beyond Impunitz: Can International Criminal Justice Prevent Future Atrocities', (2001) 95 AJIL 7-31.

Aldrich, van Baarda & Kalshoven (1995)
G.H. Aldirch, Th.A. van Baarda, F. Kalshoven, 'Conference on the Rights of Children in Armed Conflict', (1995) 89 AJIL 849-851.

Alfredson 2001
L. Alfredson, 'Sexual Exploitation of Child Soldiers: an exploration and analysis of global dimensions and trends' (2001), http://reliefweb.int/sites/reliefweb.int/files/resources/C216BEBEEF8597E1C1256DAB002D9450-csusc-exploit.pdf.

Alen *et al* 2007
A. Alen, et al, *A Commentary on the United Nations Convention on the Rights of the Child* (2007), Leiden (etc.): Martinus Nijhoff.

Alfredsson, Macalister-Smith & Grahl-Madsen 1996
G. Alfredsson, P. Macalister-Smith, A. Grahl-Madsen (eds.), *The Living Law of Nations: Essays on refugees, minorities and indigenous peoples and the human rights of other vulnerable groups: in memory of Atle Grahl-Madsen* (1996), Kehl (etc.): Engel.

Alink & van Zeden 2006
M.J. Alink, P.D.J. van Zeden, *Getuigen in het Nederlands Strafproces* (2006), Nijmegen: Wolf Legal Publishers.

Allwood, Bell-Gohan & Husain 2002
M.A. Allwood, D. Bell-Dolan, S.A. Husain, 'Children's Trauma and Adjustment Reactions to Violent and Non-Violent War Experiences', (2002) 41 *Journal of American Academy of Child and Adolescent Psychiatry* 450-457.

Alston & Goodman 2013
P. Alston, R. Goodman, *International Human Rights* (2013), Oxford: Oxford University Press.

Alvarez 2009
J.E. Alvarez, 'Alternatives to International Criminal Justice', in A. Cassese (ed.), *The Oxford Companion to International Criminal Justice* (2009), Oxford: Oxford University Press, 25-38.

Ambos 2009
K. Ambos, ''Witness Proofing' Before the ICC: Neither Legally Admissible Nor Necessary' in: C. Stahn, G. Sluiter (eds), *The Emerging Practice of the International Criminal Court* (2009), Leiden: Martinus Nijhoff Publishers, 599-614.

Ang, Berghmans & Cattrijsse 2006
F. Ang, E. Berghmans, L. Cattrijsse (eds.), *Participation Rights of Children* (2006), Antwerp (etc.): Intersentia.

Ang, Berghmans & Delplace 2006
F. Ang, E. Berghmans, M. Delplace, 'Participation Rights in the UN Convention on the Rights of the Child', in F. Ang, E. Berghmans, L. Cattrijsse (eds.), *Participation Rights of Children* (2006), Antwerp (etc.): Intersentia, 9-26.

Apfel & Aimon 1996
R.J. Apfel, B. Aimon (eds.), *Minefields in their hearts: the mental health of children in war and communal violence* (1996), New Haven: Yale University Press.

Aptel & Ladisch 2011
C. Aptel, V. Ladisch, International Center for Transitional Justice, *Children – Through a New Lens: A Child-Sensitive Approach to Transitional Justice* (2011), http://www.crin.org/docs/ICTJ_ThroughaNewLens.pdf.

Arsanjani 1999
M.H. Arsanjani, 'The Rome Statute of the International Criminal Court', 93 (1999) AJIL 22-43.

Artis 2004
J.E. Artis, 'Judging the Best Interests of the Child: Judges' Accounts of the Tender Years Doctrine, (2004) 38 *Law and Society Review* 769-806.

Arts 2006
K. Arts, 'General Introduction: A Child-Rights-Based Approach to International Criminal Accountability', in K. Arts, V. Popovski (eds.), *International Criminal Accountability and the Rights of Children* (2006), The Hague: Hague Academic Press.

Arts & Popovski 2006
K. Arts, V. Popovski (eds.), *International Criminal Accountability and the Rights of Children* (2006), The Hague: Hague Academic Press.

Avery 1983
M. Avery, 'The Child Abuse Witness: Potential For Secondary Victimization', (1983-1984) 7 *Criminal Justice Journal* 1-48.

Ayissi 2002
A. Ayissi, 'Protecting children in armed conflict: from commitment to compliance', (2002) 3 *Disarmament forum* 5-16.

Bachrach 2000
M. Bachrach, 'The Protection and Rights of Victims under International Criminal Law', (2000) 34 *The International Lawyer* 7-20.

Bair 2008
J.P. Bair, 'From the Numbers Who Died to Those Who Survived: Victim Participation in the Extraordinary Chambers in the Courts of Cambodia', (2008-2009) 31 *University of Hawai'i Law Review* 507-552.
Baker & Shalhoub-Kevorkian 1999
A. Baker, N. Shalhoub-Kevorkian, 'Effects of political and military traumas on children: The Palestinian case', 19 (1999) *Clinical Psychology Review* 935-950.
Baker 1990
A.M. Baker, 'Psychological Responses of Palestinian Children to the Environmental Stress Associated with Military Occupation', (1990) 4 *Journal of Refugee Studies* 237-247.
Bakker 2010
C. Bakker, *Prosecuting International Crimes Against Children: The Legal Framework*, Innocenti Working Paper, IWP 2010-13 (2010).
Bank & Schwager 2007
R. Bank, E. Schwager, 'Is there a Substantive Right to Compensation for Individual Victims of Armed Conflicts against a State under International Law?' (2007) 49 *German Yearbook of International Law* 367-412.
Bassiouni 2006
M. C. Bassiouni, 'International Recognition of Victims' Rights', (2006) 6 *Human Rights Law Review* 203-279.
Bassiouni 1983
M.C. Bassiouni, 'The Penal Characteristics of Conventional International Criminal Law', (1983) 15 *Case Western Reserve Journal of International Law 27-37.*
Beckmann 2008
L. Beckman, 'Public Justifiability and Children', (2008) 16 *International Journal of Children's Rights* 141-152.
Bennet Woodhouse 2006
B. Bennett Woodhouse, 'The Changing Status of the Child', in J. Todres, M.E. Wojcik, C.R. Revaz (eds.), *The U.N. Convention on the Rights of the Child - An Analysis of Treaty Provisions and Implications of U.S. Ratification* (2006), Ardsley, New York: Transnational Publishers, 51-63.
Beloof 2005
D.E. Beloof, 'The Third Wave of Crime Victims' Rights: Standing, Remedy and Review', (2005) 8/9 *Brigham Young University Law Review* 255-365.
Beresford 2005
S. Beresford, 'Child Witnesses and the International Criminal Justice System. Does the ICC Protect the most Vulnerable', (2005) 2 *Journal of International Criminal Justice* 721-748.
Bert *et al.* 1987
J.W. Berg *et al.*, Informed Consent: Legal Theory and Clinical Practice (1987), 2nd edition, New York, NY: Oxford University Press.
Bergsmo & Pejić 2008
M. Bergsmo, J. Pejić, 'Article 15 Prosecutor', in O. Triffterer, *Commentary on the Rome Statute of the International Criminal Court – Observers' Notes, Article by Article* (2008), Second Edition, München (etc.): C.H.Beck, 581-593.

Berman 1999
H. Berman, 'Health in the aftermath of violence: a critical narrative study of children of war and children of battered women', (1999) 31 *Canadian Journal of Nursing Research* 89-109.
Bílková 2007
V. Bílková, 'Victims of War and Their Right to Reparation for Violations of International Humanitarian Law', (2007) 4 *Miskolc Journal of International Law* 1-11.
Bitti 2009
G. Bitti, 'Article 21 of the Statute of the International Criminal Court and the Treatment of Sources of Law in the Jurisprudence of the ICC', in C. Stahn & G. Sluiter, *The Emerging Practice of the International Criminal Court* (2009), Leiden: Martinus Nijhoff Publishers, 285-304.
Bitti & Friman 2001
G. Bitti, H. Friman, 'Participation of Victims in the Proceedings', in R.S. Lee (ed.), *The International Criminal Court: Elements of Crimes and Rules of Procedure and Evidence* (2001), Ardsley, NY: Transnational Publishers, 456-474.
Blattman & Bowmann 2008
R. Blattman & K. Bowmann, 'Achievements and Problems of the International Criminal Court – A View from Within' (2008) 6 *Journal of International Criminal Justice* 711-730.
Bledsoe 1993
C. Bledsoe, 'Introduction', in C. Bledsoe and B. Cohen (eds.), *Social Dynamics of Adolescent Fertility in Sub-Saharan Africa* (1993), Washington: National Academy Press.
Bledsoe & Cohen 1993
C. Bledsoe & B. Cohen (eds), *Social Dynamics of Adolescent Fertility in Sub-Saharan Africa* (1993), Washington: National Academy Press.
Boyle 2006
D. Boyle, 'The Rights of Victims – Participation, Representation, Protection, Reparation' (2006) 4 *Journal of International Criminal Justice* 307-313.
Brants 2009
C. Brants, 'Transitional Justice: History-Telling, Collective Memory, and the Victim-Witness', (2013) 7 *International Journal of Conflict and Violence* 36-49.
Breen 2007
C. Breen, 'When Is a Child Not a Child? Child Soldiers in International Law', (2007) 8 *Human Rights Review* 71-103.
Breen 2003
C. Breen, The Role of NGO's in the Formulation of and Compliance with the Optional Protocol to the Convention of the Rights of the Child on Involvement of Children in Armed Conflict, (2003) 25 *Human Rights Quarterly* 453-481.
Brett 1999
R. Brett, 'Adolescents Volunteering for Armed Forces or Armed Groups', (1999) no. 852 *International Review of the Red Cross* 875-866.
Brewin *et al.* 1999
C.R. Brewin *et al.*, 'Acute Stress Disorder and Posttraumatic Stress Disorder in Victims of Violent Crime, (1999) 156 *American Journal of Psychiatry* 360-366.

Brocklehurst 2006
H. Brocklehurst, *Who's afraid of children? Children, Conflict and International Relations* (2006), Hampshire: Ashgate Publishing.
Bruck, Ceci & Hembrooke 1998
M. Bruck, S.J. Ceci, H. Hembrooke, 'Reliability and credibility of young children's reports', (1998) 53 *American Psychologist* 136-151.
Buck 2005
T. Buck, *International Child Law* (2005), London (etc.): Cavendish.

Cahn 2006
N. Cahn, 'Poor Children: Child "Witches" and Child Soldiers in Sub-Saharan Africa', (2006) 3 *Ohio State Journal of Criminal Law* 413-456.
Candel *et al.* 2004
I. Candel, H. Merckelbach, M. Jelicic, M. Limpens & K. Widderhoven, 'Children's Suggestibility For Peripheral and Central Details', (2004) 5 *The Journal of Credibility Assessment and Witness Psychology* 9-18
Capone 2013
F. Capone, *Is Anybody Playing? The Right to Reparation for child-victims of armed conflict* (2013), PhD thesis, Tilburg University..
Capone 2010
F. Capone, 'The Right to Reparation for War-Affected Children Special Focus on BIH', (2010) 1 *International Journal of Rule of Law, Transitional Justice and Human Rights* 98-110.
Carpenter 2007
R.C. Carpenter (ed.), *Born of War – Protecting Children of Sexual Violence Survivors in Conflict Zones* (2007), Bloomfield: Kumarian Press.
Carpenter 2006
R.C. Carpenter, *'Innocent Women and Children' Gender, Norms and the Protection of Civilians* (2006), Aldershot: Asghate, Hampshire.
Carpenter 2005
R. Ch. Carpenter, '"Women, Children and Other Vulnerable Groups": Gender, Strategic Frames and the Protection of Civilians as a Transitional Issue', (2005) 49 ISQ 295-334.
Carpenter 2000
R.C. Carpenter, 'Surfacing Children: Limitations of Genocidal Rape Discourse', (2000) 22 *Human Rights Quarterly* 428-477.
Cashomre & Bussey 1996
J. Cashmore, K. Bussey, 'Judicial Perceptions of Child Witnesses Competence', (1996) 20 *Law and Human Behavior* 313-334.
Cashmore & Parkinson 2007
J. Cashmore, P. Parkinson, 'What Responsibility Do Courts Have to Hear Children's Voices?', (2007) 15 *International Journal of Children's Rights* 43-60.
Cassese 2009
A. Cassese (ed.), *The Oxford Companion to International Criminal Justice* (2009), Oxford: Oxford University Press.
Cassese, Gaeta & Zappala 2008
A. Cassese, P. Gaeta, S. Zappala, *The Human Dimension of International Law. Selected Papers* (2008), Oxford (etc.): Oxford University Press.

Cassese, Gaeta & Jones 2002
A. Cassese, P. Gaeta, J. Jones (eds.), *The Rome Statute of the International Criminal Court* (2002), Volume I and II, Oxford (etc.): Oxford University Press.
Catani 2012
L. Catani, 'Victims at the International Criminal Court – Some Lessons Learned from the Lubanga Case', 10 (2012) *Journal of International Criminal Justice* 905-922.
Ceci & Bruck 1993
S.J. Ceci, M. Bruck, 'Suggestibility of the child witness: a historical review and synthesis', (1993) 113 *Psychological Bulletin* 403-439.
Chamberlayn 2014
C. Chamberlayn, *Children and the International Criminal Court* (2014), Leiden: E.M. Meijers Instituut.
Chapham & Ball 2001
A.R. Chapman, P. Ball, 'The Truth Commissions: Comparative Lessons from Haiti, South Africa, and Guatemala', (2001) 23 *Human Rights Quarterly* 1-43.
Charlow 1987
A. Charlow, 'Awarding Custody: The Best Interests of the Child and other Fictions', (1987) 5 *Yale Law & Policy Review* 267-290.
Chung 2008
C.H. Chung, 'Victims' Participation at the International Criminal Court: Are Concessions of the Court Clouding the Promise?', (2008) 6 *Northwestern Journal of International Human Rights* 459-542.
Cohn & Goodwin-Gill 1994
I. Cohn, G.S. Goodwin-Gill, *Child soldiers: the role of children in armed conflict* (1994), Oxford (etc.): Clarendon Press.
Cook & Heykoop 2010
P. Cook, C. Heykoop, 'Child Participation in the Sierra Leonean TRC', in S. Parmar et al, *Children and Transitional Justice, Truth-Telling, Accountability and Reconciliation* (2010), http://www.unicef-irc.org/publications/pdf/tj_publication_eng.pdf, 159-191.
Collbear 1992
J. Coolbear, 'Credibility of young children in sexual abuse cases: Assessment strategies of legal and human service professionals', (1992) 33 *Canadian Psychology* 151-167. First time and only once, chapter 3
Cottier & Zimmermann 2008
M. Cottier, A. Zimmermann, Article 8 War Crimes, in O. Triffterer, *Commentary on the Rome Statute of the International Criminal Court – Observers' Notes, Article by Article* (2008), Second Edition, München (etc.): C.H.Beck, 466-475.
Correa, Guillerot & Magarrell 2009
C. Correa, J. Guillerot and L. Magarrell, 'Reparations and Victim Participation: A look at the Truth Commission Experience', in C. Ferstman, M. Goetz, A. Stephens (eds.*), Reparations for Victims of Genocide, War Crimes and Crimes Against Humanity, Systems in Place and Systems in Making* (2009), Leiden (etc.): Nijhoff, 385-414.
Craig & de Búrca 2008
P. Craig, G. de Búrca, *EU Law, Text, Cases, and Materials* (2008).
Crofts 2003
T. Crofts, 'Doli Incapax: Why Children Deserve its Protection', (2003) 10 *Murdoch University Electronic Journal of Law*,
http://www.murdoch.edu.au/elaw/issues/v10n3/crofts103.txt.

Cryer *et al.* 2010
R. Cryer H. Friman, D. Robinson, *An Introduction to International Criminal Law and Procedure* (2010), 2nd edition, Cambridge (etc.): Cambridge University Press.
Cunningham 2006
L. Cunningham, 'A Question of Capacity: Towards a Comprehensive and Consistent Vision of Children and Their Status under Law', (2006) 10 *University of California Davis Journal of Juvenile Law & Policy*, 275-378.

Daly 2012
A. Daly, 'The right of children to be heard in civil proceedings and the emerging law of the European Court of Human Rights', (2012) 15 The International Journal of Human Rights, 441-461.
Dawes 1990
A. Dawes, 'The Effects of Political Violence on Children: A Consideration of South African and Related Studies', (1990) 25 *International Journal of Psychology* 13-31.
D'Cruz & Holmes 2006
L. D'Cruz, D. Holmes, *Legal Aspects of General Dental Practice* (2006), Philadelphia, PA: Elsevier.
De Berry 2001
J. De Berry, 'Child soldiers and the Convention on the Rights of the Child', (2001) 575 Annals, AAPSS 92-105.
de Brouwer & Heikkilä 2013
A de Brouwer, M. Heikkilä, *'Victim Issues: Participation, Protection, Reparation, and Assistance'*, in G. Sluiter et al. (ed.), *International Criminal Procedure – Principles and Rules* (2013), Oxford: Oxford University Press.
de Brouwer 2007
A.M.L.M. de Brouwer, 'Reparation to Victims of Sexual Violence: Possibilities at the International Criminal Court and the Trust Fund for Victims and their Families', (2007) 20 *Leiden Journal of International Law* 207-237.
de Langen 1992
M. de Langen, 'The Meaning of Human Rights for Children', in M.D.A. Freeman, P.E. Veerman (eds.), *The Ideologies of Children's Rights* (1992), Dordrecht (etc.): Nijhoff.
Delfos 2007
M. F. Delfos, 'The Developmental Damage to Children as a Result of the Violation of their Rights', in J.C.M. Willems (ed.), *Developmental and Autonomy Rights of Children – Empowering Children, Caregivers and Communities* (2007), Antwerpen (etc.): Intersentia, 39-60.
Dembour & Haslam 2004
Dembour, M.B., E. Haslam, 'Silencing Hearings? Victim-Witnesses at War Crimes Trials', (2004) 15 *European Journal of International Law* 151-177.
De Schutter 2011
O. De Schutter, *International Human Rights Law: Cases, Materials, Commentary* (2011), Cambridge (etc.): Cambridge University Press.
Detrick 1999
S. Detrick, *A Commentary on the United Nations Convention on the Rights of the Child* (1999), The Hague: Kluwer Law International.
Detrick 1992
S. Detrick (ed.), *The United Nations Convention on the Rights of the Child – A Guide to the "Travaux Préparatoires"*, (1992), Dordrecht: Nijhoff.

Dezwirek Sas, Wolfe & Gowdey 1996
L. Dezwirek Sas, D.A. Wolfe & K. Gowdey, 'Children and the Courts in Canada' (1996) 23 *Criminal Justice and Behaviour* 338-357.
DiScala & Sege 2004
C. DiScala, R. Sege, 'Outcomes in Children and Young Adults Who Are Hospitalized for Firearms-Related Injuries', (2004) 113 *Pediatrics* 1306-1312.
Dixit 2001
R.K. Dixit, 'Special Protection of Children During Armed Conflict under the Geneva Conventions Regime', (2001) 1 *ISIL Yearbook of International Humanitarian and Refugee Law*, 12-35.
Doak 2005
J. Doak, 'Victims' Rights in Criminal Trials: Prospects for Participation' (2005) 32 *Journal of Law and Society* 294-316.
Doek 2009
J.E. Doek, P. Vlaardingerbroek (eds.), *Jeugdrecht en jeugdzorg* (2009), Amsterdam: Elsevier Juridisch.
Doek 1992
J.E. Doek, 'The Current Status of the United Nations Convention on the Rights of the Child', in S. Detrick (ed.), *The United Nations Convention on the Rights of the Child – A Guide to the "Travaux Préparatoires"*, (1992), Dordrecht: Nijhoff, 632-640.
Donat-Cattin 2008, Article 68
D. Donat-Cattin, 'Article 68', in O. Triffterer, *Commentary on the Rome Statute of the International Criminal Court – Observers' Notes, Article by Article* (2008), Second Edition, München (etc.): C.H.Beck, 1275-1300.
Donat-Cattin 2008, Article 75
D. Donat-Cattin, 'Article 75', in O. Triffterer, *Commentary on the Rome Statute of the International Criminal Court – Observers' Notes, Article by Article* (2008), Second Edition, München (etc.): C.H.Beck, 1399-1412.
Donat-Cattin 1999
D. Donat-Cattin, 'The Role of Victims in ICC Proceedings', in F. Lattanzi, W. Schabas (eds.), *Essays on the Rome Statute of the International Criminal Court* (1999), Vol. I, Fagnano Alto: Il Sirente 252.
Donnelly 1986
J. Donnelly, 'International human rights: a regime analysis', (1986) 40 International Organization, 599-642.
Don Taylor III 2010
B. Don Taylor III, *Witness Proofing in International Criminal Law: Is Widening Procedural Divergence in International Criminal Tribunals a Cause for Concern* (2010), http://www.isrcl.org/Papers/2008/Taylor.pdf.
Droege 2007
C. Droege, 'Interplay between International Humanitarian Law and International Human Rights Law in Situations of Armed Conflict', (2007) 40 *Israel Law Review*, 310-355.
Drumbl 2012
M.A. Drumbl, Reimagining Child Soldiers in International Law and Policy (2012), Oxford: Oxford University Press.

Dwertmann 2010
E. Dwertmann, *The Reparation System of the International Criminal Court – Its Implementation, Possibilities and Limitations* (2010), Leiden: Martinus Hijhoff Publishers.
Dyregrov *et al.* 2000
A. Dyregrov *et al.*, 'Trauma exposure and psychological reactions to genocide among Rwandan children', (2000) 13 *Journal of Traumatic Stress* 3-21.

Eisenstat 2004
S. Eisenstat, 'Revenge, Justice and Law: Recognizing the Victim's Desire for Vengeance as a Justification for Punishment', (2004) 50 *Wayne Law Review* 1-62.
Elbedour, ten-Bensel & Maruyama 1993
S. Elbedour, R. ten-Bensel, G.M. Maruyama, 'Children at risk: Psychological coping with war and conflict in the Middle East', (1993) 22 *International Journal of Mental Health* 33-52.
Elbert *et al.* 2009
T. Elbert *et al.*, 'Trauma-related impairment in children – A survey in Sri Lankan provinces affected by armed conflict', (2009) 33 *Child Abuse & Neglect* 238-246.
Enikö 2006
F. Enikö, ‚The rising importance on the protection of witnesses in the European Union', (2006) 77 *Le Droit Pénal de l'union européenne* 313-322.
Eth & Pynoos 1985
S. Eth, R.S. Pynoos, 'Developmental perspectives on psychic trauma in children', in C. Figley (ed.), *Trauma and Its Wake – Volume I* (1985), Bristol: Brunner/Mazel, 36-52.
Evenson 2004
E.M. Evenson, 'Truth and justice in Sierra Leone: Coordination between Commission and Court', (2004) 104 *Columbia Law Review* 730-767.

Fadden, Beauchamp & King 1986
R.R. Fadden, T.L. Beauchamp, N.M.P. King, *A History and Theory of Informed Consent* (1986), New York, NY: Oxford University Press.
Fattah 2008
E. Fattah, 'Gearing Justice Action to Victim Satisfaction Contrasting Two Justice Philosophies: Retribution and Redress', in H. Katein, M. Malsch (eds.), *Crime, Victims and Justice – Essays on Principles and Practice* (2008), Hampshire: Ashgate Publishing, 16 -30.
Ferdinandusse 2004
W. Ferdinandusse, 'The Interaction of National and International Approaches in the Repression of International Crimes', (2004) 15 *European Journal of International Law* 1041-1053.
Ferrándiz & Robben 2007
F. Ferrándiz, A.C.G.M. Robben (eds.), *Multidisciplinary Perspectives on Peace and Conflict Research – A View from Europe* (2007), Bilbao: University of Deusto.
Ferstman, Goetz & Stephens 2009
C. Ferstman, M. Goetz, A. Stephens (eds.), *Reparations for Victims of Genocide, War Crimes and Crimes Against Humanity, Systems in Place and Systems in Making* (2009), Leiden (etc.): Nijhoff.

Ferstman & Goetz 2009b
C. Ferstman, M. Goetz, 'Reparations and the International Criminal Court', in C. Ferstman, M. Goetz, A. Stephens (eds.), *Reparations for Victims of Genocide, War Crimes and Crimes Against Humanity, Systems in Place and Systems in Making* (2009), 324-333.

Figley 1985
C. Figley (ed.), *Trauma and Its Wake – Volume I* (1985), Bristol: Brunner/Mazel.

Fivush 1998
R. Fivush, 'Children's recollections of traumatic and nontraumatic events', (1998) *Development and Psychopathology* 699-716.

Fletcher & Ohlin 2005
G.P. Fletcher & J.D. Ohlin, 'Reclaiming Fundamental Principles of Criminal Law in the Darfur Case' 3 (2005) *Journal of International Criminal Justice* 539-561

Fleck 2008
D. Fleck (ed.), *The Handbook of International Humanitarian Law* (2008), 2nd edition, Oxford (etc.): Oxford University Press.

Flinterman 2006
C. Flinterman, 'The Protection of Children in Times of Armed Conflict: Some Observations', in C.W. Greenbaum, P. Veerman, N. Bacon-Shnoor, *Protection of children during armed political conflict: a multidisciplinary perspective* (2006), Antwerp (etc.): Intersentia, 303-313.

Fote 1985
D.J. Fote, 'Child Witness in Sexual Abuse Criminal Proceedings: Their Capabilities, Special Problems, and Proposals for Reform', (1985-1986) 13 *Pepperdine Law Review* 157-184.

Francis 2007
D.J. Francis, ' Paper protection mechanisms: child soldiers and the international protection of children in Africa's conflict zones', (2007) 45 *Journal of Modern African Studies* 207-231.

Freeman 2007
M. Freeman, 'Article 3: The Best Interests of the Child', in A. Alen, et al, *A Commentary on the United Nations Convention on the Rights of the Child* (2007), Leiden (etc.): Martinus Nijhoff.

Freeman & Veerman 1992
M.D.A. Freeman, P.E. Veerman (eds.), *The Ideologies of Children's Rights* (1992), Dordrecht (etc.): Nijhoff.

Friman 2009
H. Friman, 'The International Criminal Court and Participation of Victims: A Third Party to the Proceedings', (2009) 22 *Leiden Journal of International Law* 485-500.

Frulli 2002
M. Frulli, 'Jurisdiction ratione personae', in A. Cassese, P. Gaeta, J. Jones (eds.), *The Rome Statute of the International Criminal Court* (2002), Volume I, 527-541.

Gallagher 2001
M.S. Gallagher, 'Soldier Boy Bad: Child Soldiers, Culture and Bars to Asylum', (2001) 13 Int J Refugee Law 310-353.

Gararina & Kostelny 1993
J. Gararina, K. Kostelny, 'Children's Response to War: What Do We Know?' in L.A. Leavitt, N.A. Fox (eds.), *The Psychological Effects of War and Violence on Children* (1993), Hillsdale, NJ: Lawrence Erlbaum Associates, In., 23-39.
Gillard 2003
E.C. Gillard, 'Reparation for violations of international humanitarian law', (2003) no. 85 IRRC 529-553.
Goldson 1996
E. Goldson, 'The Effect of War on Children', (1996) 20 *Child Abuse & Neglect* 809-819.
Goldson 1993
E. Goldson, 'War is Not Good for Children', in L.A. Leavitt, N.A. Fox, *The Psychological Effects of War and Violence* (1993), Hillsdale, New Jersey: Lawrence Erlbaum Associates, Inc., 3-22.
Goldstone 1996
Goldstone, R. J., 'Justice as a Tool for Peace-Making: Truth Commissions and International Criminal Tribunals', (1996) 28 *New York University Journal of International Law and Policy* 485-504.
Gray 1996
C. Gray, Judicial Remedies in International Law (1996), Oxford: Oxford University Press.
Greco 2007
G. Greco, 'Victims' Rights Overview under the ICC Legal Framework: A Jurisprudential Analysis', (2007) 7 *International Criminal Law Review* 531-547.
Greenbaum, Veerman & Bacon-Shnoor 2006
C.W. Greenbaum, P. Veerman, N. Bacon-Shnoor (eds.), *Protection of children during armed political conflict: a multidisciplinary perspective* (2006), Antwerp (etc.): Intersentia.
Greenwood 2008
C. Greenwood, 'Historical Development and Legal Basis', in D. Fleck (ed.), *The Handbook of International Humanitarian Law* (2008), 2nd edition, Oxford (etc.): Oxford University Press, 13-43.
Grover 2012
S. Grover, *Child Soldier Victims of Genocidal Forcible Transfer – Exonerating Child Soldiers Charged with Grave Conflict-related International Crimes* (2012), Berlin: Springer-Verlag.
Greenwood 2008a
C. Greenwood, 'Scope of Application of Humanitarian Law, in D. Fleck (ed.), *The Handbook of International Humanitarian Law* (2008), 2nd edition, Oxford (etc.): Oxford University Press, 45-78.
Guhr 2008
Guhr, A.H., 'Victim Participation During the Pre-Trial State at the International Criminal Court', (2008) 8 *International Criminal Law Review* 109-140.
Guralnick 2004
M.J. Guralnick, 'A Model of Early Intervention', in M.A. Feldman (ed.), *Early Intervention –Essential Readings in Developmental Psychology* (2004), Malden, Oxford, Carlton: Blackwell Publishing Ltd, 5-50.

Gustaffson 1999
L. Gustaffson, 'Right to Survival and Development', (1999) 15 *Journal of Medicine, Conflict and Survival* 328-335.

Haggerty *et al* 1996
R.J. Haggerty, L.R. Sherrod, N. Garmezy, M. Rutter (eds.), *Stress, Risk and Resilience in Children and Adolescents, Process Mechanisms, and Interventions* (1996), Cambridge: Cambridge University Press.

Hamilton & El-Haj 1997
C. Hamilton, T.A. El-Haj, 'Armed conflict: The protection of children under international law', (1997) 5 *International Journal of Children's Rights* 1-46.

Hamzei 2012
H. Hamzei, 'War Children's Procedural Capacities in International Proceedings', in F. Malekian, K. Nordlöf (eds.), *The Sovereignity of Children in Law*, Newcastle upon Tyne: Cambridge Scholars Publishing, 399-422.

Hamzei 2010
H. Hamzei, 'Child Victims before the International Criminal Court: Avenue to Justice for the Most Vulnerable?', in L. Hopkinns, M. Macleod, W. Turgeon (eds.), *Negotiating Childhoods*, Oxford: Inter-Disciplinary Press, 113-122.

Harvey 2003
R. Harvey, *Children and armed conflict: a short guide to international law and developments* (2003), Colchester: Children's Legal Center.

Happold 2006
M. Happold, 'The Age of Criminal Responsibility for International Crimes under International Law, in K. Arts, V. Popovski (eds.), *International Criminal Accountability and the Rights of Children* (2006), The Hague: Hague Academic Press, 69-84.

Happold 2005
M. Happold, *Child soldiers in international law* (2005), Manchester: Manchester University Press.

Happold 2000
M. Happold, 'The Optional Protocol To The Convention On The Rights Of The Child On The Involvement Of Children in Armed Conflict', (2000) 3 *Yearbook of International Humanitarian Law* 226-244.

Hafen & Hafen 1996
B.C. Hafen, J.O. Hafen, 'Abandoning Children to Their Autonomy: The United Nations Convention on the Rights of the Child', (1996) 37 *Harvard International Law Journal* 2, 449-492.

Hayner 1994
P.B. Hayner, 'Fifteen Truth Commissions – 1974 to 1994: A Comparative Study', (1994) 16 *Human Rights Quarterly* 597-655.

Heikkilä 2004
M. Heikkilä, *International Criminal Tribunals and Victims of Crime* (2004), Turku/Abo: Institute for Human Rights, Abo Akademi University.

Helle 2000
D. Helle, 'Optional Protocol on the involvement of children in armed conflict to the Convention on the Rights of the Child', (2000) no. 839 *International Review of the Red Cross* 797-823.

Heintze 2007
H. J. Heintze, 'On the Relationship between Human Rights Protection and International Humanitarian Law', in F. Ferrándiz, A.C.G.M. Robben (eds.), *Multidisciplinary Perspectives on Peace and Conflict Research – A View from Europe* (2007), Bilbao: University of Deusto, 91-116.

Heintze 1995
J.J., Heintze, 'Children Need More Protection under International Humanitarian Law – *Recent* Developments Concerning Article 38 of the UN Child Convention as a Challenge to the International Red Cross and Red Crescent Movement', (1995) 8 *Journal of International Law of Peace and Armed Conflict* 200-203.

de Hemptinne & Rindi 2006
J. de Hemptinne, F. Rindi, 'ICC Pre-Trial Chamber Allows Victims to Participate in the Investigation Phase of Proceedings', (2006) 4 *Journal of Criminal Justice* 342-350.

Henry 2009
Henry, N., 'Witness to Rape: The Limits and Potential of International War Crimes Trials for Victims of Wartime Sexual Violence', (2009) 3 *The International Journal of Transitional Justice* 114-134.

Henzelin *et al.* 2006
M. Henzelin, V. Heiskanen, G. Mettraux, 'Reparations to Victims before the International Criminal Court: Lessons from International Mass Claims Processes', (2006) 17 *Criminal Law Forum* 317-344.

Herlitz 1994
G.N. Herlitz, 'The Meaning of the Term 'Prima Facie.'' (1994) 55 *Louisiana Law Review* 391-408.

Hersch 1996
J. Hersch, *Birthright of Man, an anthology of texts or human rights prepared under the direction of Jeanne Hersch* (1996), Paris: UNESCO.

Himonga 2001
C. Himonga, C., 'Implementing the Rights of the Child in African Legal Systems: The Mthembu Journey in Search of Justice', (2001) 9 INT J. Child Right 89-122.

Hingorani 1989
R.C. Hingorani, 'Protection of children during armed conflict', in F. Kalshoven (ed.), *Assisting the Victims of Armed Conflict and Other Disasters* - Papers delivered at the International Conference on Humanitarian Assistance in Armed Conflict, The Hague, June 22-24, 1988 (1989), Dordrecht: Kluwer Academic Publishers,133-138.

Honwana 2006
B. A. Honwana, *Child Soldiers in Africa* (2006), Philadelphia: University of Pennsylvania Press.

Horn, Charters & Vahidy 2009
R. Horn, S. Charters, S. Vahidy, 'Testifying in International War Crimes Tribunal: The Experience of Witnesses in the Special Court for Sierra Leone', (2009) 3 *International Journal of Transitional Justice* 135-149.

Hussain & Herens 1997
A. Hussain, M. Herens, 'Child nutrition and food security during armed conflicts', (1997) 19 *Food, Nutrition and Agriculture* (1997) 17-25.

International Commission of Jurists 1995
International Commission of Jurists, *The International Criminal Court*, Third ICJ Position Paper (1995), http://www.iccnow.org/documents/1PrepCmt3rdPositionPaperICJ.pdf.

Jensen & Shaw 1993
P.S. Jensen, J. Shaw., 'Children as Victims of War: Current Knowledge and Future Research Needs', (1993) 32 *Journal of the American Academy of Child and Adolescent Psychiatry* 697-708.

Johansson 2009
E. Johansson, ''Doing the Right Thing' A Moral Concern from the Perspectives of Young Preschool Children', in Berthelsen, D., Brownlee, J., Johansson, E. (eds.), Participatory Learning in the Early Years (2009), New York: Taylor & Francis.

Johnstone 2004
G. Johnstone, 'How, and in What Terms, Should Restorative Justice Be Conceived?', in H. Zehr, B. Toews (eds.), *Critical issues in restorative justice* (2004), Monsey, New York: Criminal Justice Press and Willian Publishing, 5-15.

Jorda & de Hemptienne 2002
C. Jorda, J. de Hemptienne, 'The Status and Role of the Victim', in A. Cassese, P. Gaeta, J. Jones (eds.), *The Rome Statute of the International Criminal Court* (2002), Volume II, Oxford (etc.): Oxford University Press, 1387-1419.

Joseph, Cairns & McCollam 1993
S. Joseph, E. Cairns, P. McCollam, 'Political violence, coping and depressive symptomatology in Northern Irish children', (1993) 15 *Personality and Individual Differences* 471-473.

Jouet 2007
M. Jouet, 'Reconciling the Conflicting Rights of Victims and Defendants at the International Criminal Court', (2007) *St. Louis University Public Law Review* 249-308.

Kalshoven & Zegveld 2011
F. Kalshoven, L. Zegveld, *Constraints on the Waging of War* (2011), 4th edition, Cambridge: Cambridge University Press.

Kalshoven 1991
F. Kalshoven, 'State Responsibility for Warlike Acts of the Armed Forces', (1991) 40 *International and Comparative Law Quarterly* 827-858.

Kalshoven 1989
F. Kalshoven (ed.), *Assisting the Victims of Armed Conflict and Other Disasters – Papers delivered at the International Conference on Humanitarian Assistance in Armed Conflict, The Hague, 22-23 June 1988* (1989), Dordrecht (etc.): Kluwer Academic Publishers.

Kalshoven 1978
Check F. Kalshoven, *'Reaffirmation and Development of International Humanitarian Law Applicable in Armed Conflicts: The Diplomatic Conference, Geneva 1974-1977, Part II'*, (1978) 9 *Netherlands Yearbook of International Law* 107.

Kamara 2008
H. Kamara, 'The Problem of Age Determination of Juveniles and its impact on the Juvenile Justice in Sierra Leone' (2008), http://www.carl-sl.org/home/images/stories/newsletter/31st_edition_newsletter.pdf.

Kaplan 2002
H.B. Kaplan, 'Towards an Understanding of Resilience – A Critical Review of Definitions and Models', in M.D. Glantz, J.L. Johnson (eds.), *Resilience and Development, Positive Life Adaptations* (2002), New York: Kluwer Academic Publishers, 17-83.

Kaplan 2005
H.B. Kaplan, 'Understanding the Concept of Resilience', in S. Goldstein, R.B. Brooks (eds.), *Resilience in Children* (2005), 39-47.

Kaptein & Malsch 2008
H. Kaptein, M. Malsch (eds.), *Crime, Victims and Justice – Essays on Principles and Practice* (2008), Hampshire: Ashgate Publishing.

Kar 2009
N. Kar, 'Psychological impact of disasters on children: review of assessment and interventions', (2009) 5 *World Journal of Pediatrics* 5-11.

Kar, Jagadhisa & Murali 2001
N. Kar, Jagadhisha, N. Murali, 'Post-traumatic stress disorder in children following disaster', (2001) 16 *Kerala Journal of Psychiatry* 7-14.

Karp 2008
J. Karp, ' Matching Human Dignity with the UN Convention on the Rights of the Child', in Y. Ronen, C.W. Greenbaum (eds.), *The Case for the Child: Towards a New Agenda* (2008), Antwerp (etc.): Intersentia, 89-135.

Keller 2007
L.M. Keller, Seeking Justice at the International Criminal Court: Victims' Reparations, (2007) 29 *Thomas Jefferson Law Review* 189-218.

Keller 2007
L.M. Keller, 'Achieving Peace with Justice: The International Criminal Court and Ugandan Alternative Justice Mechanisms', (2007) 23, *Connecticut Journal of International Law* 209-280.

Kendall & Staggs 2005
S. Kendall, M. Staggs, *Interim Report on the Special Court for Sierra Leone* (2005), Berkeley War Crimes Studies Center, http://warcrimescenter.berkeley.edu.

King 2009
H. King, 'The Extraterritorial Human Rights Obligations of States', (2009) 9 HRLR, 512-556.

Kitzinger 1988
J. Kitzinger, 'Defending Innocence: Ideologies of Childhood', (1988) 28 *Feminist Review*, 77-87.

Kleffner 2002
J.K. Kleffner, 'Improving Compliance with International Humanitarian Law Through the Establishment of an Individual Complaints Procedure', (2002) 15 *Leiden Journal of International Law* 237-250.

Kleffner & Zegveld 2000
J.K. Kleffner, L. Zegveld, 'Establishing an Individual Complaint Procedure for Violations of International Humanitarian Law', (2000) 3 *Yearbook of International Humanitarian Law* 384-401.

Kok 2007
R.A. Kok, *Statutory limitations in international criminal law* (2007), The Hague: T.M.C. Asser Press.

Kress *et al* 2005
K. Kress *et al* (eds.), *The Rome Statute and Domestic Legal Orders: Constitutional Issues, Cooperation and Enforcement* (2005), Baden Baden: Nomos Verlagsgesellschaft.
Krieger 2006
H. Krieger, 'A Conflict of Norms: 'The Relationship Between Humanitarian Law and Human Rights Law in the ICRC Customary Law Study', (2006) 11 *Journal of Conflict & Security Law* 265-291.
Kuper 2005
J. Kuper, *Military training and children in armed conflict: law, policy and practice* (2005), Leiden: Martinus Nijhoff.
Kuper 1997
J. Kuper, *International Law Concerning Child Civilians in Armed Conflict* (1997), Oxford: Clarendon Press.
Kurth 2010
M. E. Kurth, 'The Recruitment and Use of Child Soldiers', in C. Stahn, L. van den Herik (eds.), *Future Perspectives on International Criminal Justice*, T.M.C. Asser Press (2010), 475-497.

Leach 2011
P. Leach, *Taking a Case to the European Court of Human Rights* (2011), Oxford: Oxford University Press.
Leavitt & Fox 1993
L.A. Leavitt, N.A. Fox (eds.), *The Psychological Effects of War and Violence on Children* (1993), Hillsdale, New Jersey: Lawrence Erlbaum Associates, Inc..
Leibig 2005
A. Leibig, 'Girl Child Soldiers in Northern Uganda: Do current legal frameworks offer sufficient protection?', (2005) 3 *Northwestern University Journal of International Human Rights* 1-16
Lee 2001
R.S. Lee (ed.), *The International Criminal Court: Elements of Crimes and Rules of Procedure and Evidence* (2001), Ardsley, NY: Transnational Publishers.
Letts & Miller 1976
R.M. Letts, D. Miller, 'Gunshot wounds of the extremities in children', (1976) 16 *The Journal of Trauma* 807-11.
Levine 1991
R.J. Levine, 'Informed consent: some challenges to the universal validity of the Western model' (1991) 19 *Law, Medicine & Health Care* 207-213.
Luthar 1991
S.S. Luthar, 'Vulnerability and resilience: A study of high-risk adolescents', (1991) 62 *Child Development* 600-616.

Machel 2000
G. Machel, *The Impact of Armed Conflict on Children – A critical review of progress made and obstacles encountered in increasing protection for war-affected children* (2000), http://www.strategicnetwork.org/pdf/kb5736.pdf.
Macksoud & Aber 1996
M.S. Macksoud, J.L. Aber, 'The War Experiences and Psychological Development of Children in Lebanon', (1996) 67 *Child Development* 70-88.

Magarrell 2009
L. Magarrell, 'Reparations in Theory and Practice', *Reparative Justice Series*, International Center for Transitional Justice (2009), http://ictj.org/sites/default/files/ICTJ-Global-Reparations-Practice-2007-English.pdf.
Maheu 1996
R. Maheu, 'Preface', in J. Hersch, *Birthright of Man, an anthology of texts or human rights prepared under the direction of Jeanne Hersch*, (1996), Paris: UNESCO.
Mahoney *et al* 2005
P.F. Mahoney et al (eds.), *Ballistic Trauma – A Practical Guide* (2005), 2nd edition, London: Springer.
Mann 1987
H. Mann, 'International Law and the Child Soldier', (1987) 36 *International and Comparative Law Quarterly* 32-57.
Markus Funk 2010
T. Markus Funk, Victims' Rights and Advocacy before the International Criminal Court (2010), Oxford: Oxford University Press.
Maslen 1996
S. Maslen, 'Relevance of the Convention on the Rights of the Child to Children in Armed Conflict', (1996) 6 *Transnational Law and Contemporary Problems* 329-351.
Masten, Best & Garmezy 1990
A.S. Masten, K. Best, N. Garmezy, 'Resilience and development: Contributions from the study of children who overcome adversity', (1990) 2 *Development and Psychopathology* 425-444.
Mazurana & Carlson 2010
D. Mazurana, K. Carlson, *Children and Reparation: Past Lessons and New Directions*, Innocenti Working Paper, IWP 2010-8 (2010).
Mazurana & Carlson 2009
D. Mazurana, K. Carlson, 'Reparations as a Means for Recognizing and Addressing Crimes and Grave Rights Violations against Girls and Boys during Situations of Armed Conflict and under Authoritarian and Dictatorial Regimes', in T. Rubio-Marin (ed.), *The Gender of Reparations: Unsettling sexual hierarchies while redressing human rights violations* (2009), Cambridge: Cambridge University Press, 162-214.
Mazzeschi 2003
R.P. Mazzeschi, 'Reparation Claims by Individuals for State Breaches of Humanitarian Law and Human Rights Law: An Overview' (2003) 1 *Journal of International Criminal Justice* 339-347.
McAuliffe de Guzman 2008
M. McAuliffe de Guzman, 'Article 21 Applicable Law',in O. Triffterer, *Commentary on the Rome Statute of the International Criminal Court – Observers' Notes, Article by Article* (2008), Second Edition, München (etc.): C.H.Beck, 701-712.
McCarthy 2012
C. McCarthy, *Reparations and Victim Support in the International Criminal Court* (2012), Cambridge: Cambridge University Press.
McGonigle 2009
B.N. McGonigle, 'Bridging the Divides in International Criminal Proceedings: An Examination into the Victim Participation Endeavor of the International Criminal Court' (2009) 21 *Florida Journal of International Law* 93-152.

McCallin 1995
M. McCallin, *The Reintegration of Young Ex-combatants into Civilian Life – A Report for the International Labour Office* (1995), http://repository.forcedmigration.org/show_metadata.jsp?pid=fmo:2681.
Meisel & Roth 1983
A. Meisel, L.H. Roth, 'Toward an informed discussion of informed consent: A review and critique of the empirical studies', (1983-1984) 25 *Arizona Law Review* 265-346.
Melzer 2009
N. Melzer, *Interpretive guidance on the notion of direct participation in hostilities under international humanitarian law* (2009), Geneva: International Committee of the Red Cross.
Memon & Vartoukian 1996
A. Memon & R. Vartoukian, 'The Effects of Repeated Questioning on Young Children's Eyewitness Testimony', (1996) 87 *British Journal of Psychology* 403-415.
Meron 2006
T. Meron, *The Humanization of International Law* (2006), Leiden: Nijhoff.
Meron 1994
T. Meron, 'War Crimes in Yugoslavia and the Development of International Law', (1994) 88 AJIL 78-87.
Moffet 2014
L. Moffet, *Justice for victims before the International Criminal Court* (2014), London: Routledge, Taylor & Francis Group.
Mohan 2009
M. Mohan, 'The Paradox of Victim-Centrism: Victim Participation at the Khmer Rouge Tribunal', (2009) 9 *Journal of International Criminal Justice* 733-775.
Moradi *et al.* 1999
A.R. Moradi *et al.*, 'Everyday Memory Deficits in Children and Adolescents with PTSD: Performance on the Rivermead Behavioural Memory Test', (1999) 40 *Journal of Child Psychology and Psychiatry and Allied Disciplines* 357-361.
Morrill 2005
C. Morrill, 'Perpetrators Only: the "Role" of Accused Youth in Rwanda's "Modern" *Gacaca'*, in UNICEF Innocenti Research Centre, *Expert Discussion on Transitional Justice and Children* (2005), s3.amazonaws.com/rcpp/assets/attachments/401_448_EN_original.pdf, 103-118.
Morrissey 2012
P. Morrissey, 'Applied rights in international criminal law: defence counsel and the right to disclosure', in: G. Boas, W. A. Schabas, M.P. Scharf, *International Criminal Justice – Legitimacy and Coherence* (2012), Cheltenham: Edward Elgar Publishing Limited.
Mousavi, Rastegari & Nordin 2012
S. Mousavi, B. Rastegari & R. Nordin, 'When Does Childhood Begin? A Legal Analysis on the United Nations Convention on the Rights of the Child and Islamic Republic of Iran', (2012) *Iran and Malaysia Bi-Annual Conference on Islam and Society* 1-6.
Murthy & Lakshminarayana 2006
R. S. Murthy, R. Lakshminarayana, 'Mental health consequences of war: a brief review of research findings', (2006) 5 *World Psychiatry* 25-30.

Nerlich 2009
V. Nerlich, 'The Status of the ICTY and ICTR Precedent in Proceedings before the ICC', in C. Stahn, G. Sluiter (eds.), *The Emerging Practice of the International Criminal Court* (2009), Martinus Nijhoff, 305-325.
Nolte 2013
G. Nolte, *Treaties and Subsequent Practice* (2013), Oxford: Oxford University Press.
Nosworthy 2009
D. Nosworthy (ed.), *Seen, but not Heard: Placing Children and Youth on the Security Governance Agenda* (2009), Zürich (etc.): LIT Verlag.
Nylund 1998
B.V. Nylund, 'International law and the child victim of armed conflict – Is the "First Call" for children?', (1998) 6 *International Journal of Children's Rights* 23-54.

Ohlin 2013
J.D. Ohlin, General Framework of International Criminal Procedure, in G. Sluiter et al. (ed.), *International Criminal Procedure – Principles and Rules* (2013), Oxford: Oxford University Press.
O'Kane *et al.* 2009
C. O'Kane, C. Feinstein, A. Giertsen, 'Children and Young People in Post-conflict Peacebuilding', D. Nosworthy (ed.), in *Seen, but not Heard: Placing Children and Youth on the Security Governance Agenda* (2009), Zürich (etc.): LIT Verlag, 259-284.
O'Kane, Feinstein & Giertsen 2009
C. O'Kane, C. Feinstein, A. Giertsen, 'Children and Young People in Post-conflict Peacebuilding', in D. Nosworthy (ed.), *Seen, but not Heard: Placing Children and Youth on the Security Governance Agenda* (2009), Zürich (etc.): LIT Verlag, 259-284.
Olásolo & Kiss 2010
H. Olásolo, A. Kiss, 'The Role of Victims in Criminal Proceedings before the International Criminal Court', (2010) 81 *Revue Internationale de Droit Pénal* 125-164.
Olásolo 2009
H. Olásolo, 'Systematic and Casuistic Approaches to the Role of Victims in Criminal Proceedings Before the International Criminal Court', 12 (2009) *New Criminal Law Review* 513-528.
Olusanya 2006
O. Olusanya, 'Granting Immunity to Child Combatants Supranationally', in R. Haveman, O. Olusanya (eds.), *Sentencing and Sanctioning in Supranational Criminal Law* (2006), Antwerp (etc.): Intersentia, 87-108.
Ordog *et al* 1988
G. J. Ordog et al, 'Gunshot Wounds in Children Under 10 Years of Age – A New Epidemic', (1988) 142 *American Journal of Diseases of Children* 618-622.

Radosavljevic 2008
D. Radosavljevic, 'Restorative Justice under the ICC Penalty Regime', (2008) 7 *The Law and Practice of International Courts and Tribunals* 235-255.
Rubio-Marin 2009
T. Rubio-Marin (ed.), *The Gender of Reparations: Unsettling sexual hierarchies while redressing human rights violations* (2009), Cambridge: Cambridge University Press.

Paardekooper, de Jong & Hermanns 1999
B. Paardekooper, J. T.V.M. de Jong, J.M.A. Hermanns, 'The Psychological Impact of War and the Refugee Situation on South Sudanese children in Refugee Camps in Northern Uganda: An Exploratory Study', (1999) 40 *Journal of Child Psychology and Psychiatry* 529-536.

Pare 2003
M. Pare, 'Why have street children disappeared? The role of international human rights law in protecting vulnerable groups', (2003) 11 International Journal of Children's Rights, 1-32.

Parmar *et al.* 2010
S. Parmar *et al.*, *Children and Transitional Justice, Truth-Telling, Accountability and Reconciliation* (2010),
http://www.unicef-irc.org/publications/pdf/tj_publication_eng.pdf.

Pearn 2003
J.H. Pearn, 'Children and War', (2003) 39 *Journal of Pediatrics and Child Health* 166-172.

Pellet 2002
A. Pellet, 'Applicable Law', in A. Cassese, P. Gaeta, J. Jones (ed.), *The Rome Statute of the International Criminal Court*, Volume II, 1051-1084, Oxford (etc.): Oxford University Press.

Pena & Carayon 2013
M. Pena, G. Carayon, 'Is the ICC Making the Most of Victim Participation', (2013) *The International Journal of Transitional Justice*, 1-18.

Pena 2010
M. Pena, 'Victim Participation at the International Criminal Court-Achievements Made and Challenges Lying Ahead', (2010) 16 *ILSA Journal of International and Comparative Law* 497-516.

Pfefferbaum 1997
B. Pfefferbaum, 'Posttraumatic Stress Disorder in Children: A Review of the Past 10 Years', (1997) 36 *Journal of the American Academy of Child and Adolescent Psychiatry* 1503-1511.

Pitcher 2005
G.J. Pitcher, 'Ballistic Trauma in Children', in P.F. Mahoney et al (eds.), *Ballistic Trauma – A Practical Guide* (2005), 2nd edition, London: Springer, 396-417.

Plattner 1984
D. Plattner, 'Protection of Children in International Humanitarian Law', (1984) no. 240 *International Review of the Red Cross* 140-152.

Politi & Gioia 2008
M. Politi & F. Gioia, The International Criminal Court and National Jurisdictions (2008), Hampshire: Ashgate Publishing Limited.

Poole & White 1991
D.A. Poole, L.T. White, 'Effects of question repetition on the eyewitness testimony of children and adults', (1991) 27 *Developmental Psychology* 975-986.

Preux 1995
J. Preux, 'Special protection of women and children', (1995) no. 248 *International Review of the Red Cross* 292-302.

Prime & Scanlan 2001
T. Prime, G. Scanlan, *The Law of Limitation* (2001), second edition, Oxford (etc.): Oxford University Press.
Punamäki 2002
R.L. Punamäki, 'The Uninvited Guest of War Enters Childhood: Developmental and Personality Aspects of War and Military Violence', (2002) 8 *Traumatology* 181-204.
Punamäki 1989
L. Punamäki, 'Factors affecting the mental health of Palestinian children exposed to political violence', (1989) 18 *International Journal of Mental Health* 63-79.
Pynoos *et al.* 1993
R.S. Pynoos *et al.*, 'Post-traumatic stress reactions in children after the 1988 Armenian earthquake', (1993) 163 *British Journal of Psychiatry* 239-247.

Qouta *et al* 2007
S. Qouta et al., 'Predictors of psychological distress and positive resources among Palestinian adolescents: Trauma, child and mothering characteristics, (2007) 31 *Child Abuse & Neglect* 699-717.
Qouta & El Sarraj 2006
S. Qouta, E. El Sarraj, 'Palestinian Children and Dangerous Life : Adjustment during Violent and Less Violent Times', in C.W. Greenbaum, P.Veerman, N. Bacon-Shnoor (eds.), *Protection of Children During Armed Political Conflict: A Multidisciplinary Perspective* (2006), Antwerp (etc.): Intersentia, 111-121.

Rassin & van Koppen 2002
E. Rassin, P.J. van Koppen, 'Het verhoren van kinderen in zedenzaken', in P.J. van Koppen et al, *Het Recht van Binnen – Psychologie van het Recht* (2002), Deventer: Kluwer BV, 507-530.
Resseler, Tortorici & Marcelino 1993
E.M. Resseler, J.M. Tortorici, and A. Marcelino (eds.), *Children in War: a Guide to the Provision of Services – A Study for UNICEF* (1993), http://repository.forcedmigration.org/show_metadata.jsp?pid=fmo:5191, New York: United Nations Children's Fund Programme Publications.
Ressler, Boothby & Steinbeck 1988
E.M. Ressler, N. Boothby, D.J. Steinbeck (eds.), *Unaccompanied Children: care and protection in wars, natural disasters, and refugee movements* (1988), New York, N.Y. (etc.): Oxford University Press.
Revaz & Todres 2006
C.R. Revaz, J. Todres, 'The Optional Protocols to the U.N. Convention on the Rights of the Child and the Impact of U.S Ratification', in: J. Todres, M.E. Wojcik, C.R. Revaz (eds.), *The U.N. Convention on the Rights of the Child, An Analysis of Treaty Provisions and Implications of U.S. Ratification* (2006), New York: Transnational Publishers, Inc..
Robinson 2008
D. Robinson, 'The Identity Crisis of International Criminal Law', 21 (2008) *Leiden Journal of International Law* 925-963.
Robinson 2003
D. Robinson, 'Serving the Interests of Justice: Amnesties, Truth Commissions and the International Criminal Court', 14 (2003) *European Journal of International Law* 481-505.

Roger & Triffterer 2008
S.C. Roger, O. Triffterer, 'Article 26 Exclusion of jurisdiction over persons under eighteen', in O. Triffterer, *Commentary on the Rome Statute of the International Criminal Court – Observers' Notes, Article by Article* (2008), Second Edition, München (etc.): C.H.Beck, 771-777.

Ronen & Greenbaum 2008
Y. Ronen, C.W. Greenbaum (eds.), *The Case for the Child: Towards a New Agenda* (2008), Antwerp (etc.): Intersentia.

Rosen 2005
D.M. Rosen, *Armies of the Young: Child Soldiers in War and Terrorism* (2005), New Brunswick, NJ (etc.): Rutgers University Press.

Rosenberg 2001
J.E. Rosenberg, 'Forensic Aspects of PTSD in Children and Adolescents', in Eth. Spencer (ed.), *PTSD in Children and Adolescents* (2001), Washington: American Psychiatric Publishing, 33-58.

Roth-Arriaza 2004
N. Roth-Arriaza, 'Reparations Decisions and Dilemmas', (2004) 27 *Hastings International and Comparative Law Review* 157-219.

Saathoff & Chaleby 2006
G. Saathoff, K. Chaleby, 'Tyranny and Trauma: Saddam Hussein's Legacy to Children in Kuwait', in C.W. Greenbaum, P. Veerman, N. Bacon-Shnoor (eds.), *Protection of Children During Armed Political Conflict: A Multidisciplinary Perspective* (2006), Intersentia: Antwerp, Oxford, 143-153.

Safferling 2012
C. Safferling, *International Criminal Procedure* (2012), Oxford: Oxford University Press.

Safferling 2004
C. Safferling, 'Can Prosecution be the Answer to Human Rights Violations?' (2004) 5 German Law Journal 1469-1488.

Sanin & Stirnemann 2008
K. Sanin, A. Stirnemann, 'Child Witnesses at the Special Court for Sierra Leone' War Crimes Studies center University of California, Berkeley (2008), http://socrates.berkeley.edu/~warcrime/documents/ChildWitnessReport_000.pdf.

Sanin 2005
K. Sanin, *Special Court Monitoring Program Update #57 Trial Chamber IIAFRC Trial*, 5 October 2005 http://www.ocf.berkeley.edu/~changmin/SL-Reports/057.pdf.

Saywitz, Snyder & Nathanson 1999
K.J. Saywitz, L. Snyder, R. Nathanson, 'Facilitating the Communicative Competence of the Child Witness', (1999) 3 *Applied Developmental Science* 58-68.

Schabas 2011
W. Schabas, *An Introduction to the International Criminal Court* (2011) , 4th edition, Cambridge (etc.): Cambridge University Press.

Schabas 2010
W. Schabas, *The International Criminal Court – A Commentary on the Rome Statute* (2010), Oxford (etc.): Oxford University Press.

Shann 2010
F. Shann, 'Warfare and children', (2010) 46 *Journal of Paediatrics and Child Health* 217-212.
Shaw 2008
M.N. Shaw, *International Law* (2008), 6th edition, Cambridge (etc.): Cambridge University Press.
Shelton 2006
D. Shelton, *Remedies in International Human Rights Law* (2006), Oxford (etc.): Oxford University Press.
Siegrist 2006
S. Siegrist, 'Child Participation in International Criminal Accountability Mechanisms: The Case of the Sierra Leone Truth and Reconciliation Commission' , in K. Arts, V. Popovski (eds.), *International Criminal Accountability and the Rights of Children* (2006), 53-65.
Singer 2005
P.W. Singer, *Children at War* (2005), Berkeley, California (etc.): University of California Press.
Singer 1986
S. Singer, 'The protection of children during armed conflict situations', (1986) no. 252 *International Review of the Red Cross* 133-168.
Skinner *et al* 2006a
D. Skinner et al, 'Towards a Definition of Orphaned and Vulnerable Children', (2006) 10 *Aids and Behaviour* 619-626.
Skinner *et al* 2004
D. Skinner et.al, *Defining Orphaned and Vulnerable Children* (2004), Cape Town: HSRC Publishers.
Sloane 2007
R. Sloane, 'The Expressive Capacity of International Punishment: the Limits of the National Law Analogy and the Potential of International Criminal Law', 43 (2007) Stanford Journal of International Law 39-94
Slone 2006
M. Slone, 'Promoting Children's Coping in Politically Violent Environments: Suggestions for Intervention in Educational Contexts', in C.W. Greenbaum, P. Veerman, N. Bacon-Shnoor (eds.), *Protection of Children During Armed Political Conflict: A Multidisciplinary Perspective* (2006), 169-188.
Sluiter *et al* 2013
G. Sluiter, H. Friman, S. Linton, S. Vasiliev & S. Zappalà, *International Criminal Procedure – Principles and Rules* (2013), Oxford: Oxford University Press.
Sluiter 2009
G. Sluiter, 'Human Rights Protection in the ICC Pre-Trial Phase', in C. Stahn & G. Sluiter, *The Emerging Practice of the International Criminal Court* (2009), Leiden: Martinus Nijhoff Publishers, 459-475.
Sluiter 2005
G. Sluiter, 'The Netherlands', in K. Kress *et al* (eds.), *The Rome Statute and Domestic Legal Orders: Constitutional Issues, Cooperation and Enforcement* (2005), Baden Baden: Nomos Verlagsgesellschaft, 203-233.

Smith *et al.* 2001
P. Smith *et al.*, 'War Exposure and Maternal Reactions in the Psychosocial Adjustment of Children from Bosnia-Hercegovina', (2001) 42 *Journal of Child Psychology and Psychiatry* 395-404.
Somasundaram & van de Put 2006
D.J. Somasundaram, W.A. van de Put, 'Management of trauma in special populations after disaster', (2006) 67 *Journal of Clinical Psychology* 64-73.
Sowa 2010
T. Sowa, 'Children and the Liberian Truth and Reconciliation Commission', in S. Parmar et al, *Children and Transitional Justice, Truth-Telling, Accountability and Reconciliation* (2010),
http://www.unicef-irc.org/publications/pdf/tj_publication_eng.pdf, 193-230.
Spencer 2001
Eth. Spencer (ed.), *PTSD in Children and Adolescents* (2001), Washington: American Psychiatric Publishing.
Stahn 2015
C. Stahn (ed.), *The Law and Practice of the International Criminal Court* (2015), Oxford: Oxford University Press.
Stahn & van den Herik 2010
C. Stahn, L. van den Herik (eds.), *Future Perspectives on International Criminal Justice*, T.M.C. Asser Press (2010).
Stahn & Sluiter 2009
C. Stahn & G. Sluiter, *The Emerging Practice of the International Criminal Court* (2009), Leiden: Martinus Nijhoff Publishers.
Stahn, Olásolo & Gibson 2006
C. Stahn, H. Olásolo, K. Gibson, 'Participation of Victims in Pre-Trial Proceedings of the ICC', (2006) 4 *Journal of International Criminal Justice* 219-238.
Stalford & Drywood 2009
H. Stalford, E. Drywood, 'Coming of Age?: Children's Rights in the European Union', (2009) 46 *Common Market Law Review* 143-172.
Steiner, Alston & Goodman 2008
H. Steiner, P. Alston, R. Goodman, R., *International Human Rights in Context: law, politics, morals: text and materials* (2008), Oxford (etc.): Oxford University Press.
Stichick Betancourt & Khan 2008
T. Stichick, Betancourt, K.T. Khan, 'The mental health of children affected by armed conflict: Protective processes and pathways to resilience' (2008) 20 Int. Rev. Psychiatry 317.
Strode, Slack & Essack 2010
A. Strode, C. Slack, Z. Essack, 'Child consent in South African law: implications for researchers, service providers and policy-makers', (2010) 100 South African Medical Journal 4, 247-249.
Sund 2006
L.G. Sund, 'The Rights of the Child as Legally Protected Interests', (2006) 14 International Journal of Children's Rights 327-337.

Tedeschi & Calhoun 2003
R.G. Tedeschi, L.G. Calhoun, 'The Posttraumatic Growth Inventory: Measuring the Positive Legacy of Trauma', (1996) 9 *Journal of Traumatic Stress* 445-471.

Thabet & Vostanis 2000
A.A. Thabet, P. Vostanis, 'Post Traumatic Stress Disorder Reactions in Children of War: A Longitudinal Study' (2000) 24 *Child Abuse and Neglect* 291-298.
Thabet & Vostanis 1999
A.A. Thabet, P. Vostanis, 'Post-traumatic Stress Reactions in Children of War', (1999) 49 *Journal of Child Psychology and Psychiatry and Allied Disciplines* 385-391.
Tiefenbrun 2008
S. Tiefenbrun, 'Child Soldiers, Slavery and the Trafficking of Children', (2008) 31 *Fordham International Law Journal* 415-486.
Tiefenbrun 2007
S. Tiefenbrun, 'Child Soldiers, Slavery, and the Trafficking of Children', (2007) *TJSL Legal Studies Research Paper* no. 1020341, http://papers.ssrn.com/sol3/papers.cfm?abstract_id=1020341.
Todres, Wojcik & Revaz 2006
J. Todres, M.E. Wojcik, C.R. Revaz (eds.), *The U.N. Convention on the Rights of the Child, An Analysis of Treaty Provisions and Implications of U.S. Ratification* (2006), New York: Transnational Publishers, Inc..
Tolbert 2006
D. Tolbert, 'Children and International Criminal Law: The Practice of the International Tribunal for the Former Yugoslavia (ICTY)', K. Arts, V. Popovski (eds.), *International Criminal Accountability and the Rights of Children* (2006), The Hague: Hague Academic Press, 147-154.
Traynor 2003
I. Traynor, 'In cold blood' and 'Massacre children testify in Serb trial', Guardian, 10 July 2003, http://www.guardian.co.uk/world/2003/jul/10/warcrimes.balkans, http://www.guardian.co.uk/world/2003/jul/10/balkans.
Triffterer 2008
O. Triffterer, *Commentary on the Rome Statute of the International Criminal Court – Observers' Notes, Article by Article* (2008), Second Edition, München (etc.): C.H.Beck.
Trumbull 2007
C.P. Trumbull, 'The Victims of Victim Participation in International Criminal Proceedings', (2007-2008) 29 *Michigan Journal of International Law* 777-826.
Tulkesn 2008
F. Tulkens, 'The European Convention on Human Rights and Children's Rights', in Council of Europe, *International Justice for Children* (2008), Strasbourg: Council of Europe Publishing, 17-XXX.
Tufnell 2003
G. Tufnell, 'Refugee Children, Trauma and the Law', (2003) 8 *Clinical Child Psychology and Psychiatry* 431-443.

Udombana 2006
N.J. Udombana, 'War is not Child's Play!: International Law and the Prohibition of Children's Involvement in Armed Conflict', (2006) 20 *Temple International and Comparative Law Journal* 57-109.

van Boven 2009
Th.C. van Boven, 'Victims' Rights to a Remedy and Reparation', in C. Ferstman, M. Goetz, A. Stephens (eds.), *Reparations for Victims of Genocide, War Crimes and Crimes Against Humanity, Systems in Place and Systems in Making* (2009), Leiden (etc.): Nijhoff, 19-40.

van Boven 2007
M. van Boven, 'Voorwoord namens UNICEF België', in W. Vandenhole (ed.), *Kinderrechten als mensenrechten: een multidisciplinaire verkenning* (2007), Antwerp (etc.): Intersentia, v-xxx.

van Boven 2007
Th.C. van Boven, 'Children's Rights are Human Rights; Current Issues and Developments', in J.C.M. Willems (ed.), *Developmental and Autonomy Rights of Children; Empowering Children, Caregivers and Communities* (2007), Second revised edition, Maastricht Series in Human Rights, Vol. 6, Antwerp (etc.): Intersentia, 1-10.

van Boven 1999
Th.C. van Boven, 'The Position of the Victim in the Statute of the International Criminal Court', in H. van Hebel, J. Lammers, J. Schukking (eds.), *Reflections on the International Criminal Court – Essays in Honour of Adriaan Bos* (1999), The Hague: T.M.C. Asser Press, 77-89.

van Boven 1996
Th.C. van Boven, 'The right to restitution, compensation and rehabilitation for victims of gross violations of human rights and fundamental freedoms', in G. Alfredsson, P. Macalister-Smith, A. Grahl-Madsen (eds.), *The Living Law of Nations: Essays on refugees, minorities and indigenous peoples and the human rights of other vulnerable groups: in memory of Atle Grahl-Madsen* (1996), Kehl (etc.): Engel, 339-355.

Van Bueren 2007
G. Van Bueren, *Child rights in Europe* (2007), Strasbourg: Council of Europe.

Van Bueren 1998
G. Van Bueren, *The International Law on the Rights of the Child* (1998), The Hague (etc.): Martinus Nijhoff Publishers.

Van Bueren 1994
G. Van Bueren, The International Legal Protection of Children in Armed Conflicts, (1994) 43 *International and Comparative Law Quarterly* 809-826

Van Bueren 1989
G. Van Bueren, 'Special features of the assistance and protection of children as victims of armed conflict', in F. Kalshoven (ed.), *Assisting the Victims of Armed Conflict and Other Disasters – Papers delivered at the International Conference on Humanitarian Assistance in Armed Conflict, The Hague, 22-23 June 1988* (1989), Dordrecht (etc.): Kluwer Academic Publishers, 127.

van den Herik (forthcoming 2015)
L. van den Herik, 'The unsuitability of custom as a source of International Criminal Law', in C. Bradley, I. Wuerth (eds.), *Custom in Crisis*, Oxford: Oxford University Press.

van den Herik 2012
L. van den Herik, 'Addressing 'Colonial Crimes' through Reparations', (2012) 10 *Journal of International Criminal Justice* 693-705.

Vandenhole 2007
W. Vandenhole (ed.), *Kinderrechten als mensenrechten: een multidisciplinaire verkenning* (2007), Antwerp (etc.): Intersentia.
Vandenhole 2007
W. Vandenhole, 'Het Kind en het Badwater: De Kruisbestuiving van Kinderrechten en Mensenrechten', in W. Vandenhole (ed.), *Kinderrechten als mensenrechten: een multidisciplinaire verkenning* (2007), Antwerp (etc.): Intersentia, 26-XXX.
Van den Wyngaert 2012
C. Van den Wyngaert, 'Victims Before International Criminal Courts: Some Views and Concerns of an ICC Trial Judge', (2012) 44 *Case Western Law Review* 475-496.
Van Rossum 2010
W. van Rossum. 'The clash of legal cultures over the 'best interests of the child' principle in cases of international parental child abduction', (2010) 6(2) *Utrecht Law Review* 33-55.
Vasiliev 2015
Vasiliev S., 'Victim Participation Revisited: What the ICC is Learning About Itself', C. Stahn (ed.), *The Law and Practice of the International Criminal Court* (2015), Oxford: Oxford University Press.
Verhellen 2007
E. Verhellen, 'Implementatie van Kinderrechten: óók een Akademische Verantwoordelijkheid', W. Vandenhole (ed.), *Kinderrechten als mensenrechten: een multidisciplinaire verkenning* (2007), Antwerp (etc.): Intersentia, XX.
Vollmann & Winau 1996
J. Vollmann, R. Winau, 'Informed consent in human experimentation before the Nuremberg code', (1996) 7 *British Medical Journal* 1445-1449.

Walker & Nguyen 1985
N.E. Walker, N. Nguyen, 'Interviewing The Child Witness: The Do's and the Don't's, The how's and the Why's', (1995-1996) 29 Creighton Law Review 1587-1618.
Wall 2008
J. Wall, 'Human Rights in Light of Childhood', (2008) *16 International Journal of Children's Rights* 523-543.
Walleyn *et al.* 2009
L. Walleyn et al, 'The Organisation of Legal Representation – Legal Aid and the OPCV: Counsels' Experience' (2009), http://www.scribd.com/doc/20302110/Legal-Representatives- Submission-July2009-1.
Wallneyn 2002
L. Walleyn, 'Victimes et témoins de crimes internationaux: du droit à une protection au droit à la parole', (2002) 84 No. 845 *Revue international de la Croix-Rouge* 51-78.
Wessells 2006
M.G. Wessells, *Child Soldiers: From Violence to Protection* (2006), Cambridge, MA (etc.): Harvard University Press.
Wessells 1998
M.G. Wessells, 'Children, Armed Conflict, and Peace', (1998) 35 *Journal of Peace Research* 635-646.
Werle 2005
G. Werle, Principles of International Criminal Law (2005), The Hague: TMC Asser Press

Werle 2007
G. Werle, 'Individual Criminal Responsibility in Article 25 ICC Statute', (2007) 5 *Journal of International Criminal Justice* 953-975.

Werner 2000
E.E. Werner, 'Protective Factors and Individual Resilience', in: J.P. Shonkoff, S.J Meisels (eds.), *Handbook of early child intervention* (2000), New York: Cambridge University Press, 115-132.

Werheimer 2006
E. Wertheimer, 'Of Apples and Trees: Adoption and Informed Consent', Villanova University School of Law – School of Law Working Papers (2006), Paper 68, http://law.bepress.com/cgi/viewcontent.cgi?article=1068&context=villanovalwps&sei-redir=1#search=%22adoption%20informed%20consent%20child%22.

Wheeler 2006
R. Wheeler, 'Gillick or Fraser? A plea for consistency over competence in children', (2006) 332 *British Medical Journal* 807.

Whitcomb 1986
D. Whitcomb, 'Child victims in court: the limits of innovation', (1986-1987) 70 *Judicature* 90-94.

Whitcomb 2003
D. Whitcomb, 'Legal Interventions for Child Victims', (2003) 16 *Journal of Traumatic Stress* 149-157.

Whitfield 2007
C. Whitfield, J.P. Garner, 'The early management of gunshot wounds Part II: the abdomen, extremities and special situations', (2007) 9 *Trauma* 47-71.

Willems 2007
J.C.M. Willems (ed.), *Developmental and Autonomy Rights of Children – Empowering Children, Caregivers and Communities* (2007), Antwerp (etc.): Intersentia.

Woodward & Joseph 2003
C. Woodward, S. Joseph, 'Positive change processes and post-traumatic growth in people who have experienced childhood abuse: Understanding vehicles of change', (2003) 76 *Psychology and Psychotherapy: Theory, Research and Practice* 267-283.

Yehuda 2002
R. Yehuda, 'Post-Traumatic Stress Disorder' (2002) 346 *New England Journal of Medicine* 108-114.

Yung 1983
J. Yung, 'A Comprehensive Approach to Child Hearsay Statements in Sex Abuse Cases', (1983) 83 *Columbia Law Review* 1745-1766.

Zappala 2010
S. Zappala, 'The Rights of Victims v. the Rights of the Accused', (2010) 8 *Journal of International Criminal Justice* 137-164.

Zehr & Toews (2004)
H. Zehr, B. Toews (eds.), *Critical issues in restorative justice* (2004), Monsey, New York: Criminal Justice Press and Willian Publishing.

Zeidner & Hammer 1990
M. Zeidner, A. Hammer, 'Life Events and Coping Resources as Predictors of Stress Symptoms in Adolescents', (1990) 11 *Personality and Individual Differences*, 693-703.

Zegveld 2010
L. Zegveld, 'Victims' Reparations Claims and International Criminal Courts – Incompatible Values?', (2010) 8 *Journal of International Criminal Justice* 77-111.
Zegveld 2003
L. Zegveld, 'Remedies for victims of violations of international humanitarian law', (2003) no. 851 *International Review of the Red Cross* 497-526.
Zimmermann & Arunkumar 1994
M.A. Zimmerman, R. Arunkumar, 'Resiliency Research: Implications for Schools and Policy', (1994) 8(4) *Social Polity Report*, 1-18.
Zivcić 1993
I. Zivcić, 'Emotional Reactions of Children to War Stress in Croatia', (1993) 32 *Journal of the American Academy of Child and Adolescent Psychiatry* 709-713.

United Nations Documents

- *The Millennium Development Goals Report 2008* (2008), http://www.un.org/millenniumgoals/reports.shtml.
- *The Millennium Development Goals Report 2005* (2005), http://www.un.org/millenniumgoals/reports.shtml.
- Food and Agriculture Organization of the United Nations, 'Inadequate Care', in Study on the impact of armed conflicts on the nutritional situation of children (1996), http://www.fao.org/docrep/005/w2357e/W2357E05.htm.
- UN Report of the Preparatory Committee on the Establishment of an International Criminal Court, Draft Statue & Draft Final Act, UN Doc. A/Conf.183/2/Add.1 (1995).
- Operational Guide to the Integrated Disarmament, Demobilization and Reintegration Standards, http://www.unddr.org/iddrs/iddrs_guide.php.

Secretary-General

- Report of the Special Representative of the Secretary-General for Children and Armed Conflict, UN Doc. A/68/267 (2013).
- Report of the Special Representative of the Secretary-General for Children and Armed Conflict, UN Doc. A/65/256 (2012).
- Report of the Secretary-General on children and armed conflict in Sri Lanka, UN Doc. S/2011/793 (2011).
- Report of the Secretary-General on Children and armed conflict, UN Doc. A/65/820-S/2011/250 (2011).
- Report of the Special Representative of the Secretary-General for Children and Armed Conflict, UN Doc. A/65/219 (2010).
- United Nations Office of the Special Representative of the Secretary-General for Children and Armed Conflict, Working Paper No 1, *The Six Grave Violations Against Children During Armed Conflict: The Legal Foundation* (2009), www.un.org/children/conflict/_documents/SixGraveViolationspaper.pdf.
- Statement of the UN Special Representative of the Secretary-General for Children and Armed Conflict, 5936th meeting, Agenda Children and armed conflict, UN Doc. S/PV.5936 (2008).

- UN Special Representative of the Secretary-General for Children and Armed Conflict, 'Children becoming increasingly vulnerable in conflict situations – UN envoy', (UN News Centre) 9 September 2008, http://www.un.org/apps/news/story.asp?NewsID=27985&Cr=Coomaraswamy &Cr1.
- *Guidance Note of the Secretary-General: UN Approach to Justice for Children* (2008), http://www.unhcr.org/refworld/docid/4a54bbf70.html.
- Report of the UN Secretary-General, Children and armed conflict, UN Doc. A/62/609-S/2007/757 (2007).
- Report of the Secretary-General on children and armed conflict in the Democratic Republic of the Congo, UN Doc. S/2006/389 (2006).
- Report of the Secretary-General, Children and armed conflict, UN Doc. A/59/695-S/2005/72 (2005).
- Report of the Special Representative of the Secretary-General for Children and Armed Conflict, UN Doc. A/60/335 (2005).
- UN Security Council, Special report on the events in Ituri, January 2002 - December 2003 of 16 July 2003, UN Doc. S/2004/573 (2004).
- Report of the Secretary-General, Children and armed conflict, UN Doc. A/58/546-S/2003/1053 (2003).
- Report of the Secretary-General on women, peace and security, UN Doc. S/2002/1154 (2002).
- Security Council, Report of the Secretary-General on the establishment of a Special Court for Sierra Leone, UN Doc. S/2009/915 (2000).
- General Assembly/Security Council, Report of the Secretary-General, Children and armed conflict, UN Doc. A/55/163-S/2000/712 (2000).
- Report of the Secretary General to the Security Council on the protection of civilians in armed conflict, UN Doc. S/1999/957 (1999).
- Report of the expert of the Secretary-General, Ms. Grac'a Machel submitted pursuant to General Assembly resolution 48/157, UN Doc. A/51/306 (1996).

Security Council Resolutions

- Resolution 1882 (2009), UN Doc. S/RES/1882 (2009).
- Resolution 1698 (2006), UN Doc. S/RES/1698 (2006).
- Resolution 1674 (2006), UN Doc. S/RES/1674 (2006).
- Resolution 1612 (2005), UN Doc. S/RES/1612 (2005).
- Resolution 1539 (2004), UN Doc. S/RES/1539 (2004).
- Resolution 1460 (2003), UN Doc. S/RES/1460 (2003).
- Resolution 1379 (2001), UN Doc. S/RES/1379 (2001).
- Resolution 1314 (2000), UN Doc. S/RES/1314 (2000).
- Resolution 1296 (2000), UN Doc. S/RES/1296 (2000).
- Resolution 1261 (1999), UN Doc. S/RES/1261 (1999).

Statement by the President of the Security Council

- UN Doc. S/PRST/1999/21 (1999).
- UN Doc. S/PRST/1999/6 (1999).
- UN Doc. S/PRST/1998/18 (1998).

General Assembly

- Rights of the Child, UN Doc. A/RES/66/141, A/66/PV.89 (2011).
- Report of the International Criminal Court, UN Doc. A/65/313 (2010).
- Basic Principles and Guidelines on the Right to a Remedy and Reparations for Victims of Gross Violations of International Human Rights Law and Serious Violations of International Humanitarian Law, UN Doc. A/60/147 (2005).
- General Assembly, Draft resolution referred to the High-level Plenary Meeting of the General Assembly by the General Assembly at its fifty-ninth session, 2005 World Summit Outcome, UN Doc. A/60/L.1 (2005),
- A world fit for children, UN Doc. A/RES/S-27/2 (2002).
- Report of the 1989 open-ended Working Group to the Commission on Human Rights on the question of a convention on the rights of the child, UN Doc. E/CN.4/1989/48 (1989).
- UN General Assembly, 1974 Declaration on the Protection of Women and Children in Emergency and Armed Conflict, Proclaimed by General Assembly Resolution 3318 (XXIX) of 14 December 1974, 29 UN GAOR Supp. (No. 31), at 146, UN Doc. A/9631 (1974).

ECOSOC

- ECOSOC Guidelines 2005
  ECOSOC, Resolutions and decision adopted by the Economic and Social Council at its substantive session of 2005 (29 June to 27 July 2005), Guidelines on Justice in Matters involving Child Victims and Witnesses of Crime, Resolution 2005/20, UN Doc. E/2005/INF/2/2/Add.1 (2005).

Human Rights Council

- Seventeenth session, Agenda item 5, Human rights bodies and mechanisms, Report of the Open-ended Working Group on an optional protocol to the Convention on the Rights of the Child to provide a communications procedure, UN Doc. A/HRC/17/36 (2011).
- Seventeenth session, Agenda item 5, Human Rights bodies and mechanisms, UN Doc. A/HRC/17/L.8 (2011).
- Second Session, Working Group on an optional protocol to the Convention on the Rights of the Child, Second session, Geneva, 6-10 December 2010, Proposal for a draft optional protocol prepared by the Chairperson-Rapporteur of the Open-ended Working Group on an optional protocol to the Convention on the Rights of the Child to provide a communication procedure, explanatory memorandum, UN Doc. A/HRC.WG.7/2/2 (2010).
- Report of the open-ended working group to explore the possibility of elaborating an optional protocol to the Convention on the Rights of the Child to provide a communications procedure, UN Doc. A/HRC/13/43 (2010).
- Thirteenth session, Agenda item 3, Promotion and protection of all human rights, civil, political, economic, social and cultural rights, including the right to development, UN Doc. A/HRC/RES/13/3 (2010).
- Working Group on an optional protocol to the Convention on the Rights of the Child, First Session, Geneva 14-18 December 2009, UN. Doc. A/HRC/WG7/1/CRP.5 (2009).

- Report of the United Nations Fact Finding Mission on the Gaza Conflict, Human Rights in Palestine and other Occupied Arab Territories, UN Human Rights Council, UN Doc. A/HRC/12/48 (2009).
- Eighth session, Agenda item 3, Promotion and Protection of All Human Rights, Civil, Political, Economic, Social and Cultural Rights, Including the Right to Development – Right to education in emergency situations, Report of the Special Rapporteur on the right to education, Vernor Muñoz, UN Doc. A/HRC/8/10 (2008).

UNICEF

- UNICEF 2011
  The State of the World's Children Report 2011, Adolescence An Age of Opportunity, February 2011, http://www.unicef.org/sowc2011/.
- UNICEF 2010a
  Innocenti Research Centre, *Children and Truth Commissions* (2010), www.unicef-irc.org/publications/pdf/truth_commissions_eng.pdf.
- UNICEF 2010b
  Key Principles for Children and Transitional Justice: Involvement of Children and Consideration of Children's Rights in Truth, Justice and Reconciliation Processes, Outcome of Children and Transitional Justice Conference, Harvard Law School, Cambridge, Massachusetts, USA, 27-29 April 2009, IV Specific Principles and Programmatic Recommendations, in S. Parmar et al, *Children and Transitional Justice, Truth-Telling, Accountability and Reconciliation* (2010), Annex, http://www.unicef-irc.org/publications/pdf/tj_publication_eng.pdf, 407-411.
- UNICEF 2010c
  Innocenti Research Centre, A. Michels, 'Psychosocial Support for Children" Protecting the Rights of Child Victims and Witnesses in Transitional Justice Processes', Innocenti Working Paper, IWP 2010-14 (2010).
- UNICEF 2009a
  Office of the Special Representative of the Secretary-General for Children and Armed Conflict, Machel Study 10-Year Strategic Review, Children and Conflict in a Changing World (2009), http://www.unicef.org/publications/index_49985.html.
- UNICEF 2009b
  United Nations Office on Drugs and Crime, Handbook for Professionals and Policymakers on Justice in matters involving child victims and witnesses of crime (2009), http://www.unodc.org/documents/justice-and-prison-reform/hb_justice_in_matters_professionals.pdf.
- UNICEF 2008
  UNICEF concerned over possible prosecution of child soldier (2008), http://www.un.org/apps/news/story.asp?NewsID=25496&Cr=child&Cr1=soldier.
- UNICEF 2007
  The Paris Principles and Guidelines on Children Associated with Armed Forces or Armed Groups (2007), at 7, http://www.unicef.org/emerg/files/ParisPrinciples310107English.pdf.
- *Implementation Handbook for the Convention on the Rights of the Child* (2007), 3rd edition, http://www.unicef.org/publications/files/Implementation_Handbook_for_the_Convention_on_the_Rights_of_the_Child_Part_2_of_3.pdf.

- UNICEF 2005a
Innocenti Research Centre, A. Michels, S. Siegrist, 'Expert Discussion on Transitional Justice Transitional Children', outcome document (2005), http://www.unicef-irc.org/research/pdf/TJC_Outcome_Document_FINAL.pdf.
- UNICEF 2005b
Adressing the needs of children (2005), http://www.unicef.org/crc/index_30167.html.
- UNICEF 2005b
Innocenti Insight, G. Lansdown, The Evolving Capacities of the Child (2005), http://www.unicef-irc.org/publications/pdf/evolving-eng.pdf.
- UNICEF 2005c
The State of the World's Children 2005 – Childhood under Threat (2005), http://www.childinfo.org/files/The_State_of_the_Worlds_Children_2005.pdf.
- Guide to the Optional Protocol on the Involvement of Children in Armed Conflict (2003), http://www.unicef.org/publications/index_19025.html.
- UNICEF 2002a
Innocenti Research Center, *International Criminal Justice and Children, No Peace Without Justice* (2002), http://www.unicef.org/emerg/files/ICJC.pdf.
- UNICEF 2002b
Building a World Fit for Children (2002), The United Nations General Assembly, Special Session on Children, 8-10 May 2002http://www.unicef.org/sowc06/pdfs/pub_build_wffc_en.pdf.
- UNICEF 1996
- Innocenti Studies, P. Alston, B. Gilmour-Walsh, *The Best Interests of the Child, Towards a Synthesis of Children's Rights and Cultural Values* (1996), Florence: UNICEF International Child Development Center.
- 'Children in Conflict and Emergencies'
http://www.unicef.org/protection/index_armedconflict.html.
- UNICEF in emergencies, *Humanitarian access*,
http://www.unicef.org/emerg/index_33198.html.
- Child friendly versions of the Convention on the Rights of the Child, see, http://www.unicef.org/voy/explore/rights/explore_2781.html
- Child friendly version of the United Nations Guidelines on Justice in matters involving child victims and witnesses of crime. http://www.unicef.org/voy/media/Document.doc.
- Fact sheet, http://www.unicef.org/emerg/files/childsoldiers.pdf.

UN High Commissioner for Human Rights

- Legislative History of the Convention on the Rights of the Child, Volume I, UN Doc. HR/PUB/07/1 (2007)

UN High Commissioner For Refugees

- Guidelines for Prevention and Response (2003), http://www.unhcr-centraleurope.org/en/pdf/what-we-do/caring-for-vulnerable-groups/sexual-and-gender-based-violence/unhcr-guidelines-for-prevention-and-response-to-sexual-and-gender-based-violence.html

Human Rights Committee

- *Derksen v. The Netherlands*, Communication No. 976/2001, *Derksen v. The Netherlands*, UN Doc. CCPR/C/80/D/976/2001 (2004).
- *Baban et al. v. Australia*, Communication No. 1014/2001, *Baban et al. v. Australia*, UN Doc. CCPR/C/78/D/1014/2001 (2003).
- *Darwinia Rosa Mónaco de Gallicchio v. Argentina*, Communication No. 400/1990, *Darwinia Rosa Mónaco de Gallicchio v. Argentina*, UN Doc. CCPR/C/53/D/400/1990 (1995).
- *A. and S.N. v. Norway*, Communication No. 224/1987, *A. and S.N. v. Norway*, UN Doc. CCPR/C/33/D/224/1987 (1988).
- *S.H.B. v. Canada*, Communication No. 192/1985, *S.H.B. v. Canada*, UN Doc. CCPR/C/29/D/192/1985 (1987).
- Statistical survey of individual complaints dealt with by the Human Rights Committee under the Optional Protocol to the International Covenant on Civil and Political Rights (9 April 2008), http://www2.ohchr.org/english/bodies/hrc/stat2.htm.

UN Committee on the Rights of the Child

- UN Committee on the Rights of the Child, General Comment No. 14
  General Comment NO. 14, On the right of the child to have his or her best interests taken as a primary consideration (art. 3, para. 1), UN Doc. CRC/GC/14 (2013).
- Committee on the Rights of the Child, Report and Recommendations of the Day of General Discussion on "Children of Incarcerated Parents", 30 September 2011, http://www2.ohchr.org/english/bodies/crc/docs/discussion/2011CRCDGDReport.pdf.
- UN Committee on the Rights of the Child, 'Effects of Gaza Conflict on Children "Devastating"', (UN News Centre) 13 January 2009,
  http://www.un.org/apps/news/story.asp?NewsID=29524& Cr=Gaza&Cr1=.
- UN Committee on the Rights of the Child, General Comment No. 12
  General Comment No. 12, The right of the child to be heard, UN Doc. RCR/C/GC/12 (2009).
- UN Committee on the Rights of the Child, General Comment No. 10
  General Comment No. 10, Children's rights in juvenile justice, UN Doc. CRC/C/GC/10 (2007).
- UN Committee on the Rights of the Child, General Comment No. 7
  General Comment No. 7, Implementing child rights in early childhood, UN Doc. CRC/C/GC/7/Rev.1 (2006).
- UN Committee on the Rights of the Child, General Comment No. 6
  General Comment No. 6, Treatment of unaccompanied and separated children outside their country of origin, UN Doc. CRC/C/GC/6 (2005)
- UN Committee on the Rights of the Child, General Comment No. 4
  General Comment No. 4, Adolescent health and development in the context of the Convention on the Rights of the Child, UN Doc. CRC/GC/2003/4 (2003).
- UN Committee on the Rights of the Child, CRC/C/78/Add.3, Switzerland, Consideration of Reports Submitted by States Parties under Article 44 of the Convention, Initial reports of States parties due in 1999, Switzerland, 19 October 2001.

Non-Government Organisations

International Committee of the Red Cross

International Committee of the Red Cross, Annual Report 2010 (2011), http://www.icrc.org/eng/resources/annual-report/index.jsp.
ICRC 2009
Children in war (2009), http://www.icrc.org/eng/assets/files/other/icrc_002_4015.pdf

Save the Children

Delivering Education for Children in Emergencies: A Key Building Block for the Future (2008), http://resourcecentre.savethechildren.se/content/library/documents/delivering-education-children-emergencies-key-building-block-future,
Forgotten Causalities of War: Girls in Armed Conflict (2005), http://www.peacewomen.org/assets/file/Resources/NGO/HR_ForgottenGirls_SC_2005.pdf.

Amnesty International

Amnesty International, *USA: Military Commission proceedings against Omar Khadr resume, as USA disregards its international human rights obligations*, 26 April 2010, AI Index: AMR 51/029/201, http://www.amnesty.org/en/library/asset/AMR51/029/2010/en/23618d64-1d1b-4af0-a9b5-04df1ceaddb2/amr510292010en.html
Amnesty International, *USA: Judge orders Mohammed Jawad's release from Guantánamo, Administration still mulling trial*, 30 July 2009, http://www.amnesty.org/en/library/info/AMR51/088/2009/en/refresh

Amnesty International, *United States of America – From ill-treatment to unfair trial. The case of Mohammed Jawad, child 'enemy combatant'*, 13 August 2008, AI Index: AMR 51/091/2008, http://www.amnesty.org/en/library/asset/AMR51/091/2008/en/d47d414f-693e-11dd-8e5e-43ea85d15a69/amr510912008eng.pdf

Amnesty International Kenya 2008
Amnesty International, Kenya – Concerns about the Truth, Justice and Reconciliation Commission Bill, AFR 32/009/2008, http://www.amnesty.org/en/library/asset/AFR32/009/2008/en/8903d721-2667-11dd-b995-f7269e5ea55f/afr320092008eng.pdf

THE REDRESS TRUST

Victims and the ICC: Still room for improvement – Paper prepared for the 7th Assembly of States Parties, The Hague, 14-22 November 2008, http://www.redress.org/reports/reports

The Redress Trust 2012 (In tekst veranderen, chapter II)
The Participation of Victims in International Criminal Court Proceedings (2012), http://www.redress.org/downloads/publications/121030participation_report.pdf.

The Redress Trust 2006
Victims, Perpetrators or Heroes? Child Soldiers before the International Criminal Court (2006), http://www.essex.ac.uk/armedcon/story_id/000403.pdf

REDRESS et al, Joint Letter to the ICC Prosecutor on the narrow scope of the charges brought against Mr. Lubanga, issued by Avocats Sans Frontières, Centre for Justice & Reconciliation, DRC Coalition for the ICC, International Federation of Human Rights, Human Rights Watch, REDRESS and the Women's Initiative for Gender Justice (2006), http://www.vrwg.org/smartweb/documents/members-documents

Reliefweb

Reliefweb Kenya
Reliefweb, Kenya – Analysis: Truth and consequences in Kenya, http://www.reliefweb.int/node/403351

Fédération international des droits des l'homme

FIDH 2011
FIDH Victims' Rights Before the Extraordinary Chambers in the Courts of Cambodia (ECCC) (2011), http://fidh.org/IMG/pdf/eccc_victrights_rep_nov2012_en_web.pdf

Coalition to Stop the Use of Child Soldiers

Child Soldiers - Global Report 2008
Child Soldiers - Global Report 2008 (2008), www.childsoldiersglobalreport.org/files/country_pdfs/FINAL_2008_Global_Report.pdf
Child Soldiers – Global Report 2004
Child Soldiers - Global Report 2004 (2005), www.childsoldiersglobalreport.org/files/country_pdfs/FINAL_2008_Global_Report.pdf

Human Rights First

Human Rights First, *The Case of Omar Ahmed Khadr, Canada* (2008), https://secure.humanrightsfirst.org/us_law/detainees/cases/khadr.htm

Human Rights Watch

Becker 2010
J. Becker, Children as Weapons of War, http://www.hrw.org/legacy/wr2k4/11.htm
Human Rights Watch, Releasing Jawad: A Boys life at Guantanamo (2010), http://www.hrw.org/en/news/2010/01/11/releasing-jawad-boy-s-life-guantanamo

CURE

CURE, *Child victims in the Union – Right and Empowerment – A report of the CURE project* 2009-2010, The Crime Victim Compensation and Support Authority Sweden (2010), http://www.brottsoffermyndigheten.se/default.asp?id=3251

International Center for Transitional Justice

International Center for Transitional Justice 2009
International Center for Transitional Justice, *Children and Transitional Justice* (2009), http://ictj.org/our-work/transitional-justice-issues/children-and-transitional-justice
Women's Initiatives for Gender Justice 2012
Lubanga Judgment – The Women's Initiatives Submits Observations in Reparations Proceedings in the Lubanga Case 2012, http://www.lubangatrial.org/2012/12/14/lubanga-judgment-the-womens-initiatives-submits-observations-in-reparations-proceedings-in-the-lubanga-case/

Eurochips
Eurochips 2011
Eurochips, Strengthening mutual trust in the European Judicial Area – a Green Paper on the application of EU criminal justice legislation in the field of Detention, (COM (2011) 327/3), http://ec.europa.eu/justice/newsroom/criminal/opinion/files/110510/eurochips_response_en.pdf

Cape Town Principles 1997
Cape Town Principles and Best Practices, adopted at the Symposium on the Prevention of Recruitment of Children into the Armed Forces and on Demobilization and Social Reintegration of Child Soldiers in Africa, 27-30 April 1997, Cape Town, South Africa (2009), http://www.unicef.org/emerg/files/Cape_Town_Principles(1).pdf

Council of Europe

Council of Europe Guidelines 2010
2010 Guidelines of the Committee of Ministers of the Council of Europe on child-friendly justice and their explanatory memorandum,
http://www.coe.int/t/dghl/standardsetting/childjustice/Guidelines%20on%20child-friendly%20justice%20and%20their%20explanatory%20memorandum%20_4_.pdf

International Justice for Children (2008), Strasbourg: Council of Europe Publishing

Explanatory Report on the European Convention on the Exercise of Children's Rights, http://conventions.coe.int/treaty/en/Reports/Html/160.htm

Child friendly version of the European Convention on Human Rights, http://www.eycb.coe.int/comasito/chapter_6/3.html.

Case law database relevant to children
http://www.coe.int/t/dg3/children/caselaw/CaseLawChild_en.asp

European Court of Human Rights, pending and decided Applications Allocated to a Judicial Formation,
http://www.echr.coe.int/NR/rdonlyres/92D2D024-6F05-495E-A714-4729DEE6462C/0/Pending_applications_chart.pdf,
http://www.echr.coe.int/NR/rdonlyres/7B68F865-2B15-4DFC-85E5-DEDD8C160AC1/0/Stats_EN_112011.pdf

European Commission
European Commission, An EU Agenda for the Rights of the Child
European Commission, Communication from the Commission to the European Parliament, the Council, the European Economic and Social Committee and the Committee of the Regions, An EU Agenda for the Rights of the Child, Brussels, 15.2.2011, COM(2011) 60 final

International Criminal Court

International Criminal Court homepage, http://www.icc-cpi.int/Menus/ICC/Home

Application Form for Individuals
Application Form for Individuals, http://www.icc-cpi.int/nr/exeres/e97f0ff4-9bc2-46e2-80d2-9427c67141b9.htm

Guide for the Participation of Victims
Guide for the Participation of Victims in the Proceedings of the Court which explains in detail how victims have to proceed with their applications, http://www.icc-cpi.int/Menus/ICC/Structure+of+the+Court/Victims/Participation/Booklet.htm

Representing Victims Before the International Criminal Court 2010
Office of the Public Council for Victims, *Representing Victims Before the International Criminal Court – A Manual for legal representatives* (2010), http://www.icc-cpi.int/iccdocs/PIDS/tmp/Representing%20Victims%20before%20ICC.PDF

Press Release: 14.07.2009, *Trial of Thomas Lubanga Dyilo: the Office of the Prosecutor finishes its case presentation*, http://www.icc-cpi.int/menus/icc/situations%20and%20cases/situations/situation%20icc%200104/related%20cases/icc%200104%200106/press%20releases/pr437?lan=en-GB

Trust Fund for Victims, Programme Progress Report Summer 2012
Trust Fund for Victims, Programme Progress Report Summer 2012, http://www.trustfundforvictims.org/sites/default/files/imce/TFV%20PPR%20Summer%202012%20ENG%20Final_.pdf.

2010 Trust Fund for Victims, Programme Progress Report
Trust Fund for Victims, Programme Progress Report, *Learning from the TFV's second mandate: From implementing rehabilitation assistance to reparations* (2010), http://www.trustfundforvictims.org/

Registry Facts and Figures – facts up to date as of 30 September 2010, http://www.icc-cpi.int/NR/rdonlyres/F67584DE-F045-45E2-9503-8F4D16B3DEAA/282642/RegistryFactsandFiguresEN.pdf

Assembly of States Parties, Eighth session, The Hague, 18-26 November 2009, Report of the Court on the Strategy in relation to victims, ICC-ASP/8/45, 10 November 2009

Report of the Court on the financial aspects of enforcing the Court's obligation to fund family visits to indigent detained persons, ICC-ASP/8/9, 6 May 2009

International Criminal Court, Assembly of State Parties, Report of the Court on family visits to indigent detained persons, ICC-ASP/7/24, 5 November 2008
Press Release ICC, 22 May 2007, Prosecutor opens investigation in the Central African Republic, ICC-OTP-20070522-220 http://www.icc-cpi.int/menus/icc/press%20and%20media/press%20releases/2007/prosecutor%20opens%20investigation%20in%20the%20central%20african%20republic?lan=en-GB

Strategic Plan for Outreach of the International Criminal Court, ICC-ASP/5/12, 29 September 2006

Assembly of State Parties, Establishment of a fund for the benefit of victims of crimes within the jurisdiction of the Court, and of the families of such victims, Resolution ICC-ASP/1/Res.6, adopted at the 3rd plenary meeting, on 9 September 2002.

The Trust Fund for Victims, *Assistance to children and youth*
The Trust Fund for Victims, *Assistance to children and youth*, http://www.trustfundforvictims.org/projects#Assistance%20to%20children%20and%20youth

International Criminal Court, A guide for the Participation of Victims
International Criminal Court, A guide for the Participation of Victims in the proceedings of the court, http://www.icc-cpi.int/NR/rdonlyres/8FF91A2C-5274-4DCB-9CCE-37273C5E9AB4/282477/160910VPRSBookletEnglish.pdf, at 11-12

TRC South Africa
South African Truth and Reconciliation Commission

South African TRC, Vol. 4
South African Truth and Reconciliation Commission, Truth and Reconciliation Commission of South Africa Report (1998), Vol. 4, Chapter 9, 'Special Hearing on Children and Youth', http://www.justice.gov.za/trc/report/finalreport/Volume%204.pdf

Children's hearings before the South African TRC, http://www.justice.gov.za/trc/special/index.htm#ch

Truth and Reconciliation Commission Sierra Leone

Truth and Reconciliation Commission Report For the Children of Sierra Leone (2004), http://www.unicef.org/infobycountry/files/TRCCF9SeptFINAL.pdf

TRC Sierra Leone Vol. 1, Chapter 1, Mandate
Sierra Leone TRC, *Witness to Truth: Report of the Sierra Leone Truth & Reconciliation Commission* (2004), Vol. 1, Chapter 1, 'Mandate', http://www.sierra-leone.org/Other-Conflict/TRCVolume1.pdf

TRC Sierra Leone Vol. 1, Chapter 5, Methodology and Process
Witness to Truth: Report of the Sierra Leone Truth & Reconciliation Commission (2004), Vol. 1, Chapter 5, 'Methodology and Process', http://www.sierra-leone.org/Other-Conflict/TRCVolume1.pdf

TRC Sierra Leone Vol. 2, Chapter 4, Reparations
Witness to Truth: Report of the Sierra Leone Truth & Reconciliation Commission (2004), Vol. 2, Chapter 4, 'Reparations', http://www.sierra-leone.org/Other-Conflict/TRCVolume2.pdf

TRC Sierra Leone Vol. 3B, Chapter 4 Children and the Armed Conflict in Sierra Leone
Witness to Truth: Report of the Sierra Leone Truth & Reconciliation Commission (2004), Vol. 3B, Chapter 4, 'Children and the Armed Conflict in Sierra Leone', http://www.sierra-leone.org/Other-Conflict/TRCVolume3B.pdf

Appendix 1, Statistical Appendix to the Report of the Truth and Reconciliation Commission of Sierra Leone, A Report by the Benetech Human Rights Data Analysis Group of the Truth and Reconciliation Commission (2004), http://www.sierra-leone.org/TRCDocuments.html

Truth and Reconciliation Commission of Liberia

Truth and Reconciliation Commission of Liberia Mandate, enacted on May 12, 2005, by the National Transitional Legislative Assembly, the TRC Mandate is the Act That Established the Truth and Reconciliation Commission (TRC) of Liberia, http://trcofliberia.org/about/trc-mandate.

TRC Liberia, Volume Three: Appendix
Republic of Liberia Truth and Reconciliation Commission, Volume Three: Appendices, Title II: Children, the Conflict and the TRC Children Agenda (2009), http://trcofliberia.org/reports/final-report

Overview of Legislation

Treaties, Conventions, Declarations

2010 Committee on the Rights of the Child, Rules of procedure, UN Doc. CRC/C/4/Rev.2, 2 December 2010

2010 Declaration of International Law Principles on Reparation for Victims of Armed Conflict (The Hague, Resolution 2/2010)

2009 Regulations of the Office of the Prosecutor of the International Criminal Court, Official Journal Publication ICC-BD/05-01-09

2007 Internal Rules of the Extraordinary Chambers in the Courts of Cambodia (as revised on 12 August 2011), http://www.eccc.gov.kh/en

2006 Regulations of the Registry of the International Criminal Court, Official Journal of Publication ICC-BD/03-01-06

2006 Code of Professional Conduct for Counsel, ICC-ASP/4/Res.1

2005 Regulations of the Trust Fund for Victims, ICC-Asp/4/Res.3

2005 Draft Declaration of International Law Principles on Reparation for Victims of Armed Conflict (Substantive Issues) (2010)

2005 Basic Principles and Guidelines on the Right to a Remedy and Reparations for Victims of Gross Violations of International Human Rights Law and Serious Violations of International Humanitarian Law, UN Doc. A/60/147 (2005)

2005 Act to establish the Truth and Reconciliation Commission (TRC) of Liberia (2005 TRC Act), http://allafrica.com/peaceafrica/resources/view/00010908.pdf

2004 Regulations of the International Criminal Court, Official Journal Publication ICC-BD/01-01-04

2003 Rules Governing the Detention of Persons Awaiting Trial or Appeal before the Special Court for Sierra Leone or Otherwise Detained on the Authority of the Special Court for Sierra Leone ("Rules of Detention"), (as amended on 14 May 2005), http://www.sc-sl.org/LinkClick.aspx?fileticket=sSNS1UL5T3w%3D&tabid=176

2002 Rome Statute of the International Criminal Court, 2187 UNTS 90 (Rome Statute)

2002 Rules of Procedure and Evidence of the International Criminal Court, Official Records ICC-ASP/1/3 (RPE)

2002 Elements of Crime of the International Criminal Court, Official Records ICC-ASP/1/3(part II-B)

2002 Agreement between the United Nations and the Government of Sierra Leone on the Establishment of a Special Court for Sierra Leone (with Statute), 2178 UNTS 138

2002 Rules of Procedure and Evidence of the Special Court for Sierra Leone, amended on 7 March 2003

2000 Charter of Fundamental Rights of the European Union, Official Journal of the European Communities C364/1, (18.12.2000)

2000	Optional Protocol to the Convention on the Rights of the Child on the Involvement of Children in Armed Conflict, 2173 UNTS 222
2000	Optional Protocol to the Convention on the Rights of the Child on the sale of children, child prostitution and child pornography, adopted by General Assembly Resolution 54/263, Annex II (2002), UN Doc. 54/49, Vol. III (2000)
2000	Act to establish the Truth and Reconciliation Commission in line with Article XXVI of the Lomé Peace Agreement and to provide for related matters (2000 TRC Act)
2000	Convention Concerning the Prohibition and Immediate Action for the Elimination of the Worst Forms of Child Labor (ILO Convention no. 182), 2133 UNTS 161
1999	Lomé Peace Agreement (Ratification) Act
1996	European Convention on the Exercise of Children's Rights, ETS No. 160.
1995	Rules of Procedure and Evidence of the International Criminal Tribunal for Rwanda (as amended on 9 February 2010), UN Doc. ITR/3/Rev.1 (1995)
1994	Rules of Procedure and Evidence of the International Criminal Tribunal for the Former Yugoslavia (as amended on 8 December 2010), UN Doc. IT/32/Rev.45 (2010)
1994	Statute of the International Criminal Tribunal for Rwanda ICTR Statute, 33 ILM 1602
1994	Statute of the International Criminal Tribunal for the Former Yugoslavia, 32 ILM 1192
1994	Rules of the International Criminal Tribunal for the Former Yugoslavia Governing the Detention of Persons awaiting Trial or Appeal before the Tribunal or otherwise Detained on the Authority of the Tribunal, UN Doc. IT/38Rev. 9 (2005), (as amended on 21 July 2005)
1990	African Charter on the Rights and Welfare of the Child, OAU Doc. CAB/LEG/24.9/49
1989	Convention on the Rights of the Child, 1577 UNTS 3 (CRC)
1989	Second Optional Protocol to the International Covenant on Civil and Political Rights, aiming at the abolition of the death penalty, adopted by the General Assembly Resolution 44/128 of (1989), UN Doc. A/44/49 (1989)
1985	Declaration of Basic Principles of Justice of Victims of Crime and Abuse of Power, UN General Assembly, UN Doc. A/RES/40/34 (1985)
1984	Convention against Torture and Other Cruel Inhuman or Degrading Treatment of Punishment, 1465 UNTS 85
1981	African Charter on Human and People's Rights, OAU.CAB/LEG/67/3/Rev.5 (1982), 21 ILM 59
1979	Convention on the Elimination of All Forms of Discrimination Against Women, 1249 UNTS 13
1978	American Convention on Human Rights, 1144 UNTS 123
1977	Protocol Additional to the Geneva Conventions of 12 August 1949, and Relating to the Protection of Victims of Non-International Armed Conflicts (Protocol II), 1125 UNTS 609
1977	Protocol Additional to the Geneva Conventions of 12 August 1949, and Relating to the Protection of Victims of International Armed Conflicts (Protocol I), 1125 UNTS 3

1974 Declaration on the Protection of Women and Children in Emergency and Armed Conflict, Proclaimed by General Assembly Resolution 3318 (XXIX) of 14 December 1974, 29 UN GAOR Supp. (No. 31), at 146, UN Doc. A/9631 (1974)
1966 International Covenant on Civil and Political Rights, 993 UNTS 171 (ICCPR)
1966 Optional Protocol to the International Covenant on Civil and Political Rights, 999 UNTS 302
1966 International Covenant on Economic, Social, and Cultural Rights, 993 UNTSS 3 (ICESCR)
1966 International Convention on the Elimination of all Forms of Racial Discrimination against Women, 660 UNTS 195 (CEDAW)
1961 European Social Charter, 529 UNTS 89
1959 Declaration of the Rights of the Child, Proclaimed by Genera Assembly resolution 1389(XIV) (1959), UN Doc. A/4354 (1959)
1953 Convention for the Protection of Human Rights and Fundamental Freedoms, 213 UNTS 222
1950 Convention relating to the Status of Refugees, 189 UNTS 150
1949 Geneva Convention relative to the Treatment of Prisoners of War, 75 UNTS 135
1949 Geneva Convention relative to the Protection of Civilian Persons in the Time of War, 75 UNTS 287 (Fourth Geneva Convention)
1948 Universal Declaration of Human Rights, adopted and proclaimed by General Assembly resolution 217 A (III) (1948), UN Doc. A/810 at 71 (1948)
1948 Convention on the Prevention on the Punishment of the Crime of Genocide, 78 UNTS 277
1945 Statute of the International Court of Justice, 33 UNTS 993
1924 Geneva Declaration of the Rights of the Child, League of Nations O.J. Spec. Supp. 21, at 43 (1924)

Domestic Law

Germany
2009 Gesetz über die freiwillige Gerichtsbarkeit (2009), BGBL I, 470

Netherlands
1901 Wet tot wijziging en aanvulling van de bepalingen in het Burgerlijke Wetboek omtrent de vaderlijke macht en de voogdij en daarmee samenhangende artikelen van 6 februari 1901, *Stb.* 1901, 62 (de civielrechtelijke kinderwet)
1901 Wet houdende wijziging in de bepalingen betreffende het straffen en de strafrechtspleging ten aanzien van jeugdige personen van 6 februari 1901, *Stb.* 1901, 63 (de strafrechtelijke kinderwet)
1901 Wet houdende beginselen en voorschriften omtrent maatregelen ten opzichte van jeugdige personen van 12 februari 1901, *Stb.* 1901, 64 (de zogenoemde derde Kinderwet).

Mexico
Constitution of Mexico (Constitucion Politica De Los Estados Unidos Mexicanos), http://www.constitution.org/cons/mexico.htm

Japan
Constitution of Japan, http://www.constitution.org/cons/japan.txt

South Africa
1996 Constitution of the Republic of South Africa Act, Schedule 28(1)(h), http://www.info.gov.za/documents/constitution/1996/

European Union
2003 European Union, EU Guidelines on Children and Armed Conflict, Ref. no. 15634/03, COHOM 47/PESC 762/CIVCOM302/COSDP 731, Council of the European Union, Brussels, approved by the European Union General Affairs Council, Brussels, 8 December 2003 [not published in the Official Journal], http://www.consilium.europa.eu/uedocs/cmsUpload/10019.en08.pdf,

OVERVIEW OF CASES

INTERNATIONAL COURTS AND TRIBUNALS

INTERNATIONAL CRIMINAL COURT

Situation in the Democratic Republic of the Congo

- Decision on the Applications for Participation Filed in Connection with the Investigation in the Democratic Republic of Congo by Applicants a/0189/06 to a/0198/06, a/0200/06 to a/0202/06, a/0204/06 to a/0208/06, a/0210/06 to a/0213/06, a/0215/06 to a/0218/06, a/0219/06, a/0223/06, a/0332/07, a/0334/07 to a/0337/07, a/0001/08, a/0030/08 and a/0031/08, ICC-01/04-545, 4 November 2008.
- Decision on the applications for participation filed in connection with the investigation in the Democratic Republic of Congo by Applicants a/0047/06 to a/0052/06, a/0163/06 to a/0eighteen7/06, a/0221/06, a/0226/06, a/0231/06 to a/0233/06, a/0237/06 to a/0239/06, and a/0241/06 to a/0250/06, ICC-01/04-505, 3 July 2008.
- Request for Review of the Registrar's Decision of 28 March 2998 on the Application for Legal Assistance Paid by the Court Filed by Mr. Keta on behalf of Victims a/0016/06, a/0018/06, a/0021/06, a/0025/06, a/0028/06, a/0031/06, a/0032/06, a/0034/06, a/0042/06, a/0044/06, a/0045/06, a/0142/06, a/0148/06, a/0150/06, a/0188/06, a/0199/06, a/0228/06 under Regulation 85(3) of the Regulations of the Court, ICC-01/04-494, 14 April 2008.
- Corrigendum to the 'Decision on the Applications for Participation Filed in Connection with the Investigation in the Democratic Republic of the Congo by a/0004/06 to a/0009/06, a/0016/06 to a/0063/06, a/0071/06 to a/0080/06 and a/0105/06 to a/0110/06, a/0188/06, a0128/06 to a/0162/06, a/0199/06, a/0203/06, a/0209/06, a/0214/06, a/0220/06 to a/0222/06, a/0224/06, a/0227/06 to a/0230/06, a/0234/06 to a/0236/06, a/0240/06, a/0225/06, a/0226/06, a/0231/06 to a/0233/06, a/0237/06 to a/0239/06 and a/0241/06 to a/0250/06', No. ICC-01/04-423-Corr, 31 January 2008.
- Order on the request by the OPCV for access to certain documents regarding applications a/0026/06, a/0145/06, a/0203/06 and a/0220/06, ICC-01/04-395, 17 September 2007.
- Decision on the Request of the Legal Representative of the Applicants on application process for victims'' participation and legal representation, ICC-01/04-374, 17 August 2007.
- Decision on the Applications for Participation in the Proceedings of a/0001/06, a/0002/06 and a/0003/06 in the case of the Prosecutor v. Thomas Lubanga Dyilo and of the investigation in the Democratic Republic of the Congo, ICC-01/04-177-tENG, 31 July 2006.

- Decision on the Applications for Participation in the Proceedings of VPRS 1, VPRS 2, VPRS 3, VPRS 4, VPRS 5 and VPRS 6, ICC-01/04-101-tEN-Corr, 17 January 2005.

Situation in the Democratic Republic of the Congo in the case of the Prosecutor v. Thomas Lubanga Dyilo

- Judgment on the appeal of Mr Thomas Lubanga Dyilo against his conviction, ICC-01/04-01/06-3121, 1 December 2014.
- Dissenting opinion of Judge Ušacka to the Judgment on the appeal of Mr Thomas Lubanga Dyilo against his conviction, ICC-01/04-01/06-3121-Anx2, 1 December 2014.
- Decision establishing the principles and procedures to be applied to reparations, ICC-01/04-01/06-2904, 7 August 2012.
- Decision granting leave to make representations in the reparations proceedings, ICC-01/04/01/06-2870, 20 April 2012.
- Observations on issues concerning reparations, ICC-01/04-01/06-2863, 18 April 2012.
- Observations du groupe de victimes V02 concernant la fixation de la peine et des réparations, ICC-01/04-01/06-2869, 18 avril 2012.
- Observations sur la fixation de la peine et les réparations de la part des victims a/001/06, a/003/06, a/007/06, a/0049/06, a/0149/07, a/0155/07, a/0156/07, a/0162/07, a/0149/08, a/0404/08, a/0405/08, a/0406/08, a/0407/08, a/0409/08, a/0523/08, a/0610/08, a/0611/08, a/0053/09, a/0249/09, a/0292/09, a/0398/09, et a/1622/10, 18 avril 2012.
- With Public Annexes 1 and 3 and Confidential Annex 2, Registry transmission of communications received in the context of reparations proceedings, ICC-01/04/01/06-2855, 29 March 2012.
- First Report to the Trial Chamber on applications for reparations, ICC-01/04-01/06-2847, 28 March 2012.
- Second Report of the Registry on Reparations, ICC-01/04-01/06-2806, 19 March 2012.
- Observations on Reparations in Response to the Scheduling Order of 14 March 2012, The Trust Fund for Victims, ICC-01/04-01/06-2872, 25 April 2012.
- Judgment pursuant to Article 74 of the Statute, ICC-01/04-01/06-2842, 14 March 2012.
- Office of the Prosecutor, Prosecutors Closing Statements of 25 August 2011, http://www.icc-cpi.int/iccdocs/doc/doc1210316.pdf.
- Conclusions finales de la Défense, ICC-01/04-01/06-2773-Red, 15 juillet 2011
- Redacted version of the Corrigendum of Decision on the applications by fifteen victims to participate in the proceedings, ICC-01/04-01/06-2659-ANXA-RED2, 8 February 2011.
- Redacted Decision on Intermediaries, ICC-01/04-01/06-2434-Red2, 31 May 2010.
- Discrete written application by the legal representative of victims a/0047/06, a/0048/06, a/0050/06 and a/0052/06 for participation in relation to the Special Representative of the Secretary General for the United Nations for Children and Armed Conflict, ICC-01/04-01/06-2216, 8 January 2010.
- Judgment on the appeals of Mr. Lubanga Dyilo and the Prosecutor against the Decision of Trial Chamber I of 14 July 2009 entitled "Decision giving notice of the parties and participants that the legal characterization of the facts may be subject to change in accordance with Regulation 55(2) of the Regulations of the Court, ICC-01/04-01/06-2205, 8 December 2009.

- Victims and Witnesses Unit report on confidentiality of medical records and consent to disclose medical records, ICC-01/04-01/06-2166, 15 October 2009.
- Order issuing confidential and public redacted versions of Annex A to the "Decision on the applications by 7 victims to participate in the proceedings" of 10 July 2009 (ICC-01/04-01/06-2035), ICC-01/04-01/06-2065 and ICC-01/04-01/06-2065-Anx2, 23 July 2009.
- Decision giving notice to the parties and participants that the legal characterization of the facts may be subject to change in accordance with Regulation 55(2) of the Regulations of the Court, ICC-01/04-01/06-2049, 14 July 2009.
- Decision on the applications by 7 victims to participate in the proceedings, ICC-01/04-01/06-2035, 10 July 2009.
- Decision on the request by victims a/0225/06, a/0229/06 and a/270/07 to express their views and concerns in person and to present evidence during trial, ICC-01/04-01/06-2032-Anx, 26 June 2009.
- Joint Application of the Legal Representatives of the Victims for the Implementation of the Procedure under Regulation 55 of the Regulations of the Court, ICC-01/04-01/06-1891, 22 May 2009.
- Order issuing public redacted annexes to the Decisions on the applications of victims to participate in the proceedings of 15 and 18 December 2008, ICC-01/04-01/06-1861 and ICC-01/04-01/06-1861-AnxA2, 8 May 2009.
- Decision issuing redacted and corrected versions of annex concerning applicant a/0246/06, ICC-01/04-01/06-1724-Anx3, 24 February 2009.
- Report of Ms. Elisabeth Schauer following the 6 February 2009 "Instructions to the Court's expert on child soldiers and trauma", ICC-01/04-01/06-1729-Anx1, 25 February 2009.
- Report of Ms. Elisabeth Schauer following the 6 February 2009 "Instructions to the Court's expert on child soldiers and trauma", ICC-01/04-01/06-1729, 25 February 2009.
- Instructions to the Court's expert on child soldiers and trauma, ICC-01/04-01/06-1671, 6 February 2009.
- Decision issuing redacted and corrected versions of annex concerning applicant a/0246/06, ICC-01/04-01/06-1724-Anx3, 24 February 2009.
- Prosecution's Clarifications to the 'Prosecution's Request for Non-Disclosure of the Identity of Twenty-Five Individuals providing Tu Quoque Information' filed on 19 December 2008, ICC-01/04-01/06-1650-Anx, 26 January 2009.
- Prosecution's Updated Anticipated Order of Prosecution Witnesses, ICC-01/04/01/06-1625, 19 January 2009.
- Decision on the applications by 3 victims to participate in the proceedings, ICC-01/04-01/06-1562, 18 December 2008.
- Decision on the applications by victims to participate in the proceedings, ICC-01/04-01/06-1556, 15 December 2008.
- Decision on the applications by victims to participate in the proceedings, ICC-01/04-01/06-1556-Corr-Anx1, 15 December 2008.
- Decision on Disclosure Issues, Responsibilities for Protective Measures and other Procedural Matters, ICC-01/04/01/06-1311-Anx2, 24 August 2008.
- Judgment on the appeals of the Prosecutor and The Defence against Trial Chamber I's Decision on Victims' Participation on 18 January 2008, ICC-01/04-01/06-1432, 11 July 2008.
- Decision on certain practicalities regarding individuals who have the dual status of witness and victim, ICC-01/04-01/06-1379, 5 June 2008.

- Prosecution's application for authorization to add the unredacted version of an expert report on age determination to the evidence to be relied on at the trial, ICC-01/04-01/06-1274, 10 April 2008.
- Submission of the Observations of the Special Representative of the Secretary General of the United Nations for Children and Armed Conflict pursuant to Rule 103 of the Rules of Procedure and Evidence, ICC-01/04-01/06-1229-AnxA, 18 March 2008.
- Decision on the role of the Office of Public Counsel for Victims and its request for access to documents, ICC-01/04-01/06-1211, 6 March 2008.
- Decision Inviting Observations from the Special Representative of the Secretary General of the United Nations for Children and Armed Conflict, ICC-01/04-01/06-1175, 18 February 2008.
- Victims and Witnesses Unit recommendations on psycho-social in-court assistance, ICC-01/04-01/06-1149, 1 February 2008.
- Public with confidential Prosecution and Defence only annex, Prosecution's communication of originals of incriminatory evidence disclosed to the Defence on 29 January 2008, ICC-01/04-01/06-1145, 31 January 2008.
- Decision on victims' participation, ICC-01/04-01/06-1119, 18 January 2008.
- Decision Regarding the Practices Used to Prepare and Familiarise Witnesses for Giving Testimony at Trial, ICC-01/04-01/06-1049, 30 November 2007.
- Decision on the Request of the Legal Representatives of Applicants on application process for victims' participation and legal representation, ICC-01/04-374, 17 August 2007.
- Decision of the Appeals Chamber on the Joint Application of Victims a/0001/06 to a/0003/06 and a/0105/06 concerning the "Directions and Decisions of the Appeals Chamber" of 2 February 2007, ICC-01/04-01/06-925, 13 June 2007.
- Decision on the confirmation of charges, ICC-01/04-01/06-803, 29 January 2007.
- Judgment on the appeal of Mr. Thomas Lubanga Dyilo against the decision of Pre-Trial Chamber I entitles "Second Decision on the Prosecution Requests and Amended Requests for Redactions under Rule 81, ICC-01/04-01/06-774, 14 December 2006.
- Judgment on the appeal of Mr. Thomas Lubanga Dyilo against the decision of Pre-Trial Chamber I entitles "First Decision on the Prosecution Requests and Amended Requests for Redactions under Rule 81, ICC-01/04-01/06-773, 14 December 2006.
- Decision on the Practice of Witness Familiarisation and Witness Proofing, ICC-01/04-01/06-679, 8 November 2006.
- Affaire Le Provureur c/Thomas Lubanga Dyilo, Décision du Greffier sur la demande d'aide judiciaire aux frais de la Cour déposée par la victime a/0105/06, ICC-01/04-01/06-650, 3 novembre 2006.
- Decision on applications for participation in proceedings a/004/06 to a/0009/06, a/0016/06, a/0063/06, a/0071/06 to a/0080/06 and a/0105/06 in the case of the Prosecutor v. Thomas Lubanga Dyilo, ICC-01/04-01/06-601, 20 October 2006.
- Decision on Request pursuant to Rule 103(1) of the Statute, ICC-01/04-01/06-480, 26 September 2006.
- Request submitted pursuant to Rule 103(1) of the Rules of Procedure and Evidence for leave to participate as amicus curiae in the Article 61 confirmation proceedings (with confidential annex 2), ICC-01/04-01/06-403, 8 September 2006.
- Decision on the Prosecution Request for Extension of Time, Clarification and Provision of Information, ICC-01/04-01/06-376-Corr, 1 September 2006.

- Decision on the Applications for participation in the proceedings of a/0001/06, a/0002/06 and a/0003/06, ICC-01/04-01/06-228, 28 July 2006.
- Decision on the Applications for Participation in the Proceedings submitted by VPRS 1 to VPRS 6 in the Case the Prosecutor v. Thomas Lubanga Dyilo, ICC-01/04-01/06-172, 29 June 2006.
- Registrar's Decision on Mr. Thomas Lubanga Dyilo's Application for Legal Assistance paid by the Court, ICC-01/04-01/06-63, 31 March 2006.
- Warrant of Arrest, ICC-01/04-01/06-2, 10 February 2006.
- Case Information Sheet of 15 October 2010, *The Prosecutor v. Thomas Lubanga Dyilo*, ICC-PIDS-CIS-DRC-01/004/10.

Transcripts Situation in the Democratic Republic of the Congo in the case of the Prosecutor v. Thomas Lubanga Dyilo

- ICC-01/04-01/06-T-236-Red-ENG, 27 January 2010.
- ICC-01/04-01/06-T-230-Red-ENG, 21 January 2010.
- ICC-01/04-01/06-T-229-Red-ENG, 19 January 2010.
- ICC-01/04-01/06-T-228-Red-ENG WT, 15 January 2010.
- ICC-01/04-01/06-T-227-Red-ENG, 14 January 2010.
- ICC-01/04-01/06-T-225-Red-ENG, 12 January 2010.
- ICC-01/04-01/06-T-173-ENG, 13 May 2009.
- ICC-01/04-01/06-T-172-Red-ENG, 12 May 2009.
- ICC-01/04-01/06-T-148-ENG, 13 March 2009.
- ICC-01/04-01/06-T-145-Red-ENG, 6 March 2009.
- ICC-01/05-01/06-T-135-Red-ENG, 25 February 2009.
- ICC-01/04-01/06-T-138-ENG, 22 February 2009.
- ICC-01/04-01/06-T-122-ENG, 9 February 2009.
- ICC-01/04-01/06-T-113-Red-ENG, 30 January 20.
- ICC-01/04-01/06-T-111-ENG, 29 January 2009.
- ICC-01/04-01/06-T-110-ENG, 28 January 2009.
- ICC-01/04-01/06-T-107-ENG, 26 January 2009.
- ICC-01/04-01/06-T-101-ENG, 12 January 2009.
- ICC-01/04-01/06-T-67-ENG, 9 January 2008.

Situation in the Democratic Republic of the Congo in the case of the Prosecutor v. Germain Katanga and Mathieu Ngudjolo Chui

- *Situation in the Democratic Republic of the Congo in the case of the Prosecutor v. Germain Katanga,* Dissenting opinion of Judge Christine Van den Wyngaert, ICC-01/04-01/07-3388-Anx, 26 June 2013.
- *Situation in the Democratic Republic of the Congo in the case of the Prosecutor v. Germain Katanga and Mathieu Ngudjolo Chui*, ICC-01/04-01/07-1788, 22 January 2010.
- Directions for the conduct of the proceedings and testimony in accordance with rule 140, ICC-01/04-01/07-1665, 20 November 2009.
- With confidential *ex parte* Annex only available to the Registry and to the Legal Representatives of the Victims – Grounds for the Decision on the 345 Applications for Participation in the Proceedings Submitted by Victims, ICC-01/04-01/07-1491, 23 September 2009.

- Order on the organization of common legal representation of victims, ICC-01/04-01/07-1328, 22 July 2009.
- Decision on "Mr Mathieu Ngudjolo's Complaint Under Regulation 221(1) of the *Regulations of the Registry* Against the Registrar's Decision of 18 November 2008", ICC-RoR217-02/08-8, 24 March 2009.
- Confidential, *ex parte* only available to the Defence of Mr Ngudjolo Chui and the Registrar, Decision on "Mr Mathieu Ngudjolo's Complaint Under Regulation 221(1) of the *Regulations of the Registry* Against the Registrar's Decision of 18 November 2008", ICC-ROR217/02/08-8, 10 March 2009.
- Order on the common legal representation of victims, ICC-01/04-01/07-876, 6 February 2009.
- Decision on the provisional separation of Legal Representative of Victims a/0015/08, a/0022/08, a/0024/08, a/0025/08, a/0027/08, a/0029/08, a/0032/08, a/0033/08, a/0034/08 and a/0035/08, ICC-01/04-01/07-660, 3 July 2008.
- Public Redacted Version of the Decision of the Prosecutor's Application to Redact Information Falling under Rule 77 of the Rules of Procedure and Evidence (Witness 007 and 294) of 17 June 2009 (ICC-01/04-01/07-1214-Conf-Exp), ICC-01/04-01/07-1240, 23 June 2009.
- Decision on the treatment of applications for participation, ICC-01/04-01/07-933, 27 February 2009.
- Troisième rapport du Greffe sur l'état d'avancement des demandes de visas pour les familles des personnes détenues dans la cadre des visites familiales, ICC-01/04-01/07-733, 3 novembre 2008.
- Decision on the confirmation of charges, ICC-01/04-01/07-717, 30 September 2008.
- Submissions of the Defence of Mr. Mathieu Ngudjolo in the Context of the Confirmation Hearing, ICC-01/04-01/07-699-tENG, 28 July 2008.
- Prosecution's Observations Addressing Matters that Were Discussed at the Confirmation Hearing, ICC-01/04-01/07-692, 22 July 2008.
- Registrar's decision on the indigence of Victim a/0110/08, ICC-01/04-01/07-652, 26 June 2008.
- Public Redacted Version of the "Decision on the 97 Applications for Participation at the Pre-Trial Stage of the Case", ICC-01/04-01/07-579, 10 June 2008.
- Registrar's Decision on the Indigence of Victim a/0333/07, ICC-01/04-01/07-562, 9 June 2008.
- Decision on the Applications for Participation in the Proceedings of Applicants a/0327/07 to a/0337/07 and a/0001/08, ICC-01/04-01/07-357, 2 April 2008.
- Décision du Greffier sur la demande d'aide judiciaire aux frais de la Cour déposée par M. Mathieu Ngudjolo Chui, ICC-01/04-01/07-298, 22 février 2008.
- Decision of the Registrar on the applications for legal assistance paid by the Court filed by Mr Germain Katanga, ICC-01/04-01/07-79, 23 November 2007.
- Request to the Democratic Republic of the Congo for the Arrest and Surrender of Germain Katanga, ICC-01/04-01/07-6, 6 July 2007.
- Case Information Sheet of 15 October 2010, "The Prosecutor v. Germain Katanga and Mathieu Ngudjolo Chui", ICC-PIDS-CIS-DRC2-03-004/10.

Situation in the Democratic Republic of the Congo in the case of the Prosecutor v. Bosco Ntaganda

- Decision Pursuant to Article 61(7)(a) and (b) of the Rome Statute on the Charges of the Prosecutor Against Bosco Ntaganda, 9 June 2014.
- Public Redacted Version of Prosecution's submissions on issues that were raised during the confirmation of charges hearing, 7 March 2014, ICC-01/04-02/06-276-Conf, 24 March 2014.

Transcripts Situation in the Democratic Republic of the Congo in the case of the Prosecutor v. Bosco Ntaganda

- ICC-01/04-02/06-T-10-Red-ENG WT, 13 February 2014.

Situation in Uganda

- Decision on victims' applications for participation a/0192/07 to a/0194/07, a/0196/07, a/0200/07, a/0204/07, a/0206/07, a/0209/07, a/0212/07, a/0216/07, a/0217/07, a/0219/07 to a/0221/07, a/02228/07 to a/0230/07, a/0234/07, a/0235/07, a/0237/07, a/0324/07 and a/0326/07 under rule 89, ICC-02/04-180, 10 March 2009.
- Public Document With Annex Confidential *ex parte* only available to the OPCV, OPCV Report on legal representation of victims, ICC-02/04-173, 28 November 2008.
- Decision on victims' applications for participation a/0014/07 to a/0020/07 and a/0076-07 to a/0125/07, ICC-02/04-172, 21 November 2008.
- Report on the identity documents available in the Ugandan legal and administrative system and other supporting documentation for applications for participation in proceedings in Uganda, ICC-02/04-125-Anx, 17 March 2008.
- Decision on victims' applications for participation a/0010/06, a/0064/06 to a/0070/06, a/0081/06, a/0082/06, a/0084/06 to a/0089/06, a/0091/06 to a/0097/06, a/0099/06, a/0100/06, a/0102/06 to a/0104/06, a/0111/06, a/0113/06 to a/0117/06, a/0120/06, a/0121/06 and a/0123/06 to a/0127/06, ICC-02/04-125, 14 March 2008.
- Decision on legal representation of Victims a/0090/06, a/0098/06, a/0101/06, a/0112/06, a/0118/06, a/0119/06 and a/0122/06, ICC-02/04-117, 15 February 2008.
- Decision on legal representation of Victims a/0101/06 and a/0119/06, ICC-02/04-105, 28 August 2007.
- Decision on victims' applications for participation a/0010/06, a/0064/06 to a/0070/06, a/0081/06 to a/0104/06 and a/0111/06 to a/0127/06, ICC-02/04-101, 10 August 2007.

Situation in Uganda in the case of the Prosecutor v. Joseph Kony, Vincent Otti, Okot Odhiambo, Dominic Ongwen

- *Situation in Uganda in the case of the Prosecutor v. Joseph Kony, Vincent Otti, Okot Odhiambo, Dominic Ongwen*, ICC-02/04-179, 23 February 2009.
- Public Document With Annex Confidential *ex parte* only available to the OPCV, OPCV Report on legal representation of victims, ICC-02/04-01/05-358, 28 November 2008.
- Decision on victims' applications for participation a/0010/06, a/0064/06 to a/0070/06, a/0081/06, a/0082/06, a/0084/06 to a/0089/06, a/0091/06 to a/0097/06, a/0099/06, a/0100/06, a/0102/06 to a/0104/06, a/0111/06, a/0113/06 to a/0117/06, a/0120/06, a/0121/06 and a/0123/06 to a/0127/06, ICC-02/04-01/05-282, 14 March 2008.

- Decision on victims' applications for participation a/0010/06, a/0064/06 to a/0070/06, a/0081/06 to a/0104/06 and a/0111/06 to a/0127/06, ICC-02/04-01/05-252, 10 August 2007.

Situation in the Central African Republic in the case of the Prosecutor v. Jean-Pierre Bemba Gombo

- Victims and Witnesses Unit's amended version of the "Unified Protocol on the practices used to prepare and familiarize witnesses for giving testimony at trial" submitted on 22 October 2010, ICC-01/05-01/08-1081-Anx, 7 December 2010.
- Decision on common legal representation of victims of the purpose of trial, ICC-01/05-01/08-1005, 10 November 2010.
- Decision defining the status of 54 victims who participated at the pre-trial stage, and inviting the parties' observations on applications for participation by 86 applicants, ICC-01/05-01/08-699, 22 February 2010.
- Redacted version of "Decision on legal assistance for the accused", ICC-01/05-01/08-567-Red, 26 November 2009.
- Reasons for the decision on the Applications for judicial review of Mr Jean-Pierre Bemba Gombo of 10 and 11 November 2008, ICC-01/05-01/08-310, 4 September 2009.
- Fifth Decision on Victims' Issues Concerning Common Legal Representation of Victims, ICC-01/05-01/08-322, 16 December 2008.
- Fourth Decision on Victims' Participation, ICC-01/05-01/08-320, 12 December 2008.
- Decision on Victim Participation, ICC-01/05-01/08-103-tENG-Corr, 12 September 2008.
- Registrar's Decision on the Application for Legal Assistance Paid by the Court Filed by Mr Jean-Pierre Bemba Gombo, ICC-01/05-01/08-76, 25 August 2008.

Situation in Darfur, Sudan

- Corrigendum to Decision on the Applications for Participation in the Proceedings of Applicants a/0011/06 to a/0015/06, a/0021/07, a/0023/07 to a/0033/07 and a/0035/07 to a/0038/07, ICC-02/05-111-Corr, 14 December 2007.

Situation in Darfur, Sudan in the case of the Prosecutor v. Bahar Idress Abu Garda

- Decision on Applications a/0655/09, a/0656/09, a/0736/09 to a/0747/09 and a/0750/09 to a/0755/09 for Participation in the Proceedings at the Pre-Trial Stage of the Case, ICC-02/05-02/09-255, 19 March 2010.
- Decision of the Registrar on the Indigence of Victims a/0535/09, a/0537/09, a/0538/09, a/0539/09, a/0540/09, a/0541/09, a/0542/09, a/0544/09, a/0545/09, a/0546/09, a/0547/09, a/0548/09, a/0549/09, a/0550/09, a/0551/09, a/0557/09, a/0558/09, a/0559/09, a/0560/09, a/0561/09 and a/0562/09 Represented by Mr Akin Akinbote, ICC-02/05-02/09-195, 20 October 2009.
- Decision of the Registrar on the Indigence of Victims Decision of the Registrar on the Indigence of Victims a/0552/09, a/0553/09,a/0554/09, a/0555/09, a/0556/09, a/0563/09, a/0564/09, a/0565/09, a/0566/09, a/0567/09, a/0568/09, a/0569/09, a/0570/09, a/0571/09, a/0572/09, a/0573/09, a/0574/09, a/0575/09, a/0576/09, a/0577/09, a/0578/09 Represented by Mr Franck Adaka, ICC-02/05-02/09-197, 20 October 2009.

- Decision of the Registrar on the Indigence of Victims a/0170/09, a/0171/09, a/0172/09, a/0173/09, a/0174/09, a/0175/09, a/0176/09, a/0177/09, a/0178/09, a/0179/09, a/0180/09, a/0181/09, a/0182/09, a/0183/09, a/0184/09, a/0185/09, a/0186/09, a/0187/09, a/0188/09, a/0189/09, a/0190/09, a/0191/09, a/0192/09 and a/0436/09 Represented by Mr. Brahima Kone, ICC-02/05-02/09-172, 15 October 2009.
- Decision on the 34 Applications for Participation at the Pre-Trial Stage of the Case, ICC-02/05-02/09-121, 25 September 2009.

Situation in the Republic of Kenya

- Public Redacted Version Of Corrigendum to the Report on Victims' Representations (ICC-01/09-17-Conf-Exp-Corr) and annexes 1 and 5, ICC-01/09-17-Corr-Red, 29 March 2010.

Situation in the Republic of Kenya in the case of the Prosecutor v. William Samoei Ruto and Joshua Arap Sang

- Decision on witness preparation, ICC-01/09-01/11-524.
- Annex to the Decision on witness reparation, ICC-01/09-01/11-524-Anx.

Situation in the Republic of Kenya in the case of the Prosecutor v. Francis Kirimi Mutaura and Uhuru Muigai Kenyatta

- Decision on victims' representation and participation, ICC-01/09-02/11-498

INTERNATIONAL CRIMINAL TRIBUNAL FOR THE FORMER YUGOSLAVIA

The Prosecutor v. Galić

- *The Prosecutor of the Tribunal against Stanislav Galić* (IT-98-29-I).

The Prosecutor v. Haradinaj, Balaj and Brahimaj

- *The Prosecutor of the Tribunal against Ramush Haradinaj, Idriz Balaj & Lahi Brahimaj* (IT-04-84).

The Prosecutor v. Orić

- *The Prosecutor of the Tribunal v. Naser Orić* (IT-03-068-T), Judgment, 30 June 2006.

The Prosecutor v. Tadić

- *The Prosecutor v. Dusko Tadic A/K/A "Dule"* (IT-94-1-T), Decision on the Prosecutor's Motion Requesting Protective Measures for Victims and Witnesses, 10 August 1995.

The Prosecutor v. Krajisnik

- *The Prosecutor v. Momcilo Krajisnik* (IT-00-39-T), Decision on the Defence's Request for an Order Setting Aside, in part, the Deputy Registrar's Decision of 3 February 2004

- Application for Permission to Visit a Detainee at the ICTY UN Detention Unit, www.icty.org/x/file/Legal%20Library/Detention/permission_visit_detainee_en.doc.

SPECIAL COURT FOR SIERRA LEONE

The Prosecutor v. Charles Ghankay Taylor

- The Prosecutor of the Special Court for Sierra Leone v. Charles Ghankay Taylor, Case No. SCSL-03-01-T, Judgment, 18 May 2012.

The Prosecutor v. Sesay, Kallon and Gbao

- The Prosecutor of the Special Court v. Issa Hassan Sesay, Morris Kallon Augustine Gbao, Case No. SCSL-04-15-A, Judgment, 26 October 2009.
- *The Prosecutor of the Special Court v. Issa Hassan Sesay, Morris Kallon, Augustine Gbao*, Case No. SCSL-04-15-PT, 2 March 2002.
- *The Prosecutor of the Special Court v. Issa Hassan Sesay & ORS*, Written Reasoned Ruling on the Preliminary Characterization of Expert Witness TF1-296, Case No. SCSL-04-15-T (2006), 14 July 2006.
- *The Prosecutor of the Special Court v. Issay Sesay, Morris Kallon, Augustine Gbao*, Case No. SCSL-2004-15-T, transcript of 11 April 2005.
- *The Prosecutor of the Special Court v. Issa Hassan Sesay, Morris Kallon & Augustine Gbao*, Decision on Prosecution Motion for Modification of Protective Measures for Witnesses, Case No. SCSL-04-15-PT-180, 5 July 2004.

The Prosecutor v. Brima, Kamara and Kanu

- *The Prosecutor of the Special Court v. Alex Tamba Brima, Brima Bazzy Kamara and Santigie Borbor Kanu*, Case No. SCSL-04-16-A, 22 February 2008.
- *The Prosecutor of the Special Court v. Alex Tamba Brima, Brima Bazzy Kamara and Santigie Borbor Kanu*, Case No. SCSL-04-16-T, Judgment, 20 June 2007.
- *The Prosecutor of the Special Court v. Alex Tamba Brima, Brima Bazzy Kamara, Santigie Borbor Kanu*, Case No. SCSL-2004-16-T, transcript of 26 September 2005.
- *The Prosecutor of the Special Court v. Alex Tamba Brima, Brima Bazzy Kamara, Santigie Borbor Kanu*, Case No. SCSL-2004-16-T, transcript of 8 July 2005.

The Prosecutor v. Fofana and Kondewa

- *The Prosecutor of the Special Court v. Sam Hinga Norman Moinina Fofana Allieu Kondewa*, Case no. SCSL-01-14-A, Judgment, 28 May 2008.
- *The Prosecutor of the Special Court v. Sam Hinga Norman Moinina Fofana Allieu Kondewa*, Case no. SCSL-01-14-T, Judgment, 2 August 2007.

- *The Prosecutor of the Special Court v. Sam Hinga Norman Moinina Fofana Allieu Kondewa*, Case No. SCSL-2004-14-T , transcript of 29 November 2006.
- *The Prosecutor of the Special Court v. Sam Hinga Norman Moinina Fofana Allieu Kondewa*, Case No. SCSL-2004-14-T, transcript of 9 March 2005.
- Decision on Preliminary Motion Based on Lack of jurisdiction (Child Recruitment), SCSL-2004-14-AR72(E), 31 May 2004.
- Press release SCSL, 24 June 2004, http://www.sc-sl.org/LinkClick.aspx?fileticket=TazwrTR%2bT7Q%3d&tabid=196.
- Press release SCSL, 2 November 2002, http://www.sc-sl.org/LinkClick.aspx?fileticket=XRwCUe%2BaVhw%3D&tabid=196.

European Court and Commission of Human Rights

- *Trosin v. Urkaine*, Judgment of 23 February 2012, Application no. 39758/05.
- *Thiermann and Others v. Norway*, Admissibility Decision of 8 March 2007, Application no. 18712/03.
- *Mubilanzila Mayeka and Kaniki Mitunga v. Belgium*, Judgment (Merits and Just Satisfaction) of 12 October 2006, Application no. 13178/03.
- *D., H. and others v. Czech Republic*, Judgment of 7 February 2006, Application no. 57325/00
- *S.C. v. United Kingdom*, Judgment (Merits and Just Satisfaction) of 15 June 2004, Application no. 60958/00.
- *Haase v. Germany*, Judgment (Merits and Just Satisfaction) of 8 April 2004, Application no. 11057/02.
- *Messina v. Italy* (No. 2),), Judgment of 28 September 2000, Application no. 25498/94.
- *K and T v. Finland*, Judgment (Merits and Just Satisfaction) of 12 July 2001, Application no. 25702/94.
- *V. v. United Kingdom*, Judgment (Merits and Just Satisfaction) of 16 December 1999, Application no. 24888/94.
- *T. v. United Kingdom*, Judgment (Merits and Just Satisfaction) of 16 December 1999, Application no. 24724/94.
- *A. v. The United Kingdom*, Judgment (Merits and Just Satisfaction) of 23 September 1998, Application no. 25599/94.
- *Stubbings and Others v. The United Kingdom*, Judgment (Merits) of 22 October 1996, Application no. 22083/93; 22095/93.
- *A. and B. v. The United Kingdom*, Admissibility Decision of 9 September 1996, Application no. 25599/94.
- *Stubbings v. The United Kingdom*, Admissibility Decision of 6 September 1994, Application no. 22083/93.
- *Bellet v. France*, Judgment (Merits and Just Satisfaction) of 4 December 1995, Application no. 23805/94.
- *Costello-Roberts v. UK*, Judgment of 25 March 1993, Application no. 13134/87
- *Vermeire v. Belgium*, Judgment (Merits) of 29 November 1991, Application no. 12849/87.
- *Eriksson v. Sweden*, Judgment (Merits and Just Satisfaction) of 22 June 1989, Application no. 11373/85.
- *Johnston and Others v. Ireland*, Judgment (Merits and Just Satisfaction) of 18 December 1986, Application no. 9697/82.

- *Ashingdane v. the United Kingdom*, Judgment (Merits) of 28 May 1985, Application no. 8225/78.
- *Marckx v Belgium*, Judgment (Merits and Just Satisfaction) of 13 June 1979, Application no. 6833/74.
- *Tyrer v. the United Kingdom*, Judgment (Merits) of 25 April 1978, Application no. 5856/72.
- *X and Y v. The Netherlands*, Admissibility Decision of 19 December 1974, Application no. 6753/74.
- European Court of Human Rights, pending Applications Allocated to a Judicial Formation, http://www.echr.coe.int/NR/rdonlyres/92D2D024-6F05-495E-A714-4729DEE6462C/0/Pending_applications_chart.pdf.

INTER-AMERICAN COURT OF HUMAN RIGHTS

- *Case of Vargas-Areco v. Paraguay*, Judgment (Merits, Reparations and Costs) of 26 September 2006.
- *Case of the Yean and Bosico Children v. The Dominican Republic*, Judgment of 8 September 2005.
- *Case of the "Street Children" (Villagrán-Morales et al.) v. Guatemala*, Judgment (Merits) of 19 November 1999.

HOUSE OF LORDS

- *Gillick v West Norfolk and Wisbech Area Health Authority* [1985] 3 All ER 402 (HL).

Curriculum Vitae

Helen Beckmann-Hamzei (Essen, Germany, 1980) conducted her PhD research at the Grotius Centre for International Legal Studies Leiden University, under the supervision of Professor Liesbeth Zegveld and Professor Larissa van den Herik. In addition to her research, Helen lectured in the Bachelor's and LL.M. Programmes in Public International Law. Due to generous funding of the Gieskes-foundation Helen established together with Prof. Liesbeth Zegveld the master course Protection of War Victims under International Law taught at the faculty of law at Leiden University.

Helen graduated in December 2004 at Radboud University in Nijmegen. In the spring of 2006 she completed her LL.M. (cum laude) in International and European Law at Utrecht University. Helen has working experience in the field of national, international criminal law and international humanitarian law as a result of her internships at the law offices Böhler and Wladimiroff in Amsterdam and The Hague. In 2009 Helen stayed for a few months at the Office of the Public Counsel for Victims at the International Criminal Court to do research with regard child participation in ICC proceedings. Since February 2014 she is head of the *Strategic Learning Center* (Essen, Germany), which provides advice and supervision to students and PhD candidates.

TITLES PUBLISHED IN THE SCHOOL OF HUMAN RIGHTS RESEARCH SERIES

The School of Human Rights Research is a joint effort by human rights researchers in the Netherlands. Its central research theme is the nature and meaning of international standards in the field of human rights, their application and promotion in the national legal order, their interplay with national standards, and the international supervision of such application. The School of Human Rights Research Series only includes English titles that contribute to a better understanding of the different aspects of human rights.

For previous volumes in the series, please visit http://shr.intersentia.com.

Published titles within the Series:

63. Jasper Krommendijk, *The Domestic Impact and Effectiveness of the Process of State Reporting under UN Human Rights Treaties in the Netherlands, New Zealand and Finland. Paper-pushing or policy prompting?* ISBN 978-1-78068-244-0
64. Jennifer Anna Sellin, *Access to Medicines. The Interface between Patents and Human Rights. Does one size fit all?* ISBN 978-1-78068-247-1
65. Gustavo Arosemena, *Rights, Scarcity and Justice. An Analytical Inquiry into the Adjudication of the Welfare Aspects of Human Rights* ISBN 978-1-78068-275-4
66. Etienne Ruvebana, *Prevention of Genocide under International Law. An analysis of the obligations of states and the United Nations to prevent genocide at the primary, secondary and tertiary levels* ISBN 978-1-78068-273-0
67. Evgeni Moyakine, *The Privatized Art of War. Private Military and Security Companies and State Responsibility for Their Unlawful Conduct in Conflict Areas* ISBN 978-1-78068-281-5
68. Esther Janssen, *Faith in Public Debate. On Freedom of Expression, Hate Speech and Religion in France and The Netherlands* ISBN 978-1-78068-309-6
69. Stefanie Jansen-Wilhelm, *Accepting Assistance in the Aftermath of Disasters* ISBN 978-1-78068-329-4.

www.ingramcontent.com/pod-product-compliance
Ingram Content Group UK Ltd.
Pitfield, Milton Keynes, MK11 3LW, UK
UKHW051921100926
8556IPUK00021B/1298

9 781780 683393